DAVID GLASGOW FARRAGUT
ADMIRAL IN THE MAKING

DAVID GLASGOW FARRAGUT
ADMIRAL IN THE MAKING

CHARLES LEE LEWIS

NAVAL INSTITUTE PRESS
ANNAPOLIS, MARYLAND

This book has been brought to publication with the generous
assistance of Marguerite and Gerry Lenfest.

Naval Institute Press
291 Wood Road
Annapolis, MD 21402

© 1941 by the United States Naval Institute

All rights reserved. No part of this book may be reproduced or utilized in any form or by any means, electronic or mechanical, including photocopying and recording, or by any information storage and retrieval system, without permission in writing from the publisher.

First Naval Institute Press paperback edition published in 2014.
ISBN: 978-1-59114-415-1 (paperback)
ISBN: 978-1-61251-554-0 (ebook)

The Library of Congress has cataloged the hardcover edition as follows:
Lewis, Charles Lee, 1886—
   David Glasgow Farragut.

   (Navies and men)
   Reprint of the ed. published by the United States Naval Institute, Annapolis.
   Includes bibliographies and indexes.
   CONTENTS: [1] Admiral in the making.—[2] Our first admiral
   1. Farragut, David Glasgow, 1801—1870. 2. United States—History, Naval—To 1900. 3. Admirals—United States—Biography. 4. United States. Navy—Biography.
I. Series.
E467.1.F23L48 1980   973.7'5'0924 [B]   79-6115
ISBN 0-405-13043-0 (v. 1)
ISBN 0-405-13044-9 (v. 2)

♾ Print editions meet the requirements of ANSI/NISO z39.48-1992 (Permanence of Paper).
Printed in the United States of America.

9 8 7 6 5 4 3 2 1

TO
FLORA HOODENPYL QUARLES

PREFACE

AN AUTHOR should have a good reason for launching another biography on seas already somewhat crowded with such craft. Particularly should there be justification, when the subject of his work has already been treated, as is true of Admiral Farragut.

I must confess that it was with considerable hesitation at first that I entered a field of research which had been previously cultivated by the great Mahan. But I soon discovered that, in the writing of his small biography of Farragut some fifty years ago for the *Great Commanders* series, he apparently did not have access to the large amount of source material which has become available. As a consequence this biography is by no means comparable either in scope or in treatment to his truly remarkable life of Admiral Nelson in two volumes. Still as a short compact account of Farragut's career, with the emphasis on problems of strategy, Mahan's *Admiral Farragut* still occupies an important place in naval biography. It was not displaced by the work of John Randolph Spears, another comparatively small biography, appearing in 1905, which added nothing of any consequence to the subject. Both Mahan and Spears relied largely upon the life of Farragut, written by his son Loyall and published in 1879, which was more like a compendium of source material than a finished biography. These three biographies of Farragut are the only ones worthy of consideration.

It was my good fortune to be the first investigator to read the original manuscript of *Some Reminiscences* by Admiral Farragut, after it was sold two or three years ago by the Farragut Family. Loyall Farragut quoted from this as the *Journal* in his biography of his father; but he saw fit to edit the original language at will, sometimes quite materially, and to use only those parts which he thought would enhance his father's reputation. I immediately saw that by using much of this discarded material and by using exact quotations from the manuscript, I should be able to answer some of the puzzling questions about Farragut and also at the same time make him seem more like a human being. Neither Mahan nor Spears ever saw *Some Reminiscences* and the large number of personal letters and other papers, also only recently released by the family.

Former biographers have not thought it worth while to examine the various logbooks of the ships in which Farragut served. By doing this, I discovered that, in *Some Reminiscences*, Farragut had relied largely upon his memory, and that many inaccuracies had resulted, mistakes which only the logbooks could reveal. I found also hitherto unpublished material in the archives of the United States Navy Department, in the Farragut Papers recently given to the United States Naval Academy Museum, and elsewhere.

In relating the story of Farragut's life and in portraying his character, I have endeavored to avoid glossing over his mistakes and imperfections. He was, after all, only a human being, subject to life's temptations, its suffering, sorrow, and bereavement, its happiness, ambition, and triumph. Neither have I thought it proper, merely for the sake of interest, to give so much space to the glamorous episodes that little or no attention could be devoted to the ordinary demands of the naval profession upon an officer. The reader who expects romance and adventure on every page will be disappointed. But I trust that one who is seeking a fuller understanding of the long hard years of preparation and experience and trial out of which was hammered and tempered the fine steel of Farragut's character will not be disappointed.

It was not my intention, when I commenced my researches, to write a biography which would extend beyond the usual length. But with so much new and interesting material at hand, it seemed advisable to me to attempt a work in two volumes, the first of which would cover Farragut's life up to the beginning of the Civil War, a definite line of demarcation. This period of his career has never been adequately presented. The first volume deals, accordingly, with the much longer and more varied portion of his life; the second volume, which it is hoped will in due time appear, will portray him during the crowning years of his career, as Our First Admiral.

I wish that it were practicable to mention by name all of the many persons who have generously assisted me in the collection of the material for this biography. I can state only that, without such aid, I would have been seriously handicapped and the scope of the work would have been sadly limited. I could not have written the biography at all without the help of some whose names I take pleasure in mentioning with sincere thanks. The grandniece of Admiral Farragut, Mrs. George G. Hall, and her husband most cordially received me in their home and placed at my disposal their rich store of research material, and patiently answered my numerous questions. Equally generous and helpful was Dr. Ellsworth Eliot, Jr., of New York, who, without any restrictions, permitted me to examine and use the manuscript of Farragut's *Some Reminiscences* and many other valuable Farragut papers. At the United States Naval Academy, Captain Harry A. Baldridge, U. S. Navy, the Curator, cheerfully allowed be to read the Farragut papers, recently donated to the Museum by Mr. Christian A. Zabriskie of New York. Mr. Louis H. Bolander, Assistant Librarian of the Naval Academy Library, was also extremely helpful to me in many ways. Likewise most cordial assistance was rendered me by the personnel of the Naval Records and Library of the United States Navy Department, of the National Archives, and of the Manuscript Division of the Library of Congress. Lastly, I wish to acknowledge both the assistance and the encouragement, given me by my friend, Mr. William E. Beard, journalist and author of Nashville, Tennessee.

C. L. L.

Annapolis, Maryland
March, 1941

CONTENTS

CHAPTER		PAGE
I.	Of Fighting Blood	1
II.	The Log Cabin by the River	7
III.	The Voyage on the Flatboat	12
IV.	Breaking Up the Home	16
V.	A Midshipman at the Age of Nine	22
VI.	Farragut Joins the *Essex*	25
VII.	Peace Time Cruising in the *Essex*	33
VIII.	Farragut's First Sea Fight	40
IX.	Delaware Bay to Valparaiso	49
X.	Valparaiso and Galapagos Islands	65
XI.	At Nukuhiva in the Marquesas	81
XII.	The Loss of the *Essex*	91
XIII.	An Interlude	107
XIV.	Cruising in the Mediterranean	114
XV.	Cruising in the Gulf of Mexico	140
XVI.	Hunting Pirates in the Caribbean	152
XVII.	Marriage, Promotion, and the *Brandywine*	169
XVIII.	On the Brazil Station	182
XIX.	An Ebb Tide in His Life	202
XX.	On the West India Station	207
XXI.	Home and Trouble	217
XXII.	On the Brazil Station Again	222
XXIII.	Shore Duty and Second Marriage	237
XXIV.	In the Mexican War	242
XXV.	An Ordnance Expert	251
XXVI.	Establishes Mare Island Navy Yard	256
XXVII.	Commands the Steam Sloop-of-War *Brooklyn*	267
XXVIII.	Waiting Orders	286
	Sources and Bibliography	297
	Notes	304
	Index	361

ILLUSTRATIONS

George Farragut, Father of David Glasgow Farragut 1
From the portrait by William Swain

Birthplace of David Glasgow Farragut 7
From a photograph by Thompsons, Inc.

Captain David Porter, U. S. Navy 18
From the portrait by John Wesley Jarvis

United States Frigate *Essex* 25
From the painting by Joseph Howard

Capture of the British Sloop-of-War *Alert* by the Frigate *Essex* 44
From the painting by Rodolfo Claudus

The *Essex* and Her Prizes at Nukuhiva 81
From the engraving by William Strickland of the drawing by Captain David Porter

Engagement between the *Essex* and the *Phoebe* and the *Cherub* in the Harbor of Valparaiso 97
From an old print

United States Ship of the Line *Independence* 114
From a painting by an unknown artist

Midshipman Farragut at the Age of Nineteen 140
From a portrait by F. Kuykendall

The Harbor of Rio de Janeiro 183
From a lithograph by Sarony and Company, N.Y.

French Bombardment of San Juan de Ulloa 211
From a painting in the Museum at Versailles, France

United States Ship of the Line *Delaware* 225
From the original pastel in the collection of President Franklin Delano Roosevelt

Page xiii

ILLUSTRATIONS

Mrs. David Glasgow Farragut and Her Son Loyall 240
    From an old daguerreotype

Norfolk and Portsmouth in 1851 251
    From a lithograph by E. Sachse & Co., Baltimore, Maryland

Steam Sloop-of-War *Brooklyn* 267
    From a painting by an unknown artist in the
    Officers' Club, U. S. Naval Academy

Courtesy of United States National Museum

GEORGE FARRAGUT, FATHER OF DAVID GLASGOW FARRAGUT
From the portrait by William Swain in the Smithsonian Institution, Washington, D.C.

I

OF FIGHTING BLOOD

1

A SHORT time after the War of the American Revolution began on April 19, 1775, at Lexington, there sailed up to New Orleans a small merchant vessel, which had for some time been trading between Havana and Vera Cruz. Her captain was a young swarthy man named George Anthony Magin Farragut.[1] News had travelled fast even to that distant place, then a small town of seven or eight thousand inhabitants ruled by the Spanish king. When George Farragut heard that war had broken out between Great Britain and her colonies, he at once made up his mind "to assist with his life and his fortune in the struggle for American Independence."[2]

Such a decision was natural for a man of his ancestry and character, as revealed in his short though adventurous previous career. George Farragut was then but nineteen years old, having been born on September 29, 1755, at Ciudadella on the Island of Minorca in the Mediterranean. His parents were Anthony Farragut and Juan Mesquida.[3] They were of excellent Spanish stock, long resident in the Balearic Islands. George Farragut was directly descended from Don Pedro Ferragut[4] who assisted King James I of Aragon in driving the Moors from Majorca, largest of the Balearic Islands, and from Valencia in the first half of the thirteenth century. For this he was honored by James with the office of Sergeant before the King, was granted a large estate, and at the request of the king was celebrated in verse along with the other knights by the troubadour, Mossen Jaime Febrer. Pedro Ferragut's stanza was as follows:

> "A charger's shoe is borne on his shield,
> Of purest gold, on a blood-red field,
> Set thereon with a nail of the same:

> Thus we know him, device and name.
> From Jaca, in Aragon, he came.
> At Majorca and Valencia both,
> Well he quitted his knightly troth,
> Serving as Sergeant before his liege,
> Through the conquest, in field and siege:
> Strong in battle, by plain or hold,
> Great his fame as a warrior bold,
> And a prudent captain to shun surprise;
> For years and victories made him wise.
> At every manner of arms expert,
> He did on the foe great spoil and hurt."[5]

Extending down through the fourteenth, fifteenth, sixteenth, and seventeenth centuries was a remarkably large number of Farraguts of distinction—members of the General Council of the Kingdom of Majorca, magistrates of the city of Palma, and distinguished churchmen, scholars, and soldiers.

George Farragut was sent to school for awhile at Barcelona, but overcome by the spirit of adventure, he went to sea at the age of ten. For seven years he was a seaman chiefly in the Mediterranean. He claimed[6] long years afterwards, when he was an old man nearly sixty, that he was in the Russian service during the war with Turkey, and that he was a member of the crew of the fireship which spread the flames among the Turkish ships off Cheshme in the Black Sea, where the fleet was destroyed in May, 1770. He would then have been hardly fifteen years old.

Early in 1773 George Farragut "shaped his course for the American Seas,"[7] and two years later he appeared in that city which afterwards was to be his home for many years and eventually was to become associated with the first great victory of his famous son. But just then George Farragut did not tarry long at New Orleans, his decision having been made to join the cause of the American colonies. He sailed away to Port-au-Prince, where he exchanged his cargo for cannon, small arms, and ammunition, and then in the year 1776 he proceeded to Charleston, South Carolina.

The eagerness of young Farragut to fight the British may partly be accounted for by a feeling of hatred developed in the descendant of a proud race who had lived during his early years as a subject of a nation of a different race, language, and culture. He had really been born a British subject. The Island of Minorca had been ceded to the British by the Treaty of Utrecht in 1713, and retained by them until 1756, the year following George Farragut's birth, when it was taken from the British by the French, a loss of territory for which Admiral Byng paid with his own life and honor.

A man so well provided with the implements and sinews of war was bound to be well received at Charleston at that time. Hence it was not long until George Farragut found himself a lieutenant on board a privateer of twelve guns commanded by a certain Captain Newton. He later so distinguished himself in an engagement with a British privateer, in which the latter was worsted, that his commanding officer recommended his appointment as a first lieutenant in the State Navy of South Carolina. This was in 1778, the year in which the British transferred the theater of war to the southern colonies. Then short, chunky Lieutenant Farragut became a very busy young man. He superintended the construction of galleys of war in Charleston, and when placed in command of one of them, performed valiant service in the defense of Savannah. He escaped from there when the place was captured and retired to Charleston which was soon also besieged by the British. First he fought on the water, but after the galleys had been dismantled and their cannon transferred to the army, he commanded a battery. Long years afterwards he wrote, with evident satisfaction, that he had the pleasure to believe that during the siege he "burnt as much powder and with as much annoyance to the enemy as any one officer in the American Army."[8]

All was in vain, however, for Charleston fell to the British May 12, 1780, and Farragut was made a prisoner of war. Soon exchanged, he sailed from Philadelphia on board a privateer, and in an engagement with an enemy vessel, he had his right arm badly shattered with a musket ball. For saving it from amputation he had Surgeon Ridgely to thank.

Lieutenant Farragut then left the sea, and made his way to General Francis Marion's headquarters where he served as a volunteer. This was a period of great activity, when Generals Marion, Sumter, Daniel Morgan, and Nathaniel Greene were endeavoring to reclaim South Carolina from the British. After participating in the Battle of Cowpens[9] on January 17, 1781, Farragut went to Wilmington where Governor Nash appointed him to command a company of volunteer artillery, which engaged a British detachment at Beaufort Bridge. He then raised a company of volunteer cavalry to harass the rear of General Cornwallis's army during its invasion of North Carolina. After this service, he was appointed a captain of North Carolina State Cavalry, and assisted General Marion in preserving law and order in the state. Finally, near the close of the war, he was promoted on May 5, 1783, to the rank of major of horse, to date from May 1, 1782, with the allowance of back pay due men of that rank.[10] Was there ever a more versatile, amphibious fighter than George Farragut!

2

"The peace which soon followed," complained[11] George Farragut when age had robbed him of the illusions and romance of youth, "left my adopted Country free and Independent; but your Memorialist poor and pennyless." To earn a living, therefore, he went to sea again for about seven years. Though there is no record as to what ships he sailed in and to what ports, he probably engaged in the merchant service to the West Indies, with which he was particularly familiar.

Then Fate took a hand, and set the stage for a new and entirely different scene in the drama of his life. His old acquaintance, William Blount, who was then Governor of the South Western Territory, now Tennessee, invited him to come to Knoxville. There on November 3, 1790[12] Blount appointed Farragut a Major of Militia. In the Treaty of the Holston River in 1791, a boundary between the whites and the Cherokees was agreed upon, and the following year, Farragut and Titus Ogden[13] assisted John McKee, Judge David Campbell, and Charles McClung, who had been appointed as commissioners to survey the line. But trouble again broke out with the Indians, and in 1793, Farragut served under General John Sevier in his last' expedition against the Cherokees and Creeks in northern Georgia.

In February of the year following his service under Sevier, George Farragut acquired a lot of ground in Knoxville from Colonel James White and two hundred acres on Third Creek in Knox County from Thomas King. In the following April he received a grant from North Carolina in lieu of military service during the Revolution, comprising 340 acres in Grassy Valley situated also in Knox County. Seeing himself rapidly becoming a man of property, he decided to get married. The woman he chose was Elizabeth Shine. They were married in 1795.[14]

3

Elizabeth Shine was born on June 7, 1765, in Dobbs County,[15] now Lenoir County, North Carolina, near Kinston on the Neuse River. Afterwards her parents moved with their family to what became known as Shine's Ferry[16] on the French Broad River near Old Newport, Cocke County, in what is now Tennessee. As he passed to and fro between North Carolina and the South West District on missions for Governor Blount[17] or in performance of his regular military duties, George Farragut had had many possible opportunities for making the acquaintance of Elizabeth Shine. But there is no record of the time of their first meeting, which might even have been in North Carolina during the Revolution.[18] At the time of their marriage he was forty and she thirty years old. As girls on the frontier usually married at a very early age, there were some who looked upon Elizabeth at that time as an old maid.[19]

The problem of heritable ancestral traits and character is a very complicated and doubtful one in any case; but be that as it may, biographers of David Glasgow Farragut would have done well to have given more consideration to his maternal genealogical line. It is by no means improbable that the great naval officer actually derived more of those outstanding qualities of greatness from his mother's people than from his father's side of the family, however praiseworthy this may have been. George

Farragut himself, though intrepid and charming, was lacking in that strength of character which Elizabeth Shine possessed, as will clearly appear later in this biography.

Elizabeth Shine's grandfather, Daniel Shine, came to North Carolina from Dublin, Ireland, about 1710, married Elizabeth Greene on May 15, 1715, and then settled at New Bern. Of his ten children, Elizabeth's father, John Shine, became a captain of North Carolina militia as early as December, 1754; while her Uncle Daniel Shine was, at the same time, a lieutenant colonel.[20] Colonel Shine married Barbara Franck, said to have been descended from a very distinguished family. She lived to the advanced age of ninety-five years and entertained George Washington when he made his famous southern journey.[21] Captain John Shine married first Sarah Mackelwean by whom he had two children, and after her death he married Ellenor McIver[22] by whom he had eight children, of whom Elizabeth was fifth.

After their marriage George and Elizabeth Farragut at first lived in Knoxville (soon to become the first capital of the state of Tennessee in 1796). They resided on Emmerson Street in a house of stone and logs, which George Farragut himself built so substantially that it stood the ravages of time until 1903. Here the first child, a son, was born August 23, 1797, and named William A. C. Farragut.

Selling his property in Knoxville in 1799 and 1800, George Farragut moved his family to a tract of 640 acres which he had purchased from Stockley Donelson in 1796. This land was situated on the north bank of the Holston River,[23] about fifteen miles southwest of Knoxville. There he established a new home on the great river near a place then called Stony Point,[24] which was about ten miles from Campbell's Station,[25] an important stopping place on the road leading west from Knoxville to Nashville. Here, Major Farragut was granted a license[24] by the Knoxville County Court to "keep a public ferry at his own landing." George Farragut, enamored of the sea, would have a boat even though it were only a river ferry flatboat.

BIRTHPLACE OF DAVID GLASCOW FARRAGUT

From a photograph by Thompsons, Inc. The marker was erected, on the north bank of the Holston River, fifteen miles southwest of Knoxville, Tennessee, by the Bonny Kate Chapter, Daughters of the American Revolution, and dedicated by Admiral Dewey, May 15, 1900. The old log house has long since disappeared, but Farragut may have played under the giant elm.

II

THE LOG CABIN BY THE RIVER

1

THE FARRAGUTS' log house was somewhat more pretentious than the typical frontier cabin, which was sixteen by twenty feet in dimensions.[1] Their structure was more than twice that size, being forty by twenty feet, but it was no doubt quite similar in architecture. Later, additional rooms were added.[2] The logs were notched into each other at the four corners to form the walls, and the crevices between the logs were closely packed with grass or moss mixed with clay. The ridgepole, supported in the forks of two strong tree trunks, bore a roof made of smaller logs and split wooden slabs. The window panes were of paper soaked in hog's fat or bear's grease, and the windows were protected by hinged wooden shutters. The door was thick and heavy and could be well secured. As usual, loop-holes through the walls were provided for defense against Indian attacks.

The interior was plainly and simply furnished; there were no luxuries. The chairs, tables, and beds were all made by hand. The most noticeable and perhaps the most significant objects were the spinning wheel and the loom for making the cloth for the family's clothing. Over the fireplace and near the doorway, usually suspended from stags' antlers, were the rifles with the shot pouches and the yellow powder horns and the other weapons of war and hunting. Most of the cooking was done round the hearth of the single fireplace. Hearth and home were here indeed quite synonymous terms.

It was in this log house at Stony Point that George and Elizabeth Farragut were blessed with a second son, who was born on July 5, 1801. They named him James Glasgow Farragut,[3] after James Glasgow, for a time Secretary of State of North

Carolina, with whom George Farragut had come in contact while handling land grants for the Blounts and for himself. When the little fellow was about twelve years old, he changed his name to David Glasgow Farragut, and that is the way it appears on history's roll of fame.

In the Governor William Blount Mansion in Knoxville, Tennessee, among many other objects associated with the early history of that state is a cradle[4] in which, according to tradition, young Farragut first felt that swaying motion which afterwards he experienced for so many years in a hammock on shipboard. This peculiarly constructed pine cradle is mounted on two fixed supports at each end, and thus swings very much like a sailor's hammock. If it is authentic, it was probably made by the infant's father, who was both a seaman and a carpenter.

When young Farragut became old enough to take notice of the out-of-doors spread round the log house, his earliest impressions were associated with the wide stretches of the Holston River and the Great Smoky Mountains lifting their lofty peaks in the hazy distance to the southeast. When quite young he was borne across the great stream on his father's ferryboat, and again felt that gentle rocking not unlike that he had enjoyed in his cradle when his mother lulled him to sleep at night. Such was the situation for a home which an islander and a mariner would have chosen, and it was just the environment to give sons a yearning for wider waters and larger boats.

Mrs. Farragut was accustomed to the frontier life and was inured to its hardships. She doubtless was mostly concerned over the dangers incident to occasional visits from Indian marauders, particularly with little children to be protected. Though by this time the long story of Indian massacres had practically come to an end in East Tennessee, still occasionally terror and death were brought to the outlying settlements by thieving or drunken savages. Elizabeth Farragut was a woman of great courage and resourcefulness and, when confronted with just such a peril, acted with great calmness and heroism.

The incident happened one day when Glasgow was only five years old. His older brother William was about nine; his sister

Nancy[5] was two; and his youngest brother George was less than a year old. Fortunately Mrs. Farragut discovered the Indians at some distance from the house, which they seemed to be planning to surround. Quickly she placed all the children in the loft of the log kitchen, a separate building standing not far from the house. When the Indians approached, the brave mother held a parley with them from the house, thus drawing their attention away from the place where she had concealed the children, just as a mother bird protects her young. After much parleying, the Indians said they would go away if she would give them some whiskey. So she came to the door which was securely fastened with a strong bar and chain and as she began to open the door slightly, one of the Indians struck at her with his knife. Then she quickly closed the door which shielded her from the blow, and stood there guarding her home with an axe until finally they slunk away. She then released the frightened children who had been lying "all breathless"[6] in the kitchen loft. It was a terrible ordeal for both mother and children. So indelibly written on his childish memory was every detail of the experience that nearly fifty years afterwards Farragut could vividly retell every particular of his first great adventure.

He related further that his father returned home within an hour after the Indians had departed, and that he then saw for the first time evil passion gain complete control of a man. His father became so angry that it was all his mother could do to keep him from rushing out alone in pursuit of the Indians. She finally made him understand that there were too many in the party to be mastered by less than a dozen white men. This number, she said, he could quickly collect. At length he agreed, and put on his uniform and his dragoon cask with white horse hair in the crest, an "elegant uniform,"[6] thought his little five years old son. Then he mounted his horse and rode away to collect some men. Two hours later he passed the house with eight or ten men similarly dressed. His mother put them on the trail of the Indians, and away they went in pursuit. "What became of the Indians," wrote[6] Farragut, "I don't now remember; the impression however left on my mind is that they did not leave many of them to recount the adventures of their visit to our lonely dwelling."

In later estimating Admiral Farragut's character and determining the relative extent to which he was indebted to his mother for his great success as a leader, one would do well to bear in mind not only the courage but also the self control and cool calculation displayed by the mother on this occasion as compared to the passionate foolhardiness and lack of self control on the part of the father.

2

No other noteworthy incident breaking the monotony of frontier life at Stony Point has been recorded. But there was not sufficient time for lengthy annals, for the year following the adventure with the Indians the family left their Tennessee home. Though George Farragut was "a glorious Indian hunter and a great provider in great straits for food,"[6] and had many characteristics suited to the frontier life, he was so restless that it was impossible for him to remain happily settled in one place for a very long time. It is not unlikely also that he felt himself not altogether at home among the Protestant, largely Presbyterian, settlers of that region, who were of a different race and language as well as religion. For a long time he had no doubt yearned to go to New Orleans again where he first landed on the American coast. Here he would be at home among those who spoke the Spanish tongue.[7]

Elizabeth Farragut no doubt was opposed to going so far away from her own people to what was then essentially a foreign country. But eventually circumstances arose which made it possible for George Farragut to have his way. Though this was to lead to an untimely death for his wife, it was to be a fortunate turning point in the life of young Glasgow. George Farragut's opportunity came when President Jefferson in 1803 appointed William Charles Cole Claiborne[8] to be Governor General of the Province of Louisiana. The purchase of that vast new domain had just been consummated that same year. While Claiborne was a Representative in Congress from Tennessee, he had presented a petition for George Farragut requesting pay due him for services rendered the government while he was Muster Master of the Militia of the District of East Tennessee.[9] Claiborne evidently knew George Farragut well, and the tradition is probably well founded that it was through his influence that Farragut was appointed,[10] on March 2, 1807, a sailing master in the United States Navy and ordered to duty at New Orleans.

The preceding year Claiborne had been forced to contend with the dangerous Burr Conspiracy, which came to an end only with the flight of its leader from Natchez eastward in January, 1807. In the summer of that year about the time of the arrival of George Farragut in New Orleans, Claiborne was severely wounded by Daniel Clark in a duel which arose over the Burr Affair. Claiborne, accordingly, would welcome into his service a man of Spanish[11] descent whom he could trust in the midst of a population largely Spanish and French who resented being under the American flag and remembered with pride the time when in turn the flags of their respective countries had floated over New Orleans.

III

THE VOYAGE ON THE FLATBOAT

1

GEORGE FARRAGUT did not accompany his family to New Orleans, as he had planned to do.[1] Probably it took longer to construct the flatboat than he had expected, and he did not feel that he could spare the time necessary for a long voyage on the river. So in the early summer he hastened to New Orleans to assume command of *Gunboat No. 13*,[2] and left his family to be transported to their new home under the direction of a young Kentuckian named Merrill Brady. George Farragut probably traveled to Nashville and thence by Natchez Trace to Natchez where he took a boat for New Orleans.

A keel boat or flatboat was a slow but comparatively comfortable means of transportation, particularly for women and children. This type[3] of boat had a flat bottom and a bow inclined forward about forty-five degrees. All round the upper edge was a perpendicular planking three or four feet high to serve as a bulwark. The aft section, comprising about half the boat, was roofed over, and fitted up as the living quarters. Household furniture and utensils could thus be used continuously while being transported long distances. Pens for the cow and other livestock were also provided. Food for the animals as well as ample provisions for the family had to be stored on the boat. Water could be taken directly from the river. There were two oars well forward on each side, to be used for rowing in an emergency, and directly astern was a large oar for steering, which was an important part of the equipment.

This was the kind of boat which Elizabeth Farragut and her children went aboard on a pleasant day in the early autumn of

1807. As they lived so near the river, the embarkation was comparatively easy. Mrs. Farragut could fit up the rude craft with all the comforts of their log house, and the children could take along even their pets and toys for the long journey. The oldest son, William, was then but ten; Glasgow was six; Nancy was three and a half; and the baby, George, was nearly two. When the many tearful farewells had been spoken to the friends who had gathered on the river bank, young Brady untied the boat and, as the current began to take hold, he steered for the middle of the river, and the great voyage had begun. With a sad and anxious face Elizabeth stood with her family about her, holding little George in her arms, and gazed at the receding shore line and the scenes of home fading from her sight forever. Brave, pioneer mother, she was even then carrying a fifth child, to be born November 12, 1807, and also named Elizabeth.

The danger of attack by Indians had by this time largely disappeared. General John Sevier's successful expedition against Cherokees and Creeks in 1793, and General James Robertson's Nickajack Expedition of the following year had removed this menace to navigation on the Tennessee River. There was some danger from river pirates, but they were more likely to attack the boats bearing shipments of freight; such as, corn, flax, tallow, hides, furs, dried beef, tobacco, and whiskey which was then being distilled on a large and ever increasing scale.[5] Such boats of commerce were being sent down the Cumberland, Tennessee, and Mississippi Rivers in contantly growing numbers, but they were usually accompanied by escorts armed to protect them from the inland buccaneers.

The voyage was indeed a long one, almost seventeen hundred miles, easily comparable in length to a passage across the North Atlantic. Such a voyage would take many weeks. A similar river journey of nine hundred miles from Fort Patrick Henry near Long Island on the Holston River to Nashville on the Cumberland River took four months, from December 22, 1778, to April 24, 1779.[6] It was a large expedition under command of Captain John Donelson, and its size together with Indian attacks, smallpox, and severe wintry cold doubtless prolonged the voyage unduly. Besides on the Cumberland the boats had to be rowed upstream. The Farragut family, with a steady downstream current all the way, the pleasant healthful weather of autumn, and no likely interference from the Indians, could expect to make the best of time. But they could hardly count on less than two months. Seventy-five days[7] were considered an average time for the voyage from Pittsburgh to New Orleans, a distance about equal to that from Knoxville to the same southern city.

2

It is not an exaggeration to state that such a voyage was an extraordinary experience for the whole family, but particularly for the boys of ten and six respectively. A whole boy's library of books like *Tom Sawyer* and *Huck Finn* could not match the thrills of such an adventure. In a few days they reached the confluence of the Holston and the Clinch Rivers, and then floated on the bosom of the Tennessee, the Indian name for the crooked river, which wound away to the southwest until finally it turned its course and flowed in a northerly direction to the Ohio. At that time the Tennessee followed its crooked course through a great virgin green wilderness. There was not then a single white settlement on the entire river; only a few Indian villages. In its southerly course it flowed through picturesque hills and in sight of mountains, the most striking scenery being in the vicinity of what is now Chattanooga where Lookout Mountain overlooks the great Moccasin Bend made by the stream ages ago in its struggle to break through the mountains. The northerly course was through flat country, and the scenery became more monotonous. Occasionally an Indian canoe was seen, particularly when they approached one of the villages. Frequently game appeared on the river banks, for great herds of buffalo were then numerous in the rich natural pastures, and deer and other wild beasts filled the forests. Great flocks of birds, wild turkeys and particularly wild pigeons, were to be seen; while the boys could fish from their floating home to their heart's content.

Eventually their flatboat came to the junction of the Tennessee with the Ohio, and the first stage of the voyage was successfully accomplished. Some forty miles on the Ohio brought them to the Father of Waters, the mighty Mississippi. As they floated southward, they began to make contacts with the outposts of civilization at Fort Jefferson, New Madrid, and Fort Pickering,[8] and in due time came to Natchez, and then to Baton Rouge. There was much more traffic on the Mississippi, and the monotony of the long days was frequently broken when they hailed another keelboat which they overhauled or were passed by a swifter boat. Sometimes it was a large canoe loaded with furs or other articles of trade which passed rapidly, driven by the long paddles of powerful men. The constantly increasing river traffic was the only indication that they were approaching their destination, for the great river flowed monotonously onward. But one day unexpectedly they found their flatboat being steered by the faithful Kentucky[9] pilot to a levee where the river swept in a great crescent[10] before the little city, which they were told was New Orleans, where their father and a new home awaited them.

Glasgow Farragut was old enough at the time of this voyage for it to make a lasting impression on his memory. Long years afterwards as he steamed up and down the Mississippi on board men-of-war, in his musings he must have often seen in the misty distance a vision of that old flatboat with its precious cargo floating down the river, and the tenderest emotions welled up in his heart as he thought of his brave mother, the captain of his first cruise. Thus it seems an extraordinary coincidence that young Farragut's first voyage was on the great river upon which long years afterwards he was to win imperishable fame.

IV

BREAKING UP THE HOME

1

IT WAS A strange, almost a foreign city which Mrs. Farragut and the children entered when their flatboat arrived at New Orleans. There were strong fortifications with high sloping ramparts. The Gate of France at the north was a good mile from the Gate of Tchoupitoulas at the south, and the western wall was a third of a mile from the river bank. The population then numbered about fifteen thousand,[1] largely of Spanish and French descent. They ranged in the social scale from the wholesale merchants who lived in luxury and elegance down to the adventurers and out-and-out pirates, for New Orleans was then a favorite port of the Lafittes[2] and other Baratarians. Though the streets were pompously named in honor of the princes and nobles of France, they were narrow, poorly drained breeding-places of pestilence. The architecture was rather tropical in appearance. There were steep roofs of red tiles as found in Spain. There were many picturesque balconies and verandas, and much delicately wrought metal work at gateways and lattices. The Cathedral and the Cabildo, or Municipal Hall were then considered to be among the finest buildings in North America.[3]

This was a very different environment for the Farraguts from that with which they were accustomed on the Tennessee frontier. George Farragut felt quite at home among these people of Latin culture and language; but not so poor Elizabeth who with such courage and fortitude had traveled so far from the people of her own kind in order to please her husband. Faithfully she re-established the home in new surroundings, and on November 12 bore her husband another daughter, named Elizabeth.

Where the new home was located has not been recorded, though there is a tradition that it was near the shore of Lake Pontchartrain. The proximity of the home to the lake led to an incident which was to have an important bearing on the career of Glasgow Farragut.

David Porter, Senior, father of Master Commandant David Porter, was given a warrant as sailing master in August, 1807,[4] and ordered to New Orleans, where he arrived either late in that year or early in 1808. He and George Farragut, having much in common, became warm friends. On a hot day during the ensuing summer, while Porter was fishing on the lake,[5] he suffered a sunstroke which prostrated him in his boat. It happened that Sailing Master Farragut was fishing in that vicinity, and finding his friend in this exhausted condition, he took him to his home where Mrs. Farragut nursed him as best she could in what proved to be his last illness. He was already in a very low state of health caused by consumption and, it is said,[6] really died of that disease.

Meanwhile a great tragedy befell the Farragut family. Elizabeth Farragut, strong-hearted but tender mother and faithful wife, weakened by her many household burdens and the nursing of Sailing Master Porter, fell a victim to the dreaded yellow fever. She died on Wednesday, June 22, 1808, and as fate would have it Porter died the same day. They were both buried on the morning of June 24 in the Protestant Cemetery.[7]

Glasgow, along with the other children, was removed from home during the sickness of his mother and did not know of the irreparable loss to the family until several days after she was dead.[8] It became necessary at once to provide care for the children, particularly the youngest, who were temporarily placed in different families.[9] The oldest son, William A. C., had already been provided for, having become an active midshipman on the New Orleans Station on March 14, 1808,[10] though he did not become a regular midshipman until January 16, 1809. His younger brother was soon to be even more handsomely taken care of.

2

David Porter, Junior, having been ordered by the Navy Department to take command of the Naval Station in New Orleans, arrived at that city from Pittsburgh on June 17, 1808, only five days before the death of his father.[11] Porter was greatly shocked at the tragic situation which awaited him, and it is said that he himself soon became ill of yellow fever of which he nearly died.[12] With him was his young wife whom he had recently married in Chester, Pennsylvania. He knew at first hand, therefore, what the Farraguts had done for his father in his last illness, and how sorely Mrs. Farragut was needed by her family. But he did not go immediately to George Farragut with an offer to take care of one of the children, as has been claimed.[13]

Porter first endeavored to aid George Farragut by transferring him from command of a gunboat to duty in the Navy Yard under the orders of Lieutenant Carroll, as he considered Farragut too old and infirm a man to perform the active duties required of the commander of a gunboat, though he was then not quite fifty-three years old. This was in September, 1808, and though in later official correspondence Farragut's name appears as commanding officer of two other gunboats, after July, 1809, he appears to have been retired from active service.[14] It was then that he purchased a plantation of nine hundred acres on the Pascagoula River. His land was located on the west side of the river near where it flowed into Mississippi Sound. By way of the Sound and Lake Pontchartrain it was about one hundred miles distant due east of New Orleans. This vicinity, then called Point Plaquet, became known afterwards as Farragut's Point.[15]

Some time after the Farragut family had moved to the Pascagoula River, Porter paid them a visit. He had by that time decided to offer to take one of the children and care for it as a mark of appreciation for the great kindness the Farraguts had shown his father. When the offer was put before George Farragut, he reluctantly agreed provided that Porter could induce one of them to go with him.[16] He realized, of course, that his home had been practically broken up at the death of his wife, that Porter could offer advantages that were beyond his power

Courtesy of the Curator, United States Naval Academy

CAPTAIN DAVID PORTER, U. S. NAVY
From the portrait by John Wesley Jarvis in Bancroft Hall, U. S. Naval Academy.

to give, and that it was only a matter of time before his second son would follow his older brother William, into the navy. There was little hesitation on the part of Glasgow when the opportunity presented itself. Impressed by Porter's uniform and having already become envious of the brass buttons of his older brother who had only recently received an appointment as a midshipman in February of that year, young Glasgow spoke up very promptly and said that he would go.[17] The little lad was then about eight years old. His separation from the family was made less trying by an arrangement which was then made, either the same day or soon thereafter, for the Porters to take one of the daughters also, who lived in their home in New Orleans as long as they remained on that Station. Upon their departure she was taken into the home of David Porter's sister, Margaret, who had recently married Dr. Samuel Davies Heap, the Navy Surgeon on the New Orleans Station.[18]

Glasgow[19] returned with Porter to New Orleans, where he was received by Mrs. Porter as a son[20] in her home. There is no evidence that the boy was legally adopted by the Porters. In fact, there is every indication, particularly later,[21] that he was not so adopted. But they treated the lad very well, and for this he was ever afterwards most grateful. Writing in his journal[22] forty years later, he declared, "Thus commenced my acquaintance with the celebrated Commodore David Porter, late of the United States Navy, and I am happy to have it in my power to say, with feelings of the warmest gratitude, that he ever was to me all that he promised, my 'friend and guardian.'"

3

Glasgow Farragut was not completely separated from his father, but as long as the Porters remained in New Orleans, he was often permitted to visit the plantation on the Pascagoula River. Porter permitted him sometimes to accompany him on his excursions and boat expeditions, and frequently he went sailing with his father on Lake Pontchartrain. It was during these years in the vicinity of New Orleans that young Farragut, mainly under the tutelage of his father, gained an intimate knowledge of boats and a love for the sea. He also acquired a fondness for adventure, for his father was no ordinary sailor. He was a man of recklessness of character, and on one occasion was daring enough to sail from New Orleans to Havana in his pirogue, a species of dugout canoe constructed of two pieces of wood. He was very proud of this voyage and often referred to it. When some of his friends reproached him for trusting his life and the safety of his children in the little yawl in which he cruised about the lake, he laughed and said, "Danger indeed! If you had said there was danger in going to Havana in a pirogue there would have been some sense in it; but this thing is as safe as any craft at the levee."[23]

One day he took his young sons across the lake when almost a gale was blowing. As they passed one of the gunboats, they were hailed and invited to come on board until the storm was over. To this George Farragut, displaying no uneasiness at all but having the utmost confidence in his little boat, replied that he could ride out the blow better than the gunboat could. To any one who suggested that his children were too young to be subjected to such risks he replied simply, "Now is the time to conquer their fears."[23] Like normal children, they had fears at first. Glasgow declared many years later, after he had sailed the seas through many perils, that his first experience on salt water was on Lake Pontchartrian, when he accompanied a young man whom his father had sent across the lake to clear some land on the Pascagoula plantation. On that occasion, he admitted, he had fervently hoped it would be his last voyage. He was thus indebted to his father, during those most impressionable years, for a sea-mindedness developed through a close contact with the sea and boats. He early learned resourcefulness also. If bad weather or night prevented George Farragut and his sons from returning home, they slept on the beach of one of the islands in the lake wrapped up in the boat sails. If the weather was cold, they scooped out beds in the dry sand and lay half buried there.[24] This was good training in self-reliance for an admiral in the making.

About June 21, 1810, young Farragut was entirely separated

from his family when he accompanied the Porters on their leaving New Orleans at the expiration of Master Commandant Porter's tour of duty as the commanding officer of the Naval Station at that place. Glasgow was never to see his father again. All the family life which he in childhood was to have thereafter was to be enjoyed in the home of the Porters. Even this was of very short duration, and it might be said that Glasgow Farragut never experienced the normal life of a child.

V

A MIDSHIPMAN AT THE AGE OF NINE

GLASGOW FARRAGUT's voyage with the Porter family from New Orleans to Washington was his first experience on the high sea. He was then not quite nine years old, as the Porter's left for the north near June 21, 1810.¹ They made the voyage, which lasted about one month, on the little bomb brig *Vesuvius*, which carried eleven small guns and thirty men.² The reason the passage took so long was that they sailed by way of Cuba so that Porter could stop at Havana. He called there to endeavor to collect a reward offered by both Spain and the United States for the seizure of French privateers which he had captured in the vicinity of New Orleans.

While in Havana they learned that a short time before their arrival the United States brig *Vixen*, commanded by Lieutenant John Trippe, had been fired upon and damaged by a British man-of-war. This news made a lasting impression on the young lad; long years afterwards he wrote, "I believe it was the first thing that caused bad feeling in me toward the English nation. I was too young to know anything about the Revolution; but I looked upon this as an insult to be paid in kind, and was anxious to discharge the debt with interest."³ His indignation was heightened by the thought of what might have happened if a British vessel of war had fired upon the *Vesuvius* with Mrs. Porter and her one year old son on board.

The lad also heard the angry comments of Porter on the incident. That officer had already had several unpleasant experiences with the British. When as a very young man he was making his first voyage on board a merchantman commanded by his father, an armed boat from a British man-of-war attempted to board their ship while lying in the harbor of Jeremie, Santo Domingo, and to search her for deserters. The attempt failed, but with the loss of several men, one of whom fell by the side of young Porter. On a later voyage, he had the humiliating experience of being taken by a press-crew on board a British vessel, where he was treated rather brutally; then he was fortunate enough to escape during the night and swim to a Danish merchantman. On a third voyage he had a similar experience, though he was able that time to escape very quickly and return to his shipmates. Glasgow Farragut, through his association with a man of such experiences, could hardly have failed to be moved by an act of injustice suffered from the British. His fighting spirit was fostered also through Porter, with whose prowess in battle he early became familiar. Porter had participated, under command of Captain Thomas Truxtun, in the capture of the *Insurgent* by the *Constellation* in the War with France. Later as executive officer of the schooner *Experiment* he had fought both the French and pirates in the West Indies. In the War with Tripoli he had been on the *Enterprise* when she captured an enemy polacca, and had then spent a period of imprisonment in Tripoli after the *Philadelphia,* commanded by Bainbridge, had run on the rocks and he with the other officers and crew had been captured in the harbor of Tripoli. Fortunate indeed was Glasgow Farragut in being placed under the tutelage of an officer who had so distinguished himself.

Arriving eventually at Washington, the Porters spent several months there before proceeding to Mrs. Porter's home in Chester, Pennsylvania. During this time Glasgow was placed in school in Washington. One day Porter took him with him to make a call on the Secretary of the Navy, Paul Hamilton,[4] of South Carolina. It was an interesting and somewhat dramatic moment in Glasgow's career, his first contact with the head of the service, from whom were to come the orders which were to direct and control his life and his fortunes during a long career as a naval officer. Porter introduced the little fellow to the great man as one who aspired to wear the uniform of a midshipman.

Taking the hand of the lad, who looked up appealingly at him, Secretary Hamilton promised him the appointment when he had reached the age of ten.

Hamilton more than made good this promise, for he appointed Glasgow a midshipman under a warrant dated December 17, 1810[5]; he was not ten years old until the following July 5. This was a very tender age at which to enter the naval service; but the fact has been heretofore overlooked that the muster rolls of the New Orleans Station had borne the name, "J. G. Farragut, Boy, 12 April, 1810, to 15 June, 1810."[6] The record shows also that he had not drawn rations but had received the sum of $13 for this first service in the Navy of the United States. At that time he had not reached even the age of nine.

When he was appointed a midshipman, Porter gave Farragut a beautiful gold watch inscribed "D. P. to D. G. F., U.S.N., 1810." This watch is now one of the much prized relics and memorials in the Museum of the United States Naval Academy.

It is not unlikely that Farragut's early appointment as a midshipman was due to the following incident in Porter's career. About a month after his return to Washington from New Orleans, on August 16, 1810, he wrote a letter to the Secretary of the Navy in which he practically resigned from the service. It was probably in connection with this that he called on the Secretary. The difficulty was finally adjusted by granting him, on February 1, 1811, a furlough to make a voyage on a merchant vessel. He still had visions of collecting the reward for the capture of the French privateers. So he sailed away to Havana; but was back in Chester by July 21, 1811, when he acknowledged there his orders to command the *Essex*. It is significant that the request for Glasgow's appointment as a midshipman and the granting of the appointment itself both came during this period of uncertainty, when Porter may have particularly desired to see the lad more securely provided for. Be that as it may, it was a fortunate circumstance for Glasgow that he should receive the appointment in time to accompany Porter on board the *Essex* and to be associated with him in many romantic adventures in that man-of-war.

UNITED STATES FRIGATE *Essex*
From the contemporary painting by Joseph Howard.

VI

FARRAGUT JOINS THE *ESSEX*

EARLY in August, 1811, Porter, accompanied by Midshipman Farragut, arrived in Norfolk to join the frigate *Essex*. On the ninth of that month he sent the lad aboard the vessel with the following note for Lieutenant John Downes, the executive officer: "I have sent Mr. Farragut and David Fittimary on board and beg you to take them under your particular care. When the wherry is perfectly dry, I will thank you to send her over to me every morning at ½ past 9, under charge of Mr. Farragut."[1] By virtue of his appointment as a midshipman in the United States Navy the boy had become "Mr. Farragut," though only ten years old; and in spite of his extreme youth, Porter at once intrusted him with command in a position of some responsibility. It was a propitious beginning for a career that was to end so gloriously.

Little Glasgow Farragut was a proud lad when he stepped on board the *Essex* for the first time and stood looking about him on the deck of the strange vessel. He was an appealing figure, small even for his age but well proportioned; after he became a grown man, he was only five feet, six and a half inches tall.[2] He stood there, very erect but graceful, with a charming smile on his face. This smile relieved the air of seriousness and firm resolution which his tightly closed mouth gave his countenance. His features were a mixture from his Irish and Spanish ancestry. His complexion was somewhat swarthy and his hair dark brown, though his eyes were hazel or light brown; the shape of his face was oval and his lips were thin and the mouth well formed, but his cheek bones were prominent and his nose was aquiline.

Young Farragut was wearing the undress uniform of a midshipman. His short blue coat had a standing collar with a button and a slip of lace on each side; his vest, knee breeches, and stockings were all white; his shoes, similar to what are now called slippers, were low cut; on his head he wore a plain cocked hat of the variety which had superseded the three-cornered hat of the Revolutionary days.

In his luggage, which was being brought on board that day and was soon to be stowed in his locker in the steerage, was a much more splendid outfit, his full dress uniform. This consisted of a blue coat with tails like those of the captain and the lieutenants. The lapels were short, the standing collar was decorated with a diamond about two inches square which was made of gold lace and placed on each side, the slashed sleeves had three small buttons at the bottom, and there were six buttons in front with button holes worked with gold thread. The vest and breeches were white and just like those of the lieutenants except that there were no buttons on the pockets of the vest. On these pockets the captain had four buttons and the lieutenants only three. Rank must have its privileges. He also had shoes with buckles, a grand, gold-laced, cocked hat, and a hanger, which was a short curved sword.[3]

All this grand uniform he wore when Porter came on board and ceremoniously assumed command of the *Essex*. With his officers grouped about him on the quarter-deck and the crew drawn up on their portion of the spar deck, Captain Porter then read his orders from the Secretary of the Navy, his flag was raised, and the band played.

The midshipman's youthful curiosity and his duties on board soon made him fully acquainted with the ship from stem to stern. He found out that the *Essex*'s gun deck was 141 feet long and her keel 118 feet in length, that her breadth of beam was 37 feet and depth of hold 12 feet and 3 inches, that the height between gun and lower decks was 5 feet, 9 inches, and between gun and spar decks was 6 feet at the waist and 6 feet, 3 inches, under the quarter-deck. He was told that his vessel with a tonnage of slightly over 850[4] was considerably smaller than the *Constellation* which was rated at 1265 tons. Although the *Essex* was called a thirty-two, he counted twenty-four 32-pounder carronades and two long 12-pounders on the main gun deck and sixteen 32-pounders and four long 12-pounders on the spar deck, making a total of forty-six guns.[5] It was the usual practice for American frigates, however, to carry more than their rated number of guns.

On inquiry as to the origin of the name of the *Essex*, he was told that the ship's construction grew out of the unlawful practices of France in seizing American neutral ships in an endeavor to cripple Great Britain, with which country she was then at war. In January, 1798, the American Congress without declaring war ordered the capture of French armed vessels wherever they should be met on the high sea, and in June following, to increase the navy it passed an act which authorized "the President to accept such vessels as might be built by the citizens for the national service, and to issue six per cent stock to indemnify the subscribers."[6] It was under the provisions of this law that the citizens of Salem, in Essex County, Massachusetts, built the frigate with subscriptions amounting to over $75,000,[7] the government paying about the same amount for her guns and stores. Hence the name *Essex*. She was extremely well built, civic pride and national patriotism having inspired the whole community, which was then an important shipping center. Having been launched on September 30, 1799, she was less than two years older than Midshipman Farragut himself.

The old salts on board had many stories to tell of the prowess the ship had already won both in peace and war. They could relate how she sailed from Salem on December 22 following her launching under command of Captain Edward Preble for Batavia on the Island of Java to escort home a fleet of American merchantmen, and how in carrying out this mission she became the first man-of-war of the United States to sail round the Cape of Good Hope into the Indian Ocean. They could tell how she participated in the War with Tripoli, when Stephen Decatur[8] was one of her officers, and how shortly before Porter took command of her, she brought home a distinguished passenger,

William Pinkney, late Minister to Great Britain, who was returning after diplomatic relations had been broken off with that country by the United States as a preliminary step towards the War of 1812.

"On reaching the *Essex*," wrote Farragut in his journal,[9] "I was exceedingly pleased with the ship and her officers." Among these officers were several besides Porter who were to gain distinction in the service. Those particularly worthy of mention were John Downes, first lieutenant, William Finch (Bolton), acting fourth lieutenant, and Stephen Decatur McKnight, acting fifth lieutenant. The last, a nephew of Commodore Stephen Decatur, was lost at sea in the ill-fated *Wasp* only a few years afterwards when still a very young man. Though Farragut mentions the officers of the frigate by name in his journal, he makes no reference to the midshipmen, who were twelve in number, nor to the crew, numbering about 300 men. He was probably not so well pleased with his fellow midshipmen as with the older men on the ship, for the youngsters doubtless teased the little lad as far as they dared to go with one, soon known to be the special protégé of the commanding officer. He probably was sent to look for five bells, and to find Charley Noble and ask him to report to the officer of the watch, and was made the butt of other jokes and pranks of a rougher nature.

The life of a midshipman on a frigate a hundred years ago was at best a hard one. All the midshipmen lived together in the steerage, or the "gun-room," which was a section of the berth deck just forward the wardroom. They all ate here at a messtable which was securely fastened to the floor; here also they slept in hammocks which at night were suspended from hooks attached to the beams overhead. The steerage was neither well ventilated nor adequately lighted. For heat in the cold winter months at sea, the lads had only buckets of sand in which were buried hot 24-pound shot. A midshipman rarely had any privacy for writing a letter or reading a book, for there was usually a noisy crowd in the steerage, spinning yarns, playing cards, and singing, or engaging in rough pranks on their shipmates, in ordinary horse play, and sometimes in fisticuffs. The food in port was plain but rather good. At sea, however, on a long cruise all had to subsist on hard-tack infested with weevils, tough and indigestible beef soaked in brine, squashy rice, pork and bean soup, and scouse, which was a mixture of hard-tack softened with water and of pork fat baked together in a pan. The midshipmen received a regular grog ration, and the older ones invented many ingenious ways of enjoying that of the younger ones as well as their own. Some of the "young gentlemen" had already fallen into habits of intemperance as there were temptations to drink on every side along the wharves when the ship was in port. They even went so far as to engage in dueling sometimes, in which they followed the etiquette of the code of honor as carefully as did their elders.[10]

This was the life to which Midshipman Farragut had to accustom himself. His experiences during the past two or three years had somewhat prepared him to take care of himself, and his character was already beginning to take form. He had many traits which would tend to make him popular among his fellows. He was talkative and greatly enjoyed a joke. He was naturally friendly and kind and his sympathy was quickly aroused by injustice and suffering. In fact, he found it difficult to conceal his emotions, all of which were mirrored in his face. As will be seen later, he did not know the meaning of the word "fear," and young lads soon learn to respect the anger of one ready to defend himself.

While the *Essex* was being made ready for active service, Farragut had time not only to acquaint himself with the vessel, his officers, and his shipmates, but also to learn his duties as a midshipman. Though the naval regulations of those early years state that "no particular duties can be assigned to this class of officers," the statement is largely contradicted by the following sentence: "They are promptly and faithfully to execute all the orders for the public service, of their commanding officers." In other words, as some one has aptly expressed it, "The midshipman was to do what he was told, and that damned quick," or he might feel the sting of a rope or be brought to a sudden realization of his low status in the navy by the persuasive force of an officer's boot. It would, therefore, have been better for the lads if their duties had been more specifically set down. The only specific duty stated in the regulations was that "midshipmen are to keep regular journals, and deliver them to the commanding officer at the stated periods, in due form." These were intended to give the lads some practice in writing, spelling, and composition, but they usually deteriorated into copies of the ship's log and were accordingly of little value. The last item relating to midshipmen was very general in its nature. It stated that "they are to consider it as the duty they owe to their country to employ a due portion of their time in the study of naval tactics, and in acquiring a thorough and extensive knowledge of all the various duties to be performed on board of a ship of war.'

There were many duties to be performed by the midshipmen, whether they were in the regulations or not. They had to echo the orders of the officer of the deck and see that they were obeyed promptly; at night they sometimes had to rout the members of the watch from the secluded places where they had concealed themselves for a bit of sleep. During the principal evolutions of the ship two midshipmen were ordered to the tops in advance to direct the work of the crew, and in a storm to encourage the men by taking the most dangerous places themselves on the yards. In port, they were placed in charge of every boat that left the ship and were held responsible if the boat returned with any of its crew missing. At the guns, midshipmen served as assistants to the officer commanding a division and saw to it personally that all his commands were properly executed. They had to inspect the clothing of the crew once a week; they had to serve as master's mates on watch on the forecastle, and as assistants to the officer of the deck; they had to superintend the issuing of provisions, water, and spirits; and besides they had to perform many other minor miscellaneous duties too numerous even to list. In view of these varied duties, a midshipman in the old navy of sails might almost have claimed, in the words of that fantastic mariner of the *Nancy Bell*,

> Oh, I am a cook and a captain bold,
> And the mate of the *Nancy* brig,
> And a bo'sun tight, and a midshipmite,
> And the crew of the captain's gig.[11]

The officers, however, were reminded in the regulations that they were to "consider the midshipmen as a class of officers meriting, in an especial degree, their fostering care. . . . They will see, therefore, that the schoolmasters perform their duty towards them, by diligently and faithfully instructing them in those sciences appertaining to their department; that they use their utmost care to render them proficient therein." A very young midshipman such as Farragut would receive a full measure of this "fostering care." Commodore Bolton, who was a lieutenant on the *Essex* with Midshipman Farragut, related many years afterwards to Mrs. Farragut that he once found the little fellow on watch, leaning against a gun-carriage fast asleep, and that he had covered him with his pea-jacket to protect him from the cold night air.[12]

But it would be a mistake to conclude that Farragut was then a mild little fellow who either needed, or appreciated, coddling. The truth of this is borne out in a incident which is said[13] to have happened not long after he joined the *Essex*. One day in the regular performance of his duty as midshipman of the captain's gig while the small boat was waiting at the wharf in Norfolk for the return of Porter who had gone ashore on business, some loungers about the dock began to make sport of the appearance of the young midshipman, who probably looked somewhat childishly self-conscious in his new uniform. Finally one of the number was imprudent enough to sprinkle the lad with an old water-pot. He was immediately jerked into the boat by the boat-hook of the bowman, which caught in the culprit's pocket. A general fight quickly developed, and the boat crew jumped ashore, Farragut in their midst brandishing his dirk and encouraging them on. The sailors drove their tormentors up to Market Square, where the police took a hand in the engagement and arrested all hands. The outcome was that young Farragut with all the rest was bound over to keep the peace.

One writer,[14] in further imbellishing the incident, adds that Porter was greatly pleased with the spirit displayed by the bantam midshipman and declared to Lieutenant Downes when commenting on the affair that the lad was made up of "three pounds of uniform and seventy pounds of fight."

VII

PEACE TIME CRUISING IN THE *ESSEX*

1

HAVING just returned from a foreign cruise when Porter took command of her, the *Essex* needed considerable refitting, but she was ready to sail on October 25, 1811.[1] This was to be Midshipman Farragut's first real experience at sea on a man-of-war, although he had already traveled many miles by water for a lad of his age. It was a far cry, though, from a flatboat on the Tennessee, Ohio, and Mississippi Rivers and a small bomb brig from New Orleans to Washington, to a smart frigate like the *Essex*.

Accordingly on October 25 Farragut first witnessed the operation of getting a frigate under way. He stood by Porter, ready to obey his first command, as all hands were piped to their stations. Men climbed like squirrels into the rigging in all parts of the ship and took their places on the yards ready for the command to loose the sails. He could hear below on the gun deck other sailors heaving the capstan round and raising the anchor. First the topsails were unloosed but allowed to hang down flapping in the wind until the command, "Sheet home topsails," rang out. Then the men standing by the braces and halliards came into action, and the wind began to fill the white sails. About this time, the report came from the forecastle, "Anchor's aweigh, sir," and the frigate began to move very slowly from her mooring. As the ship's head was turned towards Hampton Roads, white sails filled with wind on yard after yard. Farragut looked over the side and noted the increasing headway, as the water foamed in the wake and the shoreline rapidly receded.

When the ship came nearer the Capes, he took deep breaths of the fresh salt air and felt the deck become more unsteady under his feet. But he did not mind the swaying of the deck; he had gotten his sea legs with his father on Lake Pontchartrain and on the long voyage on the *Vesuvius*. He looked aloft and thought he had never dreamed that anything could be so beautiful as the frigate *Essex* under full sail outward bound.

But this was not to be merely a pleasure cruise. As soon as the ship had reached the open sea, and everything had been neatly stowed away and the frigate made shipshape, Porter began to discipline and exercise his crew. War with Great Britain then seemed imminent, and he wanted his men to be fully prepared. Indeed, the ship was sailing under orders to protect American commerce from improper and illegal interference of any kind. A sharp lookout was kept at all times for a British man-of-war.

On the previous May 1, the British frigate *Guerrière* had overhauled the American brig *Spitfire*, off New York harbor, and boarded her and then impressed a passenger who was a native born American citizen. On May 16 at eight o'clock in the evening, Captain John Rodgers in command of the *President*, while searching for the *Guerrière*, saw a strange vessel looming up out of the darkness. He hailed her twice, and the ship answered with a shot which struck the American frigate's mainmast. Rodgers then replied with a broadside. The ensuing battle lasted fifteen minutes before the stranger, which turned out to be the British corvette *Little Belt*, surrendered. She had lost nine killed and twenty-three wounded, and, though badly damaged, was able the next day to continue her voyage unassisted. This had increased the bitterness of the enmity between the two nations, and the *Essex* had to be ready at all times to meet a British frigate whose captain might be eager for revenge.

No time was to be lost, therefore, in disciplining the men and exercising them at the guns. In these exercises, it was Farragut's duty to serve as one of the two or three midshipmen who were assigned to assist the lieutenant in command of a division. There were six divisions: one on the quarter-deck, one on the forecastle, three on the gun deck, and one on the berth deck. All were commanded by lieutenants except the sixth which was under command of the purser. Ten or twelve men composed the crew of each gun and its opposite across the deck. In battle, when the ship maneuvered to bring this opposite broadside to bear, the crew rushed across and manned the other gun assigned to them. Each gun crew consisted of a captain and second captain, two spongers and rammers, two loaders, two train and tackle men, two crow and handspike men, and at least one powder boy. The heavier guns required more tackle and handspike men than did the carronades. Twice a day, when the weather was good, morning and evening the crew was mustered at the guns; this was called "quarters." A blast from a bugle was followed by the beating of the drum. The men at once seized their cutlasses and rushed as fast as they could to their stations. When the drum ceased, the midshipman began calling the names of his gun crew. Upon finishing, he reported to his officer of division, he in turn to the first lieutenant, and he to the captain. Then he gave the order, "Beat the retreat!" and the men returned just as precipitately to their ordinary duties or stations.

Sometimes the call to quarters was beaten at dead of night. Then the men were required to get out of their hammocks, lash them up and stow them in the nettings, and rush to their stations—all in about ten minutes. Sometimes at night also was sounded the alarm for fire drill, when officers and men were required to lose no time in gaining the stations assigned them; the marines were drawn up with fixed bayonets, the engines were prepared and the pumps examined, the first and second lieutenants were sent to the place from which the alarm was supposed to come, and other persons were dispatched to the magazines to take necessary precautionary steps for the safety of the ship.

For real exercise at the guns, general quarters was sounded. Then all the evolutions of a battle were performed with the guns. At the various orders, which were given in a long, drawling tone of voice, the guns were run in on their carriages by the tackle men, loaded and primed by the loaders with the assistance of the rammers, run out again through the gun ports, and pointed by the crow and handspike men who used quoins or little iron wedges to hold the gun at the required elevation. Occasionally the guns were really loaded with powder and ball, the magazines having been opened and the powder boys having carried the powder to the guns in their leather buckets with tight fitting lids. Then the guns roared and the men cheered when a hit was made on a floating cask or some other target. During all these exercises the marines, as the principal marksmen on board, were at their stations on the spar deck and in the tops.[2]

The first cruise was a short one, for the *Essex* was back in Norfolk on November 5. But after only a week in port, she was at sea again, cruising three or four days off the Capes and then proceeding to Chester on the Delaware River.[3] By this time Farragut was beginning to become familiar with the duties of a midshipman at sea and with the following daily routine of a man-of-war. At first break of day, the drums begin to sound and the night sentries fire off their loaded guns; reveille immediately follows; and as though this were not enough to wake the dead, the boatswain and his mates pipe long and loud and shout, "All hands, ahoy," then pipe again and cry, "All hands up hammocks, ahoy." The men work up an appetite for breakfast by a general scouring of the decks and everything that needs cleaning and putting in order. At six bells (seven o'clock) in summer and at eight bells in winter the men are piped to breakfast. The midshipmen are now aroused from sleep by a midshipman from the watch; hammock boys lash their hammocks and stow them on deck; and the midshipmen have their breakfast and then come up for fresh air and a promenade while their rooms are being holystoned and cleaned. One hour is allowed for breakfast; then the drums roll, the ensign is run up, the guard in undress is changed for one in full uniform, and the band is ordered to the quarter-deck to play music. The sailors meanwhile have begun the numberless duties of the morning.

At nine o'clock the midshipmen assemble in the forward cabin or dining room for school which is presided over by the Chaplain. The instruction, devoted mainly to navigation, lasts two hours. When the weather is sufficiently clear, they go on the spar deck at half past eleven and "take the sun" or "shoot the sun," as it is sometimes called. They are required then to work out the last day's run and the ship's position at noon. Meanwhile the sweepers are piped, the decks are swept, and grog (one gill of whiskey diluted with an equal amount of water for each man) is made ready to be served to the crew. At twelve a midshipman is sent to the captain to inform him that it is noon. A bell is then struck, which is followed by two long pipes from the boatswain and his mates; all work immediately ceases. Then the midshipmen dine in the steerage and the crew on the gun deck; the other officers have their dinner later, the lieutenants at one, when they are called by a bugle. At this time the crew must be ready to begin work again. These activities continue until supper, which is eaten between four and five o'clock by all hands.

The remainder of the day is given over to relaxation, enjoyed by officers and crew in the various parts of the ship restricted to each group. It is the time for spinning yarns, reading, music, frolic among the youngsters, or idle whiling the time away. As the sun sets, the drums roll, the colors are hauled down and the night pendant is raised, marines in undress replace those in uniform, and the band strikes up, "Hail Columbia." After half an hour of music, the boatswain's whistle and the hoarse cry, "All hands, stand by your hammocks, ahoy!" announce the approach of bedtime. At eight o'clock in winter and nine in summer, the drums beat; then at the first roll the bell is struck and the bugles are blown; at the second roll, the sentries discharge their day muskets and exchange them for loaded ones. Lights are gradually ordered put out in various parts of the ship, a midshipman being sent last to the wardroom to see that all fires are extinguished. By ten o'clock, only the tread of the officers of the watch is heard, broken each half hour by the striking of the ship's bell which is answered by the sentries' cry, "All's well; all's well."[4]

2

Porter had sailed under orders to return to Norfolk from Chester, but on November 19 new orders were dispatched commanding him to proceed to Newport, Rhode Island, and there join the squadron under command of Commodore John Rodgers.[5] Near the middle of December, with Christmas appoaching, when Porter would have much preferred to remain with his wife and two small children in their home than to be buffeted by the wintry waves of the Atlantic, he yielded to the call of duty. From the verandah of "Green Bank," the gray stone colonial home which Mrs. Porter's father had given her as a wedding present,[6] could be seen the *Essex* swinging at anchor a few hundred yards distant in the Delaware River. After the sad farewells were said, Porter and Midshipman Farragut went down to the river bank where they boarded the captain's wherry and were rowed out to the ship. Soon the frigate was in motion down the river, and when Farragut awoke the following morning, the *Essex* was bowling proudly along over the wide expanse of Delaware Bay with her nose pointed towards the Capes and the Atlantic.

It was Christmas eve when the *Essex* arrived in the vicinity of Newport. Not being able to reach the harbor that night, she came to anchor off the Bluffs. About four o'clock the next morning there began to blow in from the northeast a severe storm with sleet and snow, and the ship commenced to drift toward the shore. Another anchor was let go, but it too was dragged. At half past six a third anchor was let go and then a fourth, but in vain; the ship went ashore just off the Bluffs. Immediately she heeled over at a dangerous angle; by that time all the rigging was so clogged with ice that the masts could not be lowered, and as a consequence the main and mizzen top gallant masts were at once blown away. It was a terrifying situation, and Farragut's first experience in the perils of the sea. The wind was roaring through the rigging, white crested waves were dashing against the ship, officers were shouting commands as loud as they could. Captain Porter and Lieutenant Downes took turns on the lookout but for only a few minutes at a time because of the intensity of the cold, which was so great that one of the sailors froze to death in his hammock. Farragut never forgot the smallest detail of that night's dreadful predicament.[7]

The ship lay temporarily on a bank, and was in imminent danger of being driven further and then dashed against the ice-covered cliffs. Men were, accordingly, stationed with axes, ready to cut away the masts as a last measure. But at that critical moment the wind began to decrease in intensity, and the ship and her crew were saved from destruction. Their escape was providential, for it was a fearful storm which did great damage along the coast. The brig *Nautilus* limped into Newport, having lost all her guns which she had been forced to throw overboard to save the ship.

After Porter had gotten the *Essex* safely into port and had paid his respects to Rodgers, the Commodore returned the call and inspected the frigate. When the inspection was over, Midshipman Farragut, who was standing near, heard the big man with the black bushy eyebrows[8] compliment Porter highly on the efficiency of his crew and the smartness of his ship, while the little captain's red face beamed in appreciation. Farragut too was pleased at this recognition of the efforts which had been made to bring the discipline and gunnery to as high a state as possible. So efficient had the men become that Porter had divided them into three watches instead of the accustomed two, and so they remained as long as he commanded the *Essex*. The frigate, Farragut declared,[9] was the smartest vessel in the squadron.

During the remainder of the winter, Farragut along with the other midshipmen attended a school taught by a Mr. Adams in Newport.[10] Here the *Essex* remained until March 28, 1812, when she sailed in company with the frigate *President*, the flagship of Commodore Rodgers, for New York, where feverish preparations were made for the war which was about to begin.[11]

VIII

FARRAGUT'S FIRST SEA FIGHT

1

ON JUNE 18, 1812, the President signed the bill of Congress declaring war against Great Britain. It was the culmination of the many years of illegal interference with American commerce and impressment of American seamen into the British navy. There were contributory causes, such as, the Indian problem in the Northwest and the aggressiveness of Western politicians called "War Hawks"; but the naval officers understood best the maritime causes.

The news of the declaration of war did not reach Commodore Rodgers in New York until two days later. Only the day before, Commodore Decatur had joined him from the south with his flagship *United States,* the frigate *Congress* commanded by Captain John Smith, and the brig *Argus* under command of Lieutenant Arthur Sinclair. This squadron anchored in Sandy Hook Bay, where on June 21 it was joined by the *President,* Commodore Rodgers's flagship, and the sloop of war *Hornet,* commanded by Master Commandant James Lawrence. At three o'clock that same afternoon[1] the combined squadron put to sea in search of enemy ships.

There was great disappointment on board the *Essex* because that frigate was not able to accompany the squadron.[2] Examination had revealed that she must have a new foremast before going to sea, though as early as the middle of the preceding April it was reported that the ship was in every respect ready for action.[3] To remedy the defect the crew put forth their utmost energy, and in about two weeks the *Essex* was prepared in every respect for the exigencies of war.

Meanwhile the fighting spirit of the officers and men on the

Essex rose to a high pitch. On three successive days Porter assembled his crew, and read to them the declaration of war. After making a short patriotic speech, he asked if there was any one who wished a discharge from the service on the ground of being a British subject. No one raised his voice until the third day, when one man refused to take the oath of allegiance to the United States, and claimed that he was an Englishman. Unfortunately for the man, who was a sailmaker's mate, there was a sailor on board who declared that he was willing to make oath that he knew the man to be an American, in fact, that he had known him all his life for they came from the same town, Barnstable, in Massachusetts. In their warlike state of mind, the crew were so greatly aroused at the man's cowardly falsehood that only the interference of Captain Porter saved him from violence. As it turned out, he was not treated very gently, for Porter decided to teach him a lesson by allowing the crew to tar and feather him and then put him ashore in New York as a coward. Such a punishment was not approved, however, by the civil authorities and Porter almost got into serious legal trouble over the affair.[4]

On July 3 Captain Porter gave signal to get under way. Never before had the anchor been hoisted to the cathead with such speed nor had topsails been unfurled to the breeze more quickly than upon that occasion, so eager were all hands to get to sea. Captain Porter was then wearing his title not through courtesy as being the commanding officer of a ship, but as a real captain, he having been promoted to that rank only the day before the *Essex* sailed. So the ship sped down the lower harbor, through the Narrows, and out into the broad Atlantic, anxious to make up for lost time.

To Midshipman Farragut the first days at sea were historically significant. First came the 4th of July, which was honored with a salute at sunrise, noon, and sunset. That day also the national ensign was borne at both mainmast and foremast, and the Union Jack at the mizzen.[5] In time of war at sea the routine could not be altered nor the discipline relaxed in recognition of the national holiday. But an additional ration of grog at noon and a little more "duff" or plum pudding from the cook was quite in order. The officers fared much better on that day, and after dinner many patriotic toasts were drunk.

July 5 was young Farragut's eleventh birthday, and the little fellow held his head a bit higher and walked with a somewhat manlier stride that day. No recognition of it could be taken on a man-of-war; but Porter saw to it that the day did not pass wholly unregarded.

The *Essex* cruised to the southward. North of the Bermudas, at two o'clock in the morning of July 11, she fell in with a convoy of seven British transports en route from Barbados to Quebec. The rearmost brig, *Transport No. 299*, also known as *Samuel and Sarah*, was cut off and captured with its full crew in addition to the 197 soldiers on board.[6] The true situation was revealed at daylight when the *Essex* showed American colors. The recently captured British officers wished very much to see the American frigate engage the British escorting vessel, the 32-gun frigate *Minerva*, which they considered a good match for the *Essex*. Porter informed them that he was quite ready to engage if Captain Richard Hawkins would meet him. General quarters was then sounded, and the *Essex* bore down upon the convoy. When within gunshot, she hove to, fully expecting the *Minerva* to meet her. Then to the amazement and chagrin of the British prisoners, Captain Hawkins tacked ship and fled among the convoy. The prisoners denounced him as a coward and swore that they would report him to the Admiralty at the first opportunity;[7] but Hawkins, though not displaying valor, showed discretion in not hazarding an engagement unless he was forced to do so to protect the remainder of the convoy. Porter's crew were so disappointed that they sent a deputation to the captain begging him to attack the whole convoy. He replied that it would be madness to do so, though British historians have not been able to understand why he did not continue the attack.[8] Not wishing to be troubled with so many prisoners, Porter disarmed and paroled them, and then permitted the brig to depart under a ransom bond.

Two days later the *Essex* captured the brig *Lamprey*, laden with rum from Jamaica, bound for Halifax. After ordering her to Baltimore, Porter turned the *Essex* towards Newfoundland. In the waters of the North Atlantic between July 26 and August 9, he took the following ships: *Leander,* ordered to Cape Ann; *Hero,* burnt; *Nancy,* ransomed for $14,000; *Brothers,* made a cartel for prisoners and ordered to the United States; *King George,* ordered to Boston; and *Mary,* burnt.[9] The *Essex,* cruising under English colors, one day on the banks of Newfoundland ran in so near the British ship *Antelope,* 50 guns, that her upper ports were plainly visible; the American frigate then hove to and the *Antelope* swept by, unaware of the prize well within her grasp.[10]

2

These captures were all made without any fighting. A shot fired across the bows of a vessel was all that was required to cause her to heave to. This was sufficient to afford plenty of excitement to a lad only eleven years old, but the next capture was to be attended with real thrills. It was to be Farragut's first sea fight. On the morning of the 13th of August,[11] the *Essex* was idling along under reefed topsails. With her sails carelessly trimmed, her topgallant masts lowered, and her gun deck ports closed, at a distance she had the appearance of a merchantman.[12] Suddenly the lookout's cry, "Ship ahoy!" electrified the crew. Everyone sought a vantage point from which to see the ship. There it was far to the windward, hardly more than a speck but growing larger every minute. Porter decided to try a stratagem to lure the ship near enough for certain capture. He ordered drags to be put out astern, and then sent sailors aloft to shake out the reefs, masthead the yards, and make sail, as if the ship were trying to make her escape. Entirely deceived as to the character and intentions of the *Essex,* the approaching ship continued to bear down with all the speed she could make. Porter then ordered the crew to quarters and cleared the ship for action. However, the ports remained closed and the tompions in the guns.

Finally the pursuing ship fired a gun, the *Essex* hove to, and the former passed under the latter's stern and got on her lee quarter. Immediately Porter ordered the flag of Great Britain to be lowered and the Stars and Stripes to be raised on the *Essex*. To this the enemy raised three hearty cheers, and discharged a broadside of grape and canister. The angle of fire, however, was such that the shot did not enter the *Essex's* ports but struck her bulwarks without doing any particular damage. In response Porter ordered the helm to be put up and the gun ports to be knocked out, and then gave the completely out-maneuvered ship a smashing broadside, which practically finished the engagement. Realizing soon that she could not run away and seeing the *Essex* about to come alongside, the beaten ship struck her colors, eight minutes after the engagement had commenced. Her captain then hailed that his ship was leaking badly, and Porter sent Lieutenant Finch[13] on board to take possession. He found seven feet of water in the hold and three of her crew wounded. The prize turned out to be his Britannic Majesty's sloop *Alert*, twenty guns, commanded by Captain Thomas L. P. Laugharne.[14] As soon as possible the leak was stopped, the officers were transferred to the *Essex*, and the *Alert* was taken in tow. So the British ship which was looking for the U. S. sloop *Hornet*[15] found a ship whose sting was much more fatal.

The *Alert* was the first British man-of-war to be taken in the War of 1812, and so historically the engagement took on a significance out of all proportion to its naval importance. Porter, indeed, in writing to Secretary of the Navy Paul Hamilton of the affair, referred to it as a trifling skirmish.[16] But to Midshipman Farragut it was a memorable engagement, a detailed account of which he has left in his journal.[17] He left no record, however, as to what he did during the battle. But that he did his duty with courage all his later life bears witness.

This is exemplified in his conduct in an incident which happened a few nights afterwards, an incident which Farragut related[18] in full. It occurred while the *Essex* had many prisoners on board. In disciplining and training his crew, Captain Porter was likely to have the alarm of fire sounded at any hour of the night, and to test the nerves of the men he sometimes ordered

CAPTURE OF BRITISH SLOOP-OF-WAR *Alert* BY FRIGATE *Essex*

From the painting by Rodolfo Claudus, presented to the United States Naval Museum by the Sperry Gyroscope Company. This was Farragut's first sea battle.

smoke to be produced in the main hold that the drill might be made as realistic as possible. At the sound of the alarm, every man was required to grab his cutlass and his blanket and rush to his assigned position as fast as his legs would carry him, and there quietly await the orders of the captain and other officers. On this particular night the wisdom of such patient and careful training was to be fully demonstrated.

Suddenly in the dead of night, Farragut awoke to discover the coxswain of the captain's gig of the *Alert* standing beside his hammock and looking at him like a cat upon a mouse. He instantly noted that the man was armed with a pistol and knew that mischief was afoot. He was so frightened that he dared not move a muscle. This was fortunate, for if he had moved he would probably have been strangled. The coxswain, reassured, after awhile moved away. Then the little lad showed his courage. When he was sure that the man had gone, he slipped out of his hammock, and as quietly as a mouse crept along the dark passages of the ship to Captain Porter's cabin and told him what had happened. Porter grasped the situation in an instant, leaped from his cot, and dashed out on the berth deck, crying, "Fire! Fire!"

The dangerous situation was saved. So well trained were the men that they rushed to their stations without confusion, but the mutineering prisoners were alarmed and became so confused that all their plans were foiled. Before they fully realized what was happening, they heard Captain Porter calling the boarders to the main hatch to secure them. This was Farragut's first real achievement in the United States Navy. Nor was it a little thing to thus save his ship from disaster.

After this dangerous incident, Captain Porter decided that the *Essex* was too crowded with prisoners for either comfort or safety. So he made a cartel ship out of the *Alert* by disarming her and the crew and paroling the officers and men, 86 in number, and sent her to St. John's, Newfoundland. The ship was placed in charge of Lieutenant Stephen Decatur McKnight, who was intrusted with a letter from Captain Porter to Admiral Sir J. Y. Duckworth, commanding officer of his British Majesty's naval forces in Newfoundland waters, which explained the circumstances of the engagement.[19]

Off New York, on the afternoon of September 4, as the *Essex* was returning to a home port, some ships were discovered to the leeward. At first, it appeared as though they were engaged in battle. But Captain Porter, who went aloft to observe their movements, saw through the stratagem, a sham battle devised by an English squadron to draw the *Essex* near enough to become an easy prey. Porter, accordingly, immediately clapped on more sail and stood away. Two of the British ships did the same and followed in chase. One of them, which seems to have been the frigate *Shannon*,[20] gained on the *Essex*. When night came on, Captain Porter decided to take advantage of the foggy, rainy weather. Calling all hands on deck, he explained that he thought the situation favorable for tacking ship, smashing into the pursuing Britisher, and boarding her. Then the lights would be extinguished, and the other pursuers would run past them in the night. Preparations were then made for a night action, recognition badges and a password being furnished the men. An anchor and its cable were hoisted to a yard-arm ready to be dropped on the enemy deck, grapnels were arranged, and the guns were double-shotted. It was at best a hazardous undertaking, for the two ships might have collided in the darkness with disastrous results to both. But they did not meet. This was caused apparently by the fact that the *Shannon* also tacked in order to pursue and capture a merchant vessel. And when morning dawned, the ships were out of sight of each other.

The *Essex* sailed on to the southwestward, and on September 7 arrived safely at the mouth of Delaware Bay. As she came in, a schooner was discovered following as in chase, which turned out to be the privateer *General Armstrong*. This ship, just two years later at Horta in the Azores, was to play the leading role in one of the most glorious episodes of the War of 1812.

It was the 15th of September when the *Essex* let fall her anchor in the Delaware River, at Chester. Porter and Farragut were rowed ashore, and hurried up to "Green Bank," which they had left just before Christmas nearly a year previous. During the last cruise they had been at sea continuously for ten weeks. Eight merchant ships and one man-of-war had been captured, and five vessels which had originally been taken by Commodore Barney in the Privateer *Rossie* were recaptured. Porter estimated that he had damaged the British the round sum of $300,000.[21]

To Farragut it had been a glorious adventure. Where but in the story books could its match be found, ranging the sea in search of ships like a huntsman after game, capturing a ship of war in a stand-up fight, saving the *Essex* from attempted mutiny, and successfully escaping from a superior force? All of this he had experienced in ten weeks. Farragut had reveled in it. In spite of his age, he had become the life of the midshipmen's mess. Full of fun, he asked no quarter if it were a matter of pranks and jokes. Agile as a cat, no one could outdistance him in a climb to the top of the mast. Here, it is said,[22] he delighted to sit, gazing out over the sea and literally "rocked in the cradle of the deep." "Where's Glasgow?" Porter would ask when the lad was missed. And the quartermaster would reply, "Up on the mainmast, sir, looking for fresh air."

Three days after the arrival of the *Essex* at Chester, there appeared in the Philadelphia *Democratic Press* the following correspondence: "A passenger of the brig *Lion*, from Havannah to New York, captured by the frigate *Southampton*, Sir James Yeo, is requested to present his compliments to Captain Porter, commander of the American frigate *Essex*, and would be glad to have a tête à tête, anywhere between the capes Delaware and Havannah, where he would have the pleasure to break his own sword over his damned head, and put him down forward in irons"; and the reply: "Captain Porter, of the U.S. frigate *Essex*, presents his compliments to Sir James Yeo, commanding his B.M. frigate *Southampton*, and accepts with pleasure his polite invitation. If agreeable to Sir James, Captain Porter would prefer meeting near the Delaware, where Captain Porter pledges his honor to Sir James, that no American vessel shall interrupt their tête à tête. The *Essex* may be known by a flag, bearing the motto, '*Free trade and sailors' rights*'; and when this is struck to the *Southampton,* Captain Porter will deserve the treatment promised by Sir James."[23]

Shortly afterwards, the *Essex* went to sea and cruised about the entrance to the Delaware looking for the *Southampton.* As Sir James did not put in an appearance, Porter eventually returned to Chester. Here he soon commenced preparations for another cruise, which was to be one of the most eventful and glorious in the annals of naval history. It was to be a cruise also in which Midshipman Farragut was to have unusual experiences and weighty responsibilities for a lad of tender age.

IX

DELAWARE BAY TO VALPARAISO

1

WHILE THE crew of the *Essex* were busily engaged in making necessary repairs and Porter was swearing at the government for not having supplies awaiting the ship at Chester on her return, orders came on October 6, 1812, from Commodore William Bainbridge to "prepare the *Essex* for a long cruise."[1] On the following day the final instructions naming the points of rendezvous reached Porter, and the next day the official orders from the Secretary of the Navy also arrived. That autumn the United States fleet had been divided into three divisions. Rodgers was given command of the *President*, the *Congress*, and the *Wasp*. Decatur commanded the *United States*, the *Chesapeake*, and the *Argus*. Bainbridge's squadron was composed of the *Constitution*, the *Essex*, and the *Hornet*.[2]

According to the plan, Bainbridge's division was to go on a commerce-destroying cruise. First they were to cross the Atlantic to the Cape Verde Islands. Then they were to sail across the South Atlantic to the Brazil coast; thence proceed to the vicinity of St. Helena, or possibly make their way into the Pacific where they would prey on the British whaling industry.

For three weeks activities were redoubled on the *Essex* which resembled a bee-hive, so busy were the officers and men in finishing the repairs and in stowing all kinds of provisions which would be needed for a long voyage. As a precaution against scurvy, as much lime juice and fresh fruits and vegetables as possible were taken aboard as well as great quantities of salt beef and pork and beans, bread and drinking water. To supply the officers' table there was a cow and some milk-goats, a few hogs and poultry to be slaughtered later, and other miscellanies too numerous to mention. The ammunition, particularly the powder, had to be examined and replenished. Ample clothing for different seasons had to be provided for all hands. In fact, there seemed no end to the necessary supplies, and Midshipman Farragut sometimes wondered, as he stood on the spar deck and watched all that stuff pouring on board, how it was possible to stow it all away below decks. But it was finally finished and the ship made ready in every particular, as smart and shipshape as holystone and paintbrush could make her. The men were all in high spirits. They had been paid a part of the prize money from the last cruise, and the officers had been advanced three months' pay. Much of this had been invested in clothing and other comforts for the voyage.

Neither Farragut nor any of the other junior officers had any conception of the magnitude of the undertaking that was before them. Porter, however, certainly did. Before sailing, he wrote to his prize agent[3] that probably a more important cruise had never been undertaken by the vessels of any nation. Realizing that it would probably be a long cruise, he added that it might be many months before the *Essex* returned to the United States. The only definite information which he divulged was, "I join Bainbridge."

But Mrs. Porter was fully aware of what was to be attempted, and this made the day of parting all the more painful when it came. Even Farragut could not have been thought unmanly for his failure to restrain his tears. Mrs. Porter had always treated him very kindly and he had grown fond of the little children, William and Elizabeth, who reminded him of his own baby sister Elizabeth not much older than they. But the tearful farewells were said at last, and Porter and Farragut went aboard the *Essex* which was then quite ready for sailing. Her white sails were unfurled, and down the river she sped like some beautiful graceful bird. On the afternoon of the 28th of October[4] she passed through the Capes of the Delaware and put to sea.

2

The first point of rendezvous fixed by Commodore Bainbridge was Porto Praya in the Island of St. Jago of the Cape Verde Islands. Only two days[5] previous he had sailed for this destination from Boston with the *Constitution* and the sloop *Hornet*, of 18 guns, commanded by James Lawrence. Porter accordingly directed his course towards that same island with the full expectation of meeting Bainbridge there in due time.

The thick, windy weather which greeted the *Essex* upon entering the Atlantic developed into a gale by the morning of the 29th of October. The ship was placed under snug sail and the masts were secured by tightening the new rigging; but the heavily laden ship rolled and labored so in the great waves that a leak was opened between the cut-water and the stem. Water streamed into the coal-hole and the berth deck, damaging many of the provisions and wetting the bedding and clothing of the crew. This situation was temporarily relieved by scuttling the berth deck and the bulkhead of the coal-hole and then manning the pumps for a few minutes every two hours.

When the gale had spent itself, Porter found it advisable to modify the allowance for provisions. The allotment of a half a gallon of water a man per day and the regular rations of rum were not changed; but everything else was affected. Bread was reduced one half, though a half pound of potatoes or apples might be substituted for the remainder. Other articles were reduced one third. Orders were issued that no opportunity be missed for catching rain water for the stock. There was a standing regulation that every part of the ship must be fumigated every morning by pouring vinegar on a red-hot shot; and lime was provided for white-washing and sand for dry-rubbing. Not only the health and comfort of the men but also their discipline was early taken under consideration. A general pardon was issued for all offences to date; but that the men might understand that the millenium had not dawned and all the cats and colts had been thrown overboard, Porter assured all hands that the first man he had to punish would receive three dozen lashes.[6]

That Captain Porter knew how to administer discipline was

well known to Farragut, by experience as well as through observation, if the following incident[7] is well founded. One day on the *Essex* young Glasgow had the misfortune to have the captain catch him chewing tobacco. The telltale stains at the corners of the lad's mouth were proof positive. Quietly but firmly Porter placed his hand over Farragut's mouth, and forced him to swallow the quid. He never used tobacco in any form after that drastic but effective cure.

The day following the storm was devoted to drying the clothing and airing the bedding of the crew. Some of the powder was found to be wet, and all the guns were reloaded. Then the men were called to quarters and exercised at the great guns, for Porter did not want them to forget that it was war time and that the lookout might discover an enemy ship on the horizon at any moment.

The crew of the *Essex* then consisted of the following officers and men: a captain, five lieutenants and one lieutenant of marines, a steward, a cockswain, a cooper, a sailing-master, a chaplain, a purser, a surgeon and two surgeon's mates, twelve midshipmen, a boatswain, a gunner, a carpenter, a sail-maker, a captain's clerk, two master's mates, three boatswain's mates, two gunner's mates, a carpenter's mate, an armourer, a cook, a boatswain's yeoman, a gunner's yeoman, a carpenter's yeoman, seven quartermasters, seven quarter-gunners, two sergeants, two corporals, a drummer, a fifer, twenty-five private marines, and two hundred twenty-seven seamen, ordinary seamen, landsmen, boys, and supernumeraries. This made a total of 319.[8]

By the 2d of November the weather had grown so moderate that the provisions were brought up from below that the damaged portion might be separated from the rest and as much as possible salvaged by drying, repacking, and stowing them under tarpaulins. Measures were also taken to provide against further damage from leaks. The position of the ship was then found to be 36° 7′ north latitude and 58° 54′ west longitude by dead reckoning, and the course was changed to the southeast to cross the track of ships sailing from England to the Bermudas.

In the early morning of the following day there was great excitement when the lookout discovered a sail to the southwest. The *Essex* under full sail gave chase; but at eight o'clock the vessel turned out to be a Portuguese merchant brig, and the chase was given over. The remainder of the day was spent in ordinary routine on shipboard. And so the days went by with little to break the monotony. November 4 was such a remarkably pleasant day that Porter thought it an opportune time to try out the new suit of sails. What a beautiful inspiring picture was then to be seen in the midst of the boundless waters, a black hull with a light streak all around the gun ports, white sails billowing overhead, all inclosed with the blue sky above and dancing greenish blue waves below. Every real seaman on board could not help loving such a ship with the Star Spangled Banner rippling in the breeze above her. It was but natural that in such an environment Farragut should have acquired a fervent loyalty to that flag and a love of the American Navy.

In the afternoon of the 8th of November a sail was made out to the east northeast. In spite of the squally weather, chase was given until five o'clock. By that time the *Essex* was only about five miles to windward of the fleeing vessel. A heavy squall then came on, which was followed by nightfall, and at eight o'clock the chase was abandoned. The ship was thought to have been the American sloop of war *Wasp*, commanded by Jacob Jones, which had sailed from the Delaware a few days ahead of the *Essex*.

Nine days passed before another noteworthy incident happened. That afternoon a sail to the west southwest was sighted. By four o'clock the Americans came near enough to hail, and found her to be a Portuguese brig laden with tobacco, bound from Brazil to Gibraltar. Five days later, at daylight in the morning, Porter thought that at last a prize was about to fall into his hands, for the *Essex* had then reached the track of the Indiamen. But on speaking her, he found her to be another Portuguese ship laden with salt, bound from Lisbon to New York.

By that time the *Essex* had crossed the Horse Latitudes, or the Roaring Forties and had entered the region of the Northeast Trade Winds. On the 23d of November, the ship was in the vicinity of the Ecliptic,[9] and Farragut had one of the strangest experiences of the voyage. In the early afternoon, the ship was boarded by Neptune, god of the ocean, accompanied by his spouse, Amphitrite, and a large retinue of courtiers and servants. Masquerading in this way were those of the crew who had already "crossed the Line" and claimed the proud title of shellback. Now they were on hand to initiate into the mysteries of the noble order all the novices on board the ship. Farragut was, of course, among the novitiates who found that there was no escaping the ordeal. They were discovered by the faithful minions of Neptune whether they concealed themselves in the hold or in empty hogsheads or climbed into the tops, and dragged unceremoniously before the court of the God of the Sea, who sat majestic with trident in hand as supreme dictator of the revels.

First the unfortunate were daubed by the imps of Neptune with soap, tar, and any other disagreeable concoction that was available. Then, in turn, they were made to sit on a spar placed across a large tub filled with water, where they had the filth shaved from their faces by the official barbers armed with very dull wooden razors. Then they were ducked in the water, and allowed to participate in the initiation of the others. Unhappiest, therefore, were those who were last in line. Considerate treatment could be gained only by bribing the shellbacks with grog. That explains why, before the ceremony was half finished, both Neptune and Amphitrite were unable to stand. But the affair was conducted with less disorder than Porter had expected, and with a great deal of fun to all hands. It had proved to be a most welcome relief to the monotony of a voyage which had then already lasted nearly a month.

But the first stage of the long cruise was soon to be completed. Just three days later, at sunrise, the Island of St. Nicholas was sighted. By nightfall the ship was sailing past the sugar-loaf Isle of Sal and the irregular ragged Isle of Bonavista. The next morning the islands of Mayo and St. Jago were so near that the villages and the flocks of goats could be seen on the mountain sides, and at two o'clock the *Essex* with American colors flying rounded the point into the harbor of Porto Praya, twenty-nine days sailing from the Capes of the Delaware and a distance of over 3,500 miles.

3

Bainbridge's ships were not to be seen. There was only a small Portuguese schooner in the harbor. The *Essex* had arrived on the day set for departure from the Cape Verde rendezvous. At first, Porter thought of putting to sea immediately in order to intercept Bainbridge at the second appointed place of meeting, Fernando de Noronha, an island off the easternmost coast of Brazil. But that was about 1,400 miles distant from the Cape Verde Islands; and after a month at sea, any port however mean in appearance has its attractions. So Porter decided to send Lieutenant Downes ashore to make inquiries concerning the recent arrivals of American and British men-of-war, and establish friendly relations with the governor by promising to salute the Portuguese flag flying over the ruins of a fort in front of the town, if he would promise to return the salute gun for gun. On Downes's return, he reported that the governor was taking his siesta and could not be disturbed but that the lieutenant-governor had assured him that the salute would be returned and that Captain Porter would be received with pleasure by the governor. Downes also reported that two American privateers and a British armed schooner had recently been there, but that Bainbridge had not visited that port. Porter, accordingly, came in and anchored, and fired a salute which was promptly returned.

The *Essex* remained in the harbor until December 2. This was long enough to enable the entire crew at different times to go ashore and enjoy the sights and sounds of a foreign country. It was the first experience of this kind for Farragut, except for the brief stop at Havana with Porter two years before on the voyage from New Orleans to Washington.

Much to Porter's surprise, for the Cape Verde Islands belonged to Portugal, an ally of Great Britain, the governor received him and some of his officers in the most friendly manner, when they called officially on the morning of the twenty-eighth. Arrangements were easily made for the purchase of supplies and the securing of drinking water. Porter dined twice with the governor, who on the evening of the twenty-ninth with the ladies of his family and the officers of the garrison visited the ship. Upon his departure a salute of eleven guns was rendered, which pleased him immensely. His own military establishment was in a deplorable state. There were some thirty cannon mounted on ship's carriages so old and rotten that they were ready to fall to pieces. There was a Falstaffian army of four hundred men, who were destitute of clothing above the waist. They had hardly five good muskets among them, the rest being guns without locks, with stocks broken at the breech, or barrels tied to the stocks with leather thongs or cocoa-nut fiber. It was a comical sight to see a naked negro mounting guard and carrying only a musket barrel. To cap the climax, the cavalry was mounted on jackasses and carried broken swords.

The provisions which were secured there consisted of tropical fruits, such as, oranges, cocoa-nuts, limes, and lemons; beef and mutton, which were high in price and not very good in quality; live pigs, sheep, chickens, turkeys, and goats; and about five thousand gallons of water which was secured with considerable difficulty on account of the surf as well as the heat and the bad rum to which the watering-party was exposed. Many of the men purchased pets such as monkeys and young goats, and when fully laden and ready to sail, the *Essex*, Porter declared,[10] resembled Noah's ark.

4

In order to conceal his real intentions, Porter sailed away on the morning of December 2 to the southeast as though bound for the coast of Africa. But when out of sight of land, he changed his course to the south southwest towards Fernando de Noronha.

The next day Farragut witnessed for the first time a burial at sea. The deceased was a seaman named Levi Holmes, who had been ill most of the voyage of a paralytic seizure. The body, covered with a flag, was brought to a convenient place, on deck, where it was kept under watch until near noon. Then suddenly resounded the cry throughout the ship, "All hands, bury the dead, ahoy." The seamen assembled on the deck, looking very solemn and somewhat self-conscious. The corpse, sewed in a hammock, with a cannon ball attached to the feet, was placed on a board near the opened gangway. All were now uncovered, and the chaplain read the impressive service for the burial of the dead. When he came to the expression, "We therefore commit his body to the deep," one end of the board was raised and the hammock-covered body plunged into the sea.[11]

It soon became apparent to Captain Porter that he would be forced to order the seamen to kill all their pigs because they consumed too much water, and also the kids because they drank the milk needed for human consumption. This had to be carried out without exception though he received some moving petitions from sailors who tried to save an animal for Christmas dinner and promised that they would furnish it water from their own allowance.[12] At worst, it only meant moving forward the Christmas dinner about three weeks. Nothing was said about the monkeys, and the inroads they made on the water supply, not to mention the food supply which they frequently sampled by stealth. But they repaid for this in the amusement they afforded the crew with their antics in the rigging and throughout the ship.

Sanitation was an important factor in Porter's desire to decrease the number of livestock on board. He was greatly concerned for the health of his men, and in the very warm regions in which the *Essex* was then sailing he greatly increased their comfort at night by permitting them to sling their hammocks on the gun deck where the ventilation was much better than on the berth deck. For four or five days the ship sailed within a few degrees of the equator, and on December 11 she crossed the "Line" in the longitude of 30° west. But King Neptune did not come aboard again, as they were all shellbacks, the recent members having been somewhat prematurely initiated.

On the very next day came the most fortunate and exciting experience thus far on the cruise. At two o'clock in the afternoon a ship which looked like a British brig of war was discovered to the windward, and all sail possible was made in chase. At six o'clock the fleeing vessel displayed a signal, which Porter answered as best he could with British signals that he had learned during his previous cruise. The ship was deceived, and at sunset showed British colors. At nine o'clock, the *Essex* was within musket shot, with the men at quarters ready for action. Porter then hailed and ordered her to heave to; but she attempted to escape and it was necessary to fire a volley of musketry into her to bring her to. She turned out to be the British packet *Nocton* of ten guns and thirty-one men, bound for Falmouth. On board was specie amounting to $55,000.[13]

Porter placed Lieutenant Finch and Midshipman Conover and thirteen men as a prize crew on the packet together with seventeen of the prisoners whom he paroled; and dispatched her to the United States. The remainder of the prisoners were kept on the *Essex*, which then proceeded on her course.

On the afternoon of the 14th the lookout discovered the high peak, or Pyramid, on the Island of Fernando de Noronha. At daylight the following morning the *Essex*, disguised as a merchantman and flying British colors, entered the harbor. Porter sent Lieutenant Downes ashore in civilian clothes to gather intelligence concerning Bainbridge. He fortunately found a letter in code and partly in sympathetic ink, left with the governor by the Commodore for Porter. This appointed a third rendezvous off Cape Frio to the northward of Rio de Janeiro. Without anchoring, Porter immediately sailed away to the southward.

On this long run of about 1,400 miles to the south along the coast of Brazil only two Portuguese ships were seen. Porter boarded the second under English colors, which enabled him to secure information concerning the presence of an English sloop of war laden with specie in St. Salvador, where she had arrived in distress. From information gained from the prisoners from the *Nocton*, Porter was sure this was the *Bonne Citoyenne* and decided to sail for that port with the intention of cruising about until she came out. But thinking that probably the British sloop would be accompanied by the British ship of the line *Montague,* known to be in those waters, which would be more than a match for the *Essex,* and reflecting that his first duty after all was to proceed to the rendezvous, he continued southward.

On Christmas morning the color of the water began to indicate the proximity to land, and at noon, though the weather was hazy, high and irregular land was discovered. By four o'clock Cape Frio itself came into view.[14] The *Essex* then cruised about the entrance to Rio de Janeiro under English colors, looking out for Bainbridge and for any English ships which might appear. The first two were Portuguese, but on the twenty-ninth the British schooner *Elizabeth* was captured after a chase which lasted from early morning until nine o'clock at night. Learning that she was one of a convoy of six, from which she had just parted to return to port on account of a leak, Porter hastily placed Midshipman Clarke and six men on board her with orders to use his own discretion as to whether he would take her into Rio or directly to the United States. Three prisoners were left on her; the remainder were placed on the *Essex.* As soon as possible Porter set out in chase of the convoy, which was under escort of the three masted schooner *Juniper.* In spite of a heavy head sea and injuries to the rigging and spars Porter refused to give up the chase, which continued until January 12. Then he decided to make for St. Catharines, the fifth place of rendezvous, and skip the fourth, St. Sebastians. There he might expect to obtain wood, water, and other provisions which were beginning to be much needed.[15]

The *Essex* arrived on the 20th at St. Catharines, an island very near the coast about 500 miles below Rio de Janeiro. Porter again sent Lieutenant Downes ashore to establish proper relations with the authorities. Wood and water and rum in sufficient quantities were easily procured; but only a small amount of flour, onions, yams, hogs, and fowls were obtained. Some beef was procured, but most of it was spoiled when it came on board and had to be thrown into the sea. This attracted the sharks, one of which was about twenty-five feet long, much to the horror of the men who had been swimming near the ship. One boat with provisions was capsized in a squall with considerable loss, though the boat's crew escaped with their lives. Learning from the captain of a small vessel, lately arrived from Rio, of great activity of British men-of-war in that vicinity, Porter decided to depart immediately for fear he might be blockaded. At eight o'clock in the evening of the 25th the *Essex* got under way, and by four the following morning was clear of the islands.

It then became necessary for Porter to decide on his future course. According to the purser, there was bread for three months only at half allowance. This was not sufficient to justify Porter's going to the last rendezvous, the vicinity of the Island of St. Helena, to intercept returning Indiamen. It was too dangerous to enter a port to the north to secure provisions, and it was also hazardous to attempt to return to the United States through waters swarming with enemy ships. Porter did not know that on the previous December 29 Bainbridge had destroyed the British frigate *Java* off Bahia, Brazil, and was even then on his way back to the United States. From misinformation, he thought the *Hornet* was captured,[16] though she had remained off the harbor of St. Salvador blockading the *Bonne Citoyenne* until the 24th of January when the *Montague* appeared and she fled northward. Faced with the probability of starvation, capture, or blockade, Porter made a bold decision, to double Cape Horn and find supplies at a port in Chile. He would then play havoc with British shipping in the Pacific.

On the 26th of January, 1813, Porter turned the *Essex* to the southward and began that hazardous undertaking. A long voyage, over 2,500 miles, was ahead of the ship to Cape Horn. After two days sailing, the weather became colder, and the crew began to pull out their winter clothing. Preparations began to be made in adjustments to the rigging and the securing of the guns and the restowing of various articles on the ship for the rough weather which was expected soon to fall upon the *Essex*. Albatrosses began to appear in numbers; but unlike the "Ancient

Mariner," Porter and his men did not kill any of them. The weather was very variable, with occasional gales and heavy blows approximating storms. But the first real danger did not assail the ship until February 13 when, in the midst of a gale, she was almost driven ashore on the coast of Staten Island as she was entering the Strait of Le Maire, leading between that island and Tierra del Fuego. The passage through the strait was a terrifying experience with the hazy weather, foaming breakers, and violent wind. The *Essex* stood that first test well though such a heavy press of sail was carried as to pitch the forecastle under and the sea was so rough that no one could stand without grasping something for support. But greater trials were ahead.

For two weeks the *Essex* battled with the storms and raging seas in rounding Cape Horn, and the crew experienced all the terror and hardship so vividly portrayed in John Masefield's narrative poem, "Dauber," and in all the accounts of navigating those dangerous seas. The ship was forced as far south as 60° latitude, and had the greatest difficulty under reduced sail of making her way to the westward and then to the northward. The men suffered from the bitter cold and hail and rain and the necessity of frequently making, and taking in, sail which was wet and heavy. As for food, they had barely enough to satisfy the cravings of hunger. Though Porter increased the bread to two-thirds allowance, it was full of worms and weevil. On opening the barrels of peas and beans, he found them to contain a mass of chaff and worms. So hungry were the men that a rat was considered a dainty, and its destruction a pleasing revenge for it was discovered that these animals had destroyed some of the precious bread. Even some of the pet monkeys were sacrificed to the pangs of hunger.[17]

On the last day of February the ship had arrived at approximately 80° west and 50° south, and the weather had so moderated that Porter and his men began to rejoice over the prospects of soon being in the Pacific. Then, as though the god of storms were angry at the escape of the ship from his clutches, a tempest suddenly fell upon the vessel, which was more severe than any they had previously experienced. For three days it raged. The ship was in constant danger of being swallowed by the immense waves, or of being driven upon the coast of Patagonia. The grand climax came on March 3 at three o'clock in the morning, when only the watch was on deck. The gun deck ports were burst in; the weather quarter boat was driven onto the wheel and the lee boat was swept off its davits, though she was saved through great exertion of the crew; spare spars were washed from the chains, head-rails washed away, hammock-stanchions burst in, and the ship deluged and water-logged.[18]

Farragut declared[19] that this was the only occasion on which he had seen regular good seamen paralyzed by the fear of the sea. Many of the marines and several of the sailors were seen on their knees praying. So much water was rushing down the hatchways that one of the prisoners, the boatswain from the *Nocton*, shouted that the ship was sinking, and this was readily believed by men who had been literally washed from their hammocks at three o'clock in the morning. The hero in that emergency, to Farragut, was the boatswain's mate, William Kingsbury, who had played the part of Neptune when they "crossed the Line." "Damn your eyes, put your best foot forward, there is one side of her left yet," he shouted to the men in his stentorian voice, which was more like the roar of a lion than the cry of a human being. With the assistance of Kingsbury and some other courageous spirits, the captain, the first lieutenant, and the officers of the watch got the ship again before the wind, secured the quarter boat, and cleared up the deck. Fortunately the gale commenced to decrease at that time, and the ship was saved.

During the height of the storm a marine, Lewis Price, died and had to be buried with scant ceremony. He had been ill a long time of a pulmonary disease. There were no casualties caused by the stormy rounding of the Cape, though many had been bruised by severe falls, Porter himself having been so severely hurt by three falls during the last storm that he had to keep to his cabin.

Pleasant and temperate weather at last appeared on the 5th of March, and with good breezes from the southward the *Essex* made excellent speed along the coast of Chile. Meanwhile repairs on the ship went along rapidly, and soon all marks of her recent terrific battles with wave and wind were removed. On the morning of the following day the lofty Island of Mocha was seen, some twenty miles distant. Here Porter hoped to intercept British vessels engaged in smuggling or in whaling. After the ship had come to anchor, some of the officers discovered through their spyglasses droves of wild hogs and horses on the island, and a party, including Captain Porter, was organized to go ashore with muskets and secure fresh meat for the crew. During the expedition, a most unfortunate accident happened. According to Farragut,[20] who was a member of the party, it occurred while the men were waiting in ambush for a drove of horses to come into good range. When the horses came near, the men raised their guns and fired. Then a quarter-gunner, named James Spafford, who had strayed from the party into the woods, came out as soon as the firing had ceased. Lieutenant McKnight,[21] who was near-sighted, did not see Spafford in the dusk and fired at a wounded horse that was trying to escape. As fate would have it, the ball passed through the horse's neck and then into the breast of the quarter-gunner. McKnight exclaimed, alluding to the horse, "I have killed him!" "Yes," replied Spafford, "and you have killed me too. Please have me put into the boat and carried on board that I may die under my country's flag." McKnight, almost crazed with grief, begged Spafford's forgiveness, and rendered all the assistance possible in getting him back on board the ship. He lingered for nearly a month, dying eventually on board the *Essex* at sea on April 4.

Obtaining the fresh meat at such a dear price, Porter hastened his departure from Mocha Island, on account of bad weather, and proceeded northward. Lack of a chart and the continued bad weather prevented him from calling at the Island of St. Maria and at Concepción, off which port he was greatly disappointed at not finding any British ships. Finally, in the early morning of March 14, with English colors flying, the *Essex* looked into the semicircular bay of Valparaiso to see what shipping might be there. Discovering therein several Spanish ships, an American brig, and an English brig which appeared to be a whaler preparing to sail in a few days, Porter sailed on some thirty miles to the northward with the intention of waiting for the Britisher to come out. Farragut writes[22] that, as the *Essex* was leaving the bay, Porter called his men aft and addressed them briefly in his animated and enthusiastic manner on how much more they would enjoy the pleasures of the port by abstaining from them for yet awhile longer. He was greeted with a burst of applause in spite of the fact that their provisions were then almost expended. Farragut adds that the devotion of his men to Porter seemed to check his ambition, for he said, "No! they have suffered too much already; it would be tasking them ungenerously; I shall go in, if only to give them a run on shore." Accordingly the following day, the *Essex* returned, and entered the harbor of Valparaiso, which seemed to the crew the Valley of Paradise indeed after being at sea almost continuously for four months and a half.

X

VALPARAISO AND GALAPAGOS ISLANDS

1

PORTER sent the diplomatic Lieutenant Downes ashore to inform the governor that the *Essex* was an American frigate greatly in need of stores through the loss of the store-ship off Cape Horn. He used this approach to see just how hospitable the Spaniards would prove to be. He was well aware that the United States had recently had trouble with Spain over Florida, and that, since Great Britain had aided the Spaniards in driving Napoleon's armies out of Spain, they considered themselves the allies of England. It was a great relief, therefore, when Downes returned with the report that Chile had revolted from Spain and set up an independent government, and that every assistance possible would be rendered a ship of the United States. He was informed also that privateers, sent out by the Spanish viceroy of Peru to harass the commerce of Chile, had captured several American whalers.

Porter immediately saluted the town with twenty-one guns. This was at once returned, and Porter then went ashore to make an official call on Governor Francisco Lastre. Notice of the arrival of the *Essex* was sent to American Consul-General Poinsett in Santiago, and arrangements were made for supplying the vessel with wood and water, and fresh bread, beef, vegetables, fruit, and other supplies. Porter then hurried back on board to receive the governor, who appeared with a large retinue of officers and was saluted with eleven guns. On the evening of the following day, Porter and his officers attended a brilliant reception and dance given by the governor, during which they were favorably impressed by the dark eyes of the Chilean senoritas. On the 21st, the American Consul-General arrived from Santiago, and that evening he, in company with several American gentlemen and Don Lewis Carrera, the brother of the President of Chile, dined on board the *Essex*. About three o'clock the next day, which was Sunday, while Porter and his officers were ashore where they had gone to escort some gentlemen and ladies of the city to an entertainment which had been prepared for them on board the ship, information was brought from the *Essex* that a large frigate had appeared in the offing and was approaching the harbor. The American officers unceremoniously deserted their guests, jumped into their boats, and made all haste possible to return to the ship. Soon the *Essex* was under a cloud of canvas but the wind failed and she had to be towed out of the harbor by the boats. In an hour the ship got near enough to the stranger to learn that she was a Portuguese man-of-war from Rio de Janeiro. This was a great disappointment to all hands on board as well as to the men, women, and children who had crowded the hills about the bay to view the sea engagement.

The *Essex* did not return to her anchorage until the next day. That evening the American officers attended a dinner and ball given in their honor by the government of Chile. The dinner was served in a large tent, handsomely decorated with the flags of all nations; costly silver plate was used for the twenty courses and plenty of wine was drunk accompanied with flaming patriotic toasts by the Chileans. The ball which followed was equally splendid, and lasted until one o'clock in the morning. Porter hoped to get away early that morning, but the governor and his wife came out with a boat-load of ladies who did not wish to be cheated out of a visit to the ship, and stayed from nine until twelve. An American whale-ship then arrived, and more delay was caused, for Porter wished to secure information from her captain. This proved to be valuable, for through him it was learned that several English whalers were cruising off the coast of Peru and in the vicinity of the Galapagos Islands. Finally that afternoon the *Essex* got under way and proceeded towards the northwest. It was the 23rd of March,[1] 1813.

2

Nothing out of the ordinary happened until the second day, when at daylight a sail was seen to the northeast. Upon being overhauled, she turned out to be the American whale-ship *Charles*, from Nantucket. Captain Gardner informed Porter that, two days before, his ship in company with two other whale-ships, *Walker* and *Barclay*, had been attacked by a Peruvian and a British ship off the port of Coquimbo, and that he alone had escaped. Porter at once crowded on sail and made for that port. By eight o'clock he discovered a sail to the northward and by noon he was near enough to make out that she was a ship of war disguised as a whaler. She then raised the Spanish flag, and the *Essex* hoisted English colors while the *Charles*, sailing in company, by previous arrangement hoisted the English jack over the American flag as though to indicate that she was a captured vessel. At the distance of a mile the Spanish (or Peruvian) ship fired a shot across the bow of the *Essex*. Porter, in exasperation, was tempted to reply with a broadside, but restrained himself and only fired a few shots over her, which brought her to. Finally the second lieutenant came aboard the *Essex* with the information that his ship was the Peruvian privateer *Nereyda*, that his captain was too unwell to leave the ship, that they had captured the *Barclay* and *Walker*[2] and the latter had been taken away from them by the British privateer *Nimrod*, and that they had mistaken the *Essex* for the *Nimrod*. He added that they were allies of Great Britain and that their sole object was the capture of American ships.

As the little farce was then about played out, Porter demanded to see the first lieutenant, the captain of the *Walker* and one of the prisoners of the *Barclay* on board the *Essex*. When fully informed of the true situation, he then ordered the American flag to be raised and two shots to be fired over the *Nereyda* which was by that time almost under the muzzles of the guns of the *Essex*. Taken completely by surprise, the Peruvians lowered their colors in surrender, and Downes was sent on board to take possession.[3]

The following morning all the guns, ammunition, small arms, and light sails of the *Nereyda* were thrown overboard; the American prisoners were transferred to the *Essex*; and the Peruvian commander was directed to proceed to Lima, bearing a letter to the Viceroy in which Porter branded the attack on American commerce as piratical.

Looking into the harbor of Coquimbo, a Chilean port about 300 miles north of Valparaiso, and finding no enemy ships, Captain Porter ordered the *Charles* to anchor there and place herself under the protection of the government; but the *Essex* continued northward in search of the *Nimrod* and the two captured American whalers. Meanwhile the *Essex* was disguised by being painted and otherwise altered to look like a Spanish merchant vessel. On the morning of the 4th of April[4] off Callao, Peru, three ships were discovered attempting to enter the harbor. The leading vessel answered the description of the *Barclay*, and Porter determined to capture her. This was accomplished with comparative ease, and Midshipman Cowan and eight men were placed on board her as a crew. Points of rendezvous were arranged at Payta, Peru, and at the Galapagos Islands, and as neither the *Nimrod* nor the other captured whaler[5] appeared to be in Callao, the *Essex* and the *Barclay* sailed northward on the hunt for British whalers.

On the 11th of April both the ships arrived off Payta, having seen only a few Peruvian merchant vessels and a couple of catamarans, from whom Porter obtained information regarding the unfavorable attitude of the Peruvian government towards the United States and the absence of British ships in the vicinity of Payta, information freely given as they thought the *Essex* a British vessel for she carried the flag of that country. Porter decided therefore to change his course for the Galapagos Islands. These were situated about 500 miles to the west of the coast of Ecuador and just south of the equator. On the morning of the 17th of April the *Essex* and the little *Barclay* arrived at Chatham Island, the easternmost of the archipelago.

3

Reconnoitering the anchorage on the northwest coast of Hood Island, which was a few miles to the southwest of Chatham Island, and not finding any ships there, Porter lay to off the latter island until the following day, when he proceeded to the westward to Charles Island, another of the group. Not finding any ships in that vicinity, he sent Lieutenant Downes to Hathaway's Post Office in search of information. He returned with several papers which he took from the box nailed to a post near the landing place in the small bay, an arrangement for the exchange of information among the whalers. In this way Porter learned that, since June of the preceding year, five British whalers had stopped there on their way to Albemarle Island. The *Essex*, accordingly, sailed westward for this island, where she arrived the next morning, the distance being only about forty-five miles. This was the largest island of the group, and was shaped somewhat like a crescent. The *Essex* skirted round its southern coast and into Elizabeth Bay which lies in between that island and Narborough Island to the west. The winds were very light, and it was the afternoon of April 23 before Porter could weather the Island of Narborough and look into Banks Bay. For several nights the guns had been cleared away and the hammocks kept stowed in the nettings to be ready for enemy ships. Now as the ship doubled Turtle's Nose, the northern point of the island, the yards were manned by officers and men eagerly on the lookout for ships. But to the disappointment of everybody, not a ship was in the bay.

After reconnoitering in vain for a supply of fresh water and after catching a bountiful supply of fish of various kinds and of turtles, Porter sailed out of Banks Bay bound for James Island to the east of Albemarle Island. He had not given up hope of finding those British whalers. Finally, his luck changed. At sunrise on the 29th of April, he jumped from his cot as the cry of "Sail ho! sail ho!" rang through the ship. Soon all hands were on deck. It was to be no illusion of white sand banks seen through fog, such as had previously cheated them. It was a large ship bearing west, and immediately the *Essex* gave chase. An hour later two more ships were discovered bearing southwest. At nine o'clock the *Essex*, under English colors, overhauled the first ship which proved to be a British whaler, the *Montezuma*, with 1400 barrels of oil on board. Captain Baxter and his crew were transferred to the *Essex*, a prize crew was placed on the captured vessel, and the other two vessels were then pursued.

At 11 o'clock, it fell calm when the *Essex* was about eight miles from the fleeing ships, which the prisoners informed Porter were the *Georgiana* and the *Policy*. The first carried six 18-pounders and thirty-five men; the other had ten 6-pounders and twenty-six men. Captain Porter, fearful that the vessels might escape if a breeze sprang up, decided to attack them at once in the small boats. Seven in number, they were organized in two divisions under command of Lieutenant Downes.[6] All the officers were in the expedition except the captain, the surgeon, the purser, and the boatswain. Farragut was in the whaleboat with Downes.[7] At two o'clock in the afternoon the boats were about two miles from the ships, which then hoisted English colors and commenced firing their guns. The fire was ineffective, and Downes and his men pressed onward as fast as possible. When within hailing distance, Downes asked if they surrendered, American colors then being shown from a pike in the bow of his boat. Surprisingly, this was answered by three cheers and the cry, "We are all Americans." It developed that most of the crews of both ships were really Americans who had been pressed into the British service. And this was the reason for the slight resistance of the ships to capture. Surprise, too, contributed to Porter's success. The mate of the second ship delayed to lower his colors until he saw one of the men in the bow of the whaleboat cock his musket, when he too yielded. He was not prepared, for he had to get his guns out of the hold and mount them. "If I had been ready for you," he remarked, "some would have returned with bloody noses."

In clearing their decks for action, the British had thrown overboard several hundred Galapagos terrapins. Their appearance in the water was very strange; they floated about light as corks, stretching their long necks as high as they could for fear of drowning. They were very amusing to young Farragut, who wrote that these were the first they had seen. Many were picked up and found to provide luscious and delicious food. They walked clumsily, supporting their huge bodies about a foot from the ground on legs and feet resembling those of an elephant; the head and neck, sometimes two feet long, resembled those of a serpent.[8] They constituted a sort of climax to the strange animals which Farragut had seen on the voyage; such as, albatrosses, flying fish, dolphins, seals and sea-lions, red-headed lizards, ferocious-looking guanas, green turtles, and strange fishes too numerous to mention. As a lad, he had fully enjoyed such strange sights and the peculiar customs and appearance of the people in the places where he had landed, with whom he was able to converse through his ability to speak Spanish, his "father" tongue.

The three vessels thus far captured were estimated by Porter[9] to be worth half a million dollars, and he accordingly felt that all the hardships spent in rounding Cape Horn had not been in vain. An abundant supply of ship's articles and of provisions thus came into his hands also. Only water was still lacking. The *Georgiana* was found well adapted to being converted into a cruiser. So the ten guns from the *Policy* and all the small arms from the other vessels were placed on board her, and the alterations necessary for equipping her for war were made. Lieutenant Downes was placed in command with a crew of forty-one men. On the 8th of May she hoisted the American ensign and pendant, and saluted the *Essex* with seventeen guns, which were immediately returned. She would prove invaluable as a decoy as her appearance as a whaler was not changed. Signals were furnished all the vessels, and points of rendezvous, in case of separation, were arranged at the Island of Plata and the Bay of Tumbez off the coast of Ecuador.

On the 12th of May Porter sent the *Georgiana* under Downes on a scouting expedition through the islands, while he proceeded with the *Essex*, the *Barclay*, the *Montezuma*, and the *Policy* to Hood Island. On the way he stopped at Charles Island to again visit the famous post office, and anchored in the bay for several days. The time was spent in replenishing the supply of wood and collecting a large number of the ungainly-looking terrapins. Fresh water, that was desirable, could not be obtained; and they had to be contented with securing about 2,000 gallons of water which was filthy in appearance and filled with slime and insects. Downes came in unexpectedly, and was hurried on to Albemarle Island in search of a ship which had apparently been at Charles Island recently.

Farragut enjoyed supremely his experience on this island.[10] One day he went on an excursion in the gig with Captain Porter. As the boat was being run in onto a small beach, which had struck the captain's fancy, seals were discovered making for the water. The men were urged to try to kill one. They singled out a handsome fellow, which they proceeded to beat over the head with oars and boat-hooks. But he continued to waddle towards the water. Finally they caught him by the tail and were pulled by the beast into the water. Captain Porter fired at him when he got free of the men, but the animal escaped and was soon out of sight.

A second attempt a little later was even more ridiculous. As soon as the boat landed, a large sea-lion arose, shook his head, and prepared to escape to the water. Porter told his boat's crew that now was an opportunity for them to show their American skill. He directed that they all string themselves along the shore, and each man get ready to strike the animal on the nose, for one blow would fix him, if rightly placed. Farragut records that that blow, alas, was never given. "I took Falstaff's motto, 'Discretion is the better part of valor,'" he wrote, "and ran and seated myself in a boat, not liking the gentleman's appearance. What was my surprise to see all the men open their ranks right and left and let the lion pass; the animal with a mighty roar dashed through to the water. I had a hearty laugh at the Captain. He said I was afraid to stand on the beach, while I maintained that I never undertook anything I did not go through with."[11]

The sailors were permitted to go ashore daily for exercise

and amusement. Farragut was a member of such a party who appointed one of their number to be cook while the rest went in search of the provisions for a feast. A spring of fresh water was found about three miles from the beach. A terrapin was procured, which was cooked in his shell; and a pot-pie was made of doves which were found in abundance. For dessert they enjoyed the prickly pear which there grew very large and had a delicious flavor. Well could Farragut write many years afterwards, "These were among the happiest days of my life."[12]

The *Essex* put to sea again on the 21st of May,[13] and cruised to Hood Island and thence to Albemarle Island by way of Charles Island. On the afternoon of the 28th, south of Albemarle, a sail was discovered directly ahead to the northward. The chase continued until it grew dark at nine o'clock, when Porter directed the *Montezuma* and the *Barclay* to steer courses that might enable the ship to be again discovered the next morning. So it turned out, for the *Montezuma* signaled next day that there was a sail to the northward. Then the chase began in dead earnest. At noon the wind began to die down, and Porter, fearful that he would yet lose the prize, ordered three of his fastest boats to be lowered with as many men as they could carry, each armed with a pistol, a cutlass, and a boarding-axe. Farragut was with them.

After the boats had left, a breeze sprung up, which made possible a continuation of the chase. The *Essex* soon passed the boats, and Porter signaled to the *Montezuma* to pick them up. The ship, when overhauled, made no resistance, and her commander at once came on board at the direction of Captain Porter, the *Essex* flying English colors as usual. He was soon undeceived, and surrendered his ship, which was the letter of marque whaler *Atlantic*, carrying six 18-pounders.

Almost at the same time another sail was made out from the masthead. As soon as the *Montezuma* came up, Porter sent Lieutenant McKnight with some men on board the *Atlantic* with directions to pursue the strange sail, for the *Atlantic* was reputed to be the fastest sailer in those waters. It was then about eight o'clock and night was fast approaching. Thinking she had been lost sight of in the darkness, the vessel turned about to elude the *Essex;* but Porter had picked her out with his night-glasses and was soon alongside. The captain at first refused to come on board; but a shot between his masts and the threat of a broadside had the desired effect. The ship proved to be another British whaler, the letter of marque *Greenwich* of ten guns.

From these two vessels Porter obtained additional naval stores, provisions, clothing, eight hundred tortoises or terrapins, and best of all one hundred tons of water for which he was so greatly in need.

The two captains made a very unfavorable impression. Captain John Shuttleworth of the *Greenwich* had taken on a good stock of Dutch courage, so much in fact that when he came aboard he was so intoxicated and used such insulting language that Porter could hardly refrain from turning him out of his cabin. Captain Obadiah Weir, of the *Atlantic,* thinking that he had come aboard an English man-of-war, and wishing to make a favorable impression, admitted that he was born in America where he had a wife and family on Nantucket but declared that he was an Englishman at heart. Later they behaved so badly and used such scurrilous language that the next day Porter made "them sensible of the impropriety of their conduct, and did so without violating either the principles of humanity or the rules of war."[14] But just how Captain Porter accomplished this is left by him to the imagination of the reader.

4

Porter began to think of taking his five prizes[15] to a South American port. But there was considerable delay in getting clear of the islands because of calms and adverse currents. Porter thought that perhaps that was the reason the Spaniards called them the Enchanted Islands. On the 6th of June, Farragut records,[16] he saw a beautiful sight, a volcano in eruption, on the island of Narborough. The whole atmosphere was illuminated by it, though no flames nor sparks could be seen issuing from the crater. On June 8 the *Essex* with her convoy of prizes passed north of Abington Island, the breeze freshened, and the course was set for the Island of La Plata on the coast of Ecuador (then still subject to the viceroyalty of Peru).

After an uneventful voyage during which no ships were seen, Porter saw land on the 16th of June, and the following day looked in at the anchorage of the Island of La Plata. At this place Sir Francis Drake is said to have anchored and divided his plunder on his famous freebooting expedition; it had always been a favorite place for buccaneers. There Porter had hopes of intercepting some enemy ships as it was much frequented by vessels sailing up and down the coast. In this he was disappointed. He also failed to find water, as he had expected. So he painted the two letters S.X. large enough to be seen at a considerable distance, on a rock; and left a cryptical letter in a bottle tied to a branch of a bush, which would be understood only by Lieutenant Downes when he called there. He then proceeded southward and across the Gulf of Guyaquil to the mouth of the Tumbez River. Arriving there on the 19th, the ships came to anchor just inside the river's mouth about six miles below the village of Tumbez.

The same day a sailor named John Rodgers, who had become intoxicated through his fondness for rum, fell from the mainyard while helping to furl the mainsail and was instantly killed. He was buried ashore the next day, and his messmates placed at his head the following epitaph on a board:

Entombed here
The body of John Rodgers, seaman, who departed this life
June 19th, 1813, aged 32 years.

Without a sigh
He bid this world adieu;
Without one pang
His fleeting spirit flew.[17]

Another seaman, Samuel Croce, had previously fallen and was killed. On the 27th of May Benjamin Geers had died of convulsions, probably caused by his taking poison. Two days previous Surgeon Robert Miller had died of consumption. But the loss of life on the expedition had been very small indeed, thus far.

Friendly relations were established with the governor, who came aboard the *Essex* dressed in a uniform, the wretched appearance of which provoked the crew to laughter. He was given a salute, however, and both he and the collector of customs who accompanied him were given presents amounting to about one hundred dollars in value, and promised more. Porter then visited the village, but found conditions there so wretched that he did not dare spend the night. Meanwhile wood and water were taken on board, though with difficulty on account of the surf which frequently upset the boats and endangered the lives of the men as there were many sharks and alligators in the river. On his trip up to Tumbez, Porter killed one of the latter, which Farragut declared was sixteen feet long and nearly as large around its girth as a flour barrel.[18]

Lieutenant Downes arrived on the 24th with two prizes, the *Hector* and the *Catharine*, which he had captured near James Island. He had taken a third also, the *Rose;* but as he was encumbered with seventy-five prisoners, he found it advisable to place them on the *Rose,* after her guns and oil had been thrown overboard and her captain had been given a passport for St. Helena. Porter's fleet was thus increased to nine ships. From an unfriendly note which had reached him from the Governor of Guyaquil he saw no prospects of disposing of his prizes on the Peruvian coast. He therefore determined to send them to Valparaiso, a friendly port.

5

Finding that the *Atlantic* was far superior to the *Georgiana* in sailing, size, appearance, and other qualifications as a cruiser, Porter mounted on her twenty guns, consisting of ten 6-pounders and ten 18-pounder carronades,[20] and manned her with a crew of sixty men under the command of Lieutenant John Downes, who had been Porter's strong right arm throughout the hazardous cruise. The *Greenwich* was converted into a storeship on which were also mounted twenty guns. Downes was then ordered to take his ship, renamed the *Essex Junior,* and escort to Valparaiso the *Montezuma,* the *Policy,* the *Hector,* the *Catharine,* and the recaptured American whaler *Barclay,* where he was to make such disposition of them as circumstances and his judgment might direct. Porter was to return to the Galapagos Islands with the storeship *Greenwich* and the *Georgiana,* which being nearly full of oil Porter wished to dispatch later to the United States. Rendezvous having been arranged with Downes in the Galapagos Islands and also in the Marquesas Islands, and all the prisoners at their resquest having been sent up to Tombez, the fleet sailed on the 30th of June. They were all still in company on the 4th of July, which was celebrated with a salute of seventeen guns from the *Essex,* the *Essex Junior,* and the *Greenwich* and with a sufficient quantity of grog to enable the crew to spend the day "in the utmost conviviality."[21] On the 9th all the alterations on the *Essex Junior* and other arrangements having been completed, Porter and Downes parted company with their respective squadrons.[22]

Then came an episode in Farragut's life, so extraordinary as to outdo the inventions of fiction but well authenticated nevertheless.[28] With pardonable pride Farragut has told the story. "I was sent as prize-master to the *Barclay,*" he declared. "This was an important event in my life, and when it was decided that I was to take the ship to Valparaiso, I felt no little pride at finding myself in command at twelve years of age." Captain Gideon Randall and his mate were to remain on board; and it was arranged that they were to navigate the vessel but that Farragut was to be in control of the prize crew. Captain Randall, a man of violent temper, was very angry at having his ship sent to Valparaiso as he wished to continue his whaling. Accordingly on the day of separation he decided he would take over the ship. At young Farragut he roared, "You'll find yourself off New Zealand in the morning." That, at best, was an extremely exaggerated statement, for New Zealand was more than six thousand miles distant, and even the Flying Dutchman could hardly have made such a voyage in that short a time. Farragut replied with as strong a negative as he could muster under the circumstances. He admitted that he was afraid of the old man, as every one else was. The *Barclay* was lying still, while the other ships were fast disappearing from sight, Porter sailing to the north and Downes to the south. Another test of the courage of the lad was at hand, but he was ready to meet it. As he expressed it, "The time had come for me at least to play the man."

Mustering up his courage, he ordered Captain Randall to have the main-topsail filled and to close up with the *Essex Junior*. Angrily Randall replied, "I'll shoot any man who dares to touch a rope without my orders; I'll go my own course, and I have no idea of trusting myself with a damned nutshell." With that noble speech, he went below to get his pistols. Farragut lost no time in calling his right-hand man in the crew and explained to him the situation, ending with the demand, "I want that main-topsail filled." "Aye, aye, sir!" he answered in a clear voice that was not to be misunderstood. From that moment, Farragut's confidence was completely restored and he became absolute master of the ship. Like a veteran, he gave all the necessary commands for making sail. What a situation for a painter is that moment in Farragut's career!

To Captain Randall he sent word that if he came on deck with his pistols he would order him to be put overboard. That ended the affair. When the *Barclay* came up with the *Essex Junior* and Farragut and Randall went aboard to report to Lieutenant Downes, the old man tried to gloss it over by saying, "I was only trying to frighten the lad." Farragut replied, "Captain Downes, ask him if he thinks he succeeded; to show him that I do not fear him I am ready to go back to the ship and proceed with him to Valparaiso." "Well done, Glasgow," agreed Downes, "go back on board the *Barclay* and resume command of her; Captain Randall is only your adviser in case you become separated from me." With that understanding clearly arrived at, they returned on board, and there was no further trouble during the remainder of the voyage.

Downes was received in a very friendly manner by the authorities at Valparaiso. Open war had broken out between Peru and Chile, and commerce between the two countries had come to a stop. This made it impossible for him to sell either ships or cargo. So he dispatched the *Policy* with her cargo of oil to the United States, and moored the other ships in the harbor. Learning through letters from the American consul at Buenos Aires that on July 5 the British frigate *Phoebe* of thirty-six guns and the sloops of war *Cherub* and *Raccoon,* of twenty-four guns each, had sailed from Rio de Janeiro for the Pacific to destroy both the *Essex* and the American whalers in that ocean, Downes made all possible haste to rejoin Porter in the Galapagos Islands and report what he had learned.

6

Meanwhile Porter had not been idle since he reached Charles Island on the 12th of July, and called at the post office there. The very next day he had the good fortune to capture the British ships, *Charlton* of ten guns, *Seringapatam* of fourteen guns, and *New Zealander* of eight guns. The *Charlton* was dispatched to Rio de Janeiro with the prisoners, her captain under oath to deliver them there. The *Seringapatam,* which had originally been built as a man-of-war for Tippoo Sahib of India, Porter decided to convert to that purpose by mounting twenty-two guns on her. On the 25th he sent the *Georgiana* to the United States with oil on board worth $100,000. He then cruised about, waiting for Downes, on the lookout for other whalers; but it was not until the 14th of September that another capture was made. This was the letter of marque ship *Sir Andrew Hammond* commanded by William Porter. She had an abundant supply of wood, water, beef, pork, bread, and very strong Jamaica rum. The next day Porter ran in and anchored at Port Rendezvous on Albermarle Island. It was here on September 30 that the *Essex Junior* arrived, guided by messages in bottles which Porter had left at various points in the islands.

Farragut, of course, was with Downes, as were the rest of the prize-masters and their crews. After reading all the information which Downes brought, Porter saw no reason for changing his plan of going to the Marquesas, where he could repair the

Essex and smoke the rats out of her undisturbed. Having completely broken up the British whale-fishery on the coast of Chile and Peru with a loss to the enemy of two and a half millions of dollars[24] and the services of 360 seamen who had been released on parole, Porter could well afford to retire for refitting before running the chance of meeting a British man-of-war. Accordingly, on the 2d of October his flotilla of six ships got under way for the voyage to the Marquesas.

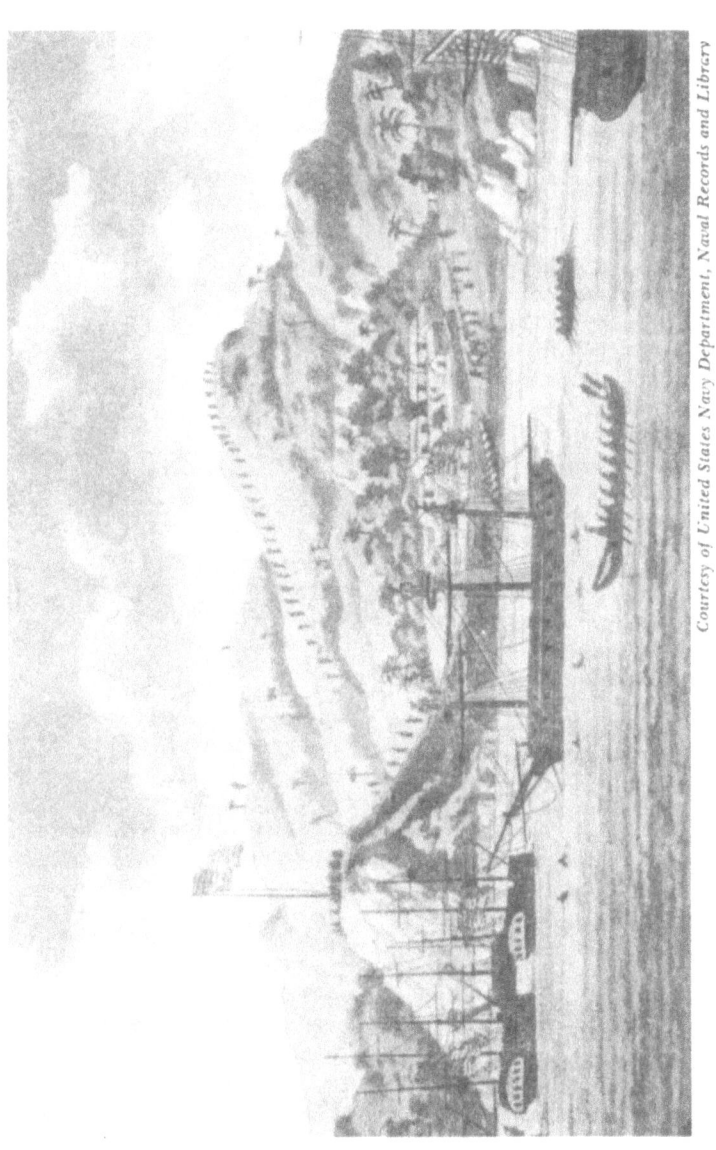

Courtesy of United States Navy Department, Naval Records and Library

THE *Essex* AND HER PRIZES AT NUKUHIVA

From the engraving by William Strickland of the drawing by Captain David Porter.

XI

AT NUKUHIVA IN THE MARQUESAS

1

ON ACCOUNT of the delay occasioned by the slow sailing of his prizes, Porter sent the *Essex Junior* on ahead on the 6th of October to the Island of St. Christiana, one of the Marquesas, where he might capture the British ship *Mary Ann*, which had been seen at Valparaiso preparing for a voyage to India. Downes was afterwards to join Porter at the Island of Nukuhiva,[1] another one of the group. Throughout the voyage the weather was remarkably pleasant, and there was not a sick man on board except a couple of the prisoners who were slightly affected with the scurvy. Nothing out of the ordinary happened that was worthy of noting in Captain Porter's *Journal*.

At twelve o'clock on the last day of the third week of the voyage, October 23, the man at the masthead first saw land to the southwest. A nearer view showed a "barren lump of rock inaccessible on all its sides, destitute of verdure, and about three miles in circuit."[2] It was far from what the seamen had been imagining since Porter had revealed their destination. The next day, however, they approached another island whose fertile valleys with trees loaded with fruits, pleasant streams, clusters of houses, and groups of natives on the hills inviting them to land seemed to fulfill their pleasurable anticipations. Porter did not land, but came in close to the shore to traffic with the natives for fruits and vegetables and their ornaments. Though they frequently repeated the word *taya*, meaning friend, it took time for them to muster up courage enough to paddle their canoes near the *Essex*. Finally their confidence was gained, and considerable trading was carried on, pieces of iron hoop and fish-hooks being most highly regarded and being exchanged for pigs, bread-fruit, feather ornaments, and many other articles. Some of them eventually came on board the ship, where they were astonished at the sight of the goats, sheep, dogs, and Galapagos tortoises.[3]

Porter reached his destination on the 25th of October when at dawn the *Essex* entered Comptroller's Bay in the Island of Nukuhiva,[4] and anchored at Port Anna Maria. Soon after anchoring, he was astonished to see a boat approaching, in which there were three white men. One of them was naked except for a loin cloth and tatooed all over like a native. Thinking they were seamen who had deserted some vessel, Porter refused to allow them to approach the ship or enter into conversation with anyone on board. On going ashore soon afterwards with four boats well armed and manned with seamen and marines, he was astonished to find that one of the white men was Midshipman John Minor Maury[5] of the United States Navy, who on furlough had sailed as an officer on an American merchantman for Canton and had been left on the island with a party of six men to gather sandalwood. All the party had been killed in warfare with the natives except Maury and another man named Baker. The third man was an English beachcomber named Wilson who had lived many years on the islands and spoke their languages so well that he proved an invaluable aid to Porter as an interpreter.

The natives, both men and women, were greatly impressed with the marching of the marines, the sound of the drum, and the firing of the muskets, when Porter put them through their exercises. It was natural for them to be interested in the warlike aspects of their visitors, for they were then at war with another tribe, called the Happahs. Their own tribe was known as the Taeehs.[6] Before Porter returned to his ship, he had made promises of protection to the natives, which were soon to lead him to participation in the war.

The valley of the Taeehs was worth fighting for. From the deck of the *Essex*, anchored in the midst of a smooth circular harbor eight or nine miles in circumference, one could see a curving beach of white sand about a mile in length. Back of this beach was a valley inclining gradually about two miles, when it divided into three or four other valleys, which were narrower and steeper and ended with the mountains, rising two to three thousand feet above the ocean and inclosing the little domain of the Taeehs. The valleys were carpeted with velvety lawns and so thickly covered with luxuriant groves of tropical fruit-bearing trees that few of the houses of the inhabitants could be seen; but some appeared on the summits of the hills, the white thatched roofs of others peeped from the heavy foliage or hung like birds' nests from the sides of the mountain forests. Down the deep, dark glens of the mountains, streams rushed and foamed in rapids and cascades. As if dominating the whole scene, a great pyramid of rock stood at the head of the valley; behind it and to the right a wall of basalt several hundred feet high crowned the highest mountain, while to the left a projecting cliff of gray stone covered with trees and parasitical hanging plants stood as if about to leap into the green valley below. It took but little imagination to picture this enchanting spot as the home of Calypso or the happy valley of the Abyssinian Prince.[7]

Into the harbor of this tropical paradise, the *Essex Junior* also sailed that same afternoon, Downes having been unsuccessful in gaining any information concerning the vessel Porter had sent him to capture. The ships were anchored about a half mile from the beach, and the next day work was commenced on the establishment of a camp on shore where the coopers, sailmakers, carpenters, and other workmen could make extensive repairs on the *Essex*. A guard of marines was placed round the camp, and work then began in earnest on the ship, lasting each day until four o'clock in the afternoon.

The Happahs immediately began to make raids in the valley, which caused Porter to strengthen the guard of the camp at night. Gattanewa, Chief of the Taeehs, daily begged for assistance. Porter had made a friend of him when he visited on board the *Essex* by presenting him with a whale's tooth, which was more esteemed there than the most valuable jewel would be cherished in Europe or America. In fact, for ten whale's teeth of large size one could purchase enough sandalwood to load a ship of 300 tons capacity, a cargo worth nearly a million dollars in China.[8] To put the old man off, Porter told him that he would bring a 6-pounder ashore, and that, if his men would carry it up to the top of a certain mountain which was pointed out to him, he would send gunners to drive away the Happahs from the hills. To his astonishment the gun was carried up the mountains, and on October 29 the ever faithful Downes with a party of forty men chiefly from the *Essex Junior* was sent to make good the promise. A decisive victory was gained over the Happahs, who had five killed; Downes did not lose a man. Within two days envoys from all the tribes on the island except the Typees came to make peace on Porter's terms. His only demands were that they would live at peace together, and bring him supplies for which he agreed to pay them with iron hoops and other articles.

On the 3rd of November more than four thousand natives from different tribes assembled at the rude camp, bringing materials with them out of which they constructed before night a dwelling-house for Captain Porter, another for the officers, a sail loft, a cooper's shop, a place for the sick, a bake-house, a guard-house, and a shed for the sentinel to walk under.[9] By this time the ship had been thoroughly smoked with charcoal and some fifteen hundred rats thus destroyed, everything such as powder and provisions having been previously removed and placed on board the prizes. The decayed main-topmast was replaced, the caulking and painting were finished, the copper on the bottom was repaired, and with the assistance of native divers even the barnacles were removed.

2

Farragut was considered too young to engage in the fighting with the native tribes, and for thus being deprived of entering into exciting adventures he and the other young midshipmen of the *Essex* "felt very indignant."[10] As to another kind of restriction which was placed upon him as soon as the ship came to anchor, he wrote, "That evening I was sent on board the Parson's ship to keep me out of the way of temptation as the women were allowed to go on board the *Essex* to the number of four hundred. Ogden, Feltus, and myself continued on board the Parson's ship for three or four days when we returned to the *Essex*."[10] With Chaplain Adams they were thus allowed to continue their studies on a taboo ship. For their relaxation they were allowed to go ashore frequently, and Farragut was able to observe the various types of islanders who thronged about the American village. The warriors were most striking in appearance, with their plumes made of the feathers of cocks and man-of-war birds, with their red or white cloaks, with their ornaments of whales' teeth or ivory suspended from their ears or worn around their necks, and with their black, highly polished spears about twelve feet in length and their richly carved clubs. Tall and well proportioned, with handsome, intelligent, and unusually expressive faces, they were extraordinary specimens of the human race. According to Farragut, he enjoyed particularly rambling about on the shore with the native boys of his own age, who taught him how to throw the spear and to walk on stilts, and how to improve in the art of swimming. These native lads had been swimming since infancy almost. Farragut often saw mothers take their little children, not more than two years old, and walk out into deep water with them on their backs and leave them there to paddle for themselves. To his great astonishment, they could even at that age swim like young ducks. Apparently it was as natural for them to swim as to eat.

Even though Farragut was not permitted to go on any of the hostile expeditions in the island, there was plenty of activity near at hand to observe. The Typees refused to be friends with the Americans, and when Porter sent to inquire why they were hostile, they sent an insulting answer calling him and his men "white lizards" and using other epithets that were too contemptible to be overlooked. Porter then arranged for the Taeehs and the Happahs to get their war canoes ready, and for the sake of the security of the village, he constructed a fort on top of a hill near by on which were mounted four guns. It was completed on the 14th of November.

That very night had been appointed by Lawson, the mate of the captured *Sir Andrew Hammond,* and his fellow conspirators among the prisoners for the capture of the *Essex Junior* and their escape to sea. On parole, they had been permitted to go about freely on shore and on board the different ships, and they had planned to get the crew of the *Essex Junior* intoxicated with rum mixed with laudanum. Then they were to seize the canoes on the beach and surprise the ship at night, and make their escape when no other vessel was ready to follow them. Porter, who had been informed of the plot almost as soon as it was formed, let them go ahead with their arrangements until the time was ripe, when he had them all sent aft, lectured them scathingly for their ingratitude, and ordered them placed in irons and given prison fare.[11] During the remainder of their stay on the island they spent their time in building a wall around the village.

On the previous day, which happened to be a Saturday, a strange sail was discovered off the mouth of the harbor. On seeing the American ships, the stranger fled under a press of sail. The *Essex Junior* immediately slipped her cables and gave chase. Farragut was permitted to accompany Downes as his aid. When the ship was overtaken, she turned out to be the American ship *Albatross,* an East India trader with a cargo of beads and other trinkets brought from Canton to exchange for sandalwood. The two ships returned to port together the following afternoon.

A remarkable event occurred on the 19th, when the American flag was raised over the fort and a salute of seventeen guns was fired from its cannon. The salute was returned by the shipping in the harbor; and Porter read a formal declaration that he had taken possession of the island for the United States.[12] The natives to whom the ceremony was explained expressed great pleasure and satisfaction at being Melleekees, as they pronounced the word "Americans."

The *Albatross* sailed on the 24th, and the following day Porter began to transfer to the *New Zealander* all the oil from the other prizes, preparatory to sending her home to the United States.

Having decided that he could no longer delay subduing the Typees, if he was to keep the friendship and respect of the other tribes, Porter took the *Essex Junior*, on November 28, and with the assistance of the Taeeh and Happah war canoes made an attack, after landing on the beach in the bay of the Typees. It was unsuccessful; Porter with his small force of thirty-five men with difficulty extricated themselves from a dangerous situation after Lieutenant Downes had suffered a broken leg. The next day Porter returned with a force of two hundred men who climbed over the mountains, and the following day swept over the valley of the Typees with fire and sword. This brought the war to a close, for the chiefs were then eager to make peace on any terms. As Farragut had no part in these expeditions, details will not be given, though the episode makes a thrilling chapter in Porter's *Journal*.[13]

3

All repairs having been completed and plenty of wood and water having been provided together with such provisions as hogs, bananas, and dried cocoanuts, an addition to the abundant supplies taken from the many prizes, Porter set December 9 as the sailing date. The prizes *Seringapatam, Sir Andrew Hammond,* and *Greenwich* were moored under the guns of the fort, and left in charge of Lieutenant Gamble of the Marines and Midshipman Feltus and twenty-one men. This arrangement was made in order that Porter might have a place to which to retire and make repairs if he were injured in a naval action with the enemy. Lieutenant Gamble was instructed to remain only five and a half months, at the expiration of which time he was to sail if he had no news from Porter.[14] The *New Zealander* was ordered to sail, when ready, with her cargo of oil to the United States.

Porter's greatest concern was to get all his men away from

the island, which had so many charms for a sailor. His first step was to stop giving liberty to the crew to go ashore at night. Three men, however, swam ashore the following night, were caught on the beach and brought aboard where they were put in irons, punished at the gangway the next morning, and set to work in chains with the prisoners. There was much grumbling at the severity of the punishment, but it served its purpose.

But there was still much restlessness and discontent on board, for the native girls lined the shore from morning till night. On Sunday, the day before the ships sailed, as was customary, several of the *Essex* crew visited on board the *Essex Junior*, where one of their number, Robert White, boasted that the crew of the *Essex* were resolved not to weigh anchor and, if compelled to go to sea, in three days they would mutiny and raise their own flag. Porter was informed of the situation, and made preparations to forestall any such trouble.

On Monday morning, he called all hands to the port side of the quarter-deck. Laying his cutlass on the capstan, he made a speech to the men with as much composure as he could command; according to Farragut,[15] the captain was shaking with anger. After telling them how necessary it was to maintain discipline, he said, "All of you who are in favor of weighing the anchor when I give the order, pass over to the starboard side; you who are of a different determination, stay on the larboard side." Every man walked over to the starboard. Then Captain Porter called up the seaman named Robert White, and in a very severe tone inquired, "How is this? Did you not tell them on the *Essex Junior* that the crew of this ship would refuse to weigh anchor?" The man in great fear answered, "No sir." "You lie, you scoundrel!" roared Porter. "Where is the list of the men who visited the *Essex Junior* on Sunday?" Ordering the men to step forward, he asked them one after the other, "Did you not hear of this thing on board of the *Essex Junior*?" "Yes, sir," was the unanimous reply. Then turning on White, Porter shouted, "Run, you scoundrel, for your life!" and away he scrambled over the starboard gangway. Porter made no great exertion to catch the fellow who swam out to a native canoe which happened to be passing.[16] If he had not been an Englishman who had joined the ship from one of the captured vessels, Porter would probably have dealt with him differently.

The Captain then made another speech to the crew, in which he praised their conduct on the cruise and held up to scorn the villainy of the man who had just fled the ship so unceremoniously. In no uncertain terms, he made them understand that he would go to any length to preserve discipline on the ship, in fact, that he was always ready "to blow them all to Hell, before they could attain their ends."[17] Then wheeling around, he ordered the capstan to be manned and the fiddle to play "The Girl I Left Behind Me." The men obeyed instantly; the anchor seemed to jump out of the water, so rapidly was it raised to the bows; sail was as quickly made, and the *Essex* moved out to sea, leaving the island of enchantment behind. "Take it altogether," wrote Farragut,[18] "it was one of the most exciting scenes I ever witnessed, and made such an impression on my young mind that the circumstance is as fresh as if it had happened yesterday."

Only one member of the crew was found missing, a lazy Negro whom Porter had taken on board at Tumbez out of charity, whose absence no one regretted. Another man was lost, however, when the *Essex* was sailing along under a fresh breeze, about twenty miles from Nukuhiva. He was a young Tahitian, named Tamaha, who had joined the ship from one of the captured vessels and had become a favorite with the sailors, whom he amused after working hours with his native dances. Soon after the *Essex* sailed he got into a difficulty with a boatswain's mate, who struck him. He was very proud, and weeping bitterly, said that no one would strike him again. When night was coming on, he jumped over the side of the ship undiscovered, and was not missed until the next morning. His loss was greatly lamented, from Captain Porter down to the youngest ship's boy. It was thought, of course, that he had drowned himself; but some years afterwards it was learned from an officer on one of the prizes left behind that, on the third day after the sailing of the *Essex*, Tamaha turned up at Nukuhiva, having swum the entire distance in spite of sharks and other perils of the sea.[19]

Porter furnished Downes with a letter giving points of rendezvous to be used in case of separation; but as it happened, the two ships rarely lost sight of each other for more than a few hours at a time during the entire voyage to the coast of Chile. The passage was entirely uneventful and monotonous, and lasted a little more than a month. But with the prospect of meeting British men-of-war almost a certainty, Porter made use of the time in drilling and disciplining his crew for any emergency that might arise. Every day they had exercises with the singlestick and small arms, and were frequently called to quarters to handle the "great guns." They were so well trained as boarders that every man was ready on call with pistol, dirk made from a file b ythe ship's armorer, and cutlass with an edge like that of a razor. "I have never been in a ship," Farragut wrote,[20] "where there were any of the *Essex* crew, that they were not the best stick players on board."

The first landfall was the Island of Mocha, on the 12th of January, 1814. The squadron turned to the northward and ran up to the Island of Santa Maria before coming to anchor. There they filled their water-casks ,and then looked into the port of Concepción where only one English vessel was to be seen. After that, the ships sailed leisurely to Valparaiso, off which they cruised about until the 3d of February,[21] when they entered the bay and anchored off the city. Thus came to an end another chapter in the famous cruise, the most successful, if not the most glorious.

XII

THE LOSS OF THE *ESSEX*

1

PORTER exchanged salutes with the battery, and paid an official call on the Governor, who returned the visit the next day with his wife and several officers. Meanwhile the *Essex Junior* was ordered to cruise off the port on the lookout for enemy merchant vessels or ships of war. No time was lost in getting the *Essex* ready for sea, though it was arranged for the crew by turns to enjoy liberty on shore. Porter was informed that nothing had been heard of the British squadron that had sailed from Rio de Janeiro and that it was supposed it had perished in rounding Cape Horn, but he was under the impression that the commanding officer had kept secret his arrival in the Pacific and fully expected him to seek the *Essex* at Valparaiso.[1]

But the British arrived somewhat sooner than Porter had planned to receive them. Finding the Chileans even more hospitable than they had been during his last visit, he decided to give a ball on board his ship on the evening of the 7th of February. In order that Lieutenant Downes might be present, he was ordered to anchor in the bay but in a position to command a full view of the sea. The dancing lasted until midnight; Downes then returned to his ship and put out to sea. Before the awnings, flags, and other decorations had been taken down and everything made shipshape on board the next morning, a signal was made from the *Essex Junior* that two ships were in sight. A gun was immediately fired to recall the half[2] of the crew who were on shore, arrangements were made for preparing the ship for action, and Porter went on board the *Essex Junior* and proceeded to reconnoiter. Finding that the ships were men-of-war and probably enemy ships, Porter ordered Downes to return to port and take up a position where he could be of the greatest service in case of an attack.

At half past seven, Porter was back on the *Essex*, which he was pleased to find completely ready for action with every man at his post. Thirty minutes later, the two ships entered the harbor. The larger ship, a frigate, ranged up to the port quarter of the *Essex*, put her helm down, and luffed up on the starboard bow within ten or fifteen feet of the American frigate.[3] The captain, wearing a pea-jacket, and standing on the after gun, shouted, "Captain Hillyar's compliments to Captain Porter, and hopes he is well." Porter replied, "Very well, I thank you." He had known Captain James Hillyar intimately in the Mediterranean. Observing that the British vessel, already closer than prudence and neutrality justified, continued to approach, Porter warned, "Sir, if you by any accident get on board of me, I assure you that great confusion will take place; I am prepared to receive you, but shall only act on the defensive." Leaning indifferently over the side of his ship, Hillyar coolly replied, "Oh sir, I have no such intentions." Again Porter warned him that, if his ship touched the *Essex*, there would be much bloodshed.[4] Though Hillyar reassured him with the same nonchalance, just then his ship was taken aback so that her jib-boom came across the forecastle of the *Essex*.

Immediately Porter called the boarders and directed them to spring on board the enemy ship the moment the hulls touched. "You have no business where you are," he cried to Hillyar; "if you touch a rope-yarn of this ship, I shall board instantly."[5] With a signal from Porter's trumpet, the kedge anchors were hoisted to the yardarms so as to be ready to grapple the enemy ship. All hands were already at quarters, and the powder-boys were stationed holding their slow matches ready to fire the guns. Then the boarders gathered with pistol and cutlass in hand, ready to board through the smoke of the first broadside. In consternation at the preparations made on the *Essex* to receive him and at the predicament in which he had placed his ship, Hillyar raised both of his hands as he explained with great alarm, "I had no intention of getting on board of you—I had no intention of coming so near you—I am sorry I came so near you."

According to Farragut,[6] a battle almost was precipitated in spite of Porter's forbearance under such aggravating circumstances. Among those summoned from the shore in the early morning was an intoxicated youth, the only one who had returned under the influence of liquor. As he looked through a gun port, he saw, or imagined that he saw, a British sailor grinning at him. "Damn you, my fine fellow, I'll stop your laughing or making faces at me," he complained and to make good his words was aiming his musket to fire, when he was seen by Lieutenant McKnight who with one blow knocked him flat on the deck. If that gun had been fired, the engagement would almost certainly have begun, and the British ship would as certainly have been taken. Her bow was exposed to a raking fire from the *Essex* and her stern was equally exposed to the *Essex Junior*, while not one of her guns could then have been brought to bear. Porter claimed that he could have either captured or destroyed her in fifteen minutes.[7]

It was fortunate for Hillyar, then, that his ship did not touch the *Essex*. As everyone waited with breathless anxiety, Captain Hillyar extricated his ship, her yards passing over those of the *Essex* without touching a rope. She then drifted between the two American ships, exposed to their broadsides; and finally anchored on the eastern side of the harbor. The other British vessel, a sloop of war, anchored within pistol shot off the port bow of the *Essex;* and Porter then ordered the *Essex Junior* to take a position so that the British sloop would be between her fire and that of the *Essex*. This annoyed her commander greatly.

2

Very friendly relations were established on shore between Captain Porter and Captain Hillyar, after the latter had assured Porter that he intended to respect the neutrality of the port. The rest of the American officers and sailors were on good terms with the officers and men of the British ships, then known to be the frigate *Phoebe* and the sloop *Cherub*. There was some rivalry in the display of mottoes. In answer to the *Essex's* motto, "Free trade and sailors' rights," the *Phoebe* raised one bearing the words, "God and country; British sailor's best rights; traitors offend both." In reply Porter hoisted this flag, "God, our country and Liberty—tyrants offend them." The crews of the respective ships amused themselves during the evenings in singing witty and sarcastic nautical songs in ridicule of each other.

Captain Hillyar went to sea on February 24 with his two ships and cruised off the harbor of Valparaiso. In an effort to provoke an engagement with the *Phoebe*, Captain Porter, on the 26th, towed one of his prizes, the *Hector*, out within reach of the British guns and burned her, and escaped easily back into the harbor. In the afternoon of the following day it looked as though this insult might lead to an engagement, for the *Phoebe* stood in for the harbor, fired a gun to windward, and raised her motto flag. But when the *Essex* sailed out to meet her, she retired and joined the *Cherub*, apparently unwilling to engage in single ship action.

The comparative strength of the opposing ships was favorable to the British. The *Phoebe* mounted thirty long 18-pounders, sixteen 32-pound carronades, one howitzer, and six 3-pounders in the tops, and carried a complement of three hundred twenty men.[8] The *Cherub* carried eighteen 32-pound carronades, eight 24-pounders, and two long 9-pounders, and a complement of one hundred eighty men. The *Essex* had forty 32-pound carronades and six long 12-pounders and a crew which had by that time been reduced to two hundred fifty-five men. The *Essex Junior* carried ten 18-pound carronades and ten short six-pounders with only sixty men. With such an advantage at long range in particular, it is surprising that Hillyar was so reluctant to engage except with two ships against one.

According to Farragut,[9] one night an expedition composed of all the ship's boats went out to board the enemy off the harbor. Captain Porter, in his boat, under muffled oars pulled near enough to the *Phoebe* to hear the men's conversation on board and learn that the crew were lying at their quarters ready for such an attack. Consequently the attempt could not be carried out and the boats returned to the *Essex*. Nothing else of interest occurred until near the last of March.

3

Realizing at last that he would not be permitted to engage the *Phoebe* alone and fearing that British re-enforcements might arrive any day, Porter decided to run the blockade with the *Essex*. A place of rendezvous with the *Essex Junior* was arranged with Downes, who was ordered to sail while the *Essex* was being pursued by the British ships.

Valparaiso Bay is not an inclosed harbor but merely an indentation in the coast, which faces the north and thus is protected by the inclosing hills, rising to a height of twelve or fifteen hundred feet, from the prevailing southerly winds throughout the year. In ordinary weather during the season when the *Essex* was blockaded there, the water in the harbor is quiet during the night, but sometimes in the afternoons the wind blows furiously through the ravines of the hills and disturbs the shipping in the anchorage.

On the 28th of March just such a wind from the southward caused the *Essex* to part her port cable and to drag her starboard anchor out toward the sea. Sail was made with all possible speed. The enemy ships were discovered near the point forming the west side of the bay, and Porter decided to try to pass to windward of them and escape to sea. The topgallant sails, which had been set over close-reefed topsails were taken in; but before they could be well secured, a squall struck the ship as she was rounding the point and, when she was inclined nearly gunwale down, away went her main-topmast into the sea and also the men on the main-topgallant yard, all of whom were drowned. Porter immediately wore ship and attempted to regain his anchorage; but, closely pursued by the British, he was not able to do so and anchored instead in a small bay on the east side of the harbor "about a quarter of a mile off shore and three quarters of a mile from a small battery."[10]

According to the generally recognized law of nations, the

neutral line of a country extends three miles, or the distance of a cannon shot, from the shore line.[11] In view of Hillyar's previous assurances, Porter had reason to believe that his vessel, which was then well within the neutral waters of Chile, would be safe from attack. But with every advantage now in his favor, Captain Hillyar no longer resisted the temptation to violate international law in order to destroy the *Essex*.

Farragut, as well as every officer and man on board, soon realized that the enemy ships, which continued to approach, were intending to attack. "Well do I remember," wrote[12] Farragut, "the awful feelings produced on me at their approach, by perceiving in the face of every one as clearly as possible even to my young mind that all was hopeless, and yet a determination equally clear to die at their guns rather than surrender. And such I believe were the feelings of the crew almost to a man." The recent weeks of waiting, during which bantering songs had been sung, hostile letters had been interchanged, and many blows exchanged between English and American boats' crews on shore, had raised the fighting spirit of the men to a very high pitch, and there was naturally no disposition to back down, now that the long awaited opportunity was at hand.

Feverish preparations were made for the dreadful work at hand with all the skill and coolness which many months of drill and discipline had developed. Flags were hoisted on every mast in answer to the display of ensigns, jacks, and motto flags on the British vessels. The enemy ships advanced with unusual caution, but finally the *Phoebe* reached a position under the stern of the *Essex*, and the *Cherub* hauled up on her starboard bow. Porter had been trying, but in vain, to get a spring on his cable,[13] when, at just six minutes to four o'clock in the afternoon, the British opened fire.

After a half hour of fighting, both the *Phoebe* and *Cherub* thought it the better part of valor to retire to repair damages. These were caused by the very effective fire of three long 12-pounders which had been moved to the stern-ports and directed at both ships, the *Cherub* having early in the action shifted her berth alongside of the *Phoebe* when she found her first position

ENGAGEMENT BETWEEN THE *Essex* AND THE *Phoebe* AND THE *Cherub* IN THE HARBOR OF VALPARAISO
From an old print, originally owned by David Glasgow Farragut.

was too hot for her. But during this first phase of the battle the *Essex* received many injuries and had many men killed or wounded, for she could oppose only three guns to two broadsides of the British. Three different times springs were attached to the cables so that the *Essex* could be turned and thus bring her own broadsides to bear on the enemy; but each time they were shot away by the excessive enemy fire. The ensign at the gaff and the motto flag at the mizzen were both shot away, but the flag bearing the words, "Free Trade and Sailors' Rights," continued to fly defiantly from the foremast. The ensign was replaced and another was made fast in the mizzen rigging, while several jacks were raised in different parts of the ship. This was a reflection of the spirit of the men of the *Essex*, all of whom Porter declared were "determined to defend their ship to the last extremity, and to die in preference to a shameful surrender."[14]

When the British had repaired their damages, they returned,[15] both ships taking up a position on the starboard quarter[16] of the *Essex* out of range of her carronades, where her stern guns could not be brought to bear and their own long guns could pour a destructive fire into the doomed American frigate. Porter, therefore, decided to get under way and attempt to close with the *Phoebe* and, if possible, even board her. Only one serviceable rope was found not to have been shot away, the flying jib-halliards; and so this was the only sail that could be hoisted. When this sail was raised, Porter ordered his cable to be cut and the *Essex* turned, bringing her broadsides to bear as she approached nearer the enemy ships. The firing then became heavy on both sides, and the losses were fearful particularly on the *Essex*, as both the *Cherub* and the *Phoebe*, because of the better condition of their sails, shifted their positions where their long guns would be most effective and the short range carronades of the *Essex* could do but little damage.

It was during this phase of the battle that Midshipman Farragut had the thrilling experiences which he so vividly described in *Some Reminiscences*.[17] He performed the duties of captain's aid, quarter-gunner, and powder-boy, and did anything else that was required of him. "I will here remark," he wrote, "the horrid impression made upon me by the death of the seaman. It was a boatswain's mate, his abdomen was taken entirely out, and he expired in a few moments; but they soon fell so fast around me that it all appeared like a dream and produced no effect on my mind. I well remember, while standing near the captain just abaft the mainmast, a shot came through the waterways which glanced upwards, killing four men who stood by the side of the gun, taking the last man in the head, and his brains flew over us both; but it made no such impression on me as the death of the first man. I neither thought of or noticed anything but the working of the guns."

Porter's losses were becoming so great, fifteen men having been killed at one gun, that he determined to run the *Essex* ashore, land his men, and then destroy the vessel. The wind was at first favorable, but when the ship was within musket shot of the shore, the wind shifted from the land and turned the ship's head toward the *Phoebe*, which then poured a raking fire into the unmanageable *Essex*. The slaughter then continued as before. About that time Downes came on board from the *Essex Junior* to receive orders, as he was under the impression that Porter would soon be forced to surrender. After ten minutes on board he was directed to return to his own ship, and to take several of the wounded in his boat. Meanwhile Porter had managed to turn the *Essex* by having a hawser bent to the sheet anchor and the anchor then cut from the bows. The broadsides of the *Essex* were thus brought to bear again but the hawser soon parted and the ship was once more drifting unmanageable and at the mercy of the enemy.

When his services were not required elsewhere, Farragut helped work a gun by running to bring powder from the boys whom he sent for more, until the Captain sent for him to carry a message. Once while he was standing beside Porter, Midshipman Isaacs came up to report that Quarter-gunner Adam Roche had deserted from his post. The Captain turned to Farragut and said simply, "Do your duty, sir." The little midshipman grabbed a pistol and rushed off in pursuit of the seaman, whom he could not find anywhere. Afterwards it was learned that he, together with six other seamen, had managed to get into the only boat that would still float and had escaped to the shore.[18]

Soon after this incident, Farragut was sent to get some gun-primers. On the way below, while going down the wardroom ladder, the captain of the gun directly opposite the hatchway was struck right in the face by an eighteen-pound shot, which knocked him on top of Farragut. "We both fell down the hatch together," wrote[18] Farragut; "I struck on my head and fortunately he fell on my hips whereas, as he was a man weighing about two hundred pounds, had he fallen directly on my body, he would have killed me. I lay there stunned for a few minutes by the blow, when awakening as it were from a dream, I ran on deck. The captain, seeing me covered with blood, asked me if I was wounded, to which I replied, 'I believe not, sir.' 'Then, my son,' said he, 'where are the tubes?' This first brought me again to my senses and I ran down again and brought them on deck. When I arrived on deck the second time, I saw the captain fall, and in my turn ran up and asked him if he was wounded; he answered me in almost the same words. 'I believe not, my son; but I felt a blow on the top of my head.' He must have been crushed down by a passing shot, as his hat was somewhat injured."

Farragut had another close call, while standing near Quartermaster Francis Bland at the wheel. The midshipman's keen eyes saw a shot coming over the fore-yard straight toward them. He yelled at the old man to jump, and at the same time tried to pull him away from danger. But he was a second too late, for the shot took off the quartermaster's right leg and came so near Farragut that it tore away his coat-tail. He assisted the stricken man below, and after the engagement learned that he had bled to death before he could be given medical attention.[19]

The conduct of most of Porter's men was heroic. Farragut, in his reminiscences, dwells with pride on the patriotic self-sacrifice of a young Scotsman, Bissley, one of whose legs was shot off near the groin. After trying to stop the bleeding by using his own handkerchief as a tourniquet, he said to his comrades,

"I left my own country and adopted the United States to fight for her. I hope I have this day proved myself worthy of the country of my adoption. I am no longer of any use to you or to her and I will not be a burthen to her, so good-by!"[19] Then he pulled himself up on the sill of a gun port and threw himself overboard.[20]

The ship had caught on fire several times during the action, and finally the flames seemed to be "bursting up each hatchway and no hopes were entertained of saving her."[21] Porter, having been informed that the fire was near the magazine, directed the men who came rushing up from below with their clothes burning to jump into the sea and swim to the shore, which was about three-quarters of a mile distant. Other members of the crew, even some of the officers, hearing the order to jump overboard, thought the ship was on the point of being blown up, and they too threw themselves into the sea. Some reached the shore in safety, but several were captured and many were drowned in the attempt. It was then, declared Farragut, that amazing powers of endurance were displayed. One instance in particular which he cites was the escape of Boatswain's Mate Kingsbury, who had behaved so bravely in the tempestuous voyage round Cape Horn. He had come with Downes on board the *Essex* late in the battle, and when the latter had returned to the *Essex Junior,* he had remained, according to his words, "to share the fate of his old ship." Though there was scarcely a square inch of his body that had escaped being burned, he plunged into the sea and swam to the shore in safety. Though deranged for several days, he ultimately fully recovered and several years later served under Farragut in the West Indies. Another seaman swam ashore with about seventeen pieces of iron scales from the muzzle of a gun, in his leg, and he too recovered, not even losing the leg.[22]

Those who remained on board heroically fought the flames and actually managed to put out the fires. The serviceable guns were then again manned, and the firing was resumed for a few minutes, when Porter decided that it was useless to sacrifice more lives and sent for his officers of divisions to consult with them on the advisability of surrendering the ship. To his surprise he found that only Lieutenant Stephen Decatur McKnight remained able to carry on the fight. Lieutenant Wilmer, after fighting gallantly, had been knocked overboard by a shot, while releasing the sheet anchor from the bows, and had been drowned. After the action, his little Negro boy, "Ruff," looking for his master, asked Farragut what had become of him and when he learned what had happened to him, he jumped overboard and deliberately drowned himself. Lieutenant John G. Cowell had lost a leg. Acting Sailing Master Edward Barnewall had been carried below with two wounds, one in the face and another in the breast. Acting Lieutenant William H. Odenheimer had just been knocked overboard, and did not regain the ship until after the surrender. "I was informed," recorded Porter, "that the cockpit, the steerage, the wardroom, and the berth deck could contain no more wounded; that the wounded were killed while the surgeons were dressing them, and that, unless something was speedily done to prevent it, the ship would soon sink from the number of shot holes in her bottom."[23]

When Captain Porter decided to surrender, he sent for Midshipman Farragut and ordered him to find the signal-book and to throw it overboard. With difficulty, he finally found it lying on the sill of a gun port and then threw it into the sea. Midshipman Isaacs and Farragut then amused themselves by throwing pistols and other small arms overboard to keep them from falling into the hands of the British. It was at twenty minutes after six P.M. that Porter "gave the painful order to strike the colors,"[24] though the enemy continued to fire for ten minutes longer and four men were killed by Porter's side.

4

When the boarding officer came on board the *Essex*, according to Farragut,[25] he ran up to Captain Porter and demanded to know how he would account for permitting members of the crew to jump overboard and swim ashore. He also demanded his sword, which Porter refused, saying, "That, sir, is reserved for your master." The battle being finished, Farragut went below, and though he had become accustomed to the scene of blood and death during the action, he "became faint and sickened"[26] when he saw the mangled bodies of his shipmates, some dead, some groaning in their agony, and others dying with patriotic expressions on their lips; such as, "Don't give her up, Logan (a nickname for Porter)" and "Hurrah for our liberty!" When he had sufficiently recovered from his first shock, he made haste to render all possible assistance to Surgeons Hoffman and Montgomery in dressing the wounds of his comrades.

Among the fatally wounded was one of Farragut's best friends, Lieutenant J. G. Cowell. "O Gatty,"[25] he said when the young midshipman spoke to him, "I fear it is all up with me." Indeed it was true, though his life might have been saved if he could have been given medical aid when he was first carried below. His leg had been shot away above the knee, and when the surgeon offered to stop attending his patient and amputate the lieutenant's leg, Cowell said, "No, no, Doctor, none of that; fair play is the jewel. One man's life is as dear as another's; and I would not cheat any poor fellow out of his turn." When his turn came an hour later, it was too late to save his life. "Thus died," Farragut declared, "one of the best of officers as well as the bravest of men."[27]

The losses had, indeed, been heavy. The slightly wounded numbered twenty-seven, and the severely wounded were thirty-nine. Thirty-one were missing, most of whom were drowned; while fifty-eight were killed outright, or afterwards died of their wounds. This was a total of one hundred fifty-five men out of the ship's complement of two hundred and fifty-five.[28] The tremendous advantages which the British had over the *Essex* is reflected in the disparity of losses, for Captain Hillyar's report[29] acknowledges the loss of only four killed and seven wounded on the *Phoebe* and one killed and three wounded on the *Cherub*. Among the killed was William Ingram, First Lieutenant of the *Phoebe*. Farragut declares that he was a very chivalrous young man who had visited the *Essex* before the battle under a flag of truce, and had been shown over the ship. His frankness and manly bearing had won the hearts of all who met him. In admiration of the *Essex*, he had remarked, "It would be the happiest moment of my life to take her to England, should she be captured in equal combat." To this Porter had replied, "Should such an event occur. I know no British officer to whom I would more readily yield the honor."[30] During the battle, while the *Phoebe* was keeping a safe distance and pounding away at the *Essex*, Lieutenant Ingram is reported to have said to his commanding officer, "It is deliberate murder to lie off at long range and fire at that ship as though she were a target. Let us bear down and board her." To this the cool and calculating Captain Hillyar, who was then about fifty years old, replied, "I have gained my reputation by several single-ship combats, and I expect to retain it on this present occasion only by an implicit obedience to orders, viz., to capture the *Essex* with the least possible risk to my vessel and crew. As I have a superior force, I have determined not to leave anything to chance, as I believe that any other course would call down on me the disapprobation of the government."[30]

Even at the comparatively safe distance from the *Essex*, a shot struck the rail of the *Phoebe* where the young lieutenant was standing, and he was so seriously wounded by a splinter that he died before the end of the engagement. So highly was he respected by his surviving recent foes that they all attended his funeral which was held on shore at the Governor's castle in Valparaiso.

In his official report, Captain Porter commended unreservedly the conduct of his officers in the engagement, and little Midshipman Farragut was mentioned by name among those who had "exerted themselves in the performance of their respective duties, and gave an earnest of their value to the service."[31]

5

Farragut went on board the *Phoebe* about eight o'clock on the following morning, and was taken to the steerage. While in tears because of the mortification at being a prisoner of war, he heard a British midshipman shouting, "A prize! a prize! Ho, boys, a fine grunter, by Jove!" He saw that the prize under the midshipman's arm was a pet pig, named "Murphy," which he had claimed as his very own. Farragut boldly demanded his pig; but the captor objected, saying, "Ah, but you are a prisoner, and your pig also." Farragut replied, "We always respect private property," meanwhile seizing the pig with the determination not to let go unless he was compelled to do so by superior force. This was rare sport for the older officers, who had gathered round. Some one cried, "Go it, my little Yankee! If you thrash Shorty, you shall have your pig." "Agreed!" said Farragut; a ring was at once formed and the fight was on.

"I soon found," wrote Farragut,[32] "that my antagonist's pugilistic education did not come up to mine. In fact, he was no match for me, and was compelled to give up the pig. So I took Master Murphy under by arm, feeling that I had, in some degree, wiped out the disgrace of our defeat. I was sent for by Captain Hillyar to come into his cabin, where Captain Porter was, and asked to take some breakfast, when, seeing my discomfiture, he remarked in a very kind manner: 'Never mind, my little fellow; it will be your turn next, perhaps.' I said I hoped so, and left the cabin to hide my emotion."

Farragut's observations on the battle, though written in his maturity long after the event, are of great interest. "In the first place," he recorded in his journal,[33] "I consider that our original and greatest error was in attempting to regain the anchorage; as, being greatly superior to the enemy in sailing qualities, I think we should have borne up and run before the wind. If we had come in contact with the *Phoebe*, we should have carried her by boarding; if she avoided us, as she might have done by her greater ability to maneuver, then we could have taken her fire and passed on, leaving both vessels behind until we replaced our topmast, by which time they would have been separated, as, unless they did so, it would have been no chase, the *Cherub* being a dull sailer.

"Secondly, when it was apparent to everybody that we had no chance of success under the circumstances, the ship should have been run ashore, throwing her broadside to the beach, to prevent raking, and fought as long as was consistent with humanity, and then set on fire. But, having determined on anchoring, we should have bent a spring on the ring of the anchor, instead of to the cable, where it was exposed and could be shot away as fast as put on. This mode of proceeding would have given us, in my opinion, a better opportunity of injuring our opponents."

As soon as arrangements could be made, Porter, his officers, and the wounded members of his crew were paroled and permitted to go ashore, on condition that the United States should bear the expenses of taking care of the wounded men. The remainder of the crew were placed under guard on a Spanish merchant vessel which Captain Hillyar hired for that purpose. The ladies of Valparaiso rendered invaluable aid in caring for the wounded, and thus saved the lives of many poor fellows. "For myself," wrote Porter,"[34] I shall never forget their gentle humanity; and if it should not be in my power to return it, I bequeath the remembrance as a legacy of gratitude to be repaid by my country."

Farragut volunteered his assistance to the surgeon to help care for the wounded in the comfortable house which had been secured for this purpose. "I never earned Uncle Sam's money so faithfully," he declared,[35] "as I did during that hospital service. I rose at daylight and arranged the bandages and plasters until eight A.M.; then after breakfast I went to work at my patients."

An agreement was made with Captain Hillyar for disarming the *Essex Junior* and converting her into a cartel ship for conveying all the prisoners under parole to some American port. The ship sailed on the 27th of April, 1814, for New York with 130[36] officers and men, all who were left of the gallant crew of the *Essex*. Among them, of course, were Porter and Farragut.

Thus ended in blood and glory the most famous cruise of an American sailing ship—a cruise which had cost the British government much in the destruction of her whaling ships, in the disruption of her trade in the Pacific, and in the dispatch of several ships of war to look for the *Essex* not only in South American waters but also in the China seas.[37] To have participated in such an odyssey and in such a desperately heroic battle, when only twelve years old, was both an unusual experience and a remarkable preparation for whatever Fate should have in store for the future. At the end of this renowned cruise, Farragut, though still a boy in years, had already reached maturity in his chosen profession.

XIII

AN INTERLUDE

1

THE HOMEWARD voyage of the *Essex Junior*, bearing the remnants of her crew as well as the survivors of the *Essex*, was comparatively uneventful. Even the wind and weather favored the war-worn seafarers. They rounded Cape Horn under topgallant studding-sails, and arrived off Sandy Hook in seventy-three days.[1]

There the vessel was overhauled by the British ship of war *Saturn*, commanded by Captain Nash, who treated Porter very courteously, furnishing him some oranges and the recent newspapers. The boarding officer examined the ship's papers and Porter's passport, and gave permission for the ship to proceed. About two hours later, however, the *Essex Junior* was brought to again, and the papers re-examined and the hold overhauled by a ship's crew and an officer. When Porter expressed his astonishment at such proceedings, he was told that Captain Nash had his motives and that Captain Hillyar had no authority to make such arrangements. He added that the passport must be taken on board the *Saturn* again, and the *Essex Junior* detained. To this Captain Porter replied, "The smallest detention will be a violation of the contract on the part of the British, and I shall consider myself a prisoner to Captain Nash and no longer on my parole."[2] Porter then offered his sword to the officer, who declined to receive it and went on board the *Saturn*. He later returned with the order from Captain Nash that the *Essex Junior* must remain under the lee of the *Saturn* during the night. Porter then declared, "I am your prisoner; I do not consider myself any longer bound by my contract with Captain Hillyar, which has thus been violated, and shall act accordingly."[2]

At seven o'clock the next morning, after breakfast, Porter ordered his boat to be manned and armed. This was the whaleboat which had the reputation of being very fast. It was evident that he had determined to make an effort to escape, and intended to make a desperate fight if pursued. His escape was not discovered on the *Saturn* for some time, as the *Essex Junior* afforded a screen. When the boat was made out from the masthead of the British ship, Captain Nash got under way and wore ship in pursuit. Luckily, just then a thick fog settled down, which enabled Porter to change his course and escape all pursuit. Farragut relates[3] that on board the *Essex Junior* not a spar of the *Saturn* could be seen, though he and his shipmates heard with anxiety every order given by the British.

Downes, who was left in command of the *Essex Junior*, took advantage of the opportunity to attempt to escape, and soon had the ship going nine knots in the direction of Sandy Hook. At eleven o'clock the lookout from the masthead discovered the broad pennant of the *Saturn* to windward. Before she was clear of the fog, Downes had given orders to take in sail and make all snug on the *Essex Junior*. After firing a gun to leeward, the *Saturn* approached and sent a boat alongside. A different officer from the one who had previously come aboard was in command. "You drift quite fast," he remarked; "we have been going nine knots for the last three hours, and yet we find you abeam with your main topsail to the mast."[3] "Yes," was the quiet reply of Downes. "And that was Captain Porter who left the ship in a boat, I suppose?" "It was," said Downes, and he left this message for your captain: "Captain Porter is now satisfied that most British officers are not only destitute of honor, but regardless of the honor of each other; he is armed and prepared to defend himself against your boats, if sent in pursuit of him; and he must be met, if met at all, as an enemy."[4] "Then, by God, you will soon be leaving too, if we don't take your boats from you," rejoined the angry boarding officer. "You had better try that," Downes remarked, coolly. "I would, if I had my way," replied the officer.[3]

Downes's self-control then deserted him, and advancing toward the British officer, he shouted, "You impertinent puppy, if you have any business to do here, do it; but if you dare to insult me again, I shall throw you overboard," accompanying the last words with an appropriate gesture. This completely took the wind out of the young officer's sails. He jumped into his boat and left the ship, and in a short time the other boarding officer came aboard and said, "Captain Nash hopes Captain Downes will excuse the youth and ignorance of the former officer, who has been ordered to send an apology for his ungentlemanly conduct."[5]

The crew was then mustered to see if all tallied with the passport, and though each man was carefully examined as he went by, no one was stopped. When the last one had passed, the officer asked one of his boat's crew, "Which is the man you spoke of as being an Englishman?" This made every one anxious, Farragut declared, lest some poor fellow might have been a deserter from the British service. But all were reassured when the sailor replied, "I never said he was an Englishman." "But," objected the officer, "you said you had sailed with him." "True enough," was the reply, "but it was out of New York." Visibly confused, the boarding officer apologized and departed.

Finally the passport was countersigned, and the *Essex Junior* was permitted to proceed. About sunset, however, another enemy frigate was encountered, and the ship had to submit to another vexatious examination. It was eight o'clock in the evening when the much harassed vessel arrived at Sandy Hook. As the night was dark and squally and no pilot could be secured, Downes took the ship in by chart alone. His adventures were not yet finished. Opposite a small battery in the Horseshoe, signal lanterns were hoisted and a boat with a light in her was sent ashore. But the light was accidentally put out, and the fort began firing on the ship. Everybody was ordered below. The firing continued until the boat could return and get another light; but not a single shot struck the vessel. This caused Farragut to conclude that "it was not as awful a thing as was supposed to lie under a battery,"[6] a judgment upon which he was to rely later in his career when a decision of the greatest importance had to be made.

Having finally convinced the battery that the ship was American, Downes decided to furl sails and remain there until morning. This was a wise decision, for the next morning when the ship entered the harbor under full sail, with colors displayed, she was again fired on by a second battery, whose aim fortunately was as bad as the first had been. In spite of both friends and foes, the *Essex Junior* completed her voyage safely and came to anchor off New York on the 7th of July, 1814, just two days after Midshipman Farragut's thirteenth birthday.

2

Upon Farragut's arrival in New York, he was surprised to learn that Captain Porter was not already there, and he began to fear that misfortune had overtaken him. But in a day or two he arrived with the report that the distance to the shore had proved to be greater than he had supposed it to be when he put off from the *Essex Junior*. After rowing and sailing his boat about sixty miles, he had made his way with difficulty through the surf and had landed near Babylon, Long Island. By that time it was sunset, and he was mistaken for a British officer by the militia, who promptly made him a prisoner. By showing his commission, he convinced them of his identity. They then gave him three hearty cheers and a salute of twenty-one guns from a small swivel cannon. They also gave him a horse to ride and an ox cart to carry his boat across to Brooklyn. When he arrived in New York, he received an enthusiastic welcome from the people, who unhitched the horses from the carriage in which he was riding, and themselves hauled him to his lodgings.[7]

In New York, Porter sold the *Essex Junior*, and the officers and men[8] dispersed to their homes under parole (except Porter and his boat's crew) to await exchange before again engaging in the war.[9] "Thus terminated one of the most eventful cruises of my life," briefly concluded Farragut.[10]

After about a week in New York,[11] Farragut accompanied

AN INTERLUDE

Porter to his home in Chester, Pennsylvania, which they had not seen for about twenty-one months. After so many diverse experiences and recent real privations, the stately Porter home, "Green Bank," was indeed a haven of rest to the weary sailors. There a surprise awaited Captain Porter, in the person of a third child only fifteen months old, whom his mother had named David Dixon Porter and who was himself to become a great naval officer and a warm personal friend and companion in arms with Farragut.

Captain Porter was not the kind of man who would tarry long at home when the military situation was so critical, and he was soon back in New York where he was ordered temporarily to command the *Fulton the First,* the steam man-of-war then under construction. Meanwhile Farragut was left in Chester and placed under the tutelage of an odd old fellow named Neif, who had been one of the celebrated guards of Napoleon Bonaparte. His pupils had no books, but were taught orally on various subjects, taking notes on which they were afterwards examined. In the afternoon he usually took them on long walks, during which Neif added to his collections of minerals and plants and talked to his scholars about mineralogy and botany. They were taught to swim and climb, and were drilled like soldiers. Though Farragut does not mention this, they were probably given instruction also in the French language. Farragut wrote that, though the course of studies was not very regular, he certainly was afforded an opportunity of gaining a great deal of useful information and worldly knowledge. "I do not regret the time passed at this school," he declared, "for it has been of service to me all through life."[12]

Residents of that neighborhood have left a traditional account[13] of Farragut's appearance at this time. According to them, he was short of stature and not very handsome in face, but he always carried himself very erect so that, as he frequently said, he would not lose even a small fraction of one of the inches of his limited height. Near the spot where Farragut went to school was the Seven Stars Tavern, a very old public house where Howe and Cornwallis had lodged in 1777 when the British army was advancing on Philadelphia from the head of the Chesapeake. Upon its porch, it was claimed, Farragut then spent many an idle hour and inside enjoyed the society of the young people of the neighborhood, who afterwards recalled with great satisfaction and pride this early association with one who had become a famous man in his generation.

While Farragut was in Chester, Porter came through with a small remnant of the old crew of the *Essex* on the way south to defend Washington from attack by the British. The young lad begged with tears in his voice, if not in his eyes, to go along too, but Porter was inexorable in his denial, saying that he was too young for land warfare. He did not miss much, however, for the Capital had already been captured and burned before Porter and his men arrived, and all that they could do was to join in the attempt to destroy the enemy vessels from the banks of the Potomac at White House, as they retired down the river.

3

But Farragut was not destined to be kept in school until the war was over. The last of November he received orders to the brig *Spark*,[14] commanded by Master Commandant Thomas Gamble. She was then lying in New York and was being fitted out to join a squadron of small vessels, which was to prey on enemy commerce. It was to be commanded by Captain Porter, who probably arranged in Washington for Farragut to be ordered to this duty to salve his feeling of disappointment at being left behind at Chester when his old shipmates were again in active service.

While the ship was being prepared, Farragut was quartered on the receiving-ship *John Adams*. This turned out to be a critical experience for Farragut. It was the first time in his naval career that he had not been under the watchful eye of Captain Porter or some schoolmaster. "I was put in a mess with a set of wild young men," Farragut wrote, "who thought the great object of youth was to be a man. And the best proof of manhood was the facility with which he could acquire the use of tobacco, whiskey, etc. Of course, with such associates, I soon became a proficient, and for two or three months there was scarcely one in the mess except my old shipmate Ogden who ever went to bed sober. Our living was wretched. We had nothing but Scotch coffee sweetened with molasses and our rations for dinner. Yet all the liquor we could raise was added to our ship's whiskey for hot stuff. The winter was intensely cold and our sufferings were great for I was not half clad. Nothing but a strict attention to my duty saved me, as my since warm friend (Wm. H. Cocke who was then First Lieutenant) has often told me."[15]

But there was to be no more active sea service in this war for Farragut, for just about the time the squadron was ready to sail peace was declared, the Treaty of Ghent having been signed on the 24th of December, though not ratified by the government of the United States until February 17, 1815.

XIV

CRUISING IN THE MEDITERRANEAN

1

THOUGH the War with Great Britain had come to an end, Farragut was immediately to participate in another war, which had been brewing for some time against Algiers. The Dey had taken advantage of the war between the United States and Great Britain to treat the former country with contempt by demanding an increase of tribute and by capturing an American merchant vessel. As soon as President Madison had his hands free to deal with Algiers, he sent a message to Congress recommending a declaration of war, which was approved by Congress on March 2, 1815.[1]

For service in the Mediterranean two squadrons were organized: one in New York under command of Commodore Stephen Decatur and the other in Boston under Commodore William Bainbridge. Though Farragut would have seen more action if he had gone with Decatur, it was his fortune to be ordered April 15, 1815, to the ship of the line *Independence*,[2] which was the flagship of Bainbridge's squadron. This ship was commanded by Captain William M. Crane, who assigned Farragut to duty as his aid. That was a great honor to be so singled out on the flagship of a squadron, and he was doubly fortunate in thus being placed under the eye of Captain Crane inasmuch as he was to be separated from his former patron, Captain David Porter, who had been appointed one of the three Navy Commissioners in Washington.

Farragut was to find the *Independence* a very different ship from the little frigate *Essex*. In fact, her tonnage of 2,257 was nearly three times that of the smaller frigate. Her length of 190

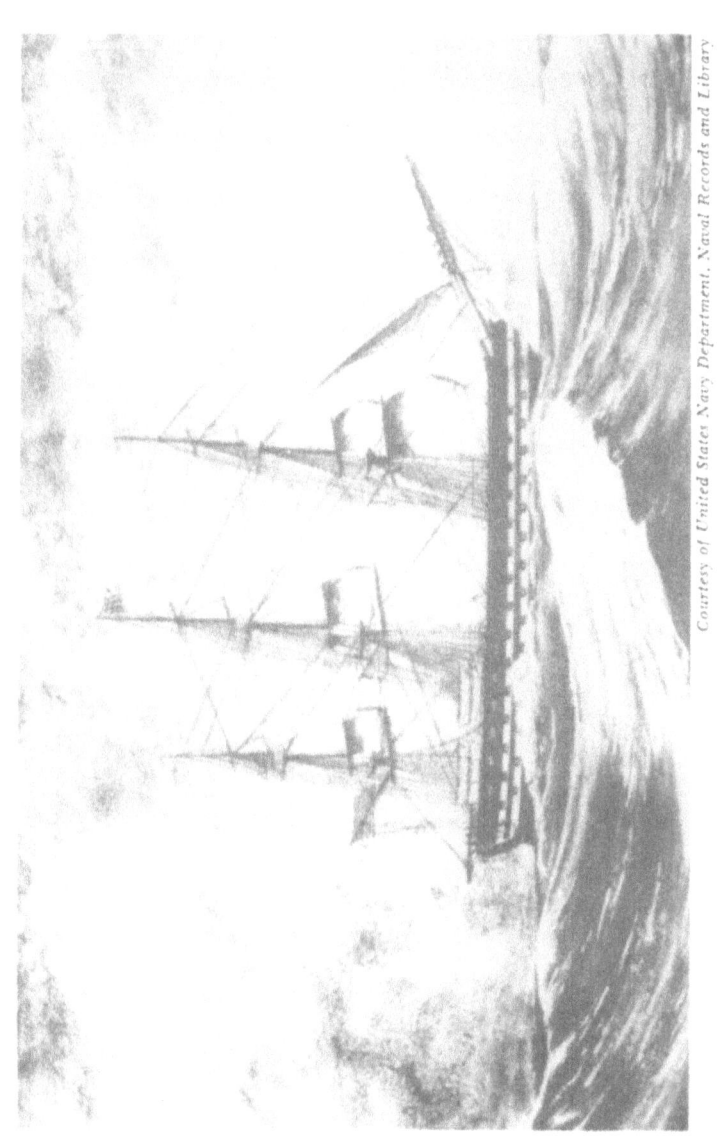

Courtesy of United States Navy Department, Naval Records and Library

UNITED STATES SHIP OF THE LINE *Independence.*

feet and beam of 50 feet were not so much greater; but she stood much higher above the water as she had one more gun deck than a frigate. She also had a much heavier battery, composed of sixty-three long 32-pounders and twenty-four 32-pounder carronades, making a total of eighty-seven guns, though she was rated as a 74-gun ship. Her officers and crew numbered about 800 men as compared to the approximate 300 on the *Essex*. She was a new ship, having been launched at Boston on the 20th of July, 1814, and having been built at a cost of $421,810. Her sister ships, *Franklin, Columbus,* and *Washington,* were laid down the same year.[3]

Big, shaggy-haired, black-eyed Commodore Bainbridge had his cabin on the spar deck, abaft the mizzenmast, under the poop deck. This was a part of that holy of holies on board a man-of-war, located abaft the mainmast and called the quarter-deck, where only the officers were permitted to congregate. But before entering these sacred precincts, each officer, even including the captain, was required to salute; and the starboard side was entirely forbidden to midshipmen. A full tier of guns was not carried on this spar deck, there being no gun ports in the waist or middle portion.

Captain Crane's cabin was aft on the deck below, called the main deck. Over the door to his cabin hung the chronometer which regulated the ship's time; and before his door constantly paced a marine who called out the half hours to the officer of the deck, and announced all visitors to the captain. Farragut went in and out of this door frequently with messages and orders from the commanding officer. Between the captain's cabin and the mainmast was the "half-deck," the port side of which was, like the quarter-deck, always kept clear. Near the foremast was the galley where the food for the commodore and the captain was prepared. And just forward on the starboard side was the brig where the offenders against the laws and rules of the ship were confined. In the beams on this deck hooks were driven where the sailors attached their hammocks at night; during the day these hammocks were placed in the nettings which ran around the bulwarks of the spar deck. A complete tier of guns was placed on this deck, and their ports, being open in favorable weather, afforded adequate ventilation.

Farthest aft on the lower gun deck, or berth deck, was the wardroom, or living quarters of the eight lieutenants, the surgeon and three assistant surgeons, the captain and two lieutenants of marines, the purser, the sailing master, the chaplain, and the commodore's secretary. Immediately forward of the foremast was the ship's main galley, where the food for the remainder of the officers and the crew was prepared and where the cooks reigned supreme. Forward of the galley was "sick bay," the realm of the surgeons. Hooks for hammocks were also attached to the beams on this deck, and the space between the guns was occupied by the mess-chests and mess-lockers of the sailors. Ventilation came through the gun ports, there being a full tier of guns on that deck also.

Below was the orlop deck, on the aftermost part of which was a large space lined with tin and called the breadroom. Forward of this were the private rooms of the wardroom officers; amidships was the cockpit which was used by the surgeons in in an engagement; then came the port and starboard steerages, occupied by the sixteen midshipmen and the three ship's clerks; next were the rooms of the boatswain, gunner, sailmaker, and carpenter; and just below "sick bay" were the sailmaker's, carpenter's, and boatswain's stores.

Still further below was the hold, in which both forward and aft were the powder magazines, accessible above by small hatches. Between the magazines were the wet provisions such as beef and pork, the chain-lockers and cable-tiers and shot-locker, and flour and dry provisions, and the spirit-room which was always under guard. Below the beams which support the tiers of the hold were the water-tanks, constructed of iron to fit the shape of the ship.

The *Independence* had three masts, on each of which square sails were carried, and differed from a frigate like the *Essex* in having taller masts and larger sails. The wheel was double and was worked by four men. Other details were similar to those on board a frigate, the only difference being that they were larger or more numerous.[4] As captain's aid, Farragut was, in a few days, thoroughly familiar with every part of this smart new ship of the line, and was the envy of the other fifteen midshipmen aboard her.

Commodore Decatur's squadron, consisting of the frigates *Guerrière*, *Macedonian*, and *Constellation*, the sloop *Ontario*, the brigs *Epervier*, *Firefly*, *Spark*, and *Flambeau*, and the schooners *Torch* and *Spitfire*, on the 20th of May, sailed from New York. Bainbridge was unable to get his squadron ready to sail from Boston until July 3. Even then he had to leave the frigate *United States* behind, and she did not reach Gibraltar until September 25. He arrived at Carthagena on August 5 with the rest of his squadron, with the exception of the *Congress*, commanded by Captain Charles Morris, which had sailed by way of Holland[5] and did not arrive until four days later. Besides the flagship *Independence*, the squadron was then composed of the frigate *Congress*, the sloop *Erie*, the brigs *Chippewa*, *Saranac*, *Boxer*, and *Enterprise*, and the schooner *Lynx*. There, at that time, were also the *Firefly*, *Spark*, and *Torch* of Decatur's squadron.

Though Bainbridge was to have commanded both squadrons upon their arrival in the Mediterranean, Decatur was not a man to remain idle when there was a chance for action and he had immediately begun operations after he arrived at Gibraltar on the 15th of June. In two weeks he captured a frigate and a brig and forced the Dey to sign a peace which brought to an end the paying of tribute by the United States to Algiers.[6]

Bainbridge learned of the conclusion of the war, on his arrival; but he proceeded with the *Independence*, *Congress*, *Erie*, *Chippewa*, and *Spark* to Algiers, and thence to Tripoli and Tunis. Though Decatur had preceded him to Tunis and Tripoli also and had exacted favorable terms before sailing away to Messina and Naples, Bainbridge learned that the appearance of his squadron so soon after that commanded by Decatur had impressed the Barbary rulers with the sea power of the United

States in such a degree that they would be more likely to respect treaties, with America in the future.

Bainbridge's squadron then crossed over to Malaga, Spain, where it arrived on the 13th of September. There he expected to meet Decatur's squadron,[7] which however was still cruising in Italian waters. According to Farragut,[8] an entertainment was given on board the *Independence* while at Malaga; but he does not mention an incident, neither pleasurable nor friendly, which is said to have happened at this time. A seaman deserted from the *Independence*, and was seized on the street of Malaga by American officers. When he declared himself to be a Spanish subject, he was released and taken to the quarters of the General of Marine. In order to force his return on board the *Independence*, Bainbridge had to threaten the governor that he would send five hundred men to take the man by force and to bombard the town, if any resistance were made.[9]

A few days afterwards, the squadron sailed to Gibraltar to await Decatur's arrival there. Meanwhile Farragut had an opportunity to visit the great fortifications, which he "examined with great interest."[10] Near the 1st of October Decatur's squadron, with the exception of the flagship, arrived; and Farragut had the pleasure, he declared, of seeing "the largest American force I have ever seen,"[11] fifteen vessels in number. Decatur himself did not arrive in the *Guerrière* until October 6, just when Bainbridge was on the point of setting sail for home with his squadron. Farragut recalled[12] how Decatur came alongside the *Independence* to make an official visit and exchange courtesies with Commodore Bainbridge, but he recorded no details as to his impressions of the romantic Decatur and his reception by the Commodore. It is claimed that Bainbridge, jealous of Decatur's successful termination of the war before the arrival of his superior officer, treated him very coldly on their meeting, and that they did not speak to each other for several years afterwards.[13] That was probably the reason why Decatur's flagship, the *Guerrière*, did not return with Bainbridge's fleet, but departed the day after it sailed. But sailing alone, he arrived home three whole days ahead of the fleet.

Bainbridge left a small squadron, composed of the *United States, Constellation, Ontario,* and *Erie,* under the command of Commodore John Shaw, to protect American interests. The *Ontario* was commanded by Captain John Downes, with whom Farragut had served in the famous cruise of the *Essex.* Thirteen ships then remained in Bainbridge's fleet on the homeward voyage. What interested Farragut most on the return passage was the exercising of the squadron by signals, the use of which "was quite a passion with Commodore Bainbridge."[14] The maneuvers consisted of "closing and spreading, general quarters, reefing top-sails, and making and shortening sail." Captain Charles Morris, who commanded the *Congress,* thought the maneuvering was not very successful. In the simple formation of sailing in three columns, it was difficult to get the ships into their proper stations and to keep them there for more than an hour at a time.[15] But it was a beautiful and inspiring picture on a clear day to be seen from the lofty spar deck of the *Independence*—white sails billowing above dark hulls, which plowed through the white-crested waves. Such a picture Farragut looked at frequently during the homeward voyage, a picture which remained imprinted on his mind all the rest of his life.[16]

The fleet separated before reaching the American coast, some ships proceeding to New York and others to Newport. Among the latter was the *Independence,* which arrived at her destination on the 15th of November, 1815, after a passage of forty days. Early in December, the flagship together with the *Congress* and *Macedonian* was ordered to Boston.[17] Meanwhile Captain Charles G. Ridgely of the *Erie* had exchanged commands with Captain Crane at Gibraltar, because of the latter's health. "We beat up to Boston in fine style," wrote Farragut[18]; "in fact, this was the first good opportunity we had of trying the sailing qualities of our ship, and they proved all that could be desired."

Although the cruise had contributed but little to the successful termination of the war, Farragut thought[18] it had been of great service to him. He prized particularly the friendship which he had formed with Midshipman William Taylor, whom he considered "one of the finest officers of his rank." Older than Farragut, he had taken the lad under his charge, had advised him, and had inspired him with sentiments of true manliness, which were the opposite of what had been presented to him on the *John Adams*. "Never having had any real love for dissipation," declared Farragut,[18] "I easily got rid of the bad influences which had assailed me in that ship."

2

Farragut was ordered to the *Macedonian*, commanded by Captain Jacob Jones, on the 18th of December, 1815; but remained on her only about a month, when he received orders on the 6th of February of the following year to the ship of the line *Washington*. She was a sister ship to the *Independence*, and the second one of this class to be launched, having been built at Portsmouth, New Hampshire. She was under the command of Captain John Orde Creighton, who chose Farragut as his aid, and she bore the broad pennant of Commodore Isaac Chauncey. Ordered to the Mediterranean as the flagship of the American squadron in those waters, she sailed from Boston about the middle of May, 1816.

She stopped, however, at Annapolis, Maryland, on May 23 to receive on board the Honorable William Pinkney, Envoy to Naples. He was being sent there to attempt to collect payment for damages which had been inflicted on American commerce when that country was under the control of Napoleon.[19] From there he was to proceed to Russia, to which country he had been appointed Minister. While at Annapolis, the *Washington* was particularly honored by a visit from President Madison, who was accompanied by his wife, the Secretary of the Navy, and two of the Navy Commissioners, Commodores John Rodgers and David Porter.[20] Farragut referred in his reminiscences to the latter in particular, calling him "my friend Commodore Porter."[21] This visit Farragut remembered vividly because of an embarrassment which he then experienced. It happened that, on that day, he went ashore with the market-boat and did not return to the ship until after his clothes-chest had been removed to the hold, "the receptacle of all encumbrances about the steerage."[21] Being thus prevented from changing into full dress, he had to appear "in rather a shabby dress," and keep himself "out of sight as much as possible."[21] As he was the Captain's aid, the latter was rather difficult. In honor of the distinguished visitors, the yards were manned and the crew was exercised at quarters, an entertainment with which all were highly pleased.

The ship remained in Annapolis until June 7, when Mr. Pinkney and his family embarked and the *Washington* sailed down the Chesapeake, bound for Gibraltar. The passage of twenty-two days was pleasant but uneventful. But the whole cruise was characterized by Farragut as disagreeable,[22] in spite of the fact that the ship behaved well and had an excellent set of officers. He disliked the way in which discipline was maintained by the Captain, with the details of which he became quite familiar as aid. Captain Creighton was known as a martinet, and his ambition was to make the *Washington* a "crack ship." According to Farragut, he achieved this end, for the ship was kept in perfect order with all the "bright work" glistening and all the decks as clean as holystoning could make them, and the crew was well-drilled and able to perform their duties with the utmost dispatch. But these results were gotten by sacrificing the comfort of every man on the ship. It became a common procedure for the officer of the watch to have his whole watch given two or three dozen lashes apiece for the fault of one man, or even for a mere accident. Sometimes all hands were kept away from their meals for eight or ten hours, and on one occasion the whole crew were kept on deck all night for several nights in succession. Farragut's experience on that ship made him determine that he would never try to have "a crack ship," if he had to resort to such inhumanity.[23]

Stopping at Gibraltar about two weeks to pick up the ships of the Mediterranean squadron except the *United States* which was at Port Mahon in the Island of Minorca, Commodore Chauncey sailed for Naples. His squadron then consisted of the frigate *Java,* under command of Captain Oliver Hazard Perry, which had been dispatched to the Mediterranean with the ratified treaty with Algiers; the frigate *Constellation;* and the sloops *Erie, Ontario,* and *Peacock.* In five days the squadron was at Naples, where Mr. Pinkney was landed with the honors due his rank, which consisted of the manning of the yards and the firing of a salute by the entire squadron.

About a month later, on August 20, the *United States* arrived and Commodore Shaw formally delivered the command of the squadron to Commodore Chauncey.[24] The squadron then sailed to Messina, Sicily, where two unfortunate events happened. Captain Perry there had a quarrel with Captain Heath, one of his marine officers, which eventually ended in a duel between the two men; and Captain Gordon, commanding the *Constellation,* died from the effects of a wound received many years previous.

In September Chauncey proceeded with his squadron to Tripoli, and to Tunis and Algiers in October. During the preceding month of August, a combined English and Dutch fleet, commanded by Lord Exmouth, had bombarded the city of Algiers and caused such severe damages to the fortifications and to the Algerian navy that the Dey had been forced to sign a treaty with England guaranteeing the complete abolition of Christian slavery. When the American squadron appeared so soon after this catastrophe, the Dey, who had not then accepted the ratified treaty with the United States, feared that his capital would again be attacked; but he was reassured by the American consul, William Shaler, that everything would be arranged without resort to force. The consul then went aboard the flagship, and the squadron departed for Gibraltar.

There Chauncey found the brig *Spark,* which had recently arrived with a letter from President Madison to the Dey, and orders appointing Shaler and Chauncey as commissioners to persuade the Dey to sign the treaty, already ratified by the United States. Though it was then late in the season and Commodore Chauncey was advised that he should go into winter quarters, he laughed at the suggestion, and taking Consul Shaler on board, sailed for Algiers with the flagship and the *Spark*. Arriving off the city on December 8, the Commodore transferred Shaler to the *Spark*, which landed him safely. But the sea was too rough for the *Washington* to anchor in the harbor, and she was forced to lay off Algiers during the remainder of the month of December. "Were I to say in one continual gale, it would scarcely be an exaggeration," declared Farragut[25]; "for though the clerk of the weather would frequently flatter us into the belief that the worst of the gale was over, just long enough to get up the light spars, the wind would return with fresh vigor, accompanied by fog and rain, with such a heavy, chopping sea at times that I thought our ship would actually roll over." During this unpleasant waiting for better weather, Farragut observed a very strange marine phenomenon. One day, three or four waves appeared to meet from different directions and then threw water forty or fifty feet into the air. Some on board thought it was caused by an earthquake, though no shock was felt at the time.

Finally at the end of December, the length of the surgeon's report convinced the Commodore that it was indeed foolish to try to cruise in those waters during the winter season, and he decided to go to Port Mahon for winter quarters, where he could refit. On the way, however, the jib-boom was carried away and a man was lost overboard; this was the only accident of the entire cruise. The *Washington* was carried into the harbor by a head wind; then her sails were clewed and furled and she was towed up to the naval station by all the boats of the other ships of the squadron which had already gone there for the winter.

During the ensuing weeks the hold was broken out and restowed, the rigging was refitted, and other routine repairs were made. The men were quartered at the Navy Yard, where two or three days in each week they were permitted to amuse themselves with such entertainments as exhibitions of jugglery and theatricals. They were allowed to go on liberty frequently in squads. Though Farragut's father was born on the Island of Minorca, no reference is made to that fact in his reminiscences.

He was then more interested in boyish escapades, one of which he relates in his journal as having taken place at that time. "On one occasion," according to this record, "some of the young officers of the *United States* invited Commodore Chauncey's son, his nephew Mr. Clinton, and myself to a ball on board. At the time we were visiting the *Ontario;* so we adjourned to the *United States*, where we enjoyed ourselves very much until about midnight, when a boat came alongside with an order from Commodore Chauncey for us to repair on board our own ship immediately. Now, Chauncey had given his son and Mr. Clinton permission to go on board the *Ontario*, and Captain Creighton, with whom I was a great favorite, had allowed me to accompany them; but the Captain, being one of those who take their text from that portion of the Bible which says, 'Whom the Lord loveth he chasteneth', in rather a literal sense, showed his displeasure as soon as I appeared, because I had 'dared to visit the *States* without his express authority.' After many angry expressions, he sent me below. As I had some curiosity to learn how the other boys would fare, I crept silently to the cabin door, and looked through the keyhole. There was Clinton sprawling on the deck, and young Chauncey standing before his father, who was bestowing on him all the angry epithets in his vocabulary, until at length he slapped him over, and, upon the boy's regaining his feet, repeated the dose. When they came into the steerage, Clinton said to Chauncey, 'Why didn't you do as I did—lie still when he first knocked you down? You might have known the old codger would knock you over again when you got up.' For this affair I was kept suspended thirty days."[26]

The restless Chauncey sailed again for Algiers on January 20, 1817, where he remained a few days only and then proceeded to Gibraltar. Remaining here a couple of months, he was back at Minorca about the middle of April. The final negotiation of the treaty with Algiers could then be considered finished business. Accordingly on the 9th of June, his squadron began an extensive cruise in the Mediterranean.[27] The educational value of such a cruise to the scenes of some of the most famous episodes in world history was inestimable to a young lad at Farragut's age, and his journal reveals how his romantic nature with its passion for the heroic expanded in such historic surroundings.

Touching at Marseilles for a short visit of four days, the squadron sailed to Leghorn, where it remained a whole month, and then proceeded to Naples. At his first visit there, just a year before, Farragut had seen Mount Vesuvius in active eruption; and this he declared[28] was alone worth a trip to Naples. On the second occasion he visited the ruined cities of Pompeii and Herculaneum, and the Palace of Murat. Very interesting also was a trip along the bay that he made with a party of officers in one of the ship's boats, which Captain Creighton kindly placed at their disposal. The boat touched at Baiae, the Baths of Nero, the Sibyl's Cave, Posilippo, and the Grotto del Cane. The latter place impressed the lad particularly. There he saw a dog thrown into spasms, when some one experimentally held its nose close to the ground and thus forced it to breathe the poisonous gas that issued from the mouth of the cave. At the Baths of Nero, he amused himself by lowering eggs in a basket three hundred feet below the surface into the waters of a hot spring where they were quickly boiled. The whole vicinity seemed as though it rested over a furnace, and when the officers went in bathing there, they could immediately feel the heat when they dug a little in the sand on the beach. Farragut declared,[29] "The pleasure which I experienced during my sojourn in the Bay of Naples left the most vivid and grateful impressions on my mind."

Chauncey sailed from Naples on the 21st of August for Gibraltar; but en route he stopped for four or five days each at Messina, Syracuse, and Tunis and for a whole week at Tripoli. None of these places impressed Farragut very favorably. The only objects of interest at Syracuse which he remembered were the old amphitheatre and Dionysius's Ear, a cavern with amazing acoustic properties. He was struck also with the filth of the city and the misery of the inhabitants.

In passing through the Straits of Messina, Chauncey placed a corporal's guard at the gangway with orders to shoot the pilot if he ran the ship aground. The Commodore did not propose to take any chances with Scylla and Charybdis, those female monsters of the ancient navigators. Tripoli, Farragut declared, had no charms for the traveler, swept as it was by the southerly winds from the nearby desert, bringing suffocating heat and burning sand. Tunis he found to be a more interesting place, with a larger Christian population. He noted that the anchorage there was safer than that at Algiers and Tripoli where ships were exposed to northern gales. The Tunisians were able to take their ships through a canal and moor them in a lake; but because of its shallow water they had to move them out to sea to take on provisions and equipment for war. Algiers he thought was better fortified than the other two Barbary seaports, but more vulnerable to attack because the depth of water permitted enemy ships to approach very near the harbor defenses.[30] At Gibraltar, Farragut was detached from the *Washington*.

3

Farragut had become a particular favorite of the Chaplain of the *Washington*, Charles Folsom,[31] who about that time had been appointed American Consul at Tunis to take the post vacated by a Mr. Anderson who wished to return to the United States. Through his great interest in Farragut, Folsom wrote a letter[32] to Commodore Chauncey, requesting that the young midshipman be permitted to accompany him to Tunis and there continue his studies with him during the winter. He pointed out that, though Farragut had been in the naval service almost since infancy, he had had but limited opportunities for improving his mind. "His prospects in life," the Chaplain continued, "depend on his merits and abilities in a peculiar manner, as he is entirely destitute of the aids of fortune or the influence of friends, other than those whom his character may attach to him." Speaking of the favorable change in character which he had noted in Farragut since he had joined the *Washington*, he declared, "His desire of cultivating his mind, which at first was feeble, has grown into an ardent zeal. His attention to his studies of late, the manner in which he has repaid my endeavors to advance his knowledge, his improving character, and his peculiar situation, have conspired to excite in me a strong interest in his welfare, and a wish to do all in my power to promote his education." Folsom, as schoolmaster on the *Washington*, had been in a position to observe Farragut very closely, and Chauncey granted his request.

Farragut and his good friend went on board the *Erie*, commanded by Master Commandant Thomas Gamble, on the 26th of October, 1817, and sailed in her by way of Malaga for Marseilles.[33] At Malaga an entertainment was given on board the *Erie* for the English Consul Kirkpatrick, whose daughter was the wife of Count de Montijo and later became the mother of a little girl who was to become Empress Eugènie of France.[34] During the mouth or so that the *Erie* lay within the mole at Marseilles, Farragut, then sixteen years old, enjoyed sight-seeing and mingling in society, an entrance to which he gained through an acquaintance with the families of Fitch and Montgomery, who were at the head of the largest American business house in the city in those days. At a dinner party at the home of the former he had a rather disagreeable experience. During the evening he was obliged to play whist; this he did merely for the sake of politeness, for he did not care for cards and did not play a good game. Great impatience was shown by other players at the way he played his hand, and remarks were made which seemed insulting to an embarrassed young man. Finally one of the players threw his cards on the table in derision of Farragut's play. This was more than he could take; so he went the man one better by throwing his cards at the fellow's head. He then apologized to Mr. Fitch and left, very regretful at having probably hurt the feelings of his host and behaved in an ungentlemanly manner, though he was really the aggrieved party whose temper had been tried to the limit.[35]

On the 22nd of December, the *Erie* sailed for Tunis where she arrived after a short passage of six days.[36] As the ship approached the coast, the town seemed to rise out of its encircling plain, with its castle commanding the harbor and the entrance to the canal, with its low, dazzling white buildings, and with lofty picturesque mountains in the distance. After receiving the salute due an American Consul, Folsom and Farragut were rowed ashore, both young enough to enjoy the experience to the fullest extent, for the new Consul was then only twenty-three years old. Farragut's sincere attachment for the young man was more like that which he might have felt for an older brother than for a chaplain and schoolmaster of the Navy.

Farragut was soon hard at work on his studies consisting of French, Italian, English literature, and Mathematics. Meanwhile he found the society of the foreign consuls very enjoyable, particularly that of the family of the Danish Counsul Gierlew, who had married the daughter of an Englishman named Robinson. Farragut stayed several weeks with them at their residence on the site of the ancient city of Carthage, situated about three miles northeast of Tunis; and spent many pleasant hours wandering about the ruins of the historic spot.

After applying himself very closely to his studies for about three months without much regular exercise, Farragut became ill and the physician recommended a trip on horseback. Folsom was eager to visit the interior of the country, and the French and Danish Consuls were invited to join the party. Having secured a passport and a guard of soldiers from the Bey and a covered cart to carry bedding and baggage, they set out on horseback on the adventurous journey.

At the end of the first day, they arrived at Toar, which was situated on a mountain of the same name in sight of Tunis. It was from here that ancient Carthage obtained its water through an aqueduct, the remains of which were to be seen here and there on the intervening plain. The captain of the escort had sent one of the soldiers ahead to the sheik of the village with the request that a house be made ready for their entertainment with cooks and other servants. On arrival, they found that a place had been selected, the occupants having been turned out and clean mats having been spread on the floors. Supper had also been prepared, apparently to the liking of the Tunisian captain. Later on the journey, on one occasion he did not like the food and had the cook bastinadoed, though Folsom interfered and stopped the punishment before it was finished. Farragut feared that such high-handed treatment of the inhabitants might lead to the murder of their entire party unless they returned by a different route.

After visiting several towns and villages in the interior and along the seacoast, they came on the ninth day to the ruins of the remarkable Roman amphitheatre of El Jem near Susa. That day had been one of the hottest Farragut had ever experienced. Only three could ride in the cart, and as Farragut was the youngest, he had continued on horseback. Though he wore a large straw hat on his head and had another tied on his back, he suffered a stroke of the sun which produced a partial paralysis of his tongue and extreme nausea. It was several hours before he could control his speech so as to talk intelligibly.

Completely worn out with fatigue, they found, when they arrived at their quarters, that the supper could not be eaten. It consisted chiefly of *couscous,* made of herbs, coarse-ground wheat, and beef and vegetables, all boiled together. The cook had upset the pepper-pot in the mess; so the Captain ordered him to eat of the mixture until he yelled with pain, and he then poured the rest of it on the poor fellow's head. Farragut was alarmed at the scowling faces of the villagers, who called all Christians "sons of dogs" and might have murdered them in their sleep had they not feared the vengeance of the Bey, under whose protection they were traveling.

The next morning, while examining the extensive ruins of the interesting example of Roman architecture, Farragut became separated from his companions. He had become tired of carrying his gun all the time and had left it in the hut where they spent the night. Fortunately he had the foresight to place his pistols in his pocket, for as he was strolling through the amphitheatre a Bedouin who had been stalking him suddenly rushed toward him with a club. When the fellow approached within a few feet of Farragut, he drew both pistols and covered his assailant, who was so surprised at the sudden turn of fortune that he fled in peril of his life. That the fellow should have made this attack almost within call of the military escort showed what would have soon been the fate of the party, if they had had no such protection. Frequently along the road they saw a pile of stones which marked the spot where some unfortunate traveler had been murdered and where, according to the custom of the country, other travelers had placed a stone as a mark of respect for the dead.

After two days at El Jem, Farragut's party proceeded to Monestin on the seashore, where the Sheik received them very hospitably. He provided for them an excellent supper, though the meats which were cut up were eaten with the fingers. The Sheik had been in Europe, however, and was acquainted with its customs; so the next day he took great pleasure in giving his guests a dinner in European style. The meat was carved, and the last course consisted of a variety of sweetmeats and excellent wine, which, according to Farragut, that particular Mohammedan drank "as freely as any Christian."[37] "Only the Europeans," he remarked, "know what good wine is, and so I send to France for my supply." On that occasion he drank a bottle of wine and four glasses full of brandy without any bad effect on him.

When they departed the following morning, the hospitable Sheik presented a gazelle to Farragut. Turning to the eastward, the party arrived about midday at a village, where they were insulted with the vilest epithets in the Arabic language. Though the Captain of the escort threatened to bastinado them all, they yelled in derision and declared they would stone the travelers. By this time the mob had become large enough to completely block the narrow street; but the escort held their ground and the Captain warned, "The first man who touches one of the travelers shall die on the spot; your streets will flow with the blood of your people; and the head of your Sheik shall pay the forfeit for your disregard of the Bey's passport." They simply hooted at the warning, and the Captain, drawing his sword, commanded "Forward!" and led the way through the mob, which parted right and left without throwing a single stone, though they continued to give vent to their feelings with angry shouts. It was a dangerous situation; the least wavering of the escort would have cost the lives of Farragut and his fellow travelers then and there.

Not daring to stop in the village, they encamped about a mile outside under a large olive tree. They had hardly finished eating some midday refreshments when they saw a party of men approaching. They got ready for another attack, when it was discovered that it was a peaceable procession led by an old man. He begged humbly for forgiveness for the insult which he said had been given by young men. Finally he was forgiven provided the future conduct of the village did not warrant a complaint to the Bey, and the agreement was ratified by eating cakes and honey with the distressed and fearful old man.

A few days afterwards, they arrived, about sunset, at the town of Sidi Solomon, situated on the western shore of the Bay of Tunis. To their astonishment, not a human being was to be seen and all the houses were closed; only cattle and hogs roamed through the streets. There was only one answer. The plague had broken out. They dared not stop for the night, though they had already spent eighteen hours in the saddle. But so fatigued were they that they took possession of a large house in the suburbs, and slept there that night. The next day they were back in Tunis.

After resting a few days, they set out again for the ruins of the ancient city of Utica. Farragut was not very favorably impressed with what he saw, noting only the remains of the seawall and the cisterns which were better preserved than those at Carthage. From here they rode to the town of Porto Farma, headquarters of small vessels engaged in the coral fishery which was carried on by Neapolitans who had a small government schooner of war stationed there for their protection. Learning that the Bey was spending a few days there, they requested the favor of showing their respects to him in person. He appointed the following morning for their reception, when they were ushered into the presence of a rather corpulent man of medium height, who appeared to be about sixty-five years old. Seated cross-legged on a low divan, he received his callers very courteously and invited them to be seated also. An easy familiar conversation about affairs of the day then followed, after which they left with a very kindly feeling for the Bey. Farragut was greatly impressed with the only ornament which he wore, a diamond on his thumb which was estimated to be worth a thousand dollars.

On the return to Tunis, they spent the night with the superintendent of a tunny fishery on the coast near Cape Sidi, who entertained them very well and served them an excellent fish for breakfast. They were then rowed about a mile out to the nets, where they saw the fishermen catch over four hundred tunnies each three to five feet long, and a sword-fish eight feet in length.

Not long after their return, the plague broke out in the city of Tunis. The Christians barricaded their homes and held communication with the outside only through their native servants. Farragut found the confinement exceedingly annoying; and he and Consul Folsom, with youthful indiscretion, went out as usual, though they were never admitted inside the barricaded homes. When the death rate reached thirty or forty persons a day, Farragut made up his mind to leave the country and rejoin the squadron.[38] The opportunity presented itself when the Danish Consul decided to depart with his family about the first of October. By that time the deaths had increased to a hundred a day.[39]

On the 9th of October, Folsom accompanied his young friend to the Goletta, where he embraced him, kissed him on both cheeks, and gave him his blessing with tears in his eyes.[40] Farragut then embarked with the Gierlews on a Genoese brig bound for Leghorn. Folsom then returned across the dreary lake to his then cheerless home, weeping and disconsolate, feeling that its light had gone out with Farragut's departure. His only comfort was that he had saved him from a threatened evil and that their pure friendship would in some way be an influence for good in his personal character and professional career. It was indeed remarkable that a young lad could have inspired such affection in an older man, who nearly fifty years afterwards would write, "I was ever on my guard, my dear Farragut, against flattering you when young, so easy was it for admiration and affection to slide into extravagant praise."[40] Folsom was not the only man who highly regarded Farragut at this time. Richard B. Jones, American Consul at Tripoli, wrote Folsom January 20, 1818, "With regard to my young friend Farragut, if he will only apply steadily to useful purposes the talents with which he is so bountifully enriched, it must, with his amiable disposition and obliging manners, insure him the respect and esteem of all who know him, and place him, at some future period, high in the niche of fame." In a later letter of May 15 of that year, he prophetically referred to him as "the young Admiral."[41]

4

The voyage in the Genoese brig was a pleasant one as far as the Island of Sardinia, where a gale forced the vessel to run into a small harbor in the Isle of Pines until it was safe to proceed. A greater peril threatened the ship off Corsica. When Farragut went on deck one evening while the ship was lying off that island, he was greatly surprised to notice that the vessel, already too close inshore, was being rapidly carried by the current toward a dangerous point of rocks. "It was a dead calm," he wrote,[42] "and all hands, including the captain, were asleep! I directed him to be called, but was informed that he had left orders not to wake him. I soon turned him out, however, but, on regaining consciousness, he was so much alarmed that he was utterly powerless to do anything. I told Mr. Gierlew that, unless the boats were got out and the vessel towed off, we should be on shore in less than an hour. This alarmed him, and he gave the necessary orders, threatening to cut off the captain's head if he refused to obey, which had the desired effect. The boats were soon out, and by hard labor we just cleared the point of rocks, while the ghastly devils on shore were looking down on us like vultures watching their prey, waiting anxiously, no doubt, to see us wrecked; but, much to their chagrin, we passed safely out of their reach. All hands went to prayers to give thanks for their delivery." They might have rendered their thanks to young Farragut, for it was indeed he who had saved their ship.

After lying off Corsica near the birthplace of Napoleon for four days, during which Farragut amused himself fishing and collecting specimens of herbs to send to Folsom, the ship sailed for Leghorn where she arrived on the 1st of November. They were immediately quarantined and were obliged to remain in the lazaretto there for forty days, which Farragut declared was more like a prison than any other place he had ever set his foot in before.[43] There he received a letter from Folsom[44] in which he told Farragut that he was as dear to him as a brother, and that his success and happiness would always make him happy and, if he proved less worthy than he had supposed, his grief and regret would be great indeed. He suggested that, when he left quarantine, he should purchase at Giuseppe Gamba's book-store in Leghorn the "Beauties of Shakespeare" and Blair's "Lectures on Rhetoric," which would serve to form his taste.

When Farragut was at last released from the lazaretto, he attended to the various requests of Folsom; such as, the delivery of attar of roses to friends and the arrangement of financial affairs. He then departed to Pisa where the naval hospital had been established, and there found Drs. Heap and Kilson and Lieutenants Cassin and Ray. The Grand Duke of Tuscany was there with his court, and many visitors had come to enjoy the gay season. Farragut, by that time an accomplished linguist, made many acquaintances among the Italian nobility. He also met Admiral Hotham and his son, and other English tourists.

Together with the other American naval officers, he was invited to a magnificent ball, given by the wealthy Countess Martioni in honor of the Grand Duke. Farragut thought everything was arranged, even the gorgeous dress of the servants, to please the eye rather than satisfy the appetite. The guests were allowed to walk through the supper-room and permitted to feast their eyes only on the preparations which had been made for the Duke and his party, the entire dinner service being made of gold. During the dancing Farragut's shoe-buckle caught in the dress of an Archduchess. He kicked off the shoe, and then gallantly knelt down and extricated it with an appropriate apology. Another apology was in order soon afterwards, when he stepped on the Duke's toe. Embarrassed at his awkwardness, he decided to leave and began to look around for his cocked hat, which he finally found was being used by the Countess Testa for a foot-warmer. "You ought to feel yourself highly complimented, young man, and should not be offended," said the Countess. But Farragut replied, "Madam, it might be so considered in your country, but not in mine."[45]

Farragut wrote in his reminiscences that he had a delightful time at Pisa until December. Then having learned that the American squadron was at Messina, Sicily, he returned to Leghorn and began to look around for transportation south. While waiting he wrote a letter[46] to his friend, Commodore David Porter, relative to his chances for an early promotion. He enclosed a letter[47] of commendation from Captain William M. Crane, assuring Porter that Farragut was a young officer of much promise, who "would do credit to a superior station in the navy."

Eventually he secured passage with Lieutenants Ray and Cassin on a small English schooner, and after what he termed in his reminiscences "a short passage," he reached his destination and reported for duty on the *Franklin* at Messina on the 15th of February, 1819.[48] Once again he became aid to Captain Gallagher, and on another ship of the line, which bore the broad pennant of Commodore Charles Stewart, Chauncey having returned home in the *Washington* the previous summer.

Farragut spent the remainder of the winter at Messina very pleasantly, attending two or three balls a week at the American Consulate and frequently visiting the arsenals to participate in athletic sports, in which he always held his own in spite of his shortness in stature.

On the 14th of April, the squadron sailed by way of Naples

to Palermo, where it remained nearly three weeks and then returned to Naples for a visit of two weeks. On the 18th of May, the *Franklin* was honored by a visit from the Emperor of Austria and the King of Naples with their respective suites.[49] The Commodore and his officers and men did all in their power to entertain their illustrious guests. Farragut was given the great honor of acting as interpreter to the Emperor, and he recalled how Prince Metternich, who was in the party, laughed at him during the tour about the ship, when he addressed the Emperor as "Mister." Farragut thought the Prince, then about fifty years old, was by no means bad looking, though he was short and stout. The only one in the party whose appearance struck him as being ridiculous was the Emperor. "He looked like a puppet," Farragut wrote.[50] "He had on a white coat with two long loops of silk cord on each shoulder, buttoned to the collar, five large stars on the breast of his coat. These were the only marks of rank he had about him and these several of the other gentlemen wore also—he wore red shorts and stockings with military boots and a cocked hat with a green plume, took short steps and absolutely looked silly. He stood about five feet five. The King of Naples was a tall raw boned, common looking man, wore a suit of blue with a red collar and cuffs."

While some guns were being fired off for the amusement of the visitors, one of the Emperor's chamberlains leaned against the wind-sail, which he thought to be a mast, and fell down into the cockpit. Though the fellow fortunately escaped with only a broken leg, the accident alarmed the party, who acted as though they feared some similar evil might have been plotted against the Emperor and the King. Calling their boats away soon after the occurrence, they returned to the city. The chamberlain was attended to by the ship's surgeon, and later removed to an apartment in Naples.

On the 1st of June, the squadron sailed for Gibraltar, whence the *Franklin* visited both Cadiz and Malaga. In August she cruised to Leghorn by way of Minorca and returned to Gibraltar on the 11th of October. There near the middle of November, Farragut was ordered by Commodore Stewart to the brig

Spark as an acting lieutenant. This, Farragut declared,[51] was one of the important events in his life, for he was then only eighteen years old. Though young in years, he felt that he was associating on an equality with men and that he had to act accordingly. Later he became executive officer on the brig, and his duties were so important that he considered that he was really in command of the ship, without bearing the responsibilities of the position. This lack of responsibility he thought a bad feature, which had ruined most promising officers. "I consider it a great advantage," he concluded, "to obtain command young, having observed, as a general thing, that persons who come into authority late in life shrink from responsibility, and often break down under its weight."[51]

Greatly to Farragut's satisfaction, the *Spark*, on approaching Malta during a cruise to that island, outsailed the English packet brig *Pigeon*, which he afterwards learned bore news of the death of George III. Rejoining the *Franklin* at Gibraltar, the brig sailed with the squadron in December to Messina, and there spent the winter.

5

In the following summer[52] of the year 1820, while the *Spark* was in the harbor of Port Mahon, Minorca, the *Guerrière*, commanded by Captain Lewis Warrington, arrived from the United States with the news that Commodore Bainbridge had arrived to take over the command of the squadron, Captain Stewart having already returned home. From Captain Warrington, Farragut obtained orders to return to the United States to take his examination for promotion to the rank of lieutenant. Not being able to return on the *Guerrière*, as that vessel had been ordered to the coast of Africa, he found it necessary to take passage on a merchantman, the *America*, on which he embarked at Gibraltar in company with two invalided sailors and the brother of one of the lieutenants of the squadron, named Seaton.

Everything went well on the voyage until the ship was only a few days' sail from home, when she sighted a suspicious-looking strange sail. The weather was perfectly calm; but the smaller vessel got out her long oars with which she approached dangerously near the *America*. By five o'clock in the afternoon, every one on board was convinced that she was a pirate, but the captain was so completely paralyzed with fright that Farragut had to take over the command of the ship. At first the captain and his mates begged Farragut to take off his uniform for fear that it would incite the pirates to wreak vengeance on the vessel. But this Farragut emphatically refused to do. He was determined to see the *America* sunk rather than surrender himself into the hands of men who might have in store for him a worse fate than death.

He accordingly mustered the crew and inquired if they would fight to defend the ship. The two navy sailors immediately placed themselves under Farragut's orders. Their example seemed to infuse new spirit into the merchant sailors, who at first were afraid to make any resistance but soon appeared willing to fight to the last gasp. The incident showed to Farragut the difference between men-of-war's men and merchant men, and led him to the conclusion that "men trained to arms will never fail, if properly led."[53]

A grindstone and a barrel of tar were gotten ready to sink the boat which they might send alongside. By that time the supposed pirate ship was near enough to hail the *America;* and this they did in Spanish, stating that they were sending a boat with an officer to come aboard. When the boat had gotten quite near, Farragut inquired in English, "Do you come as a friend?" "Yes!" replied the officer in good English. "Leave your arms in the boat then, before you come on board," warned Farragut. The officer complied, and on coming on board he turned out to be a Mr. Smith of Baltimore. His ship was a brig of war of Colombia. He brought letters which Farragut took charge of for him, and offering to supply the *America* with anything she might need, he departed. Apparently the vessel was not a pirate craft, though in those years the waters of the Caribbean were infested with them and they often sailed under the flag of some South American nation. The experience convinced Farragut that it was comparatively easy to defend a ship against pirates, if the crew did not become panic-stricken.

Arriving safe and sound in the United States, Farragut was in Washington[54] by the 28th of September when he wrote the Secretary of the Navy, officially reporting himself as a candidate for examination. And so came to a close an extremely important period in Farragut's life—a period in which his character came under the ennobling influence of Chaplain Folsom, his education was continued under very favorable circumstances, and his professional experience as an aid to four different captains of ships of the line was an unusually valuable one. At the close of those cruises in the Mediterranean, there was probably not another midshipman in the United States Navy so well equipped professionally as was David Glasgow Farragut.

XV

CRUISING IN THE GULF OF MEXICO

1

FARRAGUT was ordered to New York to take his examinations. He felt that he was qualified in seamanship, as well he might because of his many years of practical experience at sea; but he was doubtful as to his mathematics.[1] His fears were well founded, for he failed to pass, or as he expressed it, "I have been so unfortunate as not to satisfy the Board of Examiners."[2]

Very interesting light is thrown on the reasons for Farragut's failure to "satisfy" his examiners in his reminiscences.[3] As this has never been published, a full quotation will be given in order that the case may be presented in Farragut's own words. "While in New York," Farragut wrote, "Raimond (Christopher Raymond) Perry arrived and it was reported that he was to be tried for drunkenness, but I heard nothing of any charges against him yet certainly knew him to be a drunkard. One day I received a message from Captain George Washington Rodgers requesting me to call and see him, that he wished to converse with me about a report in circulation about Raimond Perry. I sent word that I would be happy to see him at my lodgings if he had any business with me. Some days after I met him in Brooklyn and he accosted me, saying that some one had set injurious reports in circulation about Capt. Perry and that officers should be careful what they said. I replied that his language did not exactly apply to me and I presumed officers were always ready to repeat what they had said when properly called on. As for myself, if Mr. Perry had anything to settle with me, I could assure him there would be no difficulty when he called. He said, I call as Captain Perry's friend. Said I, as Mr.

MIDSHIPMAN FARRAGUT AT THE AGE OF NINETEEN
From a portrait by F. Kuykendall.

Rodgers or as Captain Rodgers? He said, as Captain Rodgers. Then, sir, as Captain Rodgers I have nothing to say to you on this subject, but whenever you lay aside your official character and meet me as the friend of Mr. Perry, I shall be most happy to send a friend to settle all difficulties between him and myself.

"It will be remembered that at this time I was but eighteen years of age. Just that age when a man thinks more of himself than at any other future period. I had been the First Lieutenant of a brig of war, and acquitted myself as far as I could judge from letters received with considerable éclat, had quarreled with my Captain and triumphed over him in consequence of his beastly propensities, but I had yet a lesson to learn, that a man's personal qualifications will not bear himself against his superiors. Captain Rodgers lived with Captain Samuel Evans, who was one of my examiners and who showed me from the first moment that I saw him that he considered me a most insubordinate young man. When I came before the Board, I had the temerity to differ with my examiner, Captain Evans. I would have objected to this if I could, but it was an arrangement made between themselves and I was obliged to submit. He said that in reefing topsails I had neglected to clear away my bowlines. I declared that I did, though he might not have heard it. He swore like a mad man and said I was the most insolent young man he ever saw. I appealed to the other members who said they did not notice but were sure I did not or Captain Evans would not have been so certain. I now told that I had been First Lieutenant of a brig of war in the daily habit of reefing topsails and, if I knew nothing else, certainly I knew that, but all to no use. I could do nothing right or respectful. At length with tears in my eyes I retired, perceiving too late how fatal had been my error in not rather conciliating Captain Rodgers than insulting him, for it was apparent that his revenge was ample.

"I was accordingly rejected by a majority of the Board in obedience to their rule which I will remark is a most unjust and cruel mode of deciding the fate of a young officer. Three officers are appointed to examine a young officer. Presume (sic) that he will be judged by a majority but how different is the fact; for the convenience of these gentlemen they agree to abide by decision of each other and all depends on the examiner. If any one wishes to favor a young officer, he will let him off easily, and if on the contrary he likes to defeat him, will make his examination as difficult as possible. In fact, it puts it almost entirely in his power to pass or reject him unless the young man has a friend present on the examination to excite interest by his partiality. In my case, no doubt my pertinacity had the effect of withholding the interposition of Captain Stewart who could see no justification for the slightest insubordination of a young officer. He is one of the sternest and I think one of the most illiberal judges I have ever seen.

"I returned to Washington where I was informed that 'I had passed in Mathematics but was found otherwise deficient.' To this I objected, stating to the Secretary that they were I conceived bound to say in what I was deficient, and pledged myself to go before any board of officers he might select and that, if I did not pass above mediocre of my batch, I would consent to anything provided he would give me my rank. He said that was fair, and as I would not go to sea before there was another, if I passed agreeably to my pledge, I should have my rank but that he could not put so great an indignity on the Board as to order a new examination. I was content. . . .

"It was a good lesson that has served me much in life although it cost me dearly. It was the hardest blow I have ever sustained to my pride and the greatest mortification to my vanity. I might have deserved a rebuke, as I am told some of the members proposed, but certainly not a punishment that was to last during life."

For a few weeks Farragut doubted his ability ever to realize his ambition to make a name for himself in the Navy. He was very lonely too, feeling like "a stranger in my native land, knowing no one but Commodore Porter and his family."[1] The Porters then resided in Washington on a 110-acre estate on a hill about a mile north of the White House. On this estate, called "Meridian Hill," the Commodore had built a mansion in which he lived in comparative luxury while he was on duty as a Navy Commissioner. In 1820, when Farragut visited there for awhile, there were five children, whose ages ranged from eleven to one. That may have been one of the reasons why he did not stay long in Washington, but went down to Norfolk, possibly to pay a visit at the home of the Dixons, who were relatives of the Porters.

Farragut had been in Norfolk before. It was there that he had first joined the *Essex*, and he had been on ships that had called there on two or three other occasions. But his stay this time was to lengthen into months, during which, as he expressed it, he "received the consolation of a charming young lady, who smiled on my attentions."[4] In fact, this was the young woman of Norfolk whom he married some years later, and from that time to the beginning of the Civil War he was to look upon Norfolk as his home.

Norfolk was then a comparatively small place with a total population of about 8,500, of whom over 3,000 were negro slaves.[5] It had been a town for over a hundred years, and as destructive fires destroyed the earlier wooden buildings substantial brick structures were erected. The Norfolk *Herald*[6] in 1818 could declare with satisfaction, "Strangers were astonished at the improvement in our streets and buildings in the past eight to ten years. Where miserable hovels . . . showed their contemptible fronts, stately and elegant piles have sprung up." All the principal streets were paved, whereas a few years before one might wade ankle deep in mud at the crossings. Many of the residences were large and handsome, and were surrounded with beautiful trees and lovely flower gardens in season. There was a great deal of wealth in the town. Its harbor was one of the best on the Atlantic coast. Located at the Southern end of the Chesapeake Bay and at the mouths of the James and York Rivers, it had a strategic position for commerce in time of peace and for defense in time of war. That was the reason the Gosport Navy Yard was located there by the government. There many ships of war were constructed. Only in October preceding Farragut's arrival there, the ship of the line

Delaware had been launched at this navy yard in the presence of a great throng of 20,000 people.[7]

On the 6th of January, 1821, Farragut was ordered to report for duty at the Norfolk Station.[8] As such duty was not much to his liking, he requested, on the 26th of February, leave of absence of five or six months to visit relatives in New Orleans, whom he had not seen for eleven years. This was not granted, as his traveling allowances for the voyage home from the Mediterranean on the *America* and for his trips from New York to Washington and from there to Norfolk had not been adjusted. There had been objection to his traveling by stage by way of Richmond to Norfolk instead of by boat direct. Accordingly his seeing either of his sisters was postponed for several more years.

Farragut was looking forward to making a second attempt to pass the examinations for promotion. There is no record of his having applied to Commodore Porter for his intervention in the unfair action of the Board of Examiners the previous year. But he almost certainly brought to his attention all the details of the case upon his return to Washington. Though Porter occupied an important position as one of the three Navy Commissioners, which was indeed second only to that of the Secretary of the Navy, there was little that he could do under the peculiar circumstances. It is not improbable that he was of the opinion that the punishment was too severe but still not wholly undeserved, and that its results would do Farragut more good than harm.

Be that as it may, Farragut as early as July 20, 1821, wrote the Secretary of the Navy that he wished to report himself as a candidate "for the ensuing examinations."[9] His second attempt was successful, and he wrote from New York on October 28, "I aimed at the head but was glad to catch at number 20 out of 53."[10]

Back in Norfolk, he wrote[11] the Secretary of the Navy, on the 30th of November, requesting duty on a cruising vessel; and two days later wrote[11] him again, making a special request to serve on the *John Adams*. A month later, on January 9, David

Porter wrote[11] the Secretary, ". . . I can say with perfect confidence that Mr. Farragut has not his superior." Weeks went by with no results. On February 17 he applied[11] for duty on the *Macedonian* or any vessel which might cruise in the Gulf of Mexico. More weeks passed. Near the middle of May, he requested[11] duty on the *John Adams*. Much depressed, he wrote,[11] at the same time, to Commodore Porter that his accounts at the Navy Department had not yet been settled and he feared that his pay might be stopped, that he saw no probability of promotion for several years, and that it had become his duty to help support his sisters. His passing his examinations did not mean immediate promotion to the rank of lieutenant. His name merely was added to the list of "Midshipmen Passed for Promotion, 1821." His pay as a midshipman was only nineteen dollars a month, and under the circumstances he could be excused for looking out for his "pecuniary interest." There was also the young lady in Norfolk with whom he had fallen in love.

2

Finally on May 23[12] Farragut was ordered to report for duty on board the *John Adams*. It had been about two years since his last sea service in the Mediterranean. He was pleased to go to sea, even if it were in a frigate of twenty-eight guns and about two hundred men,[13] a vessel even smaller than the *Essex*. The *John Adams* had had an interesting history. A contractor to whom one side of the vessel was sub-let for construction, to economize, employed negroes at Charleston, where she was built in 1799, and made the moulds smaller by several inches in the beam; as a consequence the vessel sailed very much better on one tack than on the other. She had cruised in the squadrons of Truxtun, Decatur, John Rodgers, Chauncey, and many others, and about two years before Farragut joined the ship, she had carried the gallant Oliver Hazard Perry on a cruise to the mouth of the Orinoco River, during which he died of the yellow fever.

The *John Adams*, under command of Captain James Renshaw, sailed from Norfolk on the 20th of August, 1822,[14] and stopped at Charleston, where Joel R. Poinsett, the Minister to Mexico, and a Mr. Dodd, who was going to Guatemala, came on board. En route to San Juan, Puerto Rico, the ship, through an error made by the pilot, was nearly wrecked in a dangerous bay of Santo Domingo. On the way to Vera Cruz, she chased a suspicious looking brig, which was thought to be a pirate. Farragut was sent in a boat to board the stranger after she had been overhauled, and his cutter was nearly dashed to pieces against the vessel, which turned out to be a Spanish man-of-war. At that time those waters swarmed with pirates, and such mistakes were easily made as one could not know the identity of a ship from the flag she flew.

The *John Adams* arrived at Vera Cruz on the 19th of October,[15] and landed Minister Poinsett. The city had, only the previous year, been captured by General Santa Anna in the last of the series of revolutions, which led to the establishment of the independence of Mexico under Agustín Iturbide as emperor.[16] But the Viceroy of Spain still held the formidable fortress of San Juan de Ulloa, which dominated the harbor and controlled the maritime commerce of the city. In company with Minister Poinsett and Captain Renshaw, Farragut dined with General Santa Anna, whom he found to be "a young, good-looking fellow of five-and-twenty,"[17] and who then spoke enthusiastically of Emperor Iturbide, whom he later was to aid in overthrowing.

Poinsett[18] proceeded to Mexico City to present his credentials to the Emperor. The *John Adams*, after dropping down to the Island of Sacrificios for a few days, sailed on the 28th of November[19] for Tampico where the American Minister was later to rejoin the ship. On the voyage to the north, she fell in with a schooner from New York. Captain Renshaw sent Farragut to bring the master on board. The weather was then clear and there was a dead calm. As the old captain of the schooner came abroad the *John Adams*, a slight breeze from the north began to blow. Having had a great deal of experience with the fickle weather along the coast of Mexico, he immediately declared to Captain Renshaw, "I must go back to my vessel; this is a norther." Farragut just had time to take him back to his ship and to return to his own, when the norther was upon them in all its fury. Because of the fortunate warning by an experienced navigator in those waters, the ship was ready.

After riding out the gale, Captain Renshaw arrived off Tampico, which is situated on a lake, connected with the sea by an outlet[20] some six miles in length. Renshaw selected Farragut for the special duty of landing on the coast and proceeding to the city, where he was to inform Poinsett of the arrival of the ship and secure his instructions. The boat landed Farragut at what was supposed to be a suitable place, a lookout station for pilots. Hardly had he landed when the weather changed. This caused the boat to have considerable trouble in getting back to the ship, and gave Farragut much discomfort as he was dressed in summer clothing with the exception of his uniform coat and cocked hat. He had five doubloons[21] in his pocket, and for protection wore "that formidable weapon, a midshipman's dirk-sword."[22]

Farragut inquired of an old Mexican, who met him on the beach, "How far is it to Tampico?" He replied, "About ten miles." Farragut then asked if he had a horse, and received an affirmative answer; but to his inquiry concerning the furnishing of a guide the old Mexican said that it was not necessary as one merely followed the coast. A good looking horse was brought out, well equipped with a native saddle covered with skins, which could be used for a bed if needed. Farragut paid the two dollars, which had been agreed upon for hire, and started for the city.

In an hour or so, another norther was blowing furiously with a heavy rain which soaked him through and through. Eventually he reached the Panuco River, but was greatly disappointed at finding that there was not a single house or sign of life on his side of the river. He shouted himself hoarse but heard no reply above the noise of the storm and the pounding of the surf. Though tired and cold, he spread out the skins on the ground and prepared to pass a sleepless night. To his surprise, about nine o'clock he heard the splash of oars. To his hail, "Who's there?" the welcome reply was returned, "Friends; I thought you wanted to cross." "So I do," quickly added Farragut. "Then, come on. The weather is not very inviting to stay here. Turn your horse loose. He'll find his way home all right. But bring your saddle with you."[23]

Upon reaching the other side of the stream, Farragut discovered he was in a village of pilots and smugglers. He was conducted to the head man, or Mata, as he was called, who inquired what business had brought him there at that time of night. Farragut explained his connection with the ship lying off the coast, and requested that a pilot be sent when she appeared off the bar. "Very well," said the Mata. "What else?" "I wish to go to Tampico," Farragut replied. "What, to-night?" shouted the astonished Mexican. "Yes," admitted Farragut, who was not pleased with the appearance of the villagers and did not wish to spend the night among such a gang of cutthroats who might rob and murder him. "I'll see if I can find any one fool enough to accompany you,"[23] agreed the Mata, completely at a loss to understand the actions of the mad Yankee.

Meanwhile Farragut had not been reassured by the hard but inquisitive faces that had peered at him through the open door. But after awhile he was told that a fool had been found, and that in half an hour the horses would be ready for the journey. Farragut does not explain why he did not go by boat, which would seem to have been the easier method of transportation; but undoubtedly there were good reasons for not doing so.

It was ten o'clock when everything was ready for departure. After Farragut had satisfied the head man that he would pay the guide for the horses when he had reached his destination, he set out on what was to be one of the most miserable rides he ever undertook.

The distance was only nine miles; but the road, if it could be called one, led through forests of prickly pear and swamps. At least a dozen times the guide lost his way. Each time he would turn his horse around quickly, swearing at himself for losing the trail, and start out in a different direction. Farragut could dimly distinguish the fellow in the darkness by his white clothing, and each time he stopped and turned about, he feared that the man had reached a place he had chosen to rob and murder him; so he again and again drew his dirk and prepared to defend himself. At length, the guide called out, "Let go your reins and permit your horse to pick his own way along, or you will get your neck broken."[24] It soon became apparent that the route led down a hill, for sometimes Farragut's horse would settle down on his haunches and slide fifteen or twenty feet before he could get to his feet again. Several times the thick chaparral, through which they were riding, almost knocked off his cocked hat and ripped from it the lace and the cockade.

Finally, Farragut was greatly relieved to see the lights of the village of Pueblo Viejo, or old Tampico in the distance, where the guide assured him he would soon be able to enjoy some tortillas and coffee. But it was one o'clock in the morning when they arrived and Farragut was too tired and sleepy to enjoy anything but a bed.

The next morning, he learned that Minister Poinsett had not yet arrived from Mexico City, though he had already sent thirty Americans, whom he had been able to have released from the prisons of the capital city. They had arrived at Tampico with orders from Poinsett to be put on board the *John Adams*. Farragut immediately placed them in native boats and set off down the river to try to locate the ship. The sea was so rough, where it broke over the bar at the mouth of the river, that the boats could not cross. So the men were landed and conducted down the beach, whence the ship was signaled for boats to be sent to take all on board.

Having performed the first part of his mission with success, Farragut was ordered to return to Tampico to await the arrival of Poinsett, whom he was also to conduct to the ship. Having suffered so much concern over the comparatively helpless condition in which he found himself in case of attack on his first trip, Farragut took with him on his second journey his sword and a pair of pistols.

The second visit was much more satisfactory and enjoyable in every respect. It lasted for about two weeks, during which Farragut enjoyed himself at the fandangoes and parties given by the hospitable inhabitants. At the mansions of the wealthy Tampicans he improved his knowledge of the Spanish language, and after the arrival of the American Minister he improved his horsemanship in long rides to high points along the coast to discover the whereabouts of the ship. The December weather was very bad, and as Captain Renshaw was a careful navigator, it was fifteen days before the *John Adams* came in sight of the shore about the 21st of that month.

Poinsett had a quantity of bread baked in Tampico for the ship, which Farragut was ordered to convey on board. He secured boats, as before, to take Poinsett, Denis A. Smith of Baltimore, and several other Americans who had been released from prisons, down to the mouth of the river. The bread, of course, was not left behind, for fresh bread on board a man-of-war at sea in those days was a delicacy indeed.

When they arrived at the pilot station, they found that a heavy fog had settled down over the sea and the ship had not been seen since morning. To make matters worse, the surf seemed to be running so high over the bar as to make it impossible to cross. "Mata, will you take us out to the ship in the offing?" inquired Poinsett. "I will take you over the bar to the ship, if she can be found," replied the man with assurance, for he knew that the large, buoyant native launches could pass over the bar safely. "What will you charge?" further inquired the Minister. The somewhat lengthy reply was: "I will take you over the bar, pull until sunset, and, if I can find the ship, put you on board. You shall give me one hundred and fifty pesos. If I can not find her, I will return and land you, and you shall give me one hundred and fifty pesos. To-morrow morning take you out again, and go according to the same agreement until we put you on board or you get tired of attempting it." "It is a bargain,"[25] said Poinsett, concluding the conversation.

The breakers over the bar were rather terrifying, but the

launch passed over beautifully, shipping only a few gallons of water. After rowing awhile through the fog, they heard the welcome sound of a gun fired to the northeast. This was answered by a pistol-shot from the boat, and muskets, fired at regular intervals, then guided them to the *John Adams*, where they were received on board with a feeling of great relief. The bread, too, was indeed welcome, as the allowance had been reduced to half a biscuit a day to each man on board.

On the 24th of December, the *John Adams* sailed for home. Stopping at Havana five days, she arrived at Norfolk on the 23d of January, 1823.[26] The cruise had lasted five months almost to a day. It had afforded valuable experience to Farragut professionally, and given him knowledge of the Mexican coast and an insight into the character of the Mexican people, which was to be of great value to him in the future. Incidentally, it had added about four thousand miles to the extraordinary total which this young officer, then only twenty-one, had sailed in the Atlantic, the Pacific, the Mediterranean, the Caribbean, and the Gulf of Mexico. It is safe to state that no other officer of his age in the U. S. Navy held such a record.

XVI

HUNTING PIRATES IN THE CARIBBEAN

1

NOT LONG after the return of the *John Adams* to Norfolk, Farragut learned that a small squadron under the command of his old patron and friend, Commodore David Porter, was to sail to the West Indies to stamp out piracy in those waters. Norfolk was to be the port where the ships were to gather and the expedition was to be fitted out. That kind of service appealed to Farragut, and he lost no time in gaining the assistance of Commodore Porter in having him transferred[1] from the *John Adams* to the "Mosquito Fleet," as the squadron was popularly called.

Since the War of 1812, privateering had developed into outright piracy in the Caribbean, during the long struggle of the Spanish colonies to gain their independence from the mother country. It was comparatively easy for a pirate to masquerade under the flag of some South American country, and prey on the commerce of the United States. A small expedition, commanded by Commodore Oliver Hazard Perry, in 1819 came to an unsuccessful close with Perry's death caused by yellow fever, after he had made a trip up the Orinoco River to negotiate with the Venezuelan government the payment of compensation for the losses to American commerce caused by "privateers" commissioned to sail under the flag of that country. Three years later, Commodore James Biddle took a squadron into those infested waters and captured some thirty pirate vessels; but he was unable to stamp out the pirates as his frigates *Macedonian* and *Congress* could not sail with safety among the treacherous keys and even his smaller sloops and schooners were too large to be used to track down the pirates to their lairs. The unfriendly attitude of the Spanish authorities in Cuba and other islands made Biddle's work all the more difficult. So sure did they feel of protection by the authorities that a gang of them attacked a boarding party from the schooner *Alligator* in Cardenas Bay, on November 9, 1822, and killed her commanding officer, Lieutenant William Howard Allen and three· of his men, and wounded several others. A "peculiar kind of force . . . effectually to suppress" the pirates must be provided, wrote President Monroe in a special message to Congress. And on February 1, 1823, Commodore Porter was appointed to command a squadron, fitted out under the provisions of an act of Congress of the preceding December 20.

It was, indeed, a "peculiar kind of force" which assembled at Norfolk. In the squadron there were eight fast sailing schooners, or bay boats, which Porter purchased at Baltimore, ranging from 47 to 65 tons, drawing no more than seven feet of water, and carrying three guns, one of which was a "long Tom," and thirty-one men each. They were somewhat appropriately named *Fox, Greyhound, Jackall, Beagle, Terrier, Weasel, Wild Cat,* and *Ferret.* Five barges, each bearing twenty oars, had the equally picturesque names, *Mosquito, Gnat, Midge, Sandfly,* and *Gallinipper.* In New York, Porter purchased a storeship, which he named the *Decoy* to indicate her character, and armed with six guns. There he also secured a steam vessel, originally a Jersey City ferry boat, which he armed with three guns. She was a sidewheeler and was rigged as a galliot. Her speed, which enabled her to make the passage to Cuba in nine days, led Porter to call her the *Sea Gull.* Surely her appearance could not have suggested the name. For his flagship Porter had the sloop *Peacock,* commanded by Stephen Cassin, which the Commodore boarded on the 9th of February.[2]

Four days previous Farragut joined the *Greyhound,* which was commanded by Lieutenant John Porter, a brother to the Commodore. On a cold wintry day, the 15th of February,[3] the squadron sailed from Norfolk. In a few weeks that cold was to be remembered as more desirable than the hot fever-laden air of the bays and inlets in the West Indian islands. Farragut was the only officer on the *Greyhound* who had ever sailed on a schooner. That experience was of great value to him, for the squadron ran immediately into a gale. The heavy wind forced his schooner to take in all sail for an hour or two, while the other vessels were reefing their sails and making everything safe for the night. Then Farragut's commanding officer ordered sail to be clapped on, with only two reefs in the mainsail and square sail. The little schooner dashed away from the squadron like a flying fish skipping from wave to wave. Farragut thought she was carrying more sail than was wise under the circumstances; but the captain was perfectly at ease, not seeming to realize that there was any danger. When he cautiously suggested, "She does not rise to the sea," the commander replied, "If she can't carry the sail, let her drag it."[4] Though the schooner was really in danger, Farragut was struck with the humor of the situation. There sat Porter on one side of a trunk aft, wrapped up in his cloak; while he sat on the other side, also bundled up and holding an umbrella over him. Soon the squadron was entirely out of sight, and Farragut was fully convinced that he would never see daylight again. But about eight o'clock Porter went below, leaving the ship entirely in Farragut's hands. He immediately reduced sail to the foresail alone, and the little schooner "scudded through the gale like a duck."[4]

After a passage of twelve days, the *Greyhound* arrived in safety off the entrance to the Mona Passage between Puerto Rico and Haiti.[5] As she was sailing easily under her square sail, an English squadron, composed of a frigate, a sloop, and a brig, appeared in sight. When the frigate discovered the American schooner, he signaled to the brig to haul out of the line and fire a shot across the bow of the strange vessel to bring her to. Porter then proved himself as reckless as he had been during the storm. Though there was a difference of opinion as to whether the English brig had fired a shotted gun, he called his crew to quarters and gave orders, "If she fires again, return it without further command." Almost immediately, another shot boomed out across the water. "Fire," shouted Porter, "but don't hit her."[4] The brig, with her officers standing on the poop deck, was by that time within musket shot, and the cannon ball from the long gun of the *Greyhound* passed just over their heads. When one bears in mind that the English brig carried twenty guns, while the American schooner had in addition to her long gun only two 18-pounders, the recklessness, or as Farragut called it, the sauciness of Porter's act becomes evident.

The English captain, being a man of intelligence, declared to his officers, "No one but a Yankee would have done that." He might have sunk the schooner with one broadside, but he chose rather to hail her first and inquire who she was. "A United States vessel of war," was the proud reply. The Englishman then expressed his regret for firing the second gun, and sent an officer on board to explain the mistake. Farragut was amused at the anger of the opposing crews, who apparently were spoiling for a fight. When the officer returned to his ship and informed his captain that the commander of the *Greyhound* was ill, he sent the boat back with some fruit for Porter. The English coxswain, as he passed it over the side, remarked, "Here is some fruit for the shot you sent us." The boatswain, to whom he handed it, had his answer ready, "We have a gun apiece for you, and are always ready to fight or eat with you."[6]

That same night, the *Greyhound* joined a part of the squadron, which had been to the windward, and they all proceeded to San Juan. While they were lying off this place, early in March, a very unfortunate accident happened. On the 4th of March, Commodore Porter sent the *Greyhound,* commanded by his brother, into the harbor with a special mission, to convey a letter to Governor Miguel de la Torre, requesting him to furnish a list of the privateers which had been authorized to cruise from Puerto Rico. She was to wait in the harbor two days for the Governor's answer. The following day, the *Fox,* commanded by Lieutenant William H. Cocke, was also ordered to enter the harbor, apparently to bring pressure to bear on the authorities. As she gained the entrance a gun from the fort began firing on her. Cocke was struck in the shoulder, as he stood on deck, and was mortally wounded. Farragut was greatly affected by his death, for he was the young officer who had been his counselor and friend on the *John Adams* in New York eight years before, when he greatly needed the advice of an older man to keep him from forming vicious habits. He relates[6] that Admiral Sir Thomas Cochrane of the English squadron then in the harbor sent his surgeon on board to try to save the young man's life, and that all the English officers attended his funeral. He, of course, also attended. Commodore Porter exercised as much restraint as he possibly could, under the provoking circumstances, but he did make strong remonstrances and received an apologetic explanation. As an excuse, the Spaniards claimed that they had become suspicious of all small armed vessels since the arrival of the filibustering expedition the previous year in the harbor of St. Bartholomew with the object of starting a revolution in Puerto Rico. The expedition had been fitted out in the United States and sailed under the American flag. The excuse was inadequate, and the act was clearly unwarranted.[7]

2

After spending a few days at Aguadilla, Puerto Rico, where the squadron rendezvoused for the purpose of getting water and some fresh provisions, Porter divided his force into two groups, so that both the northern and southern coasts of Haiti and Cuba could be patrolled as the squadron proceeded to Key West. Farragut's schooner, the *Greyhound*, was assigned to the division which looked into all the nooks and corners of the southern route. On another schooner of this division, the *Weasel*, was Midshipman Franklin Buchanan,[8] who about forty years later was to command the Confederate naval forces in the engagement with the Union fleet commanded by Farragut in Mobile Bay. Though a careful examination was made, particularly of Cape San Antonio, the southwestern point of Cuba which was known to be one of the favorite headquarters of the pirates, apparently they had been warned to conceal all evidence of wrong-doing, for when the Americanos arrived, they saw only a few fishermen, "poor, innocent-looking fellows," whom Farragut thought were really pirates only waiting for a favorable opportunity.[9]

When the squadron reassembled at Key West, many changes were made in the personnel and in preparations for more effective boat expeditions. Fortunately for Farragut, Lieutenant Lawrence Kearny[10] was transferred from the command of the *Decoy* to the *Greyhound*. The little schooner proceeded again to the south side of Cuba, and with a watchful eye on the coast cruised all round the Isle of Pines. Discovering no pirates, Kearny sailed along the coast to the vicinity of Cape Cruz, the southeast point of Cuba. Here the *Greyhound* and her companion, the *Beagle*, came to anchor. Nothing out of the ordinary happened until one day the respective commanding officers, Kearny and J. T. Newton, went ashore in one of the boats to see if any game was to be found. Accompanied by the boat's crew, who were armed, the two officers started on their excursion. In a short time, one of the sailors, named McCabe, suddenly raised his gun as if ready to pull the trigger. "What are you aiming at?" asked Kearny. "A damned pirate, sir," he replied. "How do you know?" continued Kearny. "By his rig," said the sailor confidently. Meanwhile the fellow had faded out of the picture; but the proof that the sailor was correct was soon forthcoming.

When the party returned to their boat and were on the point of shoving off, they were fired on from the dense woods. The fire was, of course, returned, but as the pirates were well hidden by the thick screen of chaparral, its effectiveness could not be known. Farragut, on board the *Greyhound*, heard the firing, but as Captain Kearny had the only boat belonging to the schooner, he was unable to go to his assistance. Fortunately the aim of the pirates was very bad, and the party reached the schooners about dark none the worse for their experience.

But the pirates were to have their punishment the following day.

Kearny ordered Farragut to be ready with a party of men at three o'clock the next morning. A force of seventeen men was organized, composed of the marines, stewards, and boys of the two schooners. Farragut was also accompanied by Midshipman C. P. C. Harrison of the *Beagle*. According to the plan, the schooner was to be warped up inside the rocks to cover the landing, and the attacking party was to keep clear of the beach as much as possible so that they would not be mistaken for pirates and be fired on by the ship.

Being totally unfamiliar with the geography of the coast, Farragut landed his party on the beach and plunged into the chaparral, which was so thick that it was almost impassable. Forcing their way through, they were disappointed to find that they had landed on a narrow strip of land which was separated from the mainland by a lagoon. They were then compelled to struggle through the marshes and hack their way with their cutlasses through the brambles to reach the mouth of the lagoon to communicate with the ships. When they showed themselves on the beach, they came very near to being fired on from the *Greyhound*, as pirates. Luckily Kearny was able to make out Farragut's epaulet[11] through his glass, and immediately sent a boat to convey them across to the other side.

There they were joined by some men from the *Beagle* under Lieutenant Sommerville. "Nothing could exceed the ridiculous appearance we made when we got to the shore," declared[11] Farragut. "My pantaloons stuck close to my legs, my jacket was torn to pieces by the brambles, and I was loaded with mud. The men under Sommerville saluted me as their chief; but the sight was too much for their risibility, and they burst into a loud laugh as I stepped on shore literally covered with mud and rags." Farragut further relates that while he and his men were struggling through the marsh, Mr. Harrison lost one of his shoes. One of the men, in attempting to help him find it, became stuck fast with one arm and one leg in the mud and the other arm and leg projecting in the air in the most ludicrous manner imaginable.

Kearny, in order to locate the position of the pirates, entered his boat and was pulled boldly toward the shore, with his flag flying. When he had gotten just within musket range, he drew a volley of musketry and a shot from a 4-pound swivel from the pirates situated under the bluffs of the Cape. Kearny accordingly changed his plans by re-embarking all the men except Farragut's original command and Lieutenant Sommerville, whom he ordered to attack the pirates in the rear while the schooners attacked them from the front.

Farragut and his men found the ground covered with rocks which had the appearance of iron. They were honeycombed and had sharp edges which played havoc with the men's shoes that had become softened through wading in the marshes. Some of the men had their shoes cut completely off their feet by the sharp rocks; but Farragut fared better as he had put on for that day a pair of pegged Negro brogans which were better suited to such rough terrain. Also very troublesome was the thicket of cactus, whose long sharp thorns made progress slow and dangerous, and a scrubby bush, which grew so thick that they had to cut their way through with their cutlasses. When they had advanced about half a mile into the thicket, Farragut ordered his men to halt and await a prearranged signal-gun from the schooner before pushing forward as rapidly as possible. While waiting, they suddenly heard a great noise in their rear. Farragut, thinking that the pirates had somehow gotten behind him and were on the point of attacking in force, drew his men up in a position to repel such an attack. "I made a most animated speech to my men," Farragut humorously admitted,[12] "to encourage them to fight courageously, when to our inexpressible joy the noise was found to proceed from about ten thousand land crabs making their way through the briars."

Meanwhile the attack from the schooners turned out to be much more effective than the pirates had expected it could be, for they thought the ships would not be able to get close enough for their guns to reach them. But Kearny had the vessels towed in among the rocks so that in a comparatively short time the guns were blazing away at the bluffs at an effective range. It was not long until the pirates began to scatter. On the other side, Farragut's party was pressing forward as fast as possible; but the heat had become so intense that Lieutenant Sommerville fainted. In the distance, every now and then a pirate was seen in full flight, but by the time Farragut's men laboriously made their way to the beach all the pirates had escaped their clutches except two old decrepit men whose age and infirmities kept them from any punishment which they might otherwise have merited.[13] One old man appeared to Farragut to be a leper. A large black monkey was the young commander's only prize, which he captured in single combat after the animal had bitten him through the arm.

Though the pirates had disappeared, plenty of evidence against them was soon gathered. They had several houses, from fifty to one hundred feet long, a dozen boats, and all the necessary equipment for turtling and fishing. The incriminating evidence was not found in their houses but in an immense cave nearby, which was literally filled with plunder. There were many articles marked with English labels and saddles and costumes worn by the upper class of Spanish peasants. The pirates had doubtless disappeared in other caves for several were found in the vicinity, large enough to conceal a thousand men and easily defensible against a much stronger force. About all the punishment Farragut could give them, under the circumstances, was to order their houses and boats to be set on fire and destroyed and the plunder as well as their cannon to be carried on board the ships.

The remainder of the cruise was rather barren of results, though Kearny and his men kept examining various ports of Cuba until their supplies ran low, and the first of August they had to return to Key West. It was the first warlike service[14] Farragut had experienced since the bloody engagement of the

Essex with the *Phoebe* and the *Cherub* in the harbor of Valparaiso.

3

Meanwhile other detachments from the squadron were doing good work, for which Farragut gives them full credit in his journal. Off the Bay of Escondida, Lieutenant Wm. H. Watson, commanding the barges *Gallinipper* and *Mosquito,* captured a pirate schooner of sixty tons, which carried a 9-pounder and sixty men. Her commander had the reputation of being one of the most blood-thirsty pirates along the Cuban coast, and because of his atrocities was called Diablito, or the Little Devil. The barges under sail and oar rushed upon the schooner, under orders to board her. Diablito endeavored to stop them by firing his 9-pounder loaded up to the muzzle with grape shot; but his aim was bad and the only damage he did was to cut away some of the oars. Seeing that resistance was useless, the pirates began to jump overboard and attempt to swim to shore. One of the barges then boarded and captured the schooner, while the other proceeded close inshore among the fugitives who were practically annihilated, about forty being killed. Diablito was on the point of escaping when he was recognized by the Spanish pilot and shot through the head.

A few days later Lieutenant C. K. Stribling, also in command of two barges, fell in with another pirate schooner, which he chased for two hours. The pirates made good speed with their long sweeps and kept up a constant fire as they fled toward the shore. When they were finally overtaken and the Americans began to board the vessel at the stern, they jumped precipitately over the bows and scrambled ashore. One man was killed, and two were captured; the others escaped. One of the captured men, who was wounded in the arm, turned out to be the leader, named Domingo. He was a very different type of man from Diablito, being rather romantic and chivalric. Farragut relates that on one occasion he sent all the letters which he had captured, with the message, "you are a gallant set of fellows, and I have no wish to keep your letters from you but I will retain the miniature of Lieutenant G——'s[15] wife, in case I shall meet the original. I think, if she looks like the picture, I will make love to her."[16]

These incidents indicate the character of the service which Farragut and the other young officers experienced in driving the pirates off the sea lanes of the upper Caribbean. Though the pirates had lost several ships and had had several of their bases destroyed, piracy was not completely stamped out and could not be until the local governments cooperated more fully in apprehending the fleeing pirates. But Porter's squadron had given piracy in those waters the most serious blow it had thus far received.

4

When Farragut returned to Key West the second time, he met there his brother William, then a lieutenant, who had arrived from New Orleans with Lieutenant Rousseau and several midshipmen to join the squadron. Though Glasgow had not seen William since he left New Orleans with Porter thirteen years before, he knew his older brother the moment he laid eyes on him.[17] William Farragut joined the *Greyhound* but on the 18th of August[18] Porter transferred Glasgow to the steamer *Sea Gull*, then being used as his flagship. The same day Lieutenant Kearny wrote a letter[19] to Porter highly praising Farragut's conduct while under his command.

About that time, yellow fever of a malignant type appeared in the squadron. Midshipman Marshall was the first victim; and many more were to follow, for twenty-three of the twenty-five officers who took the disease died. It was equally fatal to the seamen. Though the squadron had some of the best surgeons in the service, they seemed entirely unable to cope with the disease. No one, of course, at that time understood the real cause of yellow fever. Farragut noted that it seemed to be more prevalent on the barges and that some thought this was due to the fact that the men slept in the open air. He did not agree with this theory for all the men on the *Greyhound* slept on deck. "As to myself," he declared, "I never owned a bed during my two years and a half in the West Indies, but always slept where I found the most comfortable berth."[19] The reason why the men on the barges were subject to the disease was that the boats went into the shallower waters where the yellow fever carrying mosquitoes were more likely to be found.

Only two cases were lost on the *Sea Gull*. Farragut fortunately escaped for the time being; but Porter had a very severe attack.[20] So anxious did the Secretary of the Navy become over the situation that he dispatched Commodore Rodgers and several surgeons from New York to Key West on the *Shark* near the first of October. When Porter recovered, his surgeons advised him to go north to recuperate, and Farragut accompanied him on the *Sea Gull*. The voyage turned out to be a very rough one of twenty-three days, the little steamer being unable to make much headway against the might of the tempest and the raging seas. Long stops were made at St. Mary's and Savannah. On the way up the river to Washington, Farragut came down with a light attack of the fever. In fifteen days he was able to visit his friends in Norfolk and the "charming young lady" with whom he had become engaged before the sailing of the *John Adams* from Norfolk in the summer of 1822.

There was at least one other reason Farragut was happy to be back in Norfolk; the food had been running very low, down in Key West. One of the surgeons, it is related, was walking on the beach there one morning, holding Thomas Campbell's "Pleasures of Hope" in one hand and the skull of a turtle in the other, which he apostrophized as follows: "Ah! what a noble mess this fellow would have made!"[21]

When Farragut became ill, he had left to the others the duty of getting the *Sea Gull* ready for sea. She arrived in Norfolk in January, 1824, and as Farragut was still suffering from chills and fever every third day, Porter insisted on his going to sea to get rid of them. After a rest of about six weeks, Farragut returned to the West Indies in the *Sea Gull*. Porter sailed in company in the *John Adams*, and was back again at his base at Key West by the 2d of February.[22] After the *Sea Gull* returned to duty, she made an extensive cruise, calling at the islands of St. Christopher and St. Bartholomew, coasting along the southern shores of Puerto Rico and Haiti, and visiting Santiago de Cuba. According to Farragut's reminiscences, it was not wholly dull routine. At St. Bartholomew, for instance, a large company of guests were received on board and taken on a little excursion, their first ride doubtless on a steam vessel. Refreshments were served on board, and then at sunset the officers went on shore to enjoy the hospitality of the citizens of the islands. "We frolicked all night," Farragut admitted, "going from one house to another and at daylight went on board, rigged ship and put to sea." At Santiago de Cuba, pirate hunting proved just as pleasant, for there, Farragut recorded, "also we made a display for the gratification of the inhabitants and gave them a collation as much for the holding up distinction to the pirates as anything else."

But the cruise was not all pleasure. A vessel was taken from a Colombian man-of-war, whose captain thought she was a Spanish ship sailing under false American colors. She was sent into Norfolk for identification, and Farragut afterwards learned that she was a bona fide American ship, whose papers were so illegibly signed that it was impossible to be certain of her identity.

When off the Tortugas,[23] Farragut secured leave of absence to visit his relatives in New Orleans. This was made possible by the passing of the ship *Hamlet*, of New York, bound for New Orleans with the first load of bricks for the construction of Fort Jackson below that city. This was a curious coincidence of history, for it was the forcing of his way past this fort and the consequent capture of New Orleans some forty years later that brought to Farragut his first world wide fame.

It was in May, 1824,[24] that Farragut arrived in New Orleans, and went to see his sister Nancy, then twenty years old. He told her he had recently seen her brother William and talked to her at length about himself; but she did not recognize him at all, as he had changed so much from the little lad she remembered nearly fourteen years before. But when her foster mother, Mrs.

William Boswell, saw him, she recognized him and Farragut then admitted his identity. This reunion was one of the happiest events of his life. By that time death had made cruel inroads into his family. Both his parents were dead, and his youngest brother, George Antoine, had been drowned at the age of ten. No opportunity was found for going to Pascagoula to see his other sister, Elizabeth, who then resided there in the home of a Mrs. Dupont, who had cared for her since her mother's death. His short visit of about ten days was soon passed, and he found himself on what he called "a miserable little brig" returning to duty at Key West.

There he luckily arrived just in time to find a vacancy in the command of the *Ferret*, then off Matanzas. This was occasioned by the return home of Lieutenant Silas Duncan. Farragut had considerable difficulty in securing the command from Commodore Porter, although it should have gone to him by routine agreeable to the rule that such promotions were to be made according to seniority in date of warrant and not by number in passing the examinations, a rule which had been tacitly agreed upon in the squadron. But Porter was so afraid that he would be accused of partiality to Farragut that he would not give him the command, until Captain William C. Bolton, fleet captain, declared that it rightfully belonged to Farragut. Only then did Porter reluctantly agree.

5

Farragut was overjoyed. He had reached another important milestone in his career, when he was only about twenty-three years old. Before leaving Key West, he went ashore to get some articles at the store, where Passed Midshipman John Rudd asked him to wait to see him cane Dr. H. W. Bassett. "With what?" asked Farragut. "With my umbrella," replied Rudd. "That is a bad weapon," suggested Farragut. When Bassett came in, Rudd demanded that he take back false statements he had made. The doctor refused, and went to the cooper's shop and got a rough barrel stave. But the trouble was settled without a duel, which was threatened.[27]

Farragut took passage in the *Fox* for his new command, and in a few hours after joining the *Ferret*, he went to sea in search of pirates. But they had been so frightened that they rarely ventured from their hiding places except under cover of night. So Farragut had to be content with the rather prosaic duty of escorting merchant ships from Havana and Matanzas through the dangerous waters of the Gulf as far north as the "Double-headed-shot Keys." The duty was not devoid of danger, even if there had been no pirates; Farragut had to exercise the greatest care in navigating his ship to keep from losing her on some tiny reef or key with which those waters were dotted. "It was an admirable school for a young officer," he declared, "and I realized its benefits all my life. I have never felt afraid to run a ship since, generally finding it a pleasant excitement."[28]

The yellow fever reappeared that summer, but in a milder form. Farragut had many cases on his schooner, which he treated successfully himself. There was one exception, Midshipman Minor, who would not allow him to prescribe for him because he was not a regular surgeon. When Farragut finally after several hours got the young officer ashore, it turned out that the physician had just recently arrived from the United States and had never seen a case of the yellow fever before; as a consequence the Midshipman died, but his was the only life lost on the *Ferret* while Farragut commanded her.

Returning at length to Key West,[29] Farragut was ordered to Nassau in New Providence Island, one of the Bahamas. Both going and returning, the little *Ferret* had to contend with the current of the Gulf Stream, a constant gale, and terrifying thunderstorms. At Nassau, Farragut was called upon to display his diplomatic ability in handling a rather delicate situation. While at anchor in the harbor, the acting gunner hailed an English surveying ship and declared that he was an Englishman who had deserted from H.M.S. *Pandora*. He did this foolish thing because he was angry at Farragut for not giving him permission to go ashore. Commodore Porter, however, had given strict orders that none of the men were to be allowed such a privilege during the yellow fever season. When Farragut learned what the man had done, he got under way, and when he proceeded out of the harbor and the jurisdiction of the English authorities, he called up all hands and ordered the offender to be punished. He then returned to his anchorage, where he waited two days for the English to demand the man, fully determined not to agree to such a request. Fortunately no demand for his release came, and Farragut, meanwhile learning that an English man-of-war in Havana harbor had given up an American sailor in somewhat similar circumstances, decided to offer his man to the English Commodore at Nassau. At first the Englishman was unwilling to accept the man, as he knew the worthless character of such fellows, but at the insistence of Farragut he finally consented. As a further punishment for the trouble maker, Farragut withheld the man's pay for failure to fulfill his contract with the United States government.[30]

After escorting his convoy safely, Farragut returned again to the base, and in a few days afterwards was on his way with his ship to Washington. With very favorable weather, the *Ferret* made the remarkably good passage of only five days. But the voyage ended very badly for Farragut, for he was stricken with yellow fever[31] as the ship was passing up the Potomac and was practically in sight of Washington. It was then the last of July, 1824, and Farragut had spent more than a year of very hard service in a very unhealthful climate. As a consequence he was seriously ill, and spent many weeks in a hospital in Washington. It was the last of August before he had sufficiently recovered to be able to visit his friends in Norfolk.

Meanwhile the command of the *Ferret* was taken away from him and given to Lieutenant C. H. Bell, who refused the information which Farragut offered him regarding the peculiar characteristics of the vessel and said he would find them out for himself. As a consequence he capsized the schooner north of Cuba and lost many of her crew.

On the advice of his physician, Farragut did not return for further service in the West Indies, and did not further participate in the war against the pirates which continued sporadically through the years 1824 and 1825, after which a small force patrolled the waters until 1829. Farragut, accordingly, was not with Commodore Porter on his punitive expedition to Fajardo, Puerto Rico, in November, 1824, which resulted in the court-martial of Porter, his suspension from the service for six months, and consequent resignation from the Navy.

XVII

MARRIAGE, PROMOTION, AND THE *BRANDYWINE*

1

LOGICALLY, promotion should precede marriage; but Dan Cupid often reverses the order. It was thus with Farragut. When he went down to Norfolk after his serious illness in a Washington hospital, he did not go merely to visit friends and recuperate. There was a more compelling reason than that. During his previous visits to that Southern town he had met and wooed the girl whom he wished to be his wife. She was Susan Caroline Marchant, the third daughter of Jordan and Fanny Marchant of Norfolk. On September 2, 1824[1] they were married at Trinity Church, Portsmouth, Virginia. Soon afterwards he wrote to Commodore Porter, who was then in Washington convalescing after his second attack of yellow fever, announcing his marriage. "That you may be completely happy in the character of husband," replied Porter in part, "is the sincere wish of one who feels the same interest for you as for his own son. It will afford me sincere pleasure to become acquainted with your wife and I beg to present to her the best wishes of myself and Mrs. Porter."[2] Farragut soon availed himself of the invitation implied in Porter's kind letter, and took his wife to Washington to visit the Porters at Meridian Hill. Though no one could have foreseen it, a shadow of impending trouble then hung over the Porter mansion. And the visit of the Farraguts came during the last happy weeks that the Porter family were to spend together. Soon thereafter the Commodore returned to the West Indies where the Fajardo affair brought his naval career to an unfortunate ending; the remainder of his life he spent in self-imposed exile from the United States as an officer in the Mexican Navy, American Consul-General to Algiers, and American Minister to Turkey.

As has already been suggested, Farragut's financial status at the time of his marriage was not very satisfactory. For several years, as a passed midshipman, he had occupied that station in the naval service, which has sometimes been referred to as "a sort of purgatory." He was still a warrant officer, though qualified for a commission with all the privileges and considerations accompanying such higher rank. The only change in his uniform was the placing of a star in the gold-lace diamond on his collar. He was still forced to mess in the steerage, and sometimes associate with small boys long after he was fully grown and had long ago put away childish things. That was the state of expectancy in which Farragut had lived for several years.

As a passed midshipman, his pay had been increased, however, from nineteen dollars a month and one ration a day to twenty-five dollars and two rations per diem. And when he was acting as a lieutenant, he received the pay of that rank, which was forty dollars a month and three rations each day.[3] The necessity of his contributing to the support of his sisters probably kept him from saving much; and as he received only half pay while waiting orders, he and Mrs. Farragut very likely had but little money to squander on their honeymoon.

2

But somewhat brighter days were in store for Farragut in the immediate future. On January 13, 1825, he was commissioned[4] a lieutenant, and his name stood number 22 on the list of 68 appointed that year. He had been a midshipman for more than fourteen years. This delay in being promoted Farragut thought was due, at least in part, to a statement, which Commodore Porter made after the engagement in which the *Essex* was captured, to the effect that Farragut was too young for promotion. This was a handicap against which he continued to be forced to contend; in the eyes of the government and his commanding officers he never seemed to get any older and, though he was repeatedly given favored positions on shipboard such as captain's aid and responsible duties as acting lieutenant, still he had to see midshipmen frequently promoted above him simply because they were older in years and not because they had served longer in the navy and were better qualified professionally than he. As a consequence he was twenty-three years old when his good star finally prevailed, and thenceforward he could look back on these trials as providing a better preparation for his future career in the service.

As a lieutenant, Farragut drew forty dollars a month and three rations a day; but for several months after his promotion he received only half pay as he was not on active duty. The uniform for his new rank was much more resplendent than that which he as a humble midshipman had been privileged to wear. His long-tailed coat of blue cloth had broad lapels on each of which were nine buttons; there was a button also on the high standing collar and three buttons on each of the cuffs and the flaps of the pockets; gold lace about a half an inch wide was placed around the standing collar and the cuffs, and on the left shoulder was one epaulet; the buttons were of gold with foul anchor and the American eagle surrounded by fifteen stars. The white vest was single-breasted and on each pocket there were three buttons, which were the same as those on the coat except that they were proportionately smaller. The pantaloons, which were also white, were thrust into half boots. On his head he wore a gold laced cocked hat, the lace of which was not to show more than one and a quarter inches on each side. This completed the full dress uniform except for the cut and thrust sword with yellow mountings. His undress uniform was the same with the exception that the coat had no lace and instead of a standing collar it had a rolling cape.[5] Blue pantaloons, a round hat with a cockade, and a dirk were permitted. Farragut had already become accustomed to wearing this uniform, which he had worn, at different times, for several years when on duty as an acting lieutenant.

3

It was not until the 9th of February, 1825, that Farragut felt strong enough to request active sea duty of Secretary of the Navy Southard.[6] Even then he was obliged to recall his attack of yellow fever which had left him in such a bilious condition that he had been advised to seek service in northern waters rather than in the West Indies where his health had been undermined. He reported himself ready, however, for any duty that the Secretary thought proper to assign him. When the Secretary somewhat inconsiderately ordered him to the *Decoy* for duty in the West Indies on June 27, he had to report himself in such poor health that the orders were revoked on the 6th of July.[7] Meanwhile he had been ordered to Washington on April 26 to testify in the court of inquiry called to investigate Commodore Porter's conduct at Fajardo. Farragut's testimony had but little bearing on the case as he had returned to the United States before the affair took place.

On the 6th of August, Farragut made a special request of Secretary Southard for orders to the frigate *Brandywine*.[8] This time he enclosed a sick ticket from Dr. Williamson who recommended any service but that in the West Indies. Three days later he was ordered to the beautiful new frigate, only recently built in Washington and named the *Brandywine*, "the name of a brook instead of a river," Lafayette wrote[9] home, "solely to recall my first battle and my wound." The vessel was so named because she had been selected by the United States government to transport General Lafayette home again after his epochal visit to the country which he had aided so heroically to gain its independence nearly fifty years previous. She was a 44-ton frigate with a complement of 480 officers and men and a tonnage of 1,726,[10] which made her slightly larger than the *Constitution*. She was commanded by Captain Charles Morris, who had gained fame as a midshipman on the *Intrepid* under Decatur, when the *Philadelphia* was burned in the harbor of Tripoli, and who had sustained this reputation brilliantly in the War of 1812. Because of the peculiarly patriotic mission of the *Brandywine* her officers were selected to represent as many different states as possible and, as far as practicable, they were descendants of those who had fought with distinction in the War of the American Revolution. This accounts for the large number of midshipmen ordered to her, twenty-six instead of the eight or ten usually carried by a vessel of her size. Among these was Matthew Fontaine Maury, who was later to gain world wide fame as an oceanographer and be known as the "Pathfinder of the Seas."

The *Brandywine* was not ready for sea until the first of September, and meanwhile Lafayette paid last visits to Monroe, Madison, and Jefferson, and his various presents were stowed away on board. Among these were a bear and a raccoon, not to mention Indian beads, head-dresses, and weapons, a long boat, and a hydraulic pump. President Adams insisted that he remain for a grand dinner given on the 6th of September to celebrate the great Frenchman's sixty-eighth birthday. The next day he embarked on the steamboat *Mt. Vernon,* which took him down the Potomac past Washington's home, Lafayette standing uncovered as he passed Mt. Vernon where he had so often been hospitably entertained. On the 8th of September off St. Mary's near the mouth of the Potomac, the *Brandywine* "received on board the Nation's Guest, General Lafayette"[11] and his party consisting of George Washington Lafayette, the general's son, Auguste Levasseur, M. De Scion, and two servants. Lafayette was received with full military honors; the yards were manned and a salute was fired. The Secretary of the Navy and many public officials from Washington accompanied him, and a large number of distinguished persons came down from Baltimore to bid him farewell. Refreshments were prepared on board for the numerous guests, and many speeches appropriate to the occasion were made, and farewell toasts were drunk.[12]

The following day[13] the ship sailed under a favorable wind from the mouth of the Potomac, and as she passed down the Chesapeake it seemed as if Nature had reserved to herself the honor of erecting the last of the numerous triumphal arches, dedicated to Lafayette, for the ship passed through a brilliant rainbow whose great arch seemed to be supported by the

Maryland and Virginia shores. As the *Brandywine* made her way out to the open sea, almost the last glimpse the general had of the United States was the bluffs of the York River where he had so materially aided Washington in the Battle of Yorktown.

The frigate sailed well. Farragut noted that, as she passed between the Capes out to sea, she was making eleven knots. But that very night she sprang a leak, which continued even after two or three thousand shot had been thrown overboard. It was caused by the oakum working out of the seams of the ship's sides, and for awhile it looked as if the *Brandywine* would have to return to Norfolk. This would have been rather embarrassing to Lafayette after he had taken a formal farewell of the country, but his safety could not be placed in jeopardy. Fortunately the planks of the vessel began to swell from immersion in the water and the leak diminished somewhat. As the pumps had the leak under control, Lafayette advised Captain Morris to continue the voyage.

The weather then became stormy and the sea caused the ship to roll badly. During most of the passage, the venerable general, suffering from sea-sickness and the gout, induced no doubt by the numerous public and private dinners of which he had partaken during his recent tour of the United States, was confined to his cabin. Only two days was he able to join the officers at dinner or to come on deck. Farragut and his fellow officers were thus deprived of the pleasure of listening to the reminiscences of the general's interesting and romantic career.

There was another unpleasant accident, which however affected only the midshipmen. A steward, while cleaning an officer's uniform, upset a bottle of turpentine. Its contents ran into a barrel of sugar belonging to the midshipmen's mess, and during the remainder of the voyage they were obliged to eat their desserts strongly flavored with turpentine.

Though the passage was rough, it was a comparatively short one and on the 5th of October[14] the *Brandywine* arrived off Havre. The same day the American consul and some members of the family of Lafayette came on board, and Morris, much to his relief, learned from the consul that the government had no objection to the landing of Lafayette. King Louis XVIII had died while the general was in the United States, and his successor, Charles X, was more reactionary and wished to restore the Old Régime. It was feared that Lafayette's warm reception in the United States might have made him obnoxious to Charles X who might think his democratic principles and influence dangerous to the monarchy. If Lafayette had been refused permission to land in his own country, Captain Morris was authorized to use the *Brandywine* to convey the general to any other country he might select for refuge.[15] This no doubt would have been the United States.

Farragut was sent to the authorities of the port to make sure that Lafayette could land, and to arrange for his disembarkation. The next day a steamer was sent to bring the general and his party ashore. At the end of the voyage the general was found to be "big, fat, rosy, happy, showing no signs whatever of having gone several months without sleep, talking, writing, travelling and drinking literally ten hours out of every twenty-four."[16] Before he left the ship he was presented by the midshipmen a beautiful silver urn engraved with scenes of the Capitol at Washington, Lafayette's visit to the tomb of Washington, and the arrival of the *Brandywine* at Havre. When he was requested to ask for anything he might desire as a souvenir of the voyage, he selected the flag under which he had been received on board the vessel. Lieutenant F. H. Gregory, the executive officer, ordered the national ensign to be lowered, took it in his arms, and handed it to Lafayette, saying, "Here, General, take it; we could not confide it to more glorious hands."[17]

As Lafayette left the ship he was given a major-general's salute and three rousing cheers from the crew. He was accompanied by the families of his son and son-in-law, who had come out for that purpose. With him also went Captain Morris, who had been instructed to visit the dockyards and other naval establishments in France and England, and Captain George C. Read, a passenger on the *Brandywine*, who accompanied Morris in his visits to the French navy yards before he continued to Port Mahon where he was to command one of the ships of the American squadron.

Lieutenant Gregory was left in command of the *Brandywine*. The same day he set sail,[18] rounded the grey cliff of Cape La Hève, crossed the English Channel, and proceeded through the Spithead to Cowes on the Isle of Wight. The ship arrived on the 8th of October in a gale of wind under close-reefed maintopsail and foresail. Several days were spent there calking the ship to stop her leak and render her more seaworthy. Meanwhile Farragut visited the fashionable resort of Ryde, to the east of Cowes, enjoying en route the picturesque, luxuriantly wooded shores of the Isle. He then crossed the Spithead to Portsmouth. This was the first time he had set foot on England, and he was not to return until some forty years afterwards when he was making his triumphal tour of the countries of Europe. He has but little to say in his reminiscences of Portsmouth, merely that the authorities would not permit him to visit the dockyard without permission from London. He probably did not know that it was the birthplace of Charles Dickens. The familiar names of Portsmouth and Gosport doubtless made him homesick for his adopted town in Virginia, whose naval atmosphere and topography resembled those of the great English naval base.

The *Brandywine* sailed for Gibraltar on the 22nd of October. When they took on the pilot, he said his boat would go through the Solent and the Needles round the western coast of Wight and, intercepting the frigate, take him off. Farragut offered to take the boat in tow and warned the pilot that if they once lost sight of her they would not see her again unless the captain hove to off the Needles and waited for her. The pilot scoffed at the idea; but he did not know how well the *Brandywine* sailed. She dashed out through the Spithead in a spanking breeze and rounded the island; and as Farragut had predicted, they never saw the pilot boat again. A few days out, a water-logged and abandoned vessel was overhauled, and at the request of the pilot he was placed on board her. But he too was forced to abandon her, and arrived in Gibraltar much chagrined about a week after the *Brandywine* had made port on November 2.[19]

About two weeks later she sailed in company with the *Erie*

and the ship of the line *North Carolina,* flagship of Commodore John Rodgers's squadron, to Port Mahon, where she arrived after an eleven days' passage. There she passed the winter, refitting. In the meantime she was commanded by Captain Daniel T. Patterson, old friend of the Farragut family, and by Captain George C. Read, when he arrived from France. On February 26, 1826, the frigate sailed for home, calling at Gibraltar on the 8th of March and arriving at New York on the 19th of April after an ordinary routine voyage. The only unusual feature mentioned by Farragut was the succession of gales from the southwest, which suddenly shifted to the northwest and always took the ship aback but without harm as she was always gotten round safely. During this cruise, Farragut proudly records, the *Brandywine* was probably one of the fastest sailing ships in the world. When in company with the Mediterranean Squadron, he saw her keep up with the other vessels and spare them twelve, fourteen, and even sixteen sails.[20]

On the 1st of May, the ship was moored off the New York Navy Yard, and six days later[21] Farragut was ordered to take a draft of eighty-six men and boys and three midshipmen to the Gosport Navy Yard at Norfolk in the *Telltale.* He was to remain in Norfolk only six days and return to New York by way of Washington. While at home he found that his wife had become painfully afflicted with neuralgia, and began to make arrangements to take her north for medical attention. She probably accompanied him on his return to New York, where on June 12 he wrote the Secretary of the Navy a request for leave of absence "until you may again require my services."[22] In the letter he did not mention his wife's health but states that his own health was very delicate and that there were several officers of his date who were anxious to take his place on the *Brandywine.* The request was granted, and on June 28 Farragut left that ship.[23]

4

From New York Farragut went with his wife to New Haven, Connecticut, to consult Dr. Eli Ives, who occupied the chair of Materia Medica and Botany in Yale College and was widely called into consultation in his medical practice. He was becoming known as the most learned physician of his time in the United States. The Farraguts remained in New Haven for four months, during which Farragut whiled the time away by attending the lectures of the professors at Yale College. This was a great treat to him as he had suffered from weakness of vision and nervousness ever since his sunstroke in Tunisia, after which he was never able to read or write more than a page at a time.[24] Of particular interest he found the lectures of Professor Benjamin Silliman on chemistry and mineralogy. He had occupied that chair at Yale for twenty-four years and was to retain it for twenty-seven years longer, and had founded the *American Journal of Science and Arts*, of which he was then sole editor.

Farragut does not record whether he and his wife in particular profited as much physically as they did mentally in New Haven. Apparently Mrs. Farragut received, at best, only temporary relief for her health steadily declined. In October they returned to Norfolk, where Farragut was ordered to the receiving ship *Alert* on the 29th of November. The commanding officer, Captain Kennedy, allowed him to live on board with his wife so that he could better care for her.

The Navy Yard, located at Gosport, a suburb of Portsmouth, on the Elizabeth River across from Norfolk, had by that time grown into a considerable establishment. Its most imposing structure was a huge barn-like building, called the Boat Shed, in which a frigate could be built and then launched by removing the front of the building.[25] In 1827, the first dry-dock in America was commenced there, which cost nearly a million dollars and required six years for its completion.[26] Farragut's chief activity here was the establishment of a school for the education of the boys, or apprentice seamen of the station. Farragut thus became a pioneer in this form of education, and that his school was instrumental in developing more efficient seamen and better citizens was demonstrated in the case of his most incorrigible pupil. This boy strongly objected to going to school, declaring that he had run away from home and joined the navy just to keep from being forced to be a scholar. Furthermore he never could learn his letters, and he didn't see any use of learning them anyhow. Farragut replied, "It is my duty and my pleasure to see that you go to school; and if you do not stay here the prescribed time and do your best to learn, I will not cease to punish you; and you may rest assured that it will cost you less to learn than to let it alone." This made no impression on him, and Farragut saw that he would be compelled to punish him in some way. But first he held out all the inducements that his ingenuity could devise, to all of which he answered, in his own language, "I'm damned if I will larn!"[27]

Farragut tried whipping him almost every day for awhile, and then resorted to other modes of punishment, of which ridicule accomplished more than any other. In any case, the lad was so completely conquered that he took to his books with interest and learned very rapidly. In about a year's time he was able to write a good hand and became quite expert in arithmetic. Farragut then sent him to sea with a recommendation for a position as yeoman.

Some seven years afterwards a well-dressed, handsome young fellow met Farragut on the street in Norfolk, addressed him by name, and extended his hand in greeting. Farragut shook hands with him, but the young man greeted him so warmly that he thought he had mistaken him for some old and intimate friend. "Have you not, perhaps, mistaken me for my brother William?" Farragut suggested. "Oh, no!" said he, "I make no mistake; if I did not know you, to whom I am more indebted than to any one else in the world, it would really be strange." "I have no recollection of you. What is your name?" asked Farragut, completely at sea. "I have grown probably a foot since we parted," said the young fellow, "but do you not recollect the boy who gave you so much trouble on board the *Alert*?" "Oh, yes!" rejoined Farragut, "very well; but I should never have recognized him in you." "Nevertheless," he said, "I am the same, and am ready to acknowledge you as the greatest benefactor I ever had in this world of trouble." "I am glad you have profited by the little education you have received on board the *Alert*, but I acquit you of all obligation to me, as it is highly probable that you were indebted more to your own perverse disposition than to anything else," continued Farragut; "it was that which excited my determination not to be outwitted by a boy of fifteen."

The ensuing conversation revealed that, when the young man left the Navy, he went out in an East Indiaman. On the voyage, the captain died at Batavia and the chief mate on the return trip. The lad had learned enough navigation by that time to bring the ship safely into New York, and the owners were so pleased that, in due time, they had made him captain of one of their ships in the Charleston trade.[28]

When Secretary of the Navy Southard inspected the Gosport Navy Yard, Commodore James Barron,[29] the Commandant, took him on board the *Alert* to see Farragut's school, composed at that time of thirty-seven boys. The Secretary was so pleased with the progress which they were making that he complimented Farragut for his work. That, Farragut declared, was one of the very few compliments he ever received from the Navy Department or its head, the Secretary of the Navy. Though Matthew Calbraith Perry is often referred to as the founder[30] of the apprentice-training system in the U. S. Navy, yet Farragut was engaged in practical education of apprentices a year before Perry first wrote a letter to the Secretary of the Navy relative to the needs for such training and nine years before Perry put into practice his plan in the Brooklyn Navy Yard.

Farragut's life in Norfolk during the two years he was stationed at the Navy Yard was a very quiet one, and at best a rather dull one because his weakness of vision deprived him of the pleasure of doing much reading or writing. Not many letters, aside from necessary official correspondence, written by him during this period, are extant; and probably he wrote but few. The most interesting was one to Commodore David Porter,[31] at that time General of Marine of the Republic of Mexico, a position which he had accepted after he resigned from the U. S. Navy in anger at his six months' suspension for the Fajardo affair. Farragut had received a very friendly letter[32] from Mrs. David Porter, filled with news of the family. Finding an opportunity of getting a letter to Commodore Porter who had brought his fleet to Key West, Farragut wrote to let Porter know how his family were. "I won't say, dear sir," he continued, "how much pleasure it would give me to be of any assistance to you in the world and how happy I should be at your elbow, for fear you might retort upon me by saying, 'He that saith he believe in me and doth not act accordingly is a liar.' Therefore I shall say nothing about it. But this I feel certain of, that let you go where you will, you'll be assured of carrying with you my best wishes for your triumph over your enemies or happy return to your devoted wife and family and the most greatfull (sic) feelings of an affectionate heart." Farragut would have been pleased to be with Porter then, for Mexico was engaged in a bitter struggle with Spain to maintain her independence and there were many opportunities for active service; but he had no reason for feeling under any obligation to join Porter, for the Commodore had left his oldest son William at home as a midshipman in the U. S. Navy, though he had taken two younger ones with him. Farragut asked to be remembered to one of these in particular, David Dixon Porter, then a lad only thirteen years old, who was afterwards in the Civil War to be intimately associated with Farragut and was to win distinction second only to that bestowed upon Farragut himself.

In spite of Farragut's desire to remain near his wife and endeavor to restore her to health, it was natural that he should in time begin to feel restive in a position of such inactivity. Desirous of going to sea again, he wrote[33] to the Secretary of the Navy on the 25th of May requesting orders to the 44-gun frigate *Hudson*, then fitting out for the Brazil Station. She had originally been built for the Greeks and was first named the *Liberator*. Farragut expressed his eagerness to serve on any station "except the West Indies, where I hope my long services and loss of health will prevent my returning for some time." No orders to the *Hudson* were forthcoming; in fact, Farragut had to remain at the Norfolk Navy Yard for nearly five months longer before he was ordered to sea duty.

XVIII

ON THE BRAZIL STATION

1

IT WAS NOT until the 15th of October, 1828, that Farragut received orders[1] to the *Vandalia*. She was a small sloop of 700 tons, carrying a complement of 190 officers and men and only eighteen guns.[2] Only recently had she been launched at Philadelphia and was then being rapidly fitted for sea service in South American waters. Captain John Gallagher was her commanding officer, and among the other officers Farragut was delighted to find his old friends, Lieutenant Joshua Sands and Lieutenant William H. Gardner. The latter was his brother-in-law, having married his wife's sister. The ship was not ready to sail until December 18,[3] and meanwhile Farragut had many opportunities to drop down the river to Chester and visit the family of Commodore Porter, who was still away from home on his Mexican adventure. "Green Bank" was not the same place without his old commander and patron, and Farragut thought regretfully of the misfortunes that had befallen the family in recent years and gave a sympathetic ear to Mrs. Porter's tale of disappointment and trial.

The voyage south was devoid of interest, Farragut recording in his reminiscences only his high approval of the ship as a good sailer and a prime sea-boat. But his fellow officer, Lieutenant Sands, records[4] that off Cape Frio, Brazil, a squall suddenly struck the *Vandalia* with such violence as to reduce her to double-reefed topsails. During the consequent confusion Sands was on deck and had an opportunity to observe the "cool and confident seamanship in the officer of the deck, Lieutenant David G. Farragut, who (although the captain, himself a thor-

THE HARBOR OF RIO DE JANEIRO
From a lithograph by Sarony and Company, N.Y., used as a frontispiece in *Brazil and La Plata* by C. S. Stewart (1856).

ough sailor, became somewhat excited) gave his orders through the trumpet calmly and distinctly, and with no confusion the ship in a little while was under snug sail. Young as I was, I was struck with admiration, and breathed a hope that I would some day make just such another sailor and officer—as he was my beau-ideal."

The *Vandalia* arrived at Rio de Janeiro on the 7th of February, 1829.[5] The entrance into the large and beautiful harbor is so narrow and protected by such lofty granite barriers that the aborigines called the inlet "Hidden Water" and early navigators passed it by, not suspecting its existence. Entering the harbor, Farragut saw on the right the frowning batteries of Santa Cruz Castle situated on a solid granite rock thirty feet high at the base of lofty Signal Mountain. On the opposite side was another fortress to the east of Sugar Loaf Mountain, an almost naked granite pile rising nearly a thousand feet above the water. Passing these giant warders, the ship entered the great inland elliptical lake sprinkled with green islands and surrounded by great ridges of mountains rising one above the other like the seats in an amphitheater; this was the majestic harbor of Rio. Directly in front and near the north angle of the city was the Island of Cobras (Snake Island), a strongly fortified solid rock, alongside of which the largest vessels might lie in security. There were the wharves and the dockyards, the arsenals and the naval stores. And at one of those wharves the *Vandalia* came to rest.

The city of Rio was located on the southwest side of the harbor about four miles from its entrance. It was built on a square tongue of land extending into the bay so as to have three sides of the city washed by its waters. The city had the form of a parallelogram with a fortified eminence at each corner. Most conspicuous were the Benedictine Convent, a public garden called the Passeo Publico, the reservoir, and the imperial palace. Most of the houses were constructed of stone; the streets were usually straight but most of them were narrow and dirty and only the principal ones had flagged sidewalks. The population, including slaves, was less than two hundred thousand.

The *Vandalia* remained at Rio for several weeks, taking on provisions and refitting. Meanwhile the frigate *Guerrière* and the sloop *St. Louis* arrived on the way to the Pacific Station, and Lieutenant Downing was transferred to the frigate. On account of the revolution on the Rio de la Plata, Commodore John O. Creighton had gone there with the frigate *Hudson*, the flagship, and the sloop *Boston*, and had left orders for the *Vandalia* to follow. Accordingly, on the 5th of April, she sailed away to the southward.

Seventeen days later, she was at Montevideo, then a small walled town of only some ten thousand inhabitants, which was located on a low rocky point and defended by small forts. Revolutionary disturbances extending over many years had kept the town from making much progress in spite of its rich surrounding resources. Both Argentina and Brazil wanted the territory east of the Uruguay River, known then as the Banda Oriental, of which Montevideo was the capital. The district passed into the hands of independent Brazil in 1822. But three years later the Orientals revolted, the Argentines came to their assistance, and war broke out with Brazil. This was brought to an end in 1828 through British mediation with the establishment of an independent Republic of Uruguay. Almost immediately civil war broke out in Argentina when General Lavalle, a hero of the late war, overthrew the government of Manuel Dorrego and executed him. A remarkable man, named Juan Manuel de Rosas, took up the cause of the dead Federalist leader and continued the war against the other political party, known as the Unitarians who advocated a strong central government.[6] This was the situation when Farragut's ship arrived at Buenos Aires on May 3, 1829.

The *Vandalia* anchored about five miles from the town, as she could approach no nearer because of her drawing twelve feet of water. Mr. Slocum, the American Consul, who had come out as a passenger, was then landed, and Captain Gallagher reported his arrival in person to Commodore Creighton. In the changes in personnel that were made Farragut was separated from his brother-in-law Gardner, who was transferred to the frigate *Hudson*.

The city was built on a low open grassy plain, and had narrow streets running parallel with the cardinal points of the compass. Compared to its present magnificence as the largest city in South America, it was at that time a rather mean place. Its cathedral, the largest in South America and similar to the Madeleine in Paris, was a redeeming feature. Though the *Vandalia* was off the city from time to time for five months, Farragut and his fellow officers went ashore seldom, for there was nothing going on that interested them.[7]

The city was then held by General Lavalle, while General Rosas with five hundred Guachos, or cowboys of the pampas, cut off the supplies by land. Lavalle was an experienced soldier, and not only prepared defenses by ditching the streets in all directions and by placing cannon so that they could rake every street leading into the country but also bravely led sorties which broke through the Guachos and forced them to give way to the superior discipline of trained soldiers. But these gains were only temporary. The odds were too heavy against him and supplies could be brought in only by sea. Lavalle was forced to come to terms. Though many barbarities were committed on both sides, there were also examples of chivalry and gallantry. Such was the ending of the struggle, as related by Farragut.[8] Lavalle galloped out under a flag of truce to Rosas's camp. Finding that the General was not there, he told one of his staff officers that he would await his return, if there was no objection. Adding that he had not had much rest lately, he stretched out on the ground and was soon fast asleep.

When Rosas returned, the officer informed him that Lavalle was in his tent. "And to what good fortune am I indebted for this news?" he asked, thinking that his enemy had been captured. "He came under a flag of truce, and asked permission to repose until your return," was the reply. "Very well," said Rosas, "do not allow him to be disturbed. Any one who can sleep in the tent of his most deadly enemy must be a brave man; and, let his fate be what it may, he shall have a peaceful sleep to prepare for it."⁸ When Lavalle finished his siesta, a friendly conference was held, which resulted in a peaceful understanding, at least for awhile.

The next day Farragut saw Rosas ride into the city at the head of his cowboys. The people were wild with joy; a Te Deum was sung and a high mass was celebrated in the cathedral. From that day Rosas was in fact, though not in name for some years yet, Dictator of Argentina. Farragut noted that, while the armies were being disbanded, assassinations occurred every night, and that for lack of the feeling of security in the country the currency depreciated in value and commerce decreased sadly.

Peace having been established, Commodore Creighton sailed with his squadron on the 24th of May for Rio de Janeiro, by way of Montevideo. Farragut always took great interest in the sailing qualities of the ships in which he served. The *Boston*, he learned, had made a high reputation by beating all the men-of-war on that station. He was delighted to find that the *Vandalia* was a perfect match for her while sailing in company for several days. Farragut's ship kept side by side with the *Boston*, even with a reef in the *Vandalia's* topsails to make them set better.

On this cruise the captain of the *Boston*, Master Commandant Beekman V. Hoffman, decided that he did not want to go to Rio, and in spite of all the signals from the flagship, sailed away. As his ship outsailed the *Hudson*, the Commodore could not possibly overhaul him and he was soon out of sight. Farragut thought the incident was the most flagrant breach of navy discipline he had ever witnessed. He had served under Creighton when he commanded the ship of the line *Washington* and endeavored to make her a "crack ship" by the use of the cat-o'-nine-tails and other forms of severe punishment. The Commodore could not be expected to permit such an offense to be overlooked; the following year Hoffman was cashiered. But he was eventually pardoned and died in the service.

After remaining at Rio about five weeks, the *Vandalia* returned to Montevideo and Buenos Aires where she stayed a month before returning to the Brazilian capital. Calling at Montevideo and St. Catharines, she was back at Rio on the 4th of October. There Farragut went with the Commodore and the other officers to make an official call on Emperor Dom Pedro I. They walked into the Emperor's reception room, bowing as they entered, again in the middle of the room, and a third time when directly in front of Dom Pedro. Then they backed out at the opposite side of the room, after bowing again at the same intervals. Between bows, Farragut was able to observe that the rooms were very richly decorated and the courtiers were the most gorgeously dressed persons he had ever seen. Apparently the Emperor was too dazzling for words, as he does not attempt a description of his appearance.

A few days afterwards, on the 16th of October, a Brazilian frigate arrived from England with his ten year old daughter, Dona Maria da Gloria, legitimate heir to the throne of Portugal, and his affianced second wife, Amelia, daughter of the Duke of Leuchtemberg.[9] Each fort fired a salute of one hundred guns and each ship fired twenty-one guns; the whole harbor was shrouded in a cloud of smoke almost all day. When the frigate's approach had been reported, the Emperor went out in a steamer to meet the ship and tow her into harbor.

The following day the marriage was solemnized with great magnificence. The populace turned it into a happy holiday. The houses were decorated with flags and other emblems, and arches were erected over the principal streets. A few days afterwards, Farragut was among the officers selected to accompany the Commodore to the grand audience at the Emperor's palace. The Empress stood beside Dom Pedro to receive the salutations, and Farragut thought her "a fine-looking woman, with all the animation of the French grisette."[10] Still he had not a word to say of Dom Pedro; apparently his eyes were directed only at the Empress. They then saluted the ten year old Dona Maria with the same formality, in an adjoining apartment. She appeared to Farragut to be "a little Dutch-built girl . . . with light hair and fair complexion."[11] He had seen her mother embark at Marseilles when he was there in the *Washington*. She was Dona

Maria Leopoldina, Archduchess of Austria, and had died at Rio on the 11th of December, 1826.

The *Vandalia* made two short visits to St. Salvador, or Bahia some thousand miles to the northward, the first of November and the first of December respectively. Meanwhile the *Natchez*, commanded by Alexander Claxton, arrived with Commodore Stephen Cassin, who had come out to relieve Commodore Creighton. Farragut's eyes were giving him so much trouble that he was obliged to request to be surveyed and sent home. He left the *Vandalia* on the 27th of December, 1829.[12]

2

As no man-of-war was then returning home, Farragut had to take passage on the merchant brig *Barnegat* of Boston. In her he enjoyed a very restful voyage of just fifty days. Only one incident broke the monotony of the long voyage. When the little brig was rounding Cape St. Roque, she was pursued by a craft which looked like it might be a pirate vessel. Under Farragut's direction, preparations were made to defend the ship against attack. The four 18-pounder carronades were mounted on trucks so that they could be easily moved about the deck and fired at the pirate from various quarters. The munitions consisted only of twenty-four pounds of powder and some musket balls and spike nails. For wadding the men cut up their flannel shirts. The crew consisted of six strong young men besides the officers, all of whom were willing to fight if necessary to save the ship. When the suspicious-looking stranger approached to within two miles of the *Barnegat*, a welcome breeze suddenly began, and the brig soon left her pursuer far behind. But the episode gave the men an interesting topic of conversation during the remainder of the voyage.

It was a sad home-coming for Farragut, when he arrived at Norfolk in February, 1830. He found his wife bed-ridden and still suffering from her malady, probably arthritis. After a short visit to Philadelphia where he was summoned to attend a court-martial,[13] he returned home in March, where he remained awaiting orders until December 10,[14] when he was again ordered to the Norfolk Navy Yard on the receiving ship *Congress*. Commodore Barron was still commandant of the yard, and so Farragut found himself serving again under the officer who had been a bitter enemy of Commodore Porter because of the Barron-Decatur affair. Apparently this had nothing to do with their relations, for Barron treated Farragut with kind consideration, permitting him to live with his wife on board the receiving-ship as he had previously on the *Alert*. Here they remained until August of the following year, when the frigate *Java* came in from the Mediterranean and was stationed at Norfolk as the receiving-ship. Farragut was then transferred to that frigate, also a 44-gun ship like the *Congress*.

The days passed quietly at the Navy Yard. Farragut, it seems, did not reopen the school for young apprentice seamen. But that he continued to show an unusual interest in the welfare of those entrusted to his care is attested in an interesting way by Mahan.[15] He received a letter from one who was then a midshipman under Farragut's command, who recalled, "after a lapse of nearly sixty years, the kindness, consideration, and hospitality shown him by the future admiral, who was then known through the service as the 'Little Luff' Farragut—luff being a naval abbreviation, now obsolete, for Lieutenant." The chief activity, at least the most noticeable, was the work on the great dry-dock, which was well along towards completion. For a few days there was considerable excitement during the uprising of Negroes in Southampton County, Virginia. Preparations were made to defend the Yard against attack; but the affair was soon ended with the death of the leader, old Nat Turner. This insurrection took place in the summer following the commencement on New Year's Day, 1831, of the publication in Boston of the *Liberator*, whose editor, William Lloyd Garrison, became one of the leaders of the Anti-Slavery Movement. Though Farragut did not know it then, this Nat Turner insurrection was one of the clouds in the political sky which heralded the storm that was to sweep over the United States in about thirty years and incidentally bring to him fame and fortune.

Other interesting events were taking place during these

seemingly quiet years Farragut spent at Norfolk. In 1830, the first steam locomotive made its run of fourteen miles from Baltimore to Ellicott's Mills; and the next year the first steam train ran on the Mohawk and Hudson Railway. While Farragut was on his last cruise, General Andrew Jackson, who had been a friend to George Farragut, his father, was elected President, and commenced what was called "a great political revolution." He inaugurated the "Spoils System"; he began a struggle which ended with the closing of the National Bank; and he entered into a bitter controversy with South Carolina, led by Vice President John C. Calhoun, over the question of Nullification. The great political debate between Senator Robert Y. Hayne of South Carolina and Senator Daniel Webster of Massachusetts was heard by the crowded galleries of the Senate in January, 1830, the month before Farragut's arrival home from Brazil. Norfolk could not have been a dull place to reside with such stirring events to discuss.

In the summer of 1832, Farragut decided to make another, perhaps final, attempt to secure medical relief for his suffering wife. On the 8th of June[16] he wrote to the Secretary of the Navy requesting leave of absence for two or three months so that he could take his wife to consult the "Medical Faculty of Philadelphia." He hoped that he might also secure treatment for his "diseased eyes." Leave for only one month was granted, and on June 26 he wrote from Chester where he and Mrs. Farragut were visiting the Porter family, begging for an extension of another month. Though Porter had returned home from Mexico, he was not at "Green Bank," for President Jackson had appointed him Consul-General to Algiers and then Chargé d'Affaires to Turkey. Mrs. Porter and the children had been left behind, and hospitably received Glasgow, as they called him, and the invalid wife.

Near the middle of August the Farraguts arrived at Frederick, Maryland, whence they had fled from Philadelphia because of the outbreak of cholera. Having been informed by physicians that the climate there might restore his wife's health which was adversely affected by salt air, he wrote to the Secretary, asking to be detached from the *Java* "until it may please the Navy Department to order me to sea."[17] Secretary Woodbury then[18] detached him from the *Java,* but ordered him to report to the *Vandalia* on September 15th. Farragut immediately wrote[19] begging not to be sent to sea "at present" on account of his "wife's condition"; and the Secretary very considerately revoked[20] the orders to the *Vandalia* and gave him leave of absence for two months. It would seem that the climate of Frederick did not benefit Mrs. Farragut's health as much as had been expected, for Farragut was in Washington on the 30th of August.[21] He might, however, have ridden in to the city to transact official business, and left his wife at Frederick. But they were back in Norfolk by October 4, when he wrote[22] to the Secretary reporting himself ready for duty on the *Vandalia* or the *Natchez.*

3

After waiting just two months, he was ordered on December 4 to report for duty as first lieutenant on the *Natchez.* She was an 18-gun sloop of 700 tons, similar in every respect to the *Vandalia* upon which Farragut had last served, and was commanded by Captain J. P. Zantzinger.

The failure of President Jackson to use his power to influence Congress to remove the tariff injustices against which South Carolina had so bitterly protested, and his re-election in the autumn of 1832 brought the controversy to a crisis. A South Carolina convention adopted an "Ordinance of Nullification" on November 24, which declared the tariff laws of 1828 and 1832 unconstitutional and void in South Carolina after February 1, 1833. On November 27 the state legislature passed the necessary acts for carrying the ordinance into effect. At an anniversary celebration of Jefferson's birthday on April 13, 1830, Jackson, when called upon for a toast, had responded with the significant words: "Our Federal Union: it must be preserved!" With this same end clearly in mind, he set about solving the difficult problem with the sword in one hand and the olive branch in the other. Meanwhile he had summoned General Winfield Scott to Washington. The General arrived about the middle of November, and when asked what he would advise, he suggested that reinforcements be sent to Fort Moultrie, Castle Pinckney, and the Government Arsenal at Augusta, Georgia, near the South Carolina line, and that a sloop of war and several revenue cutters be stationed off Charleston harbor to collect the duties by force, if necessary. Jackson immediately acted upon this advice by sending General Scott to Charleston to carry out his own suggestions with respect to the troops. There he arrived two days after the adoption of the ordinance by the state convention, and began to visit the forts as though on his yearly inspection tour as General in command of the Eastern Department.[23]

The *Natchez* was selected to be sent to Charleston as well as seven revenue cutters. But it was the 28th of December when she was ready to receive her crew at the Norfolk Navy Yard, and the 2d of January, 1833, when she received powder on board and dropped down to Hampton Roads and took on board Captain Zantzinger and Commodore Jesse D. Elliott, who was to be responsible for any naval operations that might be thought necessary. Jackson could hardly have approved of Elliott's selection himself, for Elliott was a member of the court-martial which suspended Porter from the Navy for the Fajardo affair. Afterwards when Porter returned from Mexico, Jackson wanted to reinstate him in the Navy, but Porter replied, "Thank you kindly, sir, beggars should not be choosers, but I would rather dig than associate with the men who sentenced me for upholding the flag." "Right, by the Eternal," said Old Hickory, "you shall not, either, if I can help it; I wouldn't associate with them myself."[24]

The *Natchez* sailed on the 5th of January with the 10-gun schooner *Experiment* in tow. The voyage in the winter season was a very unpleasant one. The towing cable parted twice. A seaman, John S. Davis, was washed overboard, and saved only through the courage of Midshipman Jarvis and the crew of a boat which was lowered to pick him up. By the 10th the gale had become a storm, and the ship lost her jib boom. The following day the *Experiment* parted company. At two o'clock the next morning such a sea struck the ship on her weather beam that the sheet anchor was moved ten or eleven inches and the quarter boat, davits and all, was rolled out of place. An hour and a half later there was an electrical discharge ten or twelve feet above the booms with such a terrific sound that the ship was thought to have been struck by lightning. At daylight the wind-mill on Cape Romaine was made out, and when ten miles from the Charleston Bar, the ship received the pilot on board. But the *Natchez* struck three times getting over the bar and lay grounded all night on the northern banks; it was not until the 19th that she finally came to anchor in Rebellion Roads.[25]

While lying off the city, the crew were exercised at small arms every morning, and at great guns in the afternoon, when the weather was favorable. The public were welcomed on board, and the boats were constantly employed in bringing out visitors where they were entertained with music and dancing. Politeness was the order of the day, and the officers and men were particularly warned against provoking any controversy or disturbance while on shore. When a fire broke out in the city on the 17th of February, Farragut was sent with the launch and first cutter, carrying fifty men, to help put out the flames. Unarmed troops from the forts were also sent by General Scott.[26] This assistance made a very favorable impression on the citizens, and afterwards it seemed to Farragut that during the remainder of his stay the chief occupation of the officers was attending parties and dances given by the Charlestonians. He was pleased particularly with an entertainment at Mrs. Rutledge's, consisting of *tableaux vivants,* or living pictures, in which a number of young ladies and gentlemen represented in appropriate costumes some well known pictures. "Nothing could have been more exquisitely executed," wrote Farragut.[27]

Meanwhile the legislature of Virginia provided for the election of a commissioner who would endeavor to persuade South Carolina to repeal the Ordinance of Nullification. Benjamin W. Leigh was elected, and went to Charleston where he worked manfully among the leaders. Jackson's friends in Congress were also working on a bill which would lower the tariff. As a consequence the leaders in Charleston had voted to suspend the operation of the ordinance until Congress could act. Senator Henry Clay's compromise tariff bill was hurried through Congress, with the assistance of Calhoun, and was ready for Jackson's signature on March 1. On March 11, the South Carolina convention reconvened, and rescinded the Ordinance of Nullification. Jackson had preserved the Federal Union, at least for twenty-eight years.

Farragut's decision, when that greater crisis arose many years later, will be more completely understood when one remembers that he was present at the very center of the controversy over nullification during its most dangerous phase. He was thoroughly conversant with the problem, and the opinions which he then formed under the influence of President Jackson, General Scott, Commissioner Leigh of Virginia, Joel R. Poinsett, and other leaders in Charleston were adhered to by him during the remainder of his life.

By the last of March conditions were approaching normal in Charleston, and on the 26th Commodore Elliott's broad pennant was lowered and he departed to the Charleston Navy Yard. A salute was fired in his honor and three cheers were given him by the crew, "by his order," Farragut parenthetically adds.[28] This is one among several flings which Farragut took at Elliott, showing a real dislike of Oliver Hazard Perry's second in command at the Battle of Lake Erie and his later enemy as well as the enemy to Decatur and David Porter. General Scott then came on board as a passenger on the ship, which sailed for Norfolk on the 4th of April. Farragut found the General "an agreeable gentleman and pleasant companion."[28] Scott had reason for feeling pleasant and making himself agreeable, for he was enjoying a great personal satisfaction in the important role he had played in helping to avert a national catastrophe. Besides he had not then come to be known as "Old Fuss and Feathers."

4

At Norfolk, the officers of the *Natchez* were given a short leave to visit their families and friends, except Farragut and Lieutenant Alexander B. Pinkham who remained and looked after the men, allowing them to go ashore in squads. When the ship arrived from Charleston, Captain Zantzinger went up to Washington where he received orders from the Secretary of the Navy to take the *Natchez* to the Brazil Station.[29] On the 8th of May the ship set sail from Hampton Roads on the long voyage to the south.

The first stop was made at Pernambuco, Brazil. Here Farragut went ashore and called on the different authorities. Conditions were comparatively quiet, though a civil war was in progress in the interior, a disturbance which lasted until 1835. Since Farragut was last in Brazil, important political changes had taken place. Dom Pedro I had become so autocratic that, on April 7, 1831, he was forced to abdicate in favor of his son, Dom Pedro II, then not six years old, and a more liberal government had been set up under an elected regency. Disorders continued in different sections of the country for several years, caused, Farragut thought, more by the brutality of the military commanders than by political dissatisfaction.

The *Natchez* drew too much water to enter within the security of the natural mole at Pernambuco, and had to remain in the uncomfortable and somewhat dangerous anchorage, where during the ship's stay a heavy swell from the south and east was constantly felt. As soon as convenient, therefore, the ship departed for Bahia, where she joined the store ship *Lexington*, bearing the broad pennant of Commodore M. T. Woolsey, and the schooner *Enterprise*, commanded by Lieutenant Samuel W. Downing.

On the 24th of June the *Natchez* sailed in company with the *Lexington* for Rio. Always eager to see how fast his ship could sail, Farragut was pleased to accept the Commodore's challenge, and with pride found that his ship outsailed the *Lexington* nine hundred yards an hour. Arriving at Rio after a nine days' sail, the ships took on stores from the public store-houses hired by the United States on the Island of Cobras. At least, they secured there what could be used. Farragut found that clothing sent out for the use of the men of the squadron was often either destroyed by rats or moths or so damaged that it was an imposition to ask the men to buy such clothes. As a consequence they were permitted to purchase better and cheaper articles on shore. So through bad administration of a department, the government lost money and every one concerned was injured except the contractor.

After ten days the ships set sail again, and on the 30th of July arrived at Buenos Aires. That same month a new Constitution was promulgated, which tended to weaken the influence and power of Rosas. Popular disorders immediately broke out, possibly instigated by the agents of Rosas. In any case, he put them down and returned at the head of a victorious army and continued to dominate the government as before.[30] Though Farragut was off Buenos Aires for many weeks and was frequently in the city, he has nothing to say, in his reminiscences, of Rosas. Instead he describes the *pamperas,* or storms that blew in from the southwest over the pampas, or great plains bordering the river, and how the ship careened considerably when they struck her. Rope made of hides was taken on, he relates, for topsail ties, sheets, trusses, and wheel-ropes; and patent lights were installed in various parts of the ship to overcome deficiencies in construction which had sacrificed both air and light for strength.

The American brig *Hyperion* came in on the 16th of October with the first official report of the death of Commodore William Bainbridge, who had died in Philadelphia on the previous July 28. On the day following the receipt of the news, the colors were half-masted, crepe was ordered to be worn thirty days, and at noon thirteen minute-guns were fired in honor of the departed Commodore. "Let his virtues be remembered," added Farragut in *Some Reminiscences,*[31] "and his faults and follies forgotten." Farragut had served under Bainbridge's command only once; that was in the squadron which arrived in the Mediterranean too late to participate in the War with Algiers, Decatur having already brought the Dey to terms. As he was then captain's aid on the flagship, Farragut had the opportunity of observing Bainbridge at close range, and knew of the coldness which developed in the long friendship between Bainbridge and Decatur and of his eventual acting as the second to Decatur in the fatal duel.[32]

Though the *Natchez* had been ordered on October 16th to depart for Montevideo, the same day news was received that a revolution had broken out in the province of Buenos Aires, and the American and British merchants petitioned Captain Zantzinger to remain. The matter was referred to the Commodore, but he had already left. While awaiting an answer, Farragut went ashore with the captain, on the first fair day they had enjoyed for weeks, and visited a comb manufactory, where these useful and ornamental articles were made of horn and shell. Farragut was greatly interested in the intricate manufacturing process as well as in the size of the larger combs which were fifteen inches from side to side.

In general, Farragut was not favorably impressed with the country on this second visit. He was somewhat concerned about the prevalence of lockjaw, smallpox, and a strange disease called *iraic*. While he was there, an Englishman had a scuffle with a Gaucho and dislocated his thumb. There was no other injury, but the man died of lockjaw in forty-eight hours. *Iraic* was said to result from the passing of a current of air through the house. One person's head might be drawn over to the shoulder, another's arm or leg might be drawn up, another might suffer from a violent ear-ache or a palsied tongue. Incredible stories were told of how the air would crack glass and even split furniture. But from the cases Farragut saw, it seemed to him that the effects were not unlike those caused by a severe cold.

Eventually the *Natchez* sailed for Montevideo on the 29th of October and thence to Rio on November 17, where on the 2d of December a salute of twenty-one guns was fired in honor of the young Emperor's eighth birthday. On the 6th of January the ship arrived again at Montevideo.[33] There Farragut was ordered by Commodore Woolsey on February 11 to leave the *Natchez* and go as a passenger to Rio on either the *Boxer* or *Enterprise*, where he was to take command of whichever of the two vessels remained on the station.[34]

Farragut had performed his responsible duties as first lieutenant, or executive officer with great success. The crew were very well disciplined, contented, and happy. When he took the trumpet and began to give commands, every man responded cheerfully and intelligently; he was like a director leading a symphony orchestra. The entrance to the harbor of Rio is quite narrow. On one occasion, Farragut took the *Natchez* out against a head wind by a difficult maneuver, called box hauling. It was done perfectly, and all hands on board felt proud that day of "Little Luff" Farragut, for the officers and crews of several English and French men-of-war were looking on with the conviction plainly written on their faces that it could not be successfully accomplished.[35]

5

The little 10-gun schooner *Boxer* of only 194 tons[36] had come to the Brazil coast recently from the East Indies, and her officers and men were to be relieved of duty to return home. The ship, however, remained at Rio and the *Enterprise* went home; and so Farragut relieved Lieutenant William F. Shields of the command of the *Boxer* on the 7th of March.[37] This was Farragut's second command, though the first, just ten years before, was a much smaller schooner, the *Ferret*, of only three guns and about 50 tons. He took great interest in his new command, and made many changes in the rigging and ballasting while he was refitting and overhauling her after her long cruise.

On the 17th of March, through invitation of Commodore Taylor[38] of the *Princess Royal*, Farragut and Captain D. Geisinger, commander of the sloop *Peacock*, went aboard the Brazilian vessel to meet the little Emperor Dom Pedro II. The shore batteries announced the departure of the Emperor and his party from the quay, and all the men-of-war manned their yards and their crews cheered him as he passed. The chief civil and military representatives of various foreign nations received him as he came aboard the ship. An abundance of delicious refreshments was served, and Farragut noted that the young Emperor and his royal sisters ate entirely too much for children of their age. After being shown about the ship and entertained by gunnery exercises, the royal visitors departed and were accorded the same ceremonies as before. Farragut sympathized with the poor Brazilian sailors who had been manning the yards from nine in the morning to four o'clock in the afternoon. He was reminded of what the frogs in the fable said to the boys who cruelly stoned them, "What is fun to you is death to us."[39]

The 44-gun frigate *Potomac*, bearing the broad pennant of Commodore John Downes, arrived in the harbor on the 26th of March, and was saluted by the *Peacock* and the *Boxer*. She was on the way home from a remarkable voyage round the world, which she had made leisurely during the years 1831 to 1834, spending much time among the islands of the Pacific.[40] The same day Commodore Woolsey arrived from Montevideo on the *Natchez*, and the bay was covered with the smoke of salutes from the forts and the other men-of-war there present. It was with a great deal of pride that Farragut, then the commanding officer of a ship, went aboard the *Potomac* to call upon his old friend Downes, with whom he had shared the hardships and the glories of the cruise of the *Essex*. They had not served together in the same ship since that famous cruise, nearly twenty years before, and they had much to talk about. Downes took great satisfaction in Farragut's progress in the service, having assisted Porter in giving the little midshipman some of his first practical lessons in his profession.

The 7th of April was celebrated at Rio as the anniversary of the abdication of Dom Pedro I in favor of his son Dom Pedro II. On that occasion the young Emperor, attended by the regents, received, in state at the palace, civil and military representatives of foreign states and other distinguished people. Farragut and several other American officers went in company with the American Chargé d'Affaires Browne, who, inasmuch as he was the oldest diplomatic representative in Brazil, had precedence and the honor of "dosing the Emperor with a speech," as Farragut expressed it.[41] After felicitating the eight year old ruler on his glorious accession to the throne of Brazil,

Browne presented ceremoniously each of the officers to his little Majesty.

In the evening a magnificent ball was given by a society, called the Defenders of the National Liberty and Independence, who celebrated the day not only in anticipation of the young Emperor's future coronation but also to keep alive the hostility to the exiled Dom Pedro I and the mother country, Portugal.[42] After a vocal concert, the ball began with the dancing of the *gavot* by two of the little princesses, which Farragut said was performed "in very pretty style." "I have never seen children in any country," he added,[41] "dance with the same grace as those of Brazil." None of the American officers danced during the evening for the simple reason that they had no partners. "The English ladies would not dance with us because they preferred their own countrymen," explained Farragut,[43] "and the Brazilians from a belief that we did not understand the figures; and there is nothing so unpleasant to a lady as the idea of making an awkward appearance on the floor and more particularly before such spectators."

With a keen eye for color and the unusual, Farragut wrote that the room prepared for the Emperor on this occasion was lined with damask silk. "The dresses of the gentlemen attached to the court," he continued, "were rich and gaudy beyond all conception. The court tailor must have been at his wit's end in getting up such a variety of designs. The coats of the subalterns had a small sprig on the collar, and then the ornamentation increased with every grade until it came to the Emperor, whose coat was so completely covered with embroidery that it would have been difficult to discover the color of the cloth. One old gentleman particularly attracted my attention. He seemed to have had his turn after the inventor of the costumes had exhausted his genius on the chamberlains. The tailor had therefore given him a coat covered indiscriminately with broad gold lace."[41]

The *Potomac* sailed for Boston on the 9th of April,[44] and just a week later, everything having been made shipshape on the *Boxer*, Farragut dropped down to Montevideo. There he joined

ON THE BRAZIL STATION 201

the sloop *Ontario* in the waters of the Rio de la Plata. On the 9th of May, her commander, William D. Salter, ordered[45] Farragut to return to Rio de Janeiro to report to Commodore Woolsey on the political situation. Here on the 8th of June Farragut received final instructions from the Commodore to take the *Boxer* home. The next day[46] he took leave of his old messmates on the *Natchez*, spread his sails, and departed from the "Hidden Water." Calling at Bahia and Pernambuco, the little *Boxer* had an uneventful passage. "On the glorious 4th," wrote[47] Farragut, "we had a grand dinner. All the officers dined together, threw all the apartments into one: passed off well, no one out of the way." Did he mean by the last phrase that no one drank too much? The ship arrived at Norfolk on the 17th of July and at the Navy Yard on the 25th. "Thus ended my command of the *Boxer*," regretfully recorded[48] Farragut, "after a most delightful little cruise of six months."

XIX

AN EBB TIDE IN HIS LIFE

WITH APOLOGIES to Shakespeare, there is a tide in the affairs of men, that must sometimes be taken at the ebb whether it leads on to fortune or not. For nearly four years after his return from the Brazil Station, Farragut found himself in a most discouraging situation. Not only was it ebb tide in his affairs, it was also ebb tide in the affairs of the United States Navy, and even in the affairs of the nation. Though Jackson said in his farewell address, "I leave this great people prosperous and happy," it was not long thereafter when the administration of his successor, President Van Buren, was called upon to cope with the panic of 1837 and the consequent unemployment and distress. The work of the navy, as in the preceding decade, continued to be devoted largely to the protection of expanding American foreign trade. For that reason, ships were kept on the Brazil Station; the *Dolphin* and the *Peacock* cruised to the Hawaiian and Marquesas Islands in 1826 and 1827 respectively; the *Vincennes* and the *Potomac* cruised round the world 1829-1830 and 1831-1834 respectively; the *Peacock* and *Boxer* went to the East Indies in 1832-1833; the *Enterprise* and *Peacock* sailed to India and China in 1835; the *Vincennes* sailed round the world again in 1835-1836; the *Columbia* and *John Adams* circumnavigated the globe by way of Zanzibar and Canton, China in 1838-1839; and the Wilkes Exploring Expedition sailed in 1838 round the Horn for three years of cruising in the Pacific.

These naval activities were carried out mainly by schooners and sloops. The ships of the line and frigates were, in the main, laid up in ordinary or were on the stocks for repairs. For example, during the years 1833 to 1836 only one ship of the line and from three to four frigates were in commission; while ten to twelve ships of the line and thirteen to fourteen frigates were either in ordinary or on the stocks. This situation resulted in two evils. In the first place, there was graft and ruinous waste in the building and repairing of ships, a system which Maury attacked with such vigor a few years later in his *Lucky Bag* articles in the *Southern Literary Messenger*[1] as eventually to bring about reforms. He proved that it cost twice as much to build a ship of war as it ought to cost and that it cost twice as much to repair one as to build her and that labor to repair cost three times as much as labor to construct. The other evil was that there were so few ships in active service, and these chiefly the smaller vessels, that a large number of officers had to be constantly kept on "waiting orders" at half pay or at navy yards where there was little to keep them properly occupied. Frequently naval officers went on cruises in merchant vessels in order to supplement their income and support their families.

This explains why Farragut was kept waiting orders for nearly four years at his home in Norfolk. The discouraging situation was made even more so by the continued decline in his wife's health. On his return he found that she had become so helpless that he had to carry her about in his arms as though she were a child. It was terribly depressing for Farragut to see her in this condition and to be incapable of doing anything to lessen her suffering. To relieve his mind somewhat and afford himself some recreation he bought a set of carpenter's tools and occupied his idle time in making repairs about the place. Like his father many years before in Tennessee, he became after a time a rather skillful carpenter.

While time hung so heavy on his hands, Farragut wrote a letter on the 6th of August, 1834, to his old friend and patron, Commodore David Porter, then American *chargé d'affaires* at Constantinople. Unfortunately this letter is no longer extant, but from Porter's reply[2] it appears that Farragut wrote particularly about his wife's illness and expressed his gratitude for all the favors he had received from Porter. Because of the close relationship existing between the two men, perhaps a rather long excerpt from this letter will be of interest. "My head, my hand, and even my pen are tired, it is almost worn out," writes Porter, then only fifty-four years old but nearly worn out by ill health and the privations of his naval career. "The continued illness of your wife is truly distressing. I know what sickness is, and I know how to sympathise with those who are afflicted. For a year past I have been bourne [sic] down with it—at one time on the verge of the grave, and the whole time afflicted with loss of speech; and even now speak with difficulty and with pain. At one time it was thought to be a paralisis [sic] of the tongue, but this was not, fortunately, the case; however, it was bad enough, and perhaps nothing but my removal to this vilage [sic][3] where the air and water are pure and excelent [sic], and living in the most persevering retirement and tranquility, have saved me. I find myself now recovering gradually but slowly, yet find myself very weak, yet I return thanks to the giver of all good, that when he deprived me of health, strength, and speech, he allowed me to retain my mind, which I am not sensible has been weakened, yet it may have been, and no one has been willing to so inform me. For you may remember how much the Bishop in 'Gil Blas' was offended when he was told that his homilies smelt of the apoplexy from which he had not been long recovered.

"However, I am getting old, have had many sorrows, much sickness and affliction, and have lasted much longer than men do under such circumstances generally; but I bear all with sufficient fortitude, and, as I have nothing to merit from fortune more than she has done for me, I have nothing to complain of on her account. I have never been elated with prosperity, and ought not, and I hope I am not depressed at the loss of worldly goods. My country has thus far taken care of me, and I hope by good conduct to merit what she has done, by endeavoring to serve her to the utmost of my power. There was a time when there was nothing that I thought too daring to be attempted for her; but those times are past, and appear only as a confused and painful dream. A retrospect of the history of my life seems a highly-coloured romance, which I should be very loth to live over again; and it would not be believed, if it was written. My sufferings in Mexico, the trials of fortitude

I underwent, exceed all belief; but now I am enjoying Elysium, compared to what I then suffered in body and in mind.

"But let it pass. They have left an impression on my mind that can never be effaced. I have been taught to admire a bold struggle with adversity as one of the most noble moral spectacles, and pride myself in acquiting [sic] myself with honour.

"I could not serve that base and unprincipled nation, for they would not let me, but I left them without a stain on my character, which was not what others, under the same circumstances, could have done.

"But where am I running to? It is time that I should stop. But before I finish my letter, my Dear Glasgow, I must say that the next thing to be admired is a grateful heart; and I am sure that I have found in yours that treasure which should be so much prized. I have allways [sic] endeavoured to do good, solely for the sake of good. I have never looked for any other return than what my feelings gave me, and to find such sentiments of gratitude from you, after all others had forgotten that they had received any benefits from me, is truly refreshing to the feelings...."

This letter from his old commander, with whom he had faced death on the *Essex*, put new courage into Farragut's heart in the "bold struggle with adversity," which he was then making in Norfolk. The only relief which he had from close confinement to his home was a visit which he made in the summer of 1835 to Washington, Georgetown, and Alexandria.[4] But his wife became so ill that he was forced to return to Norfolk in September. The distress of the family was soon afterwards greatly increased by the death of Mrs. Farragut's sister, Jane Edna. She was the wife of Passed Midshipman William D. Porter,[5] the eldest son of Commodore David Porter.

Farragut's mind was occupied somewhat during this period of inactivity by service on every court-martial that met in Norfolk; he thus became very well acquainted with that phase of his profession. Financially he managed to get along as best he could on one hundred dollars a month, which was then the pay of a lieutenant on waiting orders.[6]

Several interesting events happened in Norfolk during the four years Farragut spent continuously there. On the 15th of

September, 1836, the citizens celebrated the one hundredth anniversary of the granting of the Royal Charter to the borough. At sunrise there was a salute of twenty-six guns, and services of prayer and thanksgiving in the churches; later there was a civic procession and a military parade, while in the evening "a hundred rockets soared and exploded over the lively old borough."[7] On the 19th of April, the following year, Prince Louis Napoleon Bonaparte, then an exile but afterwards to be Emperor of France, visited the city, where he was well entertained before proceeding up the Chesapeake to Baltimore. The chief topics of conversation were bank failures and the bankruptcies of the Southern cotton merchants and the decrease in trade and the increase in unemployment. The Whigs, whose Southern leader was John Tyler of Virginia, were damning the Democrats as the originators of all the woes of the country. There was also much excited talk and speculation over the uprising in Texas and the war between that new republic and Mexico.

Farragut's financial condition was somewhat improved by his being ordered to the rendezvous at the Norfolk Navy Yard on the 18th of July, 1837.[8] But he was eager to get back to sea again, and repeatedly requested that kind of duty. He met with no success; in 1837, he was seventieth on the list of lieutenants, and there were not enough appointments to sea duty to supply half the demands. Besides there was favoritism to contend with always. Farragut wanted duty with the West India Squadron, which was then commanded by Commodore Alexander J. Dallas. "I . . . had not received orders," complained Farragut,[9] "because my date interfered with that of the First Lieutenant of the Commodore's ship. At last a Member of Congress who was a friend of the Navy made a speech attacking the Department for allowing Commodore Dallas to keep a set of young officers employed who were his favorites, whereupon changes were made, and I was ordered to the *Constellation*." Farragut applied for service particularly with the West India Squadron on the 5th of February, 1838,[10] and a little more than a month afterwards he was ordered to take passage on the sloop *Levant* for Pensacola to join that Squadron.

XX

ON THE WEST INDIA STATION

1

ON THE 10th of April, 1838, the little *Levant*, commanded by Commander Hiram Paulding, prepared to set sail from the beautiful harbor of Norfolk. Farragut, inasmuch as he was a passenger and had no duties to perform, stood on deck and looked about him at the interesting panorama. The harbor was about a mile long by three quarters of a mile wide; all along its wharves swayed back and forth the bare masts of innumerable ships of different size and character; his eyes ranged from Norfolk with its busy water front and distant church spires across to the rural village of Portsmouth on the other side and then further up to Gosport with its Navy Yard and ships and bridge. By that time the ship was under way, and was soon leaving the harbor, with the then dismantled Fort Norfolk on the right and the Doric colonnade of the new Naval Hospital on the left hand. Gathering headway as she proceeded down the Elizabeth River, she skirted Craney Island to the left, entered Hampton Roads, and eventually passed into the Chesapeake and through the Capes to the Atlantic.[1]

After a passage of seventeen days the *Levant* arrived at Pensacola and saluted the broad pennant of Commodore Dallas with thirteen guns.[2] The town was then the base of the West India Squadron, which was keeping an eye on conditions in Texas and Mexico and cooperating in trying to bring to a close the long and bloody Seminole War.

Farragut immediately reported for duty on the *Constellation*, then commanded by Lieutenant J. M. McIntosh. She was only slightly larger than the *Essex* and had had a history almost as colorful. These were the only two of the famous early frigates on which Farragut served; he was never ordered to the *Constitution.*

Two days after his arrival, Farragut obtained permission from the Commodore to visit his sister in Mississippi. He went by water to Mobile on the *Star,* and from there by stage to Pascagoula, where he arrived in the night. This was the first time he had visited his old home since childhood, and the first time he had seen his youngest sister Elizabeth since she was hardly more than an infant. She was then thirty years old and married to Celestant Dupont.[3] After spending only two days with his sister, he hurried back to Mobile and thence to Pensacola, reaching the *Constellation* in time to sail with her on her voyage to Tampico, Mexico, on the 10th of May.[4]

Arriving at Tampico just a week later, Farragut found off the town the *Natchez, Boston,* and *Ontario,* all sloops of war of the United States Navy, and the *Alcibiades* and *La Perouse* of the French Navy, France having declared a blockade of the Mexican coast in her attempt to collect claims for damages inflicted on French citizens resident in Mexico. On the 10th of June, the *Constellation* received on board $153,000 and several passengers and then sailed for home, arriving at Southwest Pass in the mouth of the Mississippi ten days later. Here the money and passengers were transferred to the steamboat *Sion,* which returned up the river to New Orleans.[5] The *Constellation* continued to Pensacola, where she arrived on the 21st of June. So satisfactory had been Farragut's performance of his duties that the Commodore selected him on the 8th of August[6] to command the sloop *Erie.*

2

This was Farragut's third command and the best up to that time. She carried eighteen guns and 140 men, and had a tonnage of about 500.[7] Prompt in the carrying out of his orders, Farragut sailed the day following his assuming command of the *Erie* and in exactly two weeks he arrived again off Tampico. Here he exchanged courtesies with the Marquis Duquesne, commanding the French brig-of-war *Laurel.* Going ashore, he was politely received by English Consul Crawford, and learned that there was more money there ready to be transported to a place of safety. Two days later he was sailing southward; early on the 26th he had a lovely view of the Perote and Orizaba mountains, at six o'clock overhauled the French brig *Valagie,* soon afterwards saw the Castle of San Juan de Ulloa and the city of Vera Cruz, and came to under the Island of Sacrificios. There he found the French Commodore Bazoche with the frigates *Herman* and *Iphigénie* and two or three brigs-of-war. Farragut called officially on the French Commodore and the Governor of Vera Cruz, and established friendly relations with the two opposing authorities. A day or two after the arrival of the *Erie,* a French barque came from Bordeaux with twenty-eight souls on board and no water. Her captain explained to Farragut that he had left France under the impression that the blockade had been lifted and that the French men-of-war could not spare any water; so Farragut as an act of charity gave him four hundred gallons. He informed the French commodore, however, that he could not market for his squadron as it was a violation of a blockade to do so. But that there might be no hard feelings, when the French brig *Dunois* arrived on the 7th of September, he sent some fruit on board and in return received a pleasant visit from the Captain and First Lieutenant, who seemed to Farragut more like men than any others he had seen in the French squadron.

Farragut occupied himself in making soundings in the vicinity of Sacrificios to find how good the anchorage was, and often went to Vera Cruz to visit American Consul Hargous, and the English Consul. He also attended the grand entertainment given in the city to celebrate Mexican independence. Finally news came of a revolution at Tampico and the request for a ship of war to protect Americans there; so he took on board a small amount of specie and sailed on the 20th of September.[8]

Arriving off Tampico seven days later, Farragut tried to cross the bar in his gig, but was warned not to attempt it, by the officers of the British ship *Satellite* which was also lying off that place. Farragut heeded their advice, for the swell was very heavy, and he then went aboard the British man-of-war.

There he learned that the town was in possession of the revolutionists under Montenegro, but that the surrounding country and the forts were in the hands of Ampudia. In the afternoon, Farragut made another attempt to cross the bar, but before he could reach it the sea began to rise again and he returned to the ship. As a norther seemed to be approaching, the *Erie* and the *Satellite* slipped their cables and put out to sea where for two days they rode out a severe gale.

It was not until the 30th of September that Farragut, accompanied by the purser and the doctor, were able to get ashore. There they learned that communication with the town had been cut off, and they were forced to go by horseback to Pueblo Viejo to advise with the American Consul. Whether they took the route of Farragut's dangerous night ride some fifteen years before, his reminiscences fail to state. Through the consul, arrangements were made with General Canales for opening communications at the river bar between the English and American consuls and their ships, and Farragut and his party returned to the *Erie*. Meanwhile, the executive officer, Lieutenant Arthur Lewis, had been confronted with a delicate diplomatic problem. General Mabia had come by sea to join the insurgents, but found the bar in possession of the government forces. If he had entered, he would have been shot and his vessel confiscated; so as an act of humanity, Lewis received him on board the *Erie*. Farragut approved the act. But no explanation is made of what happened to his companions and the boat, nor any reason given why he could not have returned by boat in safety whence he came.

Several passengers and $111,000 in specie[9] were received on board the *Erie* on October 2, and the same day Farragut sailed for South Pass where a steamer took off the passengers and specie and carried them up to New Orleans. The *Erie* continued to Pensacola where she arrived on the 18th.

3

In a couple of weeks, the little sloop set sail for Mexican waters again, and was off Tampico on the 12th of November.

FRENCH BOMBARDMENT OF SAN JUAN DE ULLOA
From a painting in the Museum at Versailles, France.

Four days later she sailed for Vera Cruz and arrived on the 25th, just two days before the French attacked the Castle. The French blockade had been effective but indecisive, and the government decided to resort to open warfare. Admiral Baudin, who had seen service in the Napoleonic Wars, was placed in command of the expedition, and upon his arrival he made feverish preparations for an early engagement. There was too much sickness among his ships' crews and the stormy wintry season was too near to permit delay. So he dispatched an ultimatum to the Mexican Government, and on the 21st of November designated noon on the 27th as the time of its expiration.

"Baudin would be undoubtedly a *rara avis* in any navy," Farragut wrote.[10] "He is about fifty years of age, has lost his right arm, looks like a north of Europe man, has a fine address, and speaks English well. He has every mark of a polished seaman and officer, with the expression of great decision, with firmness and activity to execute his well-digested plans. These were my remarks the first time I saw him, and his subsequent conduct soon proved I was right."

Baudin had been provided with a copy of the original plan of the Castle of San Juan de Ulloa. From this it was discovered that there were certain points where only five or six guns could be brought to bear on a ship, the engineer having calculated on reefs not permitting ships to take up positions there. The Mexican authorities had ordered the commander of the Castle to refrain absolutely from firing the first gun. The Admiral, accordingly, took soundings and discovered he could moor two frigates head and stern in a position where they were comparatively safe. He was seen doing this and also on shore where he went at night to take note of all weak points; but orders prevented the Mexicans from firing.[10]

This order still withheld the Mexican fire, even after an unfavorable answer had been sent to the French ultimatum; consequently on the morning of November 27th[11] Baudin, without any interference, was able to place his ships in the most advantageous positions for attacking the Castle. The nonchalance of the Mexican authorities was due in part to the generally accepted opinion that the Castle was too strong to be taken by naval attack. It was protected at that time by one hundred eighty-six guns, very thick walls, and the shoal water around the reef on which it was built. The Castle was about a half mile to seaward of the city, the approaches to which from the sea it completely commanded.

Early in the morning of the eventful day, two steamers towed the two bombers, *Cyclope* and *Vulcain*, to a position at the eastern end of the reef about a mile from the Castle. Then they took the frigates *Néréide* and *Gloire* to their positions close to the reef and about a half mile from the Castle. The third frigate, *Iphigénie*, under her own sails, took a position a little ahead of the other two frigates. Admiral Baudin was on the *Néréide*.[12] Not a shot was fired by the Mexicans, though a few well placed hits might have destroyed the steamers which played such an important role on this calm day in properly placing the sailing vessels.

Even the French civilians were taken from the city to Sacrificios, and Farragut likewise sent boats at nine o'clock in the morning to bring the Americans, he himself going along to superintend the embarkation. All these preparations were completed by noon; but it was about 2:30 in the afternoon when the engagement began at a signal from the admiral's flagship, after an offer had been received on board under a flag of truce and had been rejected as unacceptable.

At 2:35[13] clouds of smoke rose above the French ships as their guns discharged the first shower of shot and shells and bombs at the Castle. The bombardment continued for an hour without change of position. Then the *Créole*, commanded by the Prince de Joinville, which had been cruising about to the northwest of the Castle and firing at ineffective ranges, was permitted to take up a position to the southeast and enter into close action. About fifteen minutes later there was a terrific explosion of the magazine in the southeast water-battery.[14] At 4:30 a shell from the *Créole* blew up one of the towers of the Castle with heavy loss of life. The frigate *Gloire* was towed out of the fight at five o'clock. She had been seen more distinctly than the others by the crew of the *Erie*, and Farragut highly praised[15] the rapid fire she had poured into the Castle during the two hours and a half she had been in action. But the other vessels also kept up a tremendous fire, much more rapid than the Castle forts, which toward sunset discharged no more than three guns per minute. At nightfall, about six o'clock, the engagement came to a close,[16] though the bomb vessels continued to fire for two hours longer.

During the battle 7,771 round shot, 177 shell, and 302 bombs had been fired at the defenses of the Castle. The solid shot entered the soft coral walls and were imbedded there without doing much damage. But the shell penetrated the stone twelve or eighteen inches and then exploded with terrific results; sometimes large masses of stone were torn out or the wall was split from top to bottom. Little or no damage was done by the bombs which fell almost perpendicularly on the bomb-proofs.[17] Over two hundred Mexicans were dead and more were wounded;[18] out of 260 in the water batteries, only 38 had escaped being either killed or wounded.[19] Sixteen guns had been dismounted. According to the opinion of Farragut who visited the fortress the following day, four more hours of bombardment would have converted the proud Castle into a mass of rubbish, though the bomb vessels might have fired upon it for a month without success.[20] Accordingly, the Mexicans acted wisely in signing a capitulation on board the French flagship at 8:30 on the next morning.

Farragut heard the news, a little after nine o'clock, and immediately went aboard the French Admiral's ship to congratulate him on his victory. Receiving the young American officer cordially, Baudin said that he regretted that the foolishness of the Mexican government had led to the loss of so many lives, for the points of disagreement between the two nations had been acknowledged for many years. It was an interesting meeting, historically, for in later years Farragut was to gain fame in exactly the same kind of warfare, the reduction of forts with a naval force practically unsupported by an army, an achievement thought impossible before Baudin's capture of the Castle of San Juan de Ulloa.

Farragut learned on the flagship that the French losses had been only four killed and twenty-nine wounded.[21] He then went aboard the *Iphigénie* and was shown over the frigate by the first lieutenant, with whom he had become well acquainted. She was in the most exposed position during the engagement, and had received about 150 shot in her hull. Still she had only two men killed and eleven wounded. "On looking around the decks of the *Iphigénie*," wrote Farragut,[22] "which was still cleared for action, I could not help comparing her with the arrangements of our ship, the one possessing all the improvements of the day, and the other fitted up precisely as she would have been in '98. The French have no shot-boxes, watch-tubs, or wad-nests, which of themselves occupy no small space on a ship's deck. The shot are in racks made of bar iron. They use the percussion lock and fulminating tubes, and their wads are little grummets made of rope-yarns, about the size of a three-inch rope for thirty-twos, and I think a glance will suffice to show you that they are better than ours for every useful purpose; they stop the windage better, occupy less space, and take less material and time to make them. As to this simple, permanently useful lock, what shall I say? It is a simple copper hammer, pulled by a lock-string—no spring, no machinery; in fact, nothing that can become deranged. I have now seen them tested four hours—as rapid firing as I ever expect to see—and no complaint made, all the Frenchmen speaking in the highest terms of them. To my knowledge, two or three have been sent to the Department, and yet we are still using spring-locks. The first Lieutenant . . . told me that some of their guns changed their breechings seven times during the action! That with us would have been a serious affair; but, when I saw the simplicity of their arrangement, I found, as he said, that with them it was nothing. The permillion ring is removed at pleasure, and the breeching, being already spliced with an eye on each end, is shackled to the side in a moment."

Farragut wrote thus boldly to a Commodore, because he had served under him many years at the Norfolk Navy Yard and knew his interest in improvements in the naval service. "If we who wander about the world," concluded Farragut,[22] "do not keep those at home informed of the daily improvements in other navies, how can we hope to improve, particularly when we see men impressed with the idea that, because they once gained a victory, they can do it again? So they may, but I can tell them it must be with the means of 1838, and not those of 1812."

4

By the 29th of November things had so settled down in Vera Cruz that the Americans and other foreigners, even including the French, returned to the town. But on the 4th of December there was great confusion when it was learned that General Santa Anna had arrived and that General Rincon[23] had been ordered to come to Mexico City to stand trial for capitulating to the French. According to the terms he had arranged with Baudin, he was to retain command of Vera Cruz provided that all his forces, except one thousand men, retired ten leagues from the seacoast and all hostilities ceased for eight months. Farragut, accompanied by the Consul, called upon Rincon and found the report to be true. They then called on Santa Anna, who received them kindly and in the course of the conversation said, "You must tell President Van Buren and Mr. Forsyth that we are all one family, and must be united against Europeans obtaining a foothold on this continent."[24] This was a direct invoking of the Monroe Doctrine. Santa Anna further promised that American citizens would be protected against harm or loss, and told Farragut that the Mexican government disapproved the surrender and that he was determined to perish with the town rather than yield to the French demands.

Official notice of his determination had been sent by Santa Anna to Admiral Baudin, who had in turn given him until the following morning to submit. Not receiving a favorable answer, the Admiral determined to renew his attack. At six o'clock on the morning of December 5th, an expedition of 1,500 men landed in three columns under cover of a heavy fog. Two columns attacked the forts to the east and west of the city respectively, which they disarmed. The third, which was led by the Prince de Joinville, the king's son, landed on the mole, forced their way into the city, and rushed to the headquarters of Santa Anna. There his guard resisted long enough to allow him to escape in his shirt and trousers. He fled to the barracks[25] where about four hundred Mexican soldiers had gathered, and put up such a strong resistance that, when Admiral Baudin came up, he ordered a retirement as he had no intention of trying to hold the city. As the French retreated, they were fired upon from the house-tops, and as they were embarking on their boats from the mole, Santa Anna appeared with three or four hundred men just as Baudin and his staff were on the point of going aboard the Admiral's barge. Fortunately a captured Mexican cannon had been placed to cover the mole, and its fire checked the Mexicans; but in spite of losses they continued the attack. Baudin had a narrow escape; the cockswain of his barge and a midshipman standing near him were wounded and another midshipman was killed.[26] Each of the five long boats carried one 18-pound carronade. These opened fire on the Mexicans also; Santa Anna received a serious wound which resulted in the loss of his left leg, and several of his men were killed;[27] the French escaped without further loss, the fog reappearing again to their great advantage as in a Homeric battle.

The total French loss was eight killed and fifty-eight wounded; while Santa Anna admitted a loss of only thirty-one killed and twenty-six wounded.[28] Eventually a treaty was signed on March 9, 1839, in which Mexico agreed to pay $600,000 for the settlement of the French claims. Though France won, her triumph was somewhat barren for her loss in trade during the blockade and the cost of the expedition were far greater in amount than the indemnity which was thus collected.[29]

Meanwhile Farragut sailed in the *Erie* from Vera Cruz on the 17th of December,[30] ten days later was off Tampico where he stopped for only two days, and arrived at Pensacola on the 11th of January, 1839. The following day he turned over the command of the *Erie* to Commander Joseph Smoot, and returned to his home in Norfolk. From the point of view of his later career, it was the most valuable cruise he had thus far made.

XXI

HOME AND TROUBLE

1

BEFORE returning to Norfolk, Farragut took a steamer for Mobile and from there proceeded to New Orleans to see his sister Nancy.[1] This sister, he declared,[2] had always fared as her brothers when she was young and consequently had the feelings of a man rather than those of her sex. He remained with his "dear sister" about two weeks, and then returned to Mobile. Here he took passage on a boat up the Alabama River to Montgomery, where he set out by horseback across the state, towards Columbus, Georgia, and thence to Augusta in the same state. He had great difficulties in crossing the streams because of high water; rivulets that usually were not more than a few feet wide he found to be a half a mile in width with water rushing so rapidly that a horse could scarcely keep its feet.

At Augusta, he called on the family of Lieutenant William Ross Gardner who had been placed under his charge when he first went to sea in the *Natchez*. He was received with great kindness out of gratitude for the care he had taken of young Gardner. From here he continued his journey by way of Charleston and Wilmington, and at length on the ninth day after he had set out from Montgomery he arrived at Norfolk.[3] Here he found no improvement in his wife's health, and for several months he spent most of his time nursing her, though occasionally he was on duty on courts-martial.

2

Meanwhile Farragut suffered a great deal of mental anguish over a letter, which he wrote and allowed to be published over his official signature, in the New Orleans *Commercial Bulletin* of January 12, 1839. It gave an account of the French operations at Vera Cruz and contained some statements to which Admiral Baudin took violent exception. "It is said, and I believe truly," wrote Farragut in the letter, "that their (the Mexicans') surprise on the morning of the 5th ultimo was owing to Admiral Baudin saying in his last communication that he should expect an answer by eight o'clock the next morning; in consequence of which General Santa Anna directed their officers to keep their troops outside, and not enter the city until seven o'clock, but that he anticipated an attack from the French in a few minutes after the messenger left the ship. But in all this there is much recrimination. The French accuse the Mexicans of having violated their faith by arresting some of their officers at the city gate." Baudin no doubt found the following also not to his taste: "The French say their object in this attack was simply to destroy the forts to prevent their annoying them in a norther, and to take Santa Anna and Arista: and had they not attacked the Barracks, they would have accomplished their object with comparatively no loss; but as it is, they are the best judges whether or not the object was worthy the sacrifice. It has given the Mexicans great confidence, and they will find them more ready and willing for the conflict when they next assail them."

The French Admiral wrote Farragut a very strong letter in reply, in which he called him "a grave liar" and "a base calumniator."[4] Secretary J. K. Paulding wrote Farragut[5] that his published letter was one "calculated to throw doubt and suspicion, at least, on the conduct of Admiral Baudin, an officer of a foreign Government with which we are at peace." He continued that Baudin's "deportment in command of a Blockading Squadron has, it is believed, been distinguished by uniform courtesy and moderation. . . . The Department has heretofore expressed its decided disapprobation of the letter which produced the reply of Admiral Baudin, and will now take occasion to call your attention to its consequences. It has already brought you into painful collision with that officer, and will probably be the occasion of an appeal to your Government. It is moreover calculated to excite hostile feelings on the part of a nation with which we are at peace, and with which the United States have every reason to preserve a friendly understanding, and its direct tendency is to cause an interruption of that courteous intercourse which has almost always subsisted between the officers of the navies of the United States and France. For these and other reasons the Department reiterates its strong disapproval of the course you pursued on the occasion to which this letter refers. The communications of naval officers relating to public affairs should be made to their commanders or to the head of this Department and not to the Editors of newspapers for publication. Of the propriety of such publication the Department alone is to judge, and no occasion will in future be passed by, of calling to account any officer who shall so far forget the respect due to his commander, and to the head of his Department as to communicate through the newspapers that information which it is his duty to reserve for them alone."

To this rather devastating letter, Farragut admitted,[6] ". . . I can have no hesitation in acknowledging that my conduct is reprehensible for the appearance of my official signature to a publication which could be tortured into the slightest reflection on the skill, courage, and good faith of the officers of a foreign nation—but that either the one or the other of these intentions ever existed in my breast, I most solemnly deny." Farragut then attempts to shift some of the blame to the editor who "unfortunately appended his official signature" to a personal letter which he thought would be of interest to the public. Lastly, he goes into the case at great length and from his point of view explains his side fully and convincingly.

The Secretary of the Navy, however, swept aside Farragut's defense with the brief reply,[7] "The Department had no intention . . . to question the accuracy of your statements but merely to point out the impropriety and ill consequences of such publication."

A couple of months later,[8] Secretary Paulding, in answering an inquiry from Farragut as to whether the French Minister had taken any steps through the Navy Department to complain officially to the Government of the United States regarding the Baudin Affair, replied in part, " . . . As you insinuated a charge of bad faith on the part of Admiral Baudin, which appears from the official correspondence between the American authorities and the Admiral, was not well founded, it is in the opinion of the Department incumbent on you, should you renew your correspondence with the Admiral, to begin by making the explanation, when it cannot be reasonably doubted that Admiral Baudin will recall his charge of falsehood and make the *amende honorable.*"

Farragut's reply[9] restated his side of the case and declared that, though he was willing to make an explanation of the objectionable parts of his printed letter, he wished to express also in "gentlemanly language the view I took of his conduct in descending from his high station to attack an officer of my rank with such gross and insulting language." This ended the affair, so far as the naval records reveal, which has been here presented with unusual fullness because the episode has not before been published.

A month later[10] there was an indication that Farragut had no intention of again being drawn into such an indiscretion, when he wrote the Secretary of the Navy that he had that moment been informed of the appearance in the Richmond *Whig* of July 31 of an article which severely reflected on Secretary Paulding and Admiral Baudin. "I take the earliest opportunity," Farragut declared, "of disclaiming all agency in it, either directly or indirectly and of assuring the Department on my honor that I have no knowledge of the circumstances whatever." This disclaimer was immediately acknowledged as[11] "perfectly satisfactory to the Department" by Acting Secretary of the Navy Isaac Chauncey. Farragut had thus escaped another dangerous development of the affair, the political, for the feeling was then bitter between Whigs and Democrats, and Farragut's future career might conceivably have been sacrificed on the altar of party politics.

3

The climax in Farragut's troubles came in December, 1840. Probably the Baudin Affair had kept him on waiting orders until the previous month of November when he was sent to the Ordinary[12] at Norfolk. For nearly two years he had devoted most of his time to his wife, and it was fortunate, perhaps, that he was otherwise unemployed. In December she became so seriously ill that her sister, Mrs. William H. Gardner, came to see her. She also was in bad health and the shock of seeing her sister in such a desperate condition so affected her nerves that she too had to be put to bed under the care of a physician.[13] Finally, as Farragut himself pitifully records,[14] Mrs. Farragut "was taken with violent spasms which lasted three days, and on the third day, the 27th December, she terminated a life of unequaled suffering, which she bore with a resignation and patience unparalleled for sixteen years, setting an example, to all sufferers, of calmness and fortitude under the severest afflictions that would do honor to the greatest Christians."

During the long years of his wife's invalidism, Farragut had done all that was possible to relieve her suffering and supply her every comfort. His conduct fully revealed the gentleness and tenderness of his character, and favorably impressed all who knew of his family life. One woman of Norfolk declared, "When Captain Farragut dies, he should have a monument reaching to the skies, made by every wife in the city contributing a stone."[15]

After such distressing experiences, Farragut naturally wished to get away from Norfolk for awhile. He applied for sea service, and on 23rd of February,[16] 1841, he was ordered to the *Delaware*.

XXII

ON THE BRAZIL STATION AGAIN

1

THE *Delaware*, to which Farragut was ordered as executive officer, was a ship of the line of 74 guns and 2,633 tons, carrying 820 officers and men.[1] She was somewhat larger than the *Independence, Washington*, and *Franklin*, in which Farragut had served in the Mediterranean some twenty years before. The ship was delivered over to Farragut at the Norfolk Navy Yard, on the 24th of March, at the same yard where she had been launched in 1820. Setting to work immediately to overhaul and rig the vessel, he took particular pride in being able to put over the half tops in from fifteen to twenty minutes, an operation which had previously taken from four hours to half a day. On the 7th of May the crew were received on board, and on the 4th of June the ship was towed down to Hampton Roads, where Farragut spent another two months in drilling the inexperienced men at the single guns and by divisions. He also devised ingenious contrivances for hoisting the powder from the magazine, which were fully tested on the 23d of July.

On that day, the commanding officer, Captain Charles S. McCauley, gave orders that three broadsides be fired. All arrangements were made for a sham battle by sounding general quarters and clearing the ship for action. First the men were ordered to go through the motions of firing as in exercises. He then ordered the power to be hoisted and the guns to be loaded and fired as fast as possible. The main deck divisions completed three broadsides in four minutes, and the lower deck the same number in five minutes.

The firemen, boarders, and pikemen were also put through their exercises, and the small-arm men fired from six to twelve rounds. All of this was completed, the guns were reported secure, and the retreat was beaten in fifteen minutes after the first gun was fired. Farragut was rightly proud of the record.

On the morning of the 2nd of August,[2] the hoarse voice of the boatswain was heard shouting, "All hands, up anchor ahoy!" It was a proud moment for Farragut; he stood ready on the poop, trumpet in hand. The officers were called to their stations; the capstan bars were placed and manned. Farragut then brought the trumpet to his mouth and gave the order, "Heave round!" Round the capstan stepped the men to the music of the fife, chanting "Off she goes," until the anchor was apeak, when the second lieutenant, standing on the forecastle, cried, "High enough."

"Pall the capstan—unship the bars—lay aloft, topmen—lower-yard-men, in the rigging," were the successive commands given by Farragut. Soon the masts took on the appearance of living pyramids of moving seamen. When they had been given sufficient time to reach their stations Farragut shouted in a loud voice, "Trice up—layout—loose away." Immediately the studding-sails boom rose, the sail-loosers hung over the yards to untie the cords securing the sails, and then all was still. Farragut then inquired in stentorian tones, "Stand by—are you ready there, fore and aft?" "All ready, sir," replied the midshipman stationed in each of the tops, in his piping voice. "Let fall—sheet home and hoist away the topsails—cheerly with the main, cheerly," was the next command. At once the canvas fell in graceful festoons, and the men descended to the deck and began hoisting the topsails, keeping time to the music of the fifes as they played "The Girl I Left Behind Me." "Tramp the deck, boys, tramp the deck," cried the second lieutenant, as the sails were spread. "High enough with the mizzen—belay the mizzen topsail halyards," cried the fifth lieutenant. "Belay the mizzen topsail halyards," echoed a midshipman in his youthful key, and the boatswain piped, "Belay." In rapid succession the same commands were repeated for the spreading of the fore-topsails and the main-topsails.

A second time the capstan bars were placed, and Farragut

ordered, "Heave round." When the second lieutenant cried, "High enough," Farragut shouted without the aid of his trumpet, "Pall the capstan—unship the bars—forward to the cat—move, lads, move," and in a few seconds the anchor rested on the bows.

Farragut's next command was, "Man the jib halyards." "All manned, sir," replied the second lieutenant. Then came a shower of commands, "Haul taut—hoist away the jib—starboard your helm, quarter-master—jump to the braces—starboard fore braces—larboard main braces—starboard cro' jack braces, haul in." As the orders were executed, the ship's head paid round, the yards were trimmed to the wind, and she began to move gently on her way.

In the same manner sail after sail was spread to the breeze until the ship was literally under clouds of canvas, and like a graceful sea bird swept easily over the waves up the Chesapeake Bay toward Annapolis.[3] Farragut still stood motionless on the poop with his eyes roving fondly over one of the most beautiful things the hands of men have fashioned, which his commands had given life and motion, a ship of the line under full sail.

If the eyes of the ship's figurehead, carved to represent Chief Tamanend of the Delawares, had really had the power of vision, he would have seen, on the 4th of August, the towers and steeples of Annapolis rising out of the misty distance. If he had had the power of dipping far into the future, he could have seen himself set upon a pedestal in front of Bancroft Hall at the Naval Academy and later cast in bronze there as "The God of 2.5," to whom the midshipmen offer their prayers and pennies as an invocation of aid in passing their examinations and winning athletic victories.

Visitors crowded on board the *Delaware;* according to Farragut, as many as two thousand daily.[4] On the 14th the steamer *Washington* came alongside. On board her were Secretary of the Navy G. E. Badger, other members of the cabinet, and about a hundred members of Congress in addition to some

United States Ship of the Line *Delaware*
From the original pastel in the collection of President Franklin Delano Roosevelt.

hundred other gentlemen and ladies. The previous November the Whigs had overthrown the Democrats, but President Harrison had lived only a month after his inauguration and John Tyler was then President. Secretary Badger inspected the ship, while the remainder of the guests strolled about the decks talking with the sailors. After midday refreshments, the crew were put through the exercises with great guns, firing six broadsides. On the 25th, Chief Justice Taney visited the ship with several ladies and gentlemen.

On the 27th of September, two days before the ship sailed, Captain McCauley came on board with a commission as commander for Farragut and commissions as lieutenant for O. H. Berryman and Fabius Stanly. All hands were mustered, and the commissions read. In celebration, "I wet my commission with a dozen of champagne," Farragut recorded.[5] These were furnished, no doubt, to his brother officers who gathered to congratulate him. Congratulations were indeed in order. His pay was advanced from $1,800 to $2,500 a year while on sea service.[6] He was twenty-second on the list of fifty-five commanders which had been promoted that year.

Farragut had been a lieutenant for sixteen years. Certain changes had been ordered in the uniform of that rank in 1830. The most noticeable in the full dress were the changing of the one epaulet from the left to the right shoulder, the placing of an embroidered gold rope and leaves of live oak interspersed with acorns around the standing collar instead of two buttons, and the decorating of the flaps of the pockets with the embroidery of oak leaves and acorns instead of three buttons. The white pantaloons were worn over short boots or with shoes instead of being thrust into half boots; the cocked hat had no gold lace on it, but a black silk cockade with a loop formed with gold lace and a small navy button; and instead of the cocked hat a lieutenant might wear a cap around which was a band of gold lace, one and a half inches wide. In undress uniform officers might wear a "round hat" with rose-formed black silk cockades.

A few months[7] before Farragut was promoted, other changes

were ordered in the uniforms for naval officers. His full dress coat as a commander was made of the usual dark blue cloth and lined with white cloth or kerseymere. It was double-breasted and had two rows of nine buttons in each row. The standing collar, lined with white, sloped somewhat in front. The cuffs opened underneath, and had three navy buttons on top and two small ones below. There were three buttons under each pocket flap, one on each hip, one in the middle of each fold of the skirt, and one at the bottom. The pockets were in the folds of the coat. The commander's undress coat was similar except that it had a rolling collar. The vest, in full dress, was of white woolen cloth or of white kerseymere or cotton. It was single-breasted and had a sloping standing collar. Blue cloth vests, made like those for full dress, could be worn with undress, with which either white or blue double-breasted vests might be worn in cold weather. The pantaloons were made of white or blue woolen, linen, or cotton cloth. The white was worn in warm weather and the blue in cold weather, or on foreign service as directed. The pantaloons were to be worn over short boots or with shoes and white stockings.

Farragut wore two epaulets, made of gilt gold bullion, half an inch in diameter and three inches long. To indicate his rank, when the epaulets were not worn, he had shoulder straps of gold lace, half an inch wide and two and a half inches long. His cravat or stock was of black silk, above which his white shirt collar was to show. With full dress Farragut wore a black cocked hat with a black silk cockade over which was a loop of six bullions. With undress he could wear the cocked hat or a dark blue cloth cap around which was a band of gold lace one and a half inches wide. His sword had to be at least twenty-six inches long and not less than one inch wide at the hilt; the scabbard was of black leather with yellow gilt mountings; and the belt for undress was of black leather and for full dress of white webbing, both an inch and a half wide. The sword was always worn with the uniform when the officer was absent from the ship on duty, or when he was on leave at a foreign station.

In summer or in tropical climates, according to a change made in 1845, Farragut was permitted to wear a frock coat of dark blue summer cloth with medium sized buttons. In undress and without epaulets on shipboard he could wear a white straw hat.

Uniforms of the 1840's have been seldom portrayed. Photography had not then been developed, and artists usually painted only bust portraits in which but little of the uniform was displayed, the hat in particular seldom appearing; hence this rather detailed description.

On the 1st of October, the *Delaware* came to anchor again in Hampton Roads. The French frigate *Armide* and the brig *Bison* were there at that time. In the midst of a gale they were visited by the Prince de Joinville, and in spite of the violent wind the yards were manned and the ships were dressed with flags. One of the sailors was blown from the yards. At the Prince's departure two broadsides, the salute due the son of the King of France, were fired. No mention was made of his visiting the *Delaware*. Only the preceding year, the Prince had been given the honor of transporting the remains of Napoleon from St. Helena to Paris.

Robert Walsh, Esquire, Secretary of Legation at the Court of Brazil, came aboard on the 18th to take passage on the *Delaware;* and on the 22d the ship was visited by President Tyler, accompanied by Commodore Charles Morris, Captains John H. Clack and James Armstrong, and Commander C. K. Stribling. Farragut thus was afforded an opportunity to thank President Tyler personally for recently signing his commission as a commander. In honor of the distinguished guest, the ship's crew were taken through all the evolutions of an engagement, which they were then able to perform with credit, because of Farragut's untiring efforts.

2

The *Delaware* sailed away on the 1st of November,[8] for Brazil with Commodore Morris of that station on board. The voyage south was without unusual incident. Farragut recorded[9] only that, when four weeks out, the copper sheathing on the bottom began to burst off; this was caused, in his opinion, by the swelling of the felt which had been placed over it. He did not approve of felt for this purpose but of the old use of turpentine and tallow. On the 12th of December,[10] the great ship arrived in the beautiful and picturesque harbor of Rio de Janeiro.[11]

On the second day after his arrival, the Commodore visited the French, Brazilian, and Portuguese ships in the harbor, and received the salutes of each in turn. The Portuguese made the mistake of displaying the American flag, which required the *Delaware* to return their salute.

Farragut went with the Commodore and Captain McCauley on Christmas day, to take dinner with a Mr. Birckland in the country. The weather was dismal and they arrived too late for dinner, but they had a pleasant time nonetheless. The return trip was worse; the driver was drunk, the rain poured down and the wind blew and howled dismally as they passed through the forest; they were wet through and through when they arrived on board.

Farragut began the new year 1842 with a general overhauling of the ship. Just two weeks later the Emperor of Brazil with his sisters and suite, the American Minister, Mr. Hunter, and all the naval commanders visited the ship. A salute was fired for the Emperor and he and his sisters were escorted into the Commodore's cabin for refreshments; afterwards the rest of the guests were served. After spending about two hours on the ship, all the party went ashore.

On the 18th,[12] the American squadron sailed from Rio to Montevideo, where it arrived twelve days later. There Washington's birthday was celebrated with a salute, which the Montevidean and Brazilian ships also fired, but the French and English did not. A few days later Farragut went with some of the officers to see a bull-fight. They saw seven or eight bulls killed by the matadores, and two horses killed by the bulls. The precision with which the matadores always struck a fatal blow at the first attempt astonished Farragut; but bull-fighting seemed to him a barbarous sport, which he thought must have

ON THE BRAZIL STATION AGAIN

contributed to the Spaniard's reckless use of the knife and other cruel practices. Even delicate women, he noticed, did not seem to be affected by the most disgusting features of the sport. But he was amused at the baiting of a bull by five bull-dogs, when the bull kept one and sometimes two of the dogs in the air most of the time.

The *Delaware* sailed for Rio on March the 12th and arrived there the last day of the month.[12] There on the 1st of April Midshipman J. J. McCook was buried in the English cemetery with the honors accorded his rank. He was an excellent young officer, whose early death Farragut much regretted. On the 1st of June, the service of Farragut as executive officer on the *Delaware* came to an end, when he was ordered to relieve Commander Henry W. Ogden as commanding officer of the *Decatur*. He had thus finished his last duty in a subordinate position on ship board; afterwards he was always to command.

3

The sloop *Decatur*, carrying 16 guns and 150 men, was of 566 tons, and was accordingly larger than any of the three ships which Farragut had previously commanded, the *Ferret*, the *Boxer*, and the *Erie*. She was a new ship, having been launched in New York in 1839, and, to the delight of Farragut, had the reputation of being a fast sailer, having beaten the *Potomac*, the *Concord*, the *Marion*, and the *Enterprise*.[13]

Farragut first reorganized the personnel of his ship, made necessary by the discharge of several of the crew. Meanwhile he enjoyed meeting British naval officers whose ships were then at Rio, particularly Captain Bruce of the 74-gun *Agincourt*, who had been a lieutenant on the *Belvidera* during the War of 1812. When he thought his crew were ready, Farragut took his ship out on a shake-down cruise on the 13th of June which lasted twelve days.[14] The men appeared to need discipline for the punishments were frequent.

On the 1st of July, the *Decatur* sailed in company with the *Delaware* for Montevideo and arrived there after a passage of eleven days. The Fourth had been celebrated as well as possible in a severe gale at sea. Commodore Morris transferred his broad pennant to the *Decatur* which then proceeded to Buenos Aires on the 16th of July.

Much had happened there since Farragut's last visit some nine years before. Since 1835 Rosas had had the title of governor and captain-general, and enjoyed full dictatorial powers. In 1839 General Lavalle had led a formidable revolt, but he had been repeatedly defeated and finally captured and executed in 1841. After this Rosas seemed determined to exterminate all his political opponents, and there was almost constant bloodshed both in Buenos Aires and in the provinces.

Farragut went ashore frequently to make official visits, and to attend "tertulias," or evening social entertainments. He and Commodore Morris called officially on Governor Rosas. When the Commodore asked Rosas about the character of the Indians in the interior, he gave them a very interesting account of his early campaigns. He claimed that his success in dealing with the Indians had been due to his knowledge of the effect of the climate upon them. When a northeasterly wind blew, they were stubborn and unpleasant to deal with; but when there was a southwest wind, they had a happier outlook on life and were brave, generous, and honorable.

At ten-thirty, Farragut and the other officers were invited into another room, and the Commodore was left in private conference with Rosas until twelve o'clock. The Commodore told Farragut afterwards that, though Rosas seemed to throw off all restraint when entertaining a group socially, he was calm and careful in speech and manner when considering affairs of business or government. Farragut's opinion of Rosas was that he was a man of unusual intellect and energy. About most matters he was reasonable enough; but when secret societies were mentioned, he denounced them with the fury of a madman, declaring that some day they would ruin the United States.

On the 10th of August, Farragut and the Commodore visited the Governor at his *quinta*, or country house. It was an hour's trip by horseback along the muddy "Beach Road." They were welcomed into the house and at first entertained by Rosas's younger sister, Madame Marcellius. Farragut thought her a very beautiful woman; though her figure was somewhat too large, she had a pretty face with a soft expression and had easy, graceful manners, and would have been pointed out as a person of distinction in any gathering. In a few minutes the Governor's daughter, Emanuelita, came in with some young ladies, among whom were her brother's wife and her cousin Corina Rosas. Senorita Emanuelita wore a neat but plain calico dress and a white apron, and the only ornament in her hair, which was plainly dressed, was a bow of narrow ribbon on one side, such as all the ladies of Buenos Aires wore to indicate that they were Federalists. She appeared pleased to see them, and entered into a lively conversation, in which Farragut could participate with ease because of his knowledge of Spanish. She seemed to Farragut to have a better mind than her Cousin Corina, who was her dearest friend. Apparently she was admirably fitted for her most responsible duty, the entertainment of her father's guests in such a manner that they always went away pleased.

After Madame Marcellius sang and played on the guitar in very good taste, they rose to take their leave as soon as it seemed proper to do so; but were urged to remain and take breakfast, or dinner as it really was. When the Commodore was told that it would be everyday fare *à la costumbre del páis*, he accepted the invitation as he wished to learn the customs of the country. A table had been prepared by the Gauchos under a kind of summer house which was an extension of the back porch. The weather was rather raw and uncomfortable; so all sat down at the table with hats and caps on, and the natives wore their ponchos. The table was loaded with provisions; both champagne and claret flowed very freely, and there were eight dishes to each of the four courses. Emanuelita "did the honors" of the occasion, while Corina served the officers as abundantly as though they were half-starved laborers.

After breakfast, Emanuelita suggested that they visit her ballroom. This turned out to be something quite out of the ordinary. Down by the river-side they found an American brig which a gale had driven ashore. The Governor had had the ship placed on an even keel and refitted so that there was a large room eighteen by thirty, which became a ball-room, the cabin serving as a ladies dressing room. It was three o'clock in the afternoon when Farragut and the Commodore returned to the city.[15]

On the 21st of August,[16] Farragut took the Commodore to Montevideo to rejoin the *Delaware*, but eight days later the *Decatur* was back at Buenos Aires. Farragut then became very intimate with Governor Rosas and his family, spending two or three evenings a week with them. He was thus able to perform many acts of kindness for the Unitarians, or members of the opposing political party, who were in constant danger of losing their lives.

Farragut rode out to the encampment, on the 5th of October, to see the beginning of a military festival, established through the diplomacy of Madame Rosas in honor of Rosas's victories. To escape the dust, his party went to Government House where they "breakfasted" with Emanuelita and her young lady friends, and then departed after promising to return for the grand celebration on the last day of the festival.

About seven o'clock on that day, Farragut rode out to the camp. Finding the ladies not yet up, he seated himself under a tree to watch the religious ceremonies which had already begun. Near the Government House, a large canopy had been erected under which was placed an altar for divine service. To the left was a smaller altar, in front of which was a pulpit. Before each were placed handsome carpets.

When everything was in readiness about ten o'clock, bands of music began to play and soldiers began to march from all directions towards the pavilion, in front of which they were marshalled with General Rosas at their head. They were about three thousand in number, and were handsome men, well dressed, well armed, and apparently well disciplined. They constituted a reserve corps which was kept outside the city ready for any emergency that might arise. When the soldiers were in position, some senior officers carried a portrait of Rosas and placed it on the small altar, all heads meanwhile being uncovered and the national anthem being played. Two officers with swords drawn then stationed themselves near the picture as a guard of honor. They were relieved every fifteen minutes during the ceremonies which lasted until three o'clock in the afternoon.

An old priest made a long address on Rosas as the author of all the good they enjoyed and the person to whom they were to look for future benefits. God would bless the soldiers, he declared, in their great work of destroying the "savage Unitarians." When he had finished what was really a harangue to the soldiers, vivas were shouted, rockets were fired, the bands began to play, the portrait was carried away, and the soldiers retired, more than pleased that the ordeal was over, for the heat was so intense that eight of their number had been prostrated.

At three o'clock Farragut sat down to dinner with Rosas, his family, and his distinguished guests. At its close toasts were drunk to the "Illustrious restorer of the laws," in memory of the departed Madame Rosas for the good which her wisdom had brought about, and to the "Kind, amiable, and beautiful Emanuelita," all of which Farragut thought she could lay claim to except the beauty.

After dinner, the guests went over to watch the amusements at the camp, the most interesting being the Gaucho game of riding at a ring, which was called *sortija*. Young men in Gaucho costume mounted on horses richly caparisoned rode through an avenue of evergreens under three arches, placed at each end and at the middle. Each in turn at full gallop attempted to take off the small ring, suspended from the middle arch, with a short lance. During the half hour Farragut was present he noted only three failures, so dexterous were the riders.

Not so successful was an attempt to send up a balloon, which he witnessed about eight o'clock, for it rose only about fifty feet and then collapsed. An hour later Farragut was driven to another part of the encampment where a ball-room had been fitted up in an old country house. Groups of negroes and the lower class of natives were around the house, playing guitars and thumping drums and dancing. After waiting an hour for some fireworks to go off, he went into the ball-room which seemed to him creditable in every respect except for a picture hanging on one of the walls. It portrayed, in life size, a Federal soldier exultingly holding a bloody knife with which he had just cut the throat of a Unitarian lying on the ground. When Farragut saw this ghastly picture, he involuntarily shuddered, and during the rest of the night his gayety was forced and unnatural. Such a picture, he thought, would have disgraced barbarian society. But he made a night of it, and did not return to the city until seven o'clock the following morning.

The next noteworthy affair was a dance given in honor of Emanuelita, on the 5th of November, at the Victoria Theatre. Farragut went with the American Consul and several officers from his ship. The ball was opened by Emanuelita with a minuet; this was followed by quadrilles, Spanish contra-dances, waltzes, and the "minuet montenero" which is the national dance. Farragut danced the first quadrille with Emanuelita, as he had been previously honored on similar occasions.

Just a week later, Admiral Brown of the Buenos Aires navy returned from a successful expedition in pursuit of Garibaldi,[17] then a Montevidean commander. He had undertaken to carry supplies up the Parana River to Corrientes, and seeing that he was about to be overtaken, he ran his vessel up into a creek, fought desperately until he had exhausted his ammunition, and then put his crew ashore and burned his ship. The next day the Admiral landed and was greeted with huzzas, and the firing of great guns and rockets. He was then conducted to the house of the Captain of the Port, preceded by young men playing guitars and singing a song written for the occasion. On the 17th, a grand ball was given in honor of the Admiral's victory, and this Farragut attended.

During the remaining weeks of Farragut's stay at Buenos Aires, he continued his visits to the Governor's family, and rode with the ladies so often that he became an accomplished horseman. There is no indication that he became romantically inclined with respect to Emanuelita, though he evidently enjoyed her society and found the social life of Buenos Aires very pleasant during the four months which he spent there.

4

The *Decatur* having been long on the station when Farragut took command of her, it came time for her to return home. She

ON THE BRAZIL STATION AGAIN

accordingly sailed on the 21st of November, stopped at Montevideo a few days to exchange some of the officers, and proceeded to Rio where she arrived on the 15th of December. Here she remained a few days, and having taken on dispatches for the government, sailed northward on the day before Christmas. "Getting under way," Farragut recorded with pride in his journal, "was rather a difficult maneuver with us, having Rat Island on our starboard beam, a Brazilian frigate on our larboard, a sloop of war on our starboard quarter but nearly astern, and a large merchantman on our larboard quarter; the tide running flood, wind south, and lying in eleven and a half fathoms of water. The great difficulty to be apprehended was, that in such a depth of water the tide would sweep us into the hawse of the sternmost vessels before we could gather headway, as they were all lying close to us. We succeeded, however, in the following manner: hove to a short stay, set the topsails, braced the head yards slightly a-box on the larboard tack, braced the after yards sharp up on the starboard tack, and, as soon as the anchor was a-weigh, fell off to port; hove the anchor briskly up to the bows, braced around the head yards, boarded the main tack, and hauled out the spanker; boarded the fore tack, eased off the main sheet, and just cleared the stern of the frigate; so we lost nothing. Then we proceeded to cat and fish the anchor, and get all sail set, continuing to beat out of the harbor. About sunset we cleared Santa Cruz. This, I apprehend, is one of the few instances of a vessel beating out of the harbor of Rio against wind and tide."[18]

This language may not make much sense to the landlubberly reader, but it will clearly show that the maneuvering of a sailing ship was not a simple affair, and will serve to increase one's respect for the mariners in the days of sail.

The *Decatur* arrived at the Island of Maranham on the 13th of January, 1843,[19] where it stopped for three days and then proceeded to Para. Arriving there on the 19th, Farragut set out the following day with the American Consul and a small party of his officers in one of the *Decatur's* boats on an excursion of about twenty-five miles up the Parahyba River. At noon they reached Boavista where they secured paddles, entered a creek about twice the width of their boat which was bordered with India-rubber trees and cane from thirty to forty feet tall, and landed about two o'clock in the afternoon at the home of Jose Angelo. There they spent two delightful days exploring the great forests and examining the luxuriant natural growth of coffee, cocoa, and red dye annotto. On their return, they walked four miles to join the boat at Boavista, and though the sun was hot, Farragut went the whole distance with his hat off, so dense was the foliage of the forest trees. During the day they enjoyed a delicious drink made from the mucilaginous covering of the cocoa which tasted like watermelon juice, and another extraordinary beverage made from palm which had the flavor of peaches and cream mingled with wine.

Toward dusk as they were returning to the ship, Farragut heard a roaring like escaping steam, which he thought was a tide-rip. But the Consul advised that they keep close inshore for fear of being swamped. It was well that Farragut followed his advice, for the waves came rolling in four feet high. One wave passed over the boat, but they managed to ride the others and escaped disaster, though all received a good wetting.

The *Decatur* sailed for Chesapeake Bay on the 26th of January,[20] and made the voyage with only one noteworthy incident occurring. When about 150 miles to the east of Anguilla, one of the Leeward Islands, a rumbling noise was heard on deck which sounded like the shifting of chain cables or the rolling of barrels below decks. The ship shook as though it were scraping over a bank, and there was great alarm on board. It lasted only about three minutes, and must have been caused by an earthquake. An hour afterwards the northeast trade winds began to blow and dispersed the clouds. This made Farragut think there was a connection between the earthquake and the weather.

Without further incident, the *Decatur* arrived at Norfolk on the 18th of February, 1843. There his ship was laid up, and Farragut reluctantly gave up his command. It had been an interesting cruise in the smartest ship of the squadron.

XXIII

SHORE DUTY AND SECOND MARRIAGE

AFTER THE *Decatur* was laid up in Norfolk, Farragut went to Washington to endeavor to secure active duty of some kind. All his self-importance, he admitted ruefully,[1] was destroyed when he called upon Secretary of the Navy Abel P. Upshur, who laughed at his expectation of retaining command of the *Decatur*. This vessel, he learned, was to join a squadron which was to be sent to the coast of Africa under command of Captain Matthew Calbraith Perry to assist in stopping the slave trade. Farragut's name was anathema to the Perry family,[2] and for that cause alone he would not have been given the command, had there not been other reasons. Probably the real trouble was that there were too many commanders above Farragut on the list for the comparatively few commands then available for that rank, as so many ships were laid up "in ordinary," out of commission, at the navy yards.

Maury's articles on naval reform had been appearing in the *Southern Literary Messenger* in Richmond during the years 1840, 1842, and 1843, and as a result there had been a reorganization of the Navy Department in 1842 and there were other signs of an awakening interest in the development of the navy; but it was to take many years to remove the professional dry-rot and overcome the inertia of ignorance and conservatism. Though England and France were going ahead in the development of more powerful guns and ammunition and in the application of steam propulsion, the United States Navy lagged behind. The remarkable achievements of the American clipper ships under sail actually served to retard the development of steam ships in the United States, where it became a kind of patriotic slogan that American sailing ships could beat British ships propelled by steam and must continue to do so. But a beginning had been made recently in the construction of steam ships of war. The *Fulton* (second to bear that name) had been launched in 1837; the *Missouri*, launched in 1841, was destroyed by a fire at Gibraltar on August 26, 1843, only a short time after Farragut's visit to Washington; and the *Mississippi*, which was later to share in Farragut's glorious achievements in the Civil War, was also launched in 1841. In this development, it was Matthew Calbraith Perry who took the lead, and even if Farragut had not been on the Brazil Station, he probably would have been given no part in laying the foundations of the American steam navy.

Up to that time, Farragut had shown himself largely a man of action rather than a man of thought. Probably, his defective vision had much to do with this, for as a young man he was an eager student. After his unfortunate sunstroke, scientific research like that which Maury and others did with such success was impossible for him.

Not receiving orders for active service from the Secretary of the Navy, Farragut secured leave of absence and returned to Norfolk. There was then no invalid wife for him to nurse and thus occupy his time. His health was not very good, and he began to feel very lonely. Accordingly after serving on a court-martial, he went up to the mountains of Virginia and spent the summer at Fauquier Springs and the vicinity.

Meanwhile he continued to apply for active service, but without success. On the 1st of September, he learned that the command of the Norfolk Navy Yard had been vacated by Commander John L. Saunders, and he hurried to Washington to urge his claim for that appointment. Secretary Upshur had been succeeded in office by David Henshaw of Massachusetts, and when Farragut appeared before him he was told that his being from Norfolk was an insuperable obstacle to his receiving the command, as it was to be his policy to send northern officers south, and southern officers north. Farragut, again disappointed, went to Norfolk and for the first time, according to the record, participated in politics. "Lent my feeble aid," he records,[3] "to stop his (Henshaw's) confirmation by the Senate, and it was not with a little satisfaction that I heard that he had said he was not a little indebted to the officers of the navy for his rejection."

Farragut did not feel this disappointment very keenly, for he had other matters to occupy his mind just then. These were matrimonial. One of the attractions at Fauquier Springs was probably a Miss Virginia Dorcas Loyall of Norfolk, the oldest daughter of William Loyall, Esquire, of that city. In any case, they were married on December 26th, 1843, by the Reverend Upton Beall, Rector of Christ Church, Norfolk.[4] On their wedding journey they went as far north as New York, and returned home by way of Richmond.

With a wife to care for, Farragut was greatly pleased on the 17th of April, 1844,[5] to receive orders as executive officer on the ship of the line *Pennsylvania*. Under the circumstances, he was pleased also that this ship was then the receiving ship at Norfolk and he would not be separated from his bride by a voyage to some distant foreign station. The *Pennsylvania*, launched in 1837, was the largest ship of the line in the United State Navy. She had a tonnage of 3,241, and carried 120 guns and 1,100 officers and men, though the latter figure was reduced to only 125 while she was a receiving ship.[6] Captain Joseph Smoot was in command.[7] Farragut's duties were devoid of excitement, and the dull routine was broken only by entertaining distinguished visitors. Among these was President John Tyler, who was accompanied by his beautiful young wife.[8] Afterwards the same summer Governor James McDowell of Virginia visited the ship, and in the autumn a large number of Presbyterians while the Synod was meeting in Norfolk.

At that time, however, there was much to talk about. The political pot was boiling, for a presidential election was approaching, and the Whigs and the Democrats were vocal in their arguments and denunciations. The most important question was the annexation of Texas, though almost equally so was the controversy with England over the Oregon boundary and "Fifty-four Forty or Fight" was a ringing slogan of the Democrats. That same summer Samuel F. B. Morse sent the first message by electric telegraph, those memorable words, "What hath God wrought?"

On the 12th of October there was great excitement in the Farragut and Loyall households in Norfolk. That day, as Farragut recorded the event,[9] "Mrs. D. G. F. presented me with a fine Boy whose name is to be Loyall Farragut." The child was born in his Grandfather Loyall's house on East Main Street. Farragut took great pride in his son, to whom he was completely devoted during the rest of his life. The infant's early days were passed on the *Pennsylvania,* where the Farragut family then had their living quarters, in a truly nautical atmosphere. The proud father devised a little hammock in which the child swung above his mother's head during the night. By an ingenious arrangement of ropes and pulleys the hammock could be hoisted or lowered according to the child's demands for nourishment.

Immediately following Farragut's record of the birth of his son is another interesting item: "In November great excitement prevailed about the election for a President, each party claiming the victory by turns, as the news varied in favor of either party. MR. POLK, the Democratic candidate, is the successful person and the Whigs filled with chagrin and mortification are uttering their execrations on the system of making votes out of new emigrants, etc."[10] Though Farragut does not say so, it is apparent that he voted for James K. Polk of Tennessee, the state where Farragut was born and to which he was always accredited in the *Navy Registers.*

In Philadelphia, in January, 1845, the remains of Commodore David Porter were re-interred with imposing military ceremonies. He had died the previous March 3 at his diplomatic post in Constantinople, Turkey, and his body had been brought home in the sloop of war *Truxtun,* which arrived in Philadelphia only the preceding December. It seems that Farragut was unable to be present at these sad rites of the man who had been almost as a father to him, for he makes no mention of the occasion in his reminiscences.

Courtesy of Mr. and Mrs. George G. Hall

MRS. DAVID GLASGOW FARRAGUT AND HER SON LOYALL
From an old daguerreotype.

SHORE DUTY AND SECOND MARRIAGE

When Captain Smoot was detached from the *Pennsylvania*, Farragut was in command of the vessel until the 1st of October when he was ordered to the Norfolk Navy Yard as second in command to Commodore Jesse Wilkinson who had requested the Secretary of the Navy to order him to that duty. Here he remained while the country drifted rapidly into war with Mexico after the legal annexation of Texas was consummated between July 4 and December 29, 1845. Meanwhile Farragut began to dream of distinguished participation in that war which seemed imminent, a participation which he was sure would be allowed him because of his familiarity with the coast of Mexico and its harbors.

During this period of comparative leisure, internal evidence shows that he probably dictated to an amaneunsis the major portion, all in fact except the last six pages which were written in his own hand, of his autobiography, entitled *Some Reminiscences of Early Life*,[11] *by D. G. Farragut, A Captain, The United States Navy.*

XXIV

IN THE MEXICAN WAR

1

As EARLY AS August, 1845,[1] Farragut wrote Secretary of the Navy George Bancroft, informing him that he had served long in the Gulf of Mexico, and was intimately acquainted with its coasts and the character of the Mexican people, whose language he could speak. He further informed him that he was in command of the *Erie* which was off Vera Cruz when Admiral Baudin attacked the Castle of San Juan de Ulloa, and that he had recently given a copy of the plan of attack to Captain R. F. Stockton when he was ordered into the Gulf of Mexico in the steam-propeller *Princeton*. He closed his letter with the request that he be given "a command in the event of any difficulty with that country."

Months went by without any reply being received to Farragut's request. In this connection, the unfortunate controversy[2] which Farragut had with Admiral Baudin over a letter which the young officer wrote for a New Orleans newspaper and the consequent embarrassment to the Navy Department should be recalled. This had done much to counteract any favorable impressions which might have been made on that department by Farragut's letter to Commodore Barron[3] in which he recommended improvements in the United States Navy similar to those he had observed in the French Navy. This letter should have been written to the Secretary of the Navy instead of Barron, as that officer was then without much influence in the service aside from that of seniority. The contents of Farragut's letter may not have gone beyond Barron's hands.

After Congress declared war against Mexico in May, 1846, Farragut immediately applied again for a command,[4] and received only the routine "Duly noted." The war was being vigorously prosecuted on land and sea. General Zachary Taylor defeated the Mexicans at Palo Alto and at Resaca de la Palma in May and captured Monterey in September. Combined military and naval operations captured Monterey, San Francisco, and Los Angeles in California in July and August. Commodore David Conner, in command of a large squadron, established a blockade of the eastern coast of Mexico, and on the 16th of October Captain Matthew Calbraith Perry, second in command, made a successful expedition up the Tabasco River to the town of the same name.

Farragut, beginning to despair of being able to participate at all in the war, wrote again to the Secretary on November 3, repeating the contents of the letter which he had written more than a year before. He expressed the "hope that, should anything like an attack on the Castle of San Juan de Ulloa be contemplated, at some future day, I may be allowed to participate in the glorious achievement, for such I believe it will be whenever it is undertaken."[5] He referred again to his service in the Gulf of Mexico in the years 1822, 1823, and 1824 under Commodore Porter and later in 1838 and 1839 under Commodore Dallas, and to his presence in the sloop of war *Erie* at Vera Cruz when the Castle was taken by the French. "I was in the Castle a few minutes after its surrender," he wrote, "and I therefore know how vulnerable it is to ships. I was with the French officers, and saw daily all their preparations and plans of attack, all of which might be serviceable. I am proud to say I learned a good deal. The French were prepared to attack by escalade, if it had not surrendered the morning it did. This I also considered feasible, and at, perhaps, much less risk than by bombardment; but it would have been executed under cover of night. My intimate knowledge of the localities and these arrangements induces me to hope that I may have a position under whoever has the good fortune to command the squadron." He then mentioned again the plans of the attack on the Castle which he had given to Captain Stockton, who had informed him he had turned them over to Secretary Bancroft,[6] and suggested that from that document which included explanatory minutes he might learn the true condition of the Castle at the time of its surrender.

Just one week later, Secretary Mason wrote[7] Farragut that his request for duty would be granted "if an opportunity for doing so shall offer, consistently with the just rights of others." On December 29th following, the *Saratoga* arrived at Norfolk from the Brazil Station. Farragut waited patiently until the 30th of January, 1847,[8] when he wrote again to Secretary Mason, calling his attention to the fact that he had not had his proper tour of duty in command inasmuch as he had commanded the *Decatur* only eight or nine months since his promotion to commander in September, 1841. Since that time many of his juniors had been given commands, and in conclusion he added, "I now only ask for the command of the *Saratoga* that is fitting for twelve months service in the Gulf which I hope will not be considered as impinging on the rights of others." The Secretary acknowledged his application as "noted," on the 2d of February;[8] but Farragut had to wait another month, when he was finally ordered, on March 9th,[9] to command the *Saratoga*.

2

It is worthy of note that Captain Matthew Calbraith Perry arrived at Norfolk in the *Mississippi* from Mexican waters late in January, 1847, brought such pressure to bear on the Norfolk Navy Yard that repairs on his ship which ordinarily would have taken six weeks were completed in two, and then went up to Washington where he presented such a bad report of the conduct of the war by his commanding officer, Commodore Conner, that he soon returned to Vera Cruz with an order in his pocket from the Secretary placing him in command of the fleet to succeed Conner.[10] It is not unlikely that the Secretary discussed with Perry the recommendations Farragut had made with regard to an attack on the Castle of San Juan de Ulloa and his request for a command, and that Perry's later bad treatment of Farragut was in some way connected with his failure to follow such a plan. It could hardly have been due entirely to an antipathy against Farragut for what he had said about the drunkenness of his brother Raymond.[11]

Once in command, Farragut made all haste possible to get his ship to sea, taking every servant and boat's crew he could get his hands on in Norfolk. In this he received the cheerful assistance of Commodore Charles W. Skinner[12] and Captain C. K. Stribling. Even so, he had to sail ten per cent short of his complement of men, only one of whom was regularly rated a "seaman." The *Saratoga's* full complement of officers and crew numbered 210; her tonnage was 882; and she was rated a first class 20-gun sloop, though she actually carried two additional guns.[13] Although his crew were untrained, Farragut exercised them frequently on the voyage, firing at a target off the Bahama Banks, and by the time they arrived off Vera Cruz they were ready for service.

Farragut had not been able to sail from Norfolk until the 29th of March,[14] and when the *Saratoga* arrived off Vera Cruz on the 26th of April,[15] after making a rather slow passage, Farragut and his men were greeted with the sight of the American flag flying over the Castle of San Juan de Ulloa. The city and the Castle had capitulated on the 27th of March.[16]

But the navy had played only a small role in the operations, merely covering the landing of General Scott's army and lending some Paixhan guns to assist in shelling the city. After the city surrendered, the Castle ran up the white flag without attempting the slightest resistance, to the great surprise of the American leaders. It certainly substantiated Farragut's contention as to the weakness of the fortress; but all that he could say, after his late arrival, was, "I told you so." There is no record that he did this; but he shows plainly in his reminiscences that he was disappointed in not being able to put to any practical use the knowledge which he had so laboriously acquired concerning the Castle and its neighboring waters. At that time he had not foreseen war between the United States and Mexico, but he declared,[17] "I had made it a rule of my life to note these things with a view to the possible future." He bitterly complained that, when the great opportunity came for the navy to cover itself with everlasting glory, he was looked upon as a monomaniac for suggesting such a plan. "The officers in the Gulf," he continued, "who did not understand the condition of the Castle or know the people were not willing to attack the Castle because an English officer had told them it could sink all the ships in the world. It is now well known and terribly felt how sadly we have been imposed on. The navy would stand on a very different footing this day if the Castle had been attacked. It was all we could do, and should have been done at all hazards. But Commodore Conner thought differently and the old officers at home backed his opinion; but they all paid the forfeit, not one of them will ever wear an Admiral's flag, which they would have done if that Castle had been taken by the navy and there is no doubt of the result if it had been attacked."[17]

He felt that it would be only through the accomplishment of some outstanding achievement that the rank of admiral would be established in the United States Navy. Future history was to demonstrate how completely right he was, for he was to be the first to "wear an Admiral's flag," a privilege and distinction accorded him through an accomplishment below New Orleans during the Civil War much more difficult than the capture of the Castle of San Juan de Ulloa would have been for the navy.

Though Commodore Conner had already committed himself to the plan, reducing the navy to a minor role, and had actually begun operations before Perry returned from Washington to take over the command, Perry would no doubt have resented any criticism of the operations. Feeling as strongly about the matter as he did, Farragut may very likely have said something which was carried to the Commodore. The proud and volcanic Perry would have deeply resented this, and would have felt fully justified in the punishment of Farragut which he soon thereafter handed out to one whom he already disliked.

Three days after Farragut's arrival at Vera Cruz, he was ordered by Perry to blockade Tuspan, a town about one hundred and fifty miles north of Vera Cruz. At this station the *Saratoga* arrived on the 30th of April and came to anchor near the *Albany*, a sister ship, under command of Captain S. L. Breese, which had furnished a detachment of men under her commander to participate in the expedition against Tuspan the previous 18th of April. Here the *Saratoga* was kept continuously until the middle of July. Farragut was thus prevented from taking part in the expedition against Coatzacoalcos and not allowed to join the expedition against Tabasco about the middle of June, but was required to relieve the *Albany* so that Captain Breese could participate, though he did not desire to be relieved as he had already taken part in all the previous expeditions as well as the capture of Vera Cruz.[18]

On such monotonous duty, discipline was difficult to maintain on the *Saratoga*, and the entries in her logbook show that frequent punishments with the cats and the colt had to be dealt out to the crew for drunkenness, disobedience of orders, and fighting. If they could only have been allowed to fight the Mexicans, all would have been well. On the 12th of July,[19] Farragut sailed for Vera Cruz where his ship remained a couple of weeks after which he was ordered to Tabasco, probably with dispatches, for the *Saratoga* remained there only one day before returning to Vera Cruz, where she arrived at sunset on the 11th of August.

At six o'clock the following morning, the British steamer *Teviot* arrived with the Mexican General Parades on board. Inasmuch as Vera Cruz was in the control of the army, Colonel Wilson being the governor, Farragut saw no reason for interfering with the port regulations by boarding the British ship unless he was requested to do so by Governor Wilson. Later in a conversation with Farragut in the presence of Governor Wilson, Commodore Perry said, "You might have boarded the steamer." To this Farragut replied, "I did not consider it my duty to do anything of the kind unless requested to do so by the Governor. I thought the army had its own boarding officers and port regulations, which I presumed answered all their purposes. But since the Governor has been forced to displace the boarding officer, he has requested me to have all vessels boarded, as he has no competent person to perform the duty. Since that time I have given it my strict attention." Perry then said, "I will issue a circular to that effect."[20]

Still, in his letter to the Secretary of the Navy of the 18th of August,[21] Perry intimated that Farragut had neglected his duty in permitting General Parades to enter Vera Cruz and a month later Farragut had the mortification of seeing the story in the newspapers to the effect that he had been reprimanded by Perry for this neglect of duty.

Fever having broken out on the *Decatur* off Tuspan, the *Saratoga* was ordered to relieve her so she could take her sick to the hospital at Pensacola. Farragut arrived at his former station on the 1st of September. In about three weeks, the yellow fever attacked the *Saratoga*, and soon there were fifty cases on board. Farragut was among the victims.[22] His letters notifying the Commodore of the situation were not noticed, and the vessel was kept on duty "blockading and running along the coast, compelled to put to sea in gales, and kept on the blockade for two months after the fever had broken out, and treated as if nothing had occurred on board the vessel."[21] Meanwhile the sick list lengthened to ninety-nine cases. No other ship in the squadron except the *Mississippi* had more cases of the yellow fever than the *Saratoga*, and she was sent to Pensacola in August. It was very fortunate that the disease did not strike in its more virulent form; otherwise the four deaths on the *Saratoga* might have been forty or more.

It was not until the 24th of November that the *Saratoga* was relieved of the blockade duty and ordered to Vera Cruz, where however she was detained a whole month[23] before Perry finally sent her to Pensacola so that her sick could be properly taken care of. Meanwhile Farragut, completely out of patience, wrote to the Secretary of the Navy,[24] informing him that, though the *Saratoga* had been fitted out for twelve months, her rigging was beginning to give way, that more than half his crew and all his officers had been down with yellow fever, and that his commander-in-chief had not permitted the *Saratoga* to participate in the "honorable duties of the squadron" but had kept her on the blockade of Tuspan for "five and half months out of seven on the station." Farragut therefore asked that, if it was not expedient to order the *Saratoga* home for refitting, he might be relieved from the command of the ship so that his officers and men might be given more favorable consideration. "I am fully aware, sir," he concluded, "that great latitude must be given to the commander of a squadron, in order to secure his best exertions; but if he uses the trust with prejudice or partiality, there is no alternative to the subordinate but the one I seek, viz., to get from under his command, and in so doing I am anxious that those who have shared with me the evils of my command should participate in the pleasure of my relief."

Commodore Perry inclosed Farragut's letter with one he wrote to the Secretary five days later,[25] in which he declared that Farragut was mistaken in thinking that he held a prejudice against his junior officer with whom he had never before served and in whose company he did not recollect to have passed twenty-four hours in his life. He explained that all arrangements with regard to the vessels in his squadron had been made necessary by sickness and other exigencies of the service, and that "the crew of the *Saratoga* had been less exposed to the unhealthy localities of the coast than any vessel of the squadron, and had suffered less, in proportion to number, than most of them." As a parting shot, he added, "I leave it to the Department to judge of the propriety of the language and tone of the letter of Commander Farragut."

After waiting twelve days longer,[26] Perry sent the *Saratoga* to Pensacola with orders to Farragut to land his sick, take on a full supply of provisions, stores, and munitions, and then return to Vera Cruz. Farragut arrived at Pensacola on the 6th of January, 1848; but before he was ready to return to Vera Cruz he received orders from the Secretary on January 20th to take his ship to the Brooklyn Navy Yard, to convey all the sick then in the Pensacola hospital, thirty-four in number, to a northern climate.[27] The *Saratoga* was really no longer needed in Mexican waters. Scott's army had entered Mexico City on the 14th of

September, 1847. Perry, however, kept his squadron on the Mexican coast until the treaty of peace was signed on the following February 2d.

Before sailing for New York on the 31st of January, Farragut wrote a long letter to Secretary Mason[28] in which he fully explained how he had been treated by Perry. He also stated that he and Perry had served together in the same squadron more than once and besides that it was his opinion that a prejudice could easily be formed against an officer without serving with him. As to Perry's assumption that Farragut had complained because of the hardship incident to his blockade duty off Tuspan, Farragut declared that he mentioned this solely because of its connection with his being denied participation in any of the expeditions.

The *Saratoga* arrived at New York on the 19th of February, where Farragut paid off the crew and delivered the ship at the Brooklyn Navy Yard. The cruise had been, he sadly recorded,[29] "the most mortifying one" he had made since he had entered the naval service. In addition to the unhappy results of the ill-will of Commodore Perry, he had had a great deal of trouble in properly disciplining the poor crew which he had hastily collected at Norfolk. A less monotonous kind of service would have made this easier for him. During the cruise he had to rid the service of a lieutenant, a midshipman, two gunners, and a sail-maker for drunkenness, and on the very last day of his command of the *Saratoga* he had to prefer charges against his first lieutenant for that same offense. Of his crew of one hundred fifty, one hundred had been down with yellow fever. His lieutenant of marines had died on shore at Tampico, and two of his best seamen had been lost overboard on the voyage home. It had indeed been a "most mortifying" cruise.

NORFOLK AND PORTSMOUTH IN 1851
From a lithograph by E. Sachse & Co., Baltimore, Maryland.

Courtesy, The Mariners' Museum, Newport News, Va.

XXV

AN ORDNANCE EXPERT

THOUGH Secretary Mason may not have been pleased[1] with the tone of Farragut's letters concerning his treatment by Perry, Mason reappointed Farragut second in command at the Norfolk Navy Yard on the 10th of April, 1848. Farragut regretted[2] the circumstances which had led him to seek to be relieved from serving under Perry, but he was happy to return to his wife and his little three year old son in Norfolk. A few weeks afterwards, he became seriously ill of Asiatic cholera, then looked upon as a mysterious malady, the cause of which had not been determined. The following summer the disease reappeared in Norfolk in epidemic form, though not so many died of it as had in 1832 when it attacked the city with more fatal results. Surgeon George Blacknall feared that Farragut would not recover, but in spite of his weak constitution he again escaped death and, securing leave of absence,[3] went to White Sulphur Springs where he spent several weeks recuperating.

There was at that time a great deal of talk in Norfolk about the recent discovery of gold in California. Some young men and a few of the middle-aged went as quickly as possible to this new land of promise. The Farraguts could then have hardly realized, even imagined, that in a few years they would themselves be in far away California.

For two years Farragut was occupied with the monotonous routine of the Navy Yard. In November, 1849,[4] he sought a change, requesting of the Secretary of the Navy that a transfer between himself and Commander Samuel Barron, commanding the Receiving Ship *Pennsylvania,* be permitted. The request was not granted; but instead Farragut was detached from the Navy Yard on the following April 29th[5] and placed on "waiting orders." He was not relieved of duty, however, until the 24th of May.[6]

Before his detachment from the yard, a notable event occurred there in the launching of the new steam man-of-war, the *Powhatan*, on the 14th of February. The engines of the new ship were constructed at the Gosport Iron Works at a cost of over $120,000; the complete cost of the vessel was nearly $800,000. She was a sidewheel steamer of 2,415 tons, and was said to be the most beautiful ship that had been built at Norfolk. Her launching on St. Valentine's Day was a gala social event, and Commodore John D. Sloat, Commander Farragut, and Lieutenant Oliver S. Glisson opened their homes with generous hospitality and served refreshments to their numerous guests.

During the following summer, Farragut took his family to the mountains in Botetourt County, Virginia. He did not return to Norfolk until early in October[7] when he reported to Commodore Sloat as the senior officer of a board which had been selected to arrange exercises for the Ordnance Department of the Navy. Thus Farragut's early interest in improving guns and gunnery in the Navy was finally beginning to bear fruit.

A more important duty was assigned to Farragut the following March,[8] when he was ordered to Washington to draw up a book of ordnance regulations. He was, accordingly, not in Norfolk when Commodore James Barron died on the 21st of April, and ended his long career in the naval service at the age of eighty-three.

Farragut was assisted in his ordnance work in Washington by Commanders T. A. Dornin and Andrew A. Harwood and Lieutenants A. B. Fairfax and Stephen C. Rowan. After Farragut and his associates had worked on the book for several months, Commodore Lewis Warrington, Chief of the Bureau of Ordnance, died, and his successor, Commodore Charles Morris, requested that certain revisions be made. These required about six months more labor. When the work was finally finished, Commodore Morris did not approve of the drawings, which

Farragut thought were excellent illustrations, and these had to be stricken out along with other features, which to Farragut seemed the best parts of the book.

During his long stay in Washington, Farragut had an opportunity to gratify his fondness for cultural lectures. He regularly attended the evening lectures at the Smithsonian Institution, missing only one of the series. Some of the distinguished lecturers whom Farragut probably heard at that time were Dr. Elisha K. Kane, Arctic Explorer; President Mark Hopkins of Williams College; Dr. Benjamin Silliman of Yale College; and Professor Louis Agassiz of Cambridge, Massachusetts. Freely did Farragut praise the legacy of Mr. Smithson, which had thus been of such personal benefit to him. "You will rarely come away from such lectures," he declared, "without being somewhat wiser than when you went."[9] It is not unlikely that at this time Farragut became well acquainted with Lieutenant Matthew Fontaine Maury, who was then head of the Naval Observatory and had made great progress with his *Wind and Current Charts* and *Sailing Directions* which were to give him the title, "Pathfinder of the Seas." Maury was intimately associated with Professor Joseph Henry, Secretary of the Smithsonian Institution.

While in Washington, the Farragut family lived at a boarding house near Pennsylvania Avenue, where several naval officers and professors at the Smithsonian Institution had rooms with their families.

When he thought his work in Washington was nearing completion, Farragut made application for the command of the Rendezvous[10] at the Philadelphia Navy Yard, and later[11] for the command of the Ordinary at the Norfolk Navy Yard. As his ordnance duty was prolonged, neither request was granted. But when his work was finally finished, he was ordered back to Norfolk, on the 30th of April, 1852, as ordnance officer. His chief duty was to give the officers stationed there a lecture each week on gunnery. Meanwhile he served on a court-martial on the *Pennsylvania* in May, and as a member of the General Court-Martial in July.[12] Then the Chief of the Bureau of Ordnance and Gunnery, Commodore Morris, gave him an important assignment.[13] He was ordered to Fort Monroe at Old Point Comfort to superintend experiments designed to test the endurance of different kinds of guns. Here, he and his family lived at the old Hygea Hotel. Farragut was assisted in this work by Lieutenants Henry H. Bell, Percival Drayton, and William Rogers Taylor. In the Civil War, Bell was to lead one of Farragut's divisions at the passage of the forts below New Orleans, and Drayton was to be his fleet captain in the Battle of Mobile Bay.

The results of these experiments, which extended over nearly a year, were published by the Bureau of Ordnance in a pamphlet, entitled *Experiments to Ascertain the Strength and Endurance of Navy Guns*. By bursting one or two guns of each class in a series of discharges, many preconceived ideas were completely disproved with regard to the theory that the endurance of a gun depended on its tensile strength. The only recognition Farragut received was in the preliminary statement to the effect that the pamphlet was the "substance of the report made by Commander D. G. Farragut, assisted by" Lieutenants Drayton, Bell, and Taylor. The work appears to have been soon forgotten. Also forgotten was his connection with the book of ordnance regulations, for after ten years another board made some changes to adapt the regulations to steam and big guns and removed the names of the original board. "I do not care for the praise that such a volume might win," complained Farragut;[14] "but I despise the spirit that prompts those who have a little temporary power about the seat of government to purloin the credit due to others."

About this time, Lieutenant John Adolphus Dahlgren was beginning his experiments at the Washington Navy Yard on a gun of greater size, whose curve of pressure would give greater strength at the breech. So important did his discovery prove to be that it revolutionized the designing of ordnance and eventually gave Dahlgren so much distinction that the work of other pioneers like Farragut was completely overshadowed and sometimes entirely forgotten.

After concluding his experiments at Old Point Comfort, Farragut resumed his weekly lectures on gunnery at the Norfolk

Navy Yard. In the following spring when England and France joined Turkey in the war against Russia, known as the Crimean War, Farragut became very desirous of going to the seat of the war so that he could see how the newest French and English guns stood the test of war service. In April, he therefore wrote explaining to Secretary Mason the benefits to be derived from such an assignment of duty and set forth his own qualifications for such a service. He mentioned in particular his long interest in the subject and his ability to speak French, Spanish, and Italian. "I am aware that I am asking a great deal of the Department," he concluded;[15] "but as I have been in the service since I was nine years of age, I feel that my name and character are equally well known to the Department and the Navy; upon which I most respectfully rely for your favorable consideration of my request to be attached to any commission that may be sent for the above-named purposes, or to be appointed to any command destined for the seat of war."

No action on Farragut's suggestion was taken by the Navy Department,[16] whose eyes were then directed to the Far East rather than the Near East. That very month, Commander J. Kelly of the *Plymouth* was assisting British naval vessels in defending foreign lives and property at Shanghai. The preceding month Perry signed the historic treaty with Japan, the result of naval force and diplomacy. Farragut's feud with Perry had deprived him of the slightest opportunity to participate in this famous expedition.

"At this critical period of naval progress," writes Mahan,[17] "when sail was manifestly giving place to steam, when the early attempts at ironclad batteries were being made, and the vast changes in armament that have since taken place were certainly, though as yet dimly, indicated, it did not appear to the Government of the United States a matter of sufficient importance to inquire, on the spot, into the practical working of the new instruments under the tests of war."

XXVI

ESTABLISHES MARE ISLAND NAVY YARD

1

INSTEAD of ordering Farragut to the Near East to observe the Crimean War, the Navy Department sent him in the opposite direction to California. It was a coincidence, no doubt, and not an evidence of displeasure, for it was an important duty,[1] to which he was ordered, the establishment of a new navy yard in that newly acquired territory. As early as June 17, 1854,[2] he was instructed to be ready for duty in California, and on the following 6th of July he was ordered to report in person at the Navy Department. He spent the remainder of July in Washington conferring with Secretary of the Navy J. C. Dobbin and Commodore Joseph Smith, Chief of the Bureau of Yards and Docks. There were endless details to be arranged regarding the plans for the yard, the purchase of materials, and the personnel, some of whom had to be transported to this distant station. For a time Farragut was ill at the Willard Hotel,[3] but he was able to arrive in Norfolk by steamer on the 30th of July. On the 9th of August he was officially detached from his duty at the Norfolk Navy Yard.

It was a busy time in the Farragut family, for Mrs. Farragut and the nine year old son Loyall were also to go along on the long journey. All preparations were completed by the 16th of August when the family embarked on a steamer for New York where they arrived in time to sail August 19th on the *Star of the West*[4] of the Nicaragua Line. This was the ship which a few years afterwards played such a dramatic role in the opening scene of the Civil War at Charleston, South Carolina.

After the Mexican War, the extension of slavery in the new

territory became a burning political and social issue. Henry Clay's Compromise of 1850 brought about a temporary solution, but thoughtful people feared that the smoldering fire of angry passions might soon burst into flames. The "Underground Railroad" was established in violation of the Fugitive Slave Law, which had been passed by Congress. Harriet Beecher Stowe's *Uncle Tom's Cabin* was published in 1852. The Farraguts were well aware of the problems of the day, but during their long stay in distant California they lost touch with the situation which grew rapidly worse with the bloody conflict in Kansas. By leaving Norfolk at that time, they also missed the dreadful epidemic of yellow fever which ravaged that city in the summer of 1855, spreading terror and death among its citizens; for a time there were as many as a hundred deaths a day.[5]

After an uneventful voyage, the *Star of the West* arrived, on the 29th of August, at San Juan del Nord, Nicaragua. Here began the hardships of the journey. All the passengers were transferred to two old fashioned stern-wheel steamers for the voyage up the San Juan River. There were no accommodations, and the Farraguts as well as the other passengers had to camp out on deck with their baggage, where they were protected from the heavy dew at night only by an awning. With difficulty the boats scarcely made headway against the current of the river. The landscape was strange and interesting. For long stretches the river seemed walled in between ramparts of dense tropical foliage matted with vines, in which monkeys, parrots, and other birds of brilliant plumage were to be seen. The male passengers, most of whom carried revolvers, amused themselves by shooting at the lazy alligators which lay basking in the hot sun.

On the afternoon of the following day, the rapids of Castillo Viejo were reached, where everything had to be carried around the falls to other steamers. It was nightfall when the weary passengers reached the mouth of Lake Nicaragua. Here they were again transferred to a small side-wheel steamer which conveyed them across the lake to a small place on the west shore called Virgin Bay. The crowded condition on this little steamer was very trying to Farragut who had not recovered from his recent serious illness. His wife improvised a temporary shelter on deck under the guard rails, protected by an umbrella and shawls, and here spent most of the night fanning him and administering to his needs. After arriving in the early morning, the passengers had to be carried ashore in a large iron barge, pulled back and forth by natives along a line extended from the steamer to the shore.

The trials of the passengers were not ended here, where they found, instead of the elegant Concord coaches pictured by the transportation company, merely canvas covered wagons. These were for the women and children; horses and mules were provided for the men. The company had constructed a fairly good road over the mountains. But the wagons were constantly stopping to repair the harness or rest the teams, and so the party did not reach San Juan del Sur on the Pacific until ten o'clock at night. They then had to go to a primitive hotel where the sleeping apartments consisted of one large room with partitions of cotton cloth and deal bunks with canvas bottoms instead of bedsteads.

The town was picturesquely situated on some high cliffs overlooking an indentation in the coast which hardly deserved to be called a harbor, as it would afford little protection from a westerly storm. Here the Farraguts impatiently waited until September 2, when a gun was heard in the offing and the San Francisco steamer *Cortez*, commanded by Captain Cropper, appeared as it rounded the northern headland. After a voyage of twelve days, they arrived in San Francisco.[6]

On the 16th of September, Farragut took official command of Mare Island and warned all squatters to remove from it.[7] The site for this navy yard on the Pacific Coast had been chosen by a commission of three naval officers. Mare Island, which they had selected, is situated in San Pablo Bay, about thirty miles from San Francisco by the inland route. The island, almost a peninsula as it is connected with the mainland by an immense marsh, is three miles long and only half a mile wide.

On the 18th of September the *Warren* arrived and was moored

ESTABLISHES MARE ISLAND NAVY YARD

near the proposed site of the new yard. This sailing vessel, which was then the receiving ship at San Francisco, was placed at the disposal of Farragut by the Navy Department to be used as living quarters by him and his family.[8] The captain's cabin was extended to the mainmast, and here the family lived very comfortably for six or seven months. Then they moved ashore to a small cottage where they lived for some two years until the Commandant's house was finished.

It was the 28th of October when the first work on the yard began with the digging of the foundation for the Carpenter's Shop. Not until the 26th of December was the foundation of the Blacksmith Shop commenced.[9] On the 27th of April, 1855, the cornerstone of this first permanent building erected in the Navy Yard was laid with appropriate ceremonies, during which Farragut made a short speech on the importance of the new yard to California and the country at large. There was at that time no place on the Pacific coast where cruisers could be repaired or properly supplied.[10] The construction of the Blacksmith Shop took about a year, being finished near the 15th of December, 1855. The Commandant's House was completed the following 7th of March, and the Carpenter's Shop soon thereafter.

Building materials were low in cost, but laborers demanded high wages. The workmen were not permitted to live on the island, and many of them settled in the small town of Vallejo, the nearest point to the island. It had once been the capital of California and was proud of its State House. The boats carrying the workmen back and forth to work made a lively scene each morning and evening. The little old town took on new life, and a boom in real estate began on a small scale. Farragut took advantage of this and invested some of his savings in town lots from which his family profited in later years. It was in this small town that he joined the Masonic Lodge.

Farragut threw himself into his work with his usual energy. No detail was too small for his notice, as his extensive correspondence with the Secretary of the Navy clearly shows. He established very cordial relations with the workmen and made them feel that they could approach him with their complaints and would receive justice without respect to person. He had the confidence of all his subordinates, who enjoyed his generous and unconventional hospitality.[11] Farragut's energy and cordiality were increased, no doubt, by the remarkable improvement in his health, which was in a very low state when he arrived in California. The many years of service in tropical countries, and the attacks of yellow fever and cholera had practically made an invalid of him; but the change to an invigorating climate and frequent exercise on horseback restored him to health.

On the 8th of October, 1855, Farragut was commissioned captain to date from the 14th of the preceding September.[12] The satisfaction which he felt at this promotion was somewhat spoiled by hearing that his brother, Willam A. C. Farragut, was among the forty-nine officers which the famous "Retiring Board" recommended to be dropped from the navy. Though he had been in the service longer than his brother Glasgow, he had never risen above the rank of lieutenant. "That he has not rendered equivalent service for his pay is most true," Farragut wrote[13] to the Secretary of the Navy, "but that he is one of those 'whose disability has been produced by his own misconduct or indiscretion' is *not* true—and all I ask is that he should have been placed on the Furlough list or given a pension. His disease was contracted in the hardest service I have ever engaged in, 'Boat service in the Gulf of Mexico.' I served two years there during which time I never knew the luxury of a Bed, but always slept in my own coat on the Deck or elsewhere, when the time arrived for such indulgence. The consequence was, that I took the Yellow Fever but my Brother took the Rheumatism. I recovered but he never did; since then he has spent more than half his life in Bed, sometimes he walks on crutches. He is, and always has been, a sober and moral man. I am aware that not an Officer on the Board ever saw my Brother; they took their evidence from the Register, which is certainly enough to show that he is worthless to the service. But to drop him from the list is to throw him on the cold charity of the world and his relations for the support of his family, as his infirmities render him helpless. I beg to refer you to Commodore Rousseau for the truth of my statement in relation to the above facts. If it is possible for you to do anything in his case consistent with your duty and sense of justice, I trust it will be done." This sincere, straightforward letter probably had much to do with the placing of Lieutenant William A. C. Farragut's name on the "Reserved List."[14]

2

Farragut's ordinary activities and duties at the Navy Yard were considerably interfered with during the year 1856 by the conflict between the Vigilance Committee and the Law and Order Party representing the state and municipal officials in San Francisco. Though Farragut had no sympathy for the desperate and lawless characters, whose outrages in the city had caused the organization of the Vigilance Committee, he believed that as a Federal officer he had no right lawfully to interfere in the affairs of a state, even when asked to do so by its Governor to suppress an insurrection, without the authorization of the President of the United States. Without telegraphic communications between Washington and San Francisco, no such authorization could be obtained for the emergency which suddenly developed in the summer of that year.

When, after a clash between the Vigilance Committee and the Law and Order Party, Dr. R. P. Ashe, the Navy Agent, and Judge D. S. Terry, of the Supreme Court of California, were imprisoned by the Vigilantes, Commander E. B. Boutwell, in command of the *John Adams* which happened then to be at San Francisco, wrote a letter to the Committee on June 21.[15] In this he called their attention to the fact that Ashe was a Navy Agent for that station and that his imprisonment would interfere with the performance of his duties as a Federal officer. Soon thereafter Ashe was released. But Judge Terry was still held in their custody, and on the 28th of June Boutwell felt it his duty to write a letter to the Executive Committee of the Vigilantes, requesting that they deal with Judge Terry as a prisoner of war and place him on board the *John Adams*. In conclusion he threatened that it might become necessary for him to use all the power at his command "to save the life of a native-born American citizen, whose only offense is believed to be in his efforts to carry out the law, obey the Governor's proclamation, and defend his own life."[16] This letter was transmitted to Farragut for his information by the Executive Committee, who called his attention to its "extraordinary logic and menacing tone."

Early in June, Boutwell had taken the *John Adams* to the Navy Yard for some slight repairs, and was there when Governor Johnson called on Farragut for assistance in suppressing the "Revolutionary movement" in San Francisco. "Captain Farragut and myself concluded," Boutwell wrote,[15] "that, under the circumstances, authority must be received from the Navy Department before we could act." As no such authorization, in the meantime, had been received, Farragut found it necessary to restrain Boutwell, and accordingly on the 1st of July wrote him that he could not agree that he had any right to interfere. "In all cases within my knowledge," Farragut added,[17] "the Government of the United States has been very careful not to interfere with the domestic troubles of the States, when they were strictly domestic and no collision was made with the laws of the United States, and has always been studious of avoiding, as much as possible, collision with State rights principles."

The same day,[18] Farragut wrote to the Executive Committee of the Vigilantes, in answer to their communication, informing them that he had written to Commander Boutwell on the subject. He called their attention to the fact that they were denying to Judge Terry his rights as plainly guaranteed by the Constitution, and that the Constitution gave the United States government the obligation of guaranteeing to each state a Republican form of government and of protecting it against domestic violence whenever the legislature or the governor (if the legislature was not in session) requested such assistance. Each Federal officer, he declared, had to decide for himself, when so far removed from the seat of government in Washington, what action to take in such an emergency. "But you may be assured, gentlemen," he diplomatically concluded, "that I shall always be ready to pour oil on the troubled waters, rather than do aught to fan the flame of human passions, or add to the chances of the horrors of civil war."

Boutwell wrote to Farragut, the following day,[19] to explain that at the time he wrote to the Vigilance Committee he thought he was under the command of Commodore William Mervine. But as a matter of fact the Commodore, who was in command of the Pacific Squadron, was on the 1st of July at Valparaiso. Boutwell also contended that his attempt to obtain the release was not fundamentally different from Farragut's offer to serve on a committee to settle the controversy between the two factions.

To this letter, Farragut immediately replied the same day[20] in a long letter, going fully into the case and explaining the necessity for restraint. He particularly stressed the impression which Boutwell's letter had made on the Vigilantes that he intended to fire on the city, an action which might have brought injury and possibly death to many innocent people. Farragut assured him that he was still under Commodore Mervine's command, but that he was under his control so long as he remained in those waters. "It is the duty of the superior officer present to act according to the best judgment for the general good," explained Farragut. "He alone is responsible, after an appeal is made to him, and not the junior. That there was ever any disrespect intended by you, never entered my mind. That you are besought by the Government party to blow the town down, I am well aware. But that we should act in our public capacity with unbiased judgment is only called for the louder. The people on both sides are violent, and it therefore becomes us to be cool and temperate."

Farragut, however, made arrangements for carrying out any orders he might receive from the Navy Department to restore order by force of arms. He ordered Boutwell not to sail until he received orders from him to do so. He wrote to Commander Samuel Swartwout at Seattle to bring the *John Hancock* to San Francisco. Also he made sure that the batteries of the *Warren* and the *Decatur*, which was then at the Navy Yard, were in good order and that both vessels had plenty of ammunition. These latter preparations were made particularly for the protection òf four million dollars in gold at the Navy Yard if it became necessary to move the money there from the Branch Mint at San Francisco in the *John Adams*. At the request of Judge McAllister of the Circuit Court of the United States, Farragut gave orders to Commander Boutwell to assist the United States Marshal in executing a writ of *habeas corpus* for the person of Judge Terry, if it became necessary to effect his release in that way.[21]

All these preparations had much to do with influencing the Vigilantes to vote to release Judge Terry on the 7th of August, for they did not know just what action might be taken against them. After his liberation, the Judge went for safety on board the *John Adams* from which he was transferred to the Sacramento steamer. The Vigilantes, a few days afterwards, demobilized their armed forces, and in a month or so normal conditions were reestablished.

Farragut was gratified to receive from the Secretary of the Navy, about the 1st of September, a letter which fully approved his conduct during the past trying weeks.[22] Commander Boutwell's prompt action demanding the release of the Navy Agent was approved. "The spirit manifested by you in regard to the release of Judge Terry was generous, and, no doubt, originated in patriotic motives. You could not, however, properly have resorted to force in his behalf," declared the Secretary.[23] Farragut's stand in this matter was also thus vindicated. Other letters of approval[24] from the Secretary were received by Farragut. "It is all an officer has a right to hope for under such circumstances, and I deem it of the first importance that an officer should discipline himself to do his duty to the Government irrespective of his own feelings, for in civil dissensions it is impossible to satisfy either party,"[25] concluded Farragut.

3

Meanwhile work had been continued at the Navy Yard, and about the 22d of September, 1856, the basin and railway were ready for testing, when the *Warren* was taken up for that purpose. After that it was not an unusual thing to see one of the celebrated clipper ships, which became famous for their quick voyages around the Horn, in Farragut's new dock. The *Flying Cloud* and the *Flying Fish* were among the many which received repairs there.

When the *Susquehanna,* one of the ships of Perry's famous expedition to Japan, stopped at San Francisco in 1854, on the return voyage, she did not come up to Mare Island; but Farragut made an official call on board the vessel at Benecia. She was then commanded by Commander Franklin Buchanan, who in the Civil War was to command the Confederate naval forces which fought Farragut in the Battle of Mobile Bay. Loyall Farragut accompanied his father on his official visit, and was struck with the excellent appearance of Buchanan's ship whose decks were as white as snow and whose brass work shone like gold. The next year the ships of John Rodgers' scientific expedition came up to the yard.

The year after Farragut had finished his new dock, he was much gratified to have a visit from the Russian ship *Dwina* which had to have her bottom looked at and some repairs made. The ship was on her voyage home after an absence of five years. Captain Butakoff was highly pleased with the facilities afforded him, and on his departure he saluted the American flag with thirteen guns, which the *Warren* returned.[26]

Several months later another foreign ship visited San Francisco. This was the French frigate *Persevante,* flagship of Rear Admiral Lugeol. Farragut made the usual official call on the admiral, which was returned at the Navy Yard, where all the honors due his rank were accorded the admiral. He was astonished, he declared, at the energy of a people displayed in so short a time, in constructing a work so essential in the development of the commerce of the Pacific.[27]

Farragut recorded nothing else out of the ordinary as having happened at the Navy Yard during the remainder of his command. Not long before his detachment, he and his son made a very enjoyable trip through Calaveras County, Mrs. Farragut having returned home to Norfolk on account of the serious illness of her father.

On the 19th of May, 1858,[28] Farragut wrote the Secretary that he was ready for sea service whenever the Department saw fit to order him to that duty. "We have built a Navy Yard," he proudly declared, "capable of performing with its appliances the repairs required of any yard in the East; and it would have been my proudest feeling to build a ship of war of the native woods that can be collected in our immediate vicinity before my departure; but as that is out of the question now for me to do, I hope it will be done before long by some other commandant." He apparently realized that it was time for his tour of duty to come to an end, and before his letter could have reached the Secretary, orders for his detachment were dispatched on the 29th of May. These orders were received by Farragut on July 3; but Captain R. B. Cunningham did not arrive to relieve him until two weeks later.[29] On the 20th of August Farragut and his son embarked on the mail steamer *Golden Age* for the Isthmus of Panama; this they crossed and then took the steamer *George Law* for New York.

Here they were met by Mrs. Farragut. It was a happy reunion. While they were in New York, they saw the parade celebrating the successful laying of the Atlantic cable. Cyrus W. Field, and Captain Hudson and his officers of the *Niagara*, who laid the cable in the western half of the Atlantic, were the lions of the hour. They rode up Broadway in barouches drawn by handsome horses, and were applauded by the citizens who thronged the streets.

Farragut had returned after completing a difficult duty with distinction. This had been the first real opportunity he had been afforded to show that he was an officer above the ordinary. He had made such a favorable impression on Commodore Joseph Smith, Chief of the Bureau of Yards and Docks, that some years later when an officer was to be chosen to command the expedition against New Orleans it was Smith who assured the Secretary of the Navy that Farragut was the officer above all others for that important command.

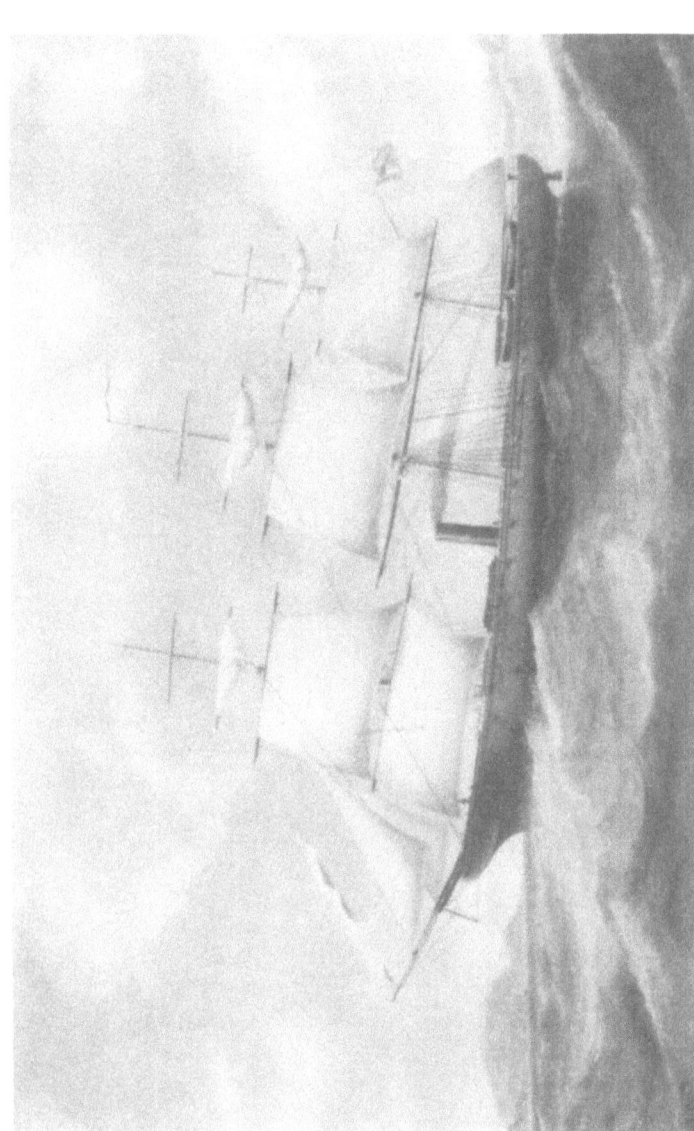

THE STEAM SLOOP-OF-WAR *Brooklyn*

From a painting in the Officers' Club, United States Naval Academy, presented by Jacob Westervelt Clark of New York in the name of his grandfather, Jacob Aaron Westervelt, the builder of the *Brooklyn*.

XXVII

COMMANDS THE STEAM SLOOP-OF-WAR *BROOKLYN*

1

AFTER THE Farraguts arrived in New York, they went up to Poughkeepsie[1] where they remained several weeks. But by the 11th of December[2] they were back home again in Norfolk after an absence of more than four years. Young Loyall was then a lad of fourteen, who had traveled extensively but very little compared to the miles his father had covered by the time he had reached that age. They returned to a city which had been decimated by the yellow fever three years before, when two-thirds of the whites and one-third of the whites and blacks together had died of the disease.[3] They came back to a town seething with political discussion. Predominantly Whig in politics, in 1848 its citizens had celebrated the election of General Zachary Taylor as President with a grand display of fireworks and a torch-light procession. But with the successive elections of two Democrats, Pierce and Buchanan, to the Presidency, the Whig party was practically dead and new political alignments had to be made. For four years the Farraguts had been out of touch with the discordant state of affairs, the continued troubles in Kansas, the fury aroused in the North over the Dred Scott Decision, and the Panic of 1857 which was caused by the discovery of gold in California. But they soon found themselves engulfed in the whirlpool of political strife which was threatening the very foundations of the national government.

Farragut also returned to Norfolk a captain, then the highest rank in the naval service. There were thirty-eight captains ahead of him on the list of eighty-one; but in the last few years he had made rapid strides towards the top. Changes had been made in the regulations for uniforms in 1852, changes more marked than those of 1841. The full dress coat was of blue cloth, lined with white silk serge, and was double-breasted with nine navy buttons in each of two rows on the breast. The skirts of the coat were more distinctly cutaway than previously; the standing collar sloped upwards and backwards as before, but it had a strip of gold lace an inch and a half wide around the top and down the front and lace one-half an inch wide around the bottom instead of being plain as before; and around each sleeve to indicate the rank were three stripes of gold lace three-quarters of an inch wide and separated by a space of half an inch from each other, this being a distinctly new addition. The blue pantaloons were made loose to be worn over boots or shoes. Those made for captains had a stripe of gold lace down the outer seams, an inch and a half wide. White pantaloons were to be worn in the tropics and during the summer in northern waters. The vest was white and single-breasted with a standing collar, and was not to show below the coat. Black cocked hats, bound with black silk lace and decorated with a black silk cockade, a tassel of gold and blue bullions, and a loop of gold bullions, were always worn with the full dress. Captains wore two epaulets of gold on which were embroidered in silver the design of the eagle and anchor and a star. Farragut's sword was the cut and thrust blade with a half-basket hilt and white grip; his scabbard was of black leather with yellow mountings. The sword-belt of black glazed leather was worn over the coat. The cravat, or stock of black silk or satin was not tied in front in the full dress as the collar fitted tightly over it.

Even greater changes were made in the undress uniform. The coat was a frock-coat, or Prince Albert, as the style came to be called. It was lined with black silk serge and was double-breasted with nine buttons in each of the two rows. As in full dress, there was a button behind on each hip and one near the bottom of each fold, and the same indication of Farragut's rank of captain on the sleeves and in the epaulets. The pantaloons were the same as for full dress except that there were no stripes of gold lace down the seams. The vest could be either white or blue to match the pantaloons. A cocked hat could be worn, or a cap of blue cloth with a patent-leather visor. Farragut's cap had a band of gold lace around it and on the front was the design of the eagle and anchor embroidered in silver and surrounded by a gold embroidered wreath of oak and olive leaves. When the epaulets were not worn with the undress, Farragut wore shoulder-straps of blue cloth, bordered with an embroidery of gold in which was the eagle-anchor design in silver. The sword and belt were worn as in full dress.

A third uniform, called service dress, had the rolling collar and other features of undress, except that caps instead of cocked hats were worn with it. Swords and epaulets could be worn with it, if the officer wished to do so. Double-breasted jackets of blue cloth or white drill, with rolling collar and the required number of buttons, could be worn as service dress when at sea, except at general muster or when in charge of the deck. Shoulder-straps instead of epaulets were always to be worn with the jackets. In summer or in tropical climates white straw hats could be worn on shipboard.[4]

Farragut was not to remain in Norfolk unemployed, for on the 9th of December[5] the Secretary of the Navy ordered him to report to Commodore S. F. Breese at the New York Navy Yard and there take command of the steamer *Brooklyn* on New Year's Day, 1859. He was thus enabled to spend at least a part of the Christmas season with his family and their relatives and friends in Norfolk.

2

The command of the *Brooklyn* was to be an entirely new and different experience for Farragut. It was, moreover, an honor to have been selected for such a command. The *Brooklyn* was the first of the five[6] new screw sloops-of-war, authorized by Congress in 1857, to be gotten ready for service. They were to be the most powerful ships in the United States Navy, and it was peculiarly fortunate for Farragut to have command of the first one and thus become familiar with the new type of man-of-war, for early in the Civil War these vessels and others like them were to become the backbone of the fleet with which he won remarkable victories. Though there had been steam war vessels in the navy for several years, Farragut had not had the privilege of serving in one previously except in the crude little steamer in Porter's Mosquito Fleet for a short time in 1823.

When Farragut first walked on board the *Brooklyn*, it was as though he were stepping into a new age, the age of steam. Though called a sloop and rigged to carry sails as an auxiliary motive power, the *Brooklyn* was a larger vessel than the average ship of the line of the age of sail. She was 233 feet in length and 43 feet in beam, and had a displacement tonnage of 2,686. Her battery consisted of twenty-two 9-inch Dahlgren shell guns, and one heavy 12-pounder and one light 12-pounder. Strangely new to Farragut was the telescopic smokestack, which was seven feet in diameter and extended some fifty feet above the grate bars. It was connected with the two vertical boilers, designed by Chief Engineer Daniel B. Martin, which furnished power for two direct-acting, horizontal, condensing, cross-head engines. Her screw propeller was fourteen and a half feet in diameter, and developed a maximum speed of eleven knots, though the average was only about seven knots. The fuel was anthracite coal.[7] The engines were in charge of Chief Engineer Joshua Follansbee and seven assistant engineers. Farragut's other officers were five lieutenants, a surgeon and two assistant surgeons, a purser, and a marine officer.[8]

Farragut had some correspondence with the Secretary of the Navy and with Commander Matthew Fontaine Maury, early in January, concerning the trial of an instrument for ascertaining deep sea temperatures, which had been sent to the Observatory by the Dutch Society for the promotion of physical researches.[9] But it was not until the 26th of January, at one o'clock in the afternoon, that Farragut took official command of the *Brooklyn*.[10] Ten days later he sailed from New York[11] on a trial run to Beaufort, South Carolina. Farragut steamed out of port, but when at sea he hoisted his sails also. It was a strange sight to the old tars to see a ship under full sail with smoke pouring out of her smokestack, as she bowled along on her course. Many a curse was leveled at this newfangled contraption which fouled the decks and the sails with its smoke and cinders. Still they were forced to approve of the ease with which they moved out of the harbor and out to sea, no longer a slave to the wind.

After a run of six days,[12] the *Brooklyn* arrived off Beaufort, and Farragut reported to the Secretary that the vessel had performed to his "perfect satisfaction."[12] He had made "ten knots and more," presumably under steam power alone. But the propeller had occasionally made a thumping noise; this was the only fault he had thus far found with the ship. The *Brooklyn*, which was the first of its size to enter those waters, remained for about a week off Beaufort, whose citizens treated Farragut and his officers and men with warm Southern hospitality and made their visit very agreeable. Farragut then sailed[13] with papers from the State Department for Port au Prince and Aux Cayes where he was to communicate with American commercial agents in Hayti.

Arriving at Port au Prince, after a voyage of just a week, Farragut was informed by Consul Lewis that the country was quite tranquil after the successful revolution which had been effected without bloodshed. President Geffrard had succeeded Emperor Saluke,[14] who had fled to Jamaica in an English storeship. A few days later, Farragut with some of his officers made an official call on the new president. Finding that the people considered the revolution as a blessing and were pleased with President Geffrard as one who would end the oppression of the former Emperor and as a man of mixed blood would bring to a close the war of color, Farragut concluded that the revolution would be comparatively permanent and sailed for Aspinwall, Panama.[15]

After watering in the great harbor of Porto Bello, made forever famous by Sir Francis Drake, the *Brooklyn* proceeded to Vera Cruz, where she arrived about the first of April.[16] Here Farragut wrote the Secretary a long report on the three months' cruise of the *Brooklyn*, which was by no means so favorable as the short report he had sent from Beaufort. He made numerous suggestions as to changes and improvements throughout the vessel.[17] At that time, conditions in Mexico were very much unsettled. In Vera Cruz, the legal president, Benito Juarez, leader of the liberal Constitutional Party, had his headquarters; while in Mexico City was the head of the Clerical Party, General Miramon, who had established himself by force of arms as the successor to the presidency. The United States recognized the government of Juarez and despatched to Vera Cruz Robert M. McLane as minister. Farragut was instructed to place the *Brooklyn* at the disposal of Minister McLane so that he might keep in touch with events in the civil war then in progress and with the American consuls who were trying to protect the interests of American citizens in Mexico. Through his knowledge of the character of the Mexican people which he had gained through many years of service on that coast and through his ability to speak the Spanish language, Farragut was of great assistance to McLane, with whom he enjoyed most cordial relations.[18]

In June, McLane sent Farragut in company with representatives of other nations to present an official letter from him to General Robles of the Miramon party, who was in command of the operations against Vera Cruz, and whose camp was then about thirty miles distant from the city. He had illegally held up the transport of specie from Mexico City under *conducta* to prominent business men in Vera Cruz. Robles had the good sense to listen to reason and the money was released. Farragut's contribution to the successful negotiations was so noteworthy that he received a very cordial letter of thanks from four American citizens whose property had thus been placed in "imminent danger."[19] To this Farragut gracefully but modestly replied that he thanked them for their appreciation of "the small service" which he had rendered in "the line of duty, carrying out the wishes of the U. S. Minister." "Had there been a necessity for further action," he added,[20] "I trust that the Navy would not have been found indifferent either to the call of their countrymen or that of humanity, from any quarter."

Later in the month of June, Farragut wrote[21] the Secretary that he had taken Minister McLane on board the *Brooklyn* and had tried to make him comfortable, but that, since the rainy season had set in, McLane had been compelled to go ashore to reside. Farragut then took occasion to criticize the *Brooklyn* very severely. "The word comfort," he declared, "does not apply to my appartment (sic). It has never been dry since I left New York; it is too dark to write in without candles, and then in this climate the heat is beyond endurance. It is the first time in my life that I ever complained of my accommodations. I have commanded vessels from 45 tons and have never known anything like the discomfort I am now subjected to in a ship of 2,000 tons." He further informed the Secretary that by the 25th of July he would be compelled to go to Pensacola for coal and provisions, but that he would be absent from his station no longer than was necessary to make the trip north under sail and to return under sail and steam.

On the 15th of July Farragut reported to the Secretary by telegraph[22] that the *Brooklyn* had just arrived in Pensacola. There she remained for several days[23] before returning to Vera Cruz, but on the 7th of September[24] she was back again in Pensacola. A week later[25] the ship was ordered to the Brooklyn Navy Yard where she arrived on the 26th of September.[26]

3

While Farragut was in New York, two very unpleasant experiences were forced upon him. The first was a quarrel with one of his officers, Lieutenant W. N. Jeffers. Because of the controversial nature of this episode, which has not hitherto been published, rather copious quotations will be made from the correspondence. The opening gun was fired by Lieutenant Jeffers, who wrote to the Secretary of the Navy on the 2nd of November:[27] "Considering myself outraged by a most arbitrary and unjust act of Captain D. G. Farragut, I appeal to you for relief. On Monday evening, the 31st ult., on returning from shore, I was informed by the Executive Officer of the ship that he had been directed to order me not to leave the ship except by special permission of the Captain. Not being informed of any reason for this invidious distinction, I the next morning appealed to the Commandant of the station; directly after the receipt of this communication Captain Farragut sent for me and in the most excited manner informed me that he 'would not permit me to treat him with contempt by passing him on shore without saluting him,' and after some further conversation ordered me 'to go below and consider myself suspended from duty.' His personal peculiarities, arising from a very nervous and excitable temperament, I can easily overlook; but, Sir, the suspension from duty was from injustice. I did meet Captain Farragut on shore, *but he was not in uniform as I am prepared to prove.* Furthermore, I was in citizen's dress—gray coat, slouched hat on, and I am not aware that there is any law or usage requiring an officer to recognize another officer when out of uniform or authorizing a senior to thrust his acquaintance upon an unwilling junior. Military rank gives no social standing; and since Captain Farragut some time ago, unprovoked, grossly insulted me in the most ill bred manner I have never spoken to him or permitted him to speak to me except upon duty. I therefore submit to the Honorable, the Secretary of the Navy whether an officer of nearly twenty years' service shall be arbitrarily punished by his commanding officer, or as an alternative forced to associate with him."

As much more serious trouble soon followed, Farragut had no time to answer Jeffers' letter, which was forwarded to him by the Secretary, until the 21st of November. He was then at sea in the *Brooklyn* off Vera Cruz. Inclosed were the two charges which he had preferred against Lieutenant Jeffers: "Treating with contempt his superior officer", "Failure to salute him or recognize him as his commanding officer two or three times", and "Scandalous conduct tending to the destruction of good morals." On the occasion in question, Farragut declared, "I was dressed in my undress uniform, with an overcoat on, which was also uniform except that I had not the straps on the shoulders, which I had forgotten were required to be on the overcoat." He furthermore affirmed that the complaints which Jeffers had written to Flag Officer Samuel L. Breese and to the Secretary to the effect that he had "treated him in a tyrannical manner, had insulted him without provocation, and that he had in consequence thereof never allowed the said Captain Farragut to speak to him from that time"—all were "utterly false."

Two days afterwards, Jeffers wrote the Secretary that he had received a copy of the charges preferred against him by Farragut, and that he was ready for a court-martial if the Secretary thought such a procedure would "advance the interests or vindicate the discipline of the service." He declared that he was prepared to show that the charges, "if not false, at least were frivolous and vexatious." In conclusion, he wrote, "I respectfully request that I may be detached from the *Brooklyn* and ordered to any other ship of the squadron."

It took several weeks for this letter to be forwarded to Farragut by the Secretary, and it was not until the 22nd of January, 1860, that Farragut, still off Vera Cruz, wrote the Secretary, ". . . As much as I desire to get rid of Lieutenant Jeffers, I have no disposition to do an injustice to others, and Commander Turner[28] anticipates nothing less than the destruction of the harmony of a most happy ship by the exchange. I shall therefore await your further instructions on the subject."

So the case rested for several weeks, when on the 25th of April Jeffers wrote Farragut: "Several months having elapsed since the commencement of what I confess was on my part an angry correspondence, and being now convinced that it arose from a mutual misconception: first, on my part, of the original cause of the quarrel and secondly on yours of what you considered an intentional official disrespect which I hereby entirely disclaim, I therefore take leave to propose that a joint application be made to the Honorable Secretary of the Navy for the withdrawal of this correspondence from the files of the Department. Whether you accede to this proposition or not, I freely admit that my letter of November 2, 1859, to the Honorable Secretary of the Navy was written under the influence of excitement caused by what I thought at the time an injustice and that I regret its angry tenor."

Farragut naturally accepted this proposal, and inclosed Jeffers' letter with one he sent to the Secretary on the 27th of April, in which he wrote: "... As I have never had any disposition to injure Lieutenant Jeffers beyond what I considered due to the service for his unaccountable conduct to me, for which he now after a long lapse of time expresses his regrets both verbally and by letter, if it meets your approbation I will be glad to withdraw the letters which accompanied those of Lieutenant Jeffers, at the same time that his are withdrawn, also the charges consequent upon those letters." The episode was then brought to a close by a letter of May 16 from the Secretary to Farragut, stating in part: "... As the letters which Lieutenant Jeffers and yourself mutually request permission to withdraw have become a part of the Department, your request cannot be complied with. No action, however, will be taken on the matter of the complaint."

4

A much more serious incident happened not long after the commencement of the Jeffers affair. This other "melancholy affair"[29] began on the *Brooklyn* on the 7th of November, the day the ship was to have sailed from New York with Minister McLane and his family on board. Apparently the *Brooklyn* had been ordered to New York to take McLane back to his post in Mexico. While the vessel was lying off Staten Island, where she had been detained by a slight accident to her machinery, several of the crew became intoxicated with liquor which had been smuggled on board. The crew consisted at that time of 267 sailors and 46 marines.[30] George Ritter, a seaman who had been locked up for drunkenness, became so abusive and noisy that a corporal of marines, named Charles Cooper, placed a wooden gag in his mouth. The Officer of the Deck had ordered him to be gagged, according to Farragut,[31] who declared that the man had not only been drunk but was fighting and, when the corporal tried to take him in custody, he resisted and was very difficult to manage. Either as a consequence of the gag or from the effects of the intoxication Ritter died, and the crew were greatly aroused as they thought he had been too roughly treated. Farragut, who was at the time having tea with McLane in his cabin, heard the sound of angry voices and the trampling of feet on deck. Realizing that something was seriously wrong, he seized a cutlass and ran to the mainmast where he confronted the angry sailors, some of whom in the darkness where they could not be identified shouted for the "murderer" to be handed over to them. The marines and other officers having by that time joined Farragut, he told the men that the case would be fully investigated and justice administered. The crew thereupon dispersed quietly.

Farragut then sent for Coroner Heslewood to come aboard and make an investigation. He assisted the coroner's jury in making their inquest which lasted most of the night, and at their request sent the body of Ritter ashore for further examination. Fearing that some violence might be done Corporal Cooper by the crew, Farragut sent him early in the morning with an explanatory letter to the Commandant of the Brooklyn Navy Yard[32] whom he requested to protect the man and hold him until he should be demanded by the authorities of the civil law. But as soon as Cooper was put ashore at the Ferry Company's dock from the captain's gig, he was arrested by the quarantine police, who were under the impression that he was trying to escape to New York, and he was placed in jail on Staten Island.

The coroner then summoned Farragut to send ashore as witnesses for further investigation some of the seamen who were prisoners on board the ship. Farragut replied that these men were under confinement for various offenses, and that, if the jury considered their testimony necessary, they could be removed from the ship only through *habeas corpus* proceedings. Having made these arrangements and believing that "further delay might prove injurious to the public interests,"[33] Farragut put to sea the same morning, of the 8th of November, and proceeded with Minister McLane to Vera Cruz.

When the *Brooklyn* had departed, the coroner announced a verdict that the "deceased came to his death by violence at the hands of Charles Cooper,"[34] and the jury passed a resolution which declared that Farragut's action in refusing to send the witnesses ashore was "entitled not only to the censure but the contempt of all American citizens."³⁵

5

On the run down to Vera Cruz, Farragut discovered that one of the crew named Williams had been inciting the seamen to mutiny by writing doggerel verse about their wrongs. He was placed in confinement, and there was no more trouble on that score. After stopping two days at Key West to coal ship, the *Brooklyn* arrived at Vera Cruz on the 21st of November. Remaining here until the McLane-Juarez treaty was concluded on the 12th of December, Farragut sailed with the treaty and dispatches for the State Department and arrived at New Orleans on the 18th.

It so happened that his brother, William A. C. Farragut, was then at the point of death. Captain Farragut, unaware of the true situation, did not hurry to his brother's bedside on his arrival and when he visited his home the following day, he found that he was dead.³⁶ They had not seen each other for many years, and it was peculiarly unfortunate that they should have thus been deprived of this last meeting. The only consolation which the younger brother felt was that he could be of some service to the bereaved family in their hour of great need.

On the day before Christmas, the *Brooklyn* departed for Mexican waters again. After the ship had been at Vera Cruz about three weeks, Minister McLane was ordered to return to Washington to explain the treaty which was meeting with much opposition in the Senate. Boarding the *Brooklyn*, McLane instructed Farragut to land a force at Tampico, on the way north, to protect the consulate and American citizens, as an attack was being threatened on the place by the forces of General Miramon. Farragut accordingly left a boat there, fully equipped with a boat gun and small arms and twenty-two sailors and marines. Perhaps not strangely, he selected Lieutenant Jeffers to command this landing party.³⁷ When Farragut arrived at the mouth of the Mississippi, he found the channel blocked with vessels which had recently gone aground. After trying in vain to get through Southwest Pass, the *Brooklyn* successfully entered through Pass à l'Outre (now called North Pass), and landed Minister McLane. The ship then proceeded to Pensacola, where she arrived on the 29th of January.[38]

Mrs. Farragut was on hand there to greet her husband and her son Loyall, who had been cruising with his father in the *Brooklyn* since she sailed from New York on the preceding 8th of November. At Pensacola, Farragut busied himself with taking on supplies and making repairs in order that he might be ready to take McLane back to his post in Mexico. But Farragut was soon to learn that he was not through with the Ritter affair.

Meanwhile Mrs. Farragut and Loyall went to Pascagoula where they made a visit of three months with Farragut's sister, Mrs. Gurlie. She lived in a house picturesquely situated on the river, and entertained them with her customary generosity. Like her brother Glasgow, she was full of energy and vivacity and had many of the attributes of a born leader. Her neighbors had great respect for her and came to her for advice and help in emergencies. At West Pascagoula was the grave of George Farragut, and the site of his old home, nothing of which then remained but the foundation, overgrown with weeds.

6

After Corporal Cooper had been in jail for several days, he was released by United States District Judge Samuel R. Betts, before whom he was brought on a writ of *habeas corpus*, as no witnesses appeared against him. Cooper was immediately taken into custody by an officer of the navy under direction of Commandant Breese of the Navy Yard and placed in confinement on the *North Carolina*, the station ship.[39] Here he remained until about the middle of January when he was again turned over to the civil authorities who again placed him in the Richmond County jail on Staten Island. On the 25th of January, District Attorney Winant wrote the Secretary of the Navy requesting that the witnesses be produced before the grand jury which would be convened on the third Tuesday in the following February. In reply, Secretary Toucey requested[40] the names of the witnesses, which Winant sent on the 1st of February. Not hearing anything further, Winant wrote again, three weeks later, stating that the grand jury was in session and inquiring as to the prospects of obtaining the attendance of the witnesses.

Meanwhile Toucey had ordered Farragut to take the *Brooklyn* to New York, and he had sailed from Pensacola on the 19th of February.[41] Accordingly Toucey wrote Winant on the 23d that the *Brooklyn* was on the way to New York, and that upon her arrival there the presence of the required witnesses could be secured. Not hearing from Toucey by the time Cooper's case came before the grand jury, Winant was forced to discharge Cooper as he could not produce any witnesses. Immediately he wisely disappeared from Staten Island and parts thereunto adjacent.

Four days later, the *Brooklyn* arrived in New York on the 27th of February, and the same day Farragut wrote Winant that "such witnesses as may be required from the crew in the case of George Ritter are subject to any legal demand that may be made for them, and those whom you may deem necessary will be forthwith discharged from the naval service and forwarded to you."[42]

The trial began on the 1st of March. Cooper, for whose rearrest a warrant had been issued, could not be found; and as it was necessary to have some person to try, Sergeant Edward Ray of the Marines was charged with having been a party to Ritter's death. During the trial Farragut testified that gagging was not allowed on board his vessel without direct orders from him, and that he had never authorized it. Charles Clark, however, testified that he had received, from Captain Farragut and all the Lieutenants except Mitchell, orders to gag a dozen or so men.[43] Evidently a great deal of feeling had been aroused against Farragut among some of the seamen on the *Brooklyn*, and during the trial he was treated by some of the lawyers as though he himself were on trial.[44] At the end of the trial which lasted nine days, Sergeant Ray was committed on a charge of assault and battery with intent to kill, but released on bail.

Captain Farragut and Lieutenant William Mitchell "were held on their own recognizances to appear at the next term of the court in the event of the Grand Jury inculpating them in homicide."[45] As for Ray, while he was in charge of a police officer before he had procured bail, he made his escape, and that ended his case.[46]

No action was taken against Farragut and Mitchell, though Secretary Toucey as an expression of his displeasure ordered Farragut's detachment from the command of the *Brooklyn*.

Reconsidering the matter, however, he telegraphed Commandant Breese on the 8th of March: "Until further advised, retain Captain Farragut's detachment sent by to-night's mail," and on the following day he wrote to Breese to return to him the order detaching Farragut from his command. The same day he telegraphed Breese to direct Captain Farragut to proceed immediately with the *Brooklyn* to Hampton Roads. Farragut certainly had a close shave; detachment under such circumstances would surely have been a black mark on his record, one that he might have found it difficult to overcome in the future.

Mr. Charles O'Conor, who aided Farragut legally, refused a fee, saying, "Sir, it has been such a pleasure for me to defend such a frank man that I will not accept a cent."[47] The case was treated very seriously by the newspapers—particularly the *Evening Post* and the *Tribune*. In the latter paper, then edited by Horace Greeley, there appeared an editorial on March 10, 1860, entitled *Discipline in the Navy*, which was leveled, perhaps, not so much at Farragut as at the Secretary of the Navy and the Democratic administration in Washington, to which Greeley was then violently opposed. "The recent case of homicide on board the steam frigate *Brooklyn*," ran the editorial, "is not one to pass over in silence. We are not—at least north of the Mason and Dixon's Line—a cruel people, but we are rapidly gaining the reputation, whether we deserve it or not, of an indifference to human suffering. The cruelty not unfrequently practised on board of American merchant vessels is frightful. ... It is a safe conclusion that the ship on board which discipline is maintained by manslaughter is officered by men utterly unfit to be trusted with authority over others. We have been accustomed to think that on board our naval vessels such a state of things as disgraces our commercial marine, and has made it a byword abroad could not occur. The character of the officers was supposed to be a sufficient guaranty against cruel treatment of the men, while their number put out of the question any plea of the necessity for unusual severity. This notion, it seems, was not altogether a correct one. The abuses of the merchant service are creeping into the navy, if the state of things on board of the *Brooklyn* are any indication of the general condition of that branch of the service where such abuses are least excusable. As the navy is neither useful nor ornamental, it will lose its hold upon public respect when it ceases to be a school of subordination and discipline. So far as the published evidence before the Staten Island Justices shows, the man Ritter, who was killed on board the *Brooklyn,* was guilty of no worse crime than getting drunk, and using some offensive language toward a superior officer. Both actions are indefensible, and deserving of punishment, though the penalty for the first misdemeanor, we cannot help thinking, would, if applied without respect of person, sometimes find subjects in the ward-rooms and possibly in the cabins of our men-of-war."

The editorial, after reviewing the case of George Ritter in detail, continues, "It seems that the possibility of a fatal result from the use of such an instrument (the gag) is not unknown in the navy, as Captain Farragut of the *Brooklyn* testified that, though gagging is one of the usages of the service, no officer has any authority to give an order for its application, and that no order had emanated from him for its use in this case. Here, then, we have the fact of the death of a man, by a cruel and unusual punishment, and on evidence of such lax discipline in the navy that inferior officers usurp the authority of their superiors, even to the exercise of power over life and death. If the courts of law have jurisdiction here over this case, as one of alleged murder, the Navy Department, it strikes me, have also a duty in regard to it in relation to discipline among its officers."

To this criticism in the newspapers, Farragut replied, "I am at all times ready to answer to the laws of my country for any cruelty, and I feel assured that no one who knows me will believe me guilty of cruelty to anything, least of all to my fellow man. So long as I stand acquitted in my own mind before my Maker, I shall be content, and I feel entire confidence that my countrymen who seek the truth in forming a judgment will protect me with their respect and good will."[48]

7

As soon as possible, Farragut sailed from New York, though a high wind was blowing. "I would sooner go to sea in a gale," he wrote,[49] "than encounter any more annoyances from the civil authorities." When the *Brooklyn* arrived off the Hook, there was no boat to take the pilot off; so Farragut took him on to Norfolk, where he arrived early in the afternoon of the 12th after a run of only 28 hours. Through an oversight in reading his orders, Farragut went on to Norfolk instead of stopping at Hampton Roads, and was prevented from returning immediately to the Roads by a heavy snow storm.[50] The Secretary wrote Farragut his disapproval of this act as well as of his taking the *Brooklyn* up to the Battery before sailing from New York, both of which acts he declared were "in direct violation of orders."[51] By that time poor Farragut must have felt that all the cards were against him.

A few days afterwards the *Brooklyn* sailed, with Minister McLane on board, for Vera Cruz once again, where she arrived on the 28th of March.[52] There Farragut learned that the siege of Vera Cruz had been raised and that General Miramon was in retreat. He was also informed that Lieutenant Jeffers and his men had returned from Tampico. The men returned on the British gunboat *Jasper*, but Jeffers, ill of rheumatism, had been delayed and did not arrive until the 24th of April[53] on a coasting brig. He had then been transferred to the *Saratoga*. While off Vera Cruz, Farragut, worn out by his recent annoyances, was attacked by a fever "from which he barely recovered."[54]

In May and June, Farragut conveyed McLane in the *Brook-*

lyn to visit Merida, Campeche, and other places. After returning to Vera Cruz from Campeche, Farragut declared, "I can't help loving my profession, but it has materially changed since the advent of steam. I took as much pleasure in running into this port the other day in a gale of wind as ever a boy did in any feat of skill. The people seemed astonished. McLane said he would sooner have done it than anything else—except to take a ship."[55] Farragut established very intimate and pleasant relations with McLane, and placed himself entirely under his orders. When he was afterwards criticized for being under the authority of a civilian, Farragut answered: "I can only say that I am always at the service of the country in doing my duty, and would rather be subject to the directions of an intelligent man, appointed by the Government for a purpose on account of his qualifications than to be under some old fool who has floated up to his position without the first requisites, the only merit that he possesses being that he had been in the navy all his life without having done anything to recommend him either to the Government or to his brother officers."[55]

After the *Brooklyn* had returned to Norfolk near the first of August, the Secretary ordered[56] Farragut to be in readiness to convey the members of a scientific expedition, which the government was sending to explore a route across the Isthmus of Chiriqui, to their base on the Gulf of Mexico. Lieutenant Jeffers was the hydrographer of the expedition, which was to be under the command of Captain Frederick Engle, who was junior to Farragut. A senior officer would thus be compelled by the orders of a junior to take the *Brooklyn* wherever the latter desired. Whether this was merely an error on the part of the Secretary of the Navy or possibly arranged to punish Farragut for recent annoyances he had caused the Secretary cannot now be proved.[57] Farragut had very friendly feelings for Engle, whom he had known for a long time; but he did not think it was proper for him to overlook the embarrassing situation and wrote a letter of protest to the Secretary.[58]

Not wishing to delay the sailing of the *Brooklyn*, which had been provisioned at the Norfolk Navy Yard and had then dropped down to Hampton Roads to receive the personnel and equipment of the expedition, Farragut proceeded to sea on the 13th of August,[59] and arrived eleven days[60] later at Chiriqui, Boca del Toro, Panama. With the exception of a trip across to Aspinwall (now called Colon) between the 12th and 17th of September, the *Brooklyn* remained at the base at Boca del Toro until the middle of October when she returned to Aspinwall. Arriving here, Captain Farragut, on the 20th of October,[60] turned over the command of the *Brooklyn* to Captain W. S. Walker, whom the Secretary had ordered to relieve him. "It affords me pleasure," wrote[60] Engle to the Secretary, "to say to you that Capt. Farragut has afforded me every facility for fulfilling my duty with energy and dispatch. He is an able and accomplished seaman, and runs his ship with the ability and confidence of one."

XXVIII

WAITING ORDERS

AFTER giving up the command of the *Brooklyn,* Farragut returned to New York in the steamer *Northern Light,*[1] where he reported himself to the Secretary of the Navy, on the 2nd of November, as "waiting orders." Receiving no reply, he wrote again to the Secretary just a week later, stating that, if the Department had no objections, he wished to go to Norfolk to meet the *Brooklyn* when she arrived at that port, because he had left all his personal belongings on the ship for the accommodation of his successor and the members of the Chiriqui expedition who had lived in the cabin with him. To this the Secretary rather testily replied, ". . . There is no objection to your going to Norfolk or anywhere in the United States providing you comply with the General Order dated 30 January, 1846."[2] Two days later Farragut acknowledged this letter from Poughkeepsie, New York, where he had gone to join his wife who was then residing there in order that Loyall might attend the Dutchess County Academy. In his acknowledgment, Farragut requested to be registered on the books of the purser at the Norfolk Station that he might draw his pay there. The Secretary coldly replied, ". . . You are informed that the Fourth Auditor is the proper officer to whom you must reply as to the transfer of your account."[3]

Farragut soon realized that he would not receive orders for active service from the Secretary, who was apparently displeased not only with the unfortunate incidents connected with his command of the *Brooklyn* but also with his request to be relieved of his command of that vessel. He accordingly returned to Norfolk to wait for a more favorable turn of Fortune's wheel. Meanwhile he would get along as best he could on the annual pay of $3,000, which a captain then drew while he was "waiting orders."

Farragut, of course, was delighted to be able to return to his family, whom he had scarcely seen for the past two years. He arrived a month or so too late to join in celebrating his son's sixteenth birthday. During those two years events had happened which tended to widen the breach between the North and the South. John Brown had made his raid into Virginia to liberate slaves, in October, 1859; had been captured with his men at Harper's Ferry by Colonel Robert E. Lee in command of a company of United States Marines; and had been hanged at Charlestown, Virginia, on the following December 2. After a hard fought Presidential campaign "Honest Old Abe, the Rail-Splitter" defeated the three other candidates who opposed him, receiving a safe majority of the electoral votes though only about 40 per cent of the popular vote. Farragut apparently did not vote, as he was then still in New York state. If he had done so, it is likely that he would have cast his vote for John Bell of Tennessee,[4] the nominee of the Constitutional Union Party, who recognized "no political principle other than the Constitution of the country, the union of the States, and the enforcement of the laws."

More momentous events were soon to follow. South Carolina seceded from the Union on the 20th of December, and by the following February 1, 1861, Mississippi, Florida, Alabama, Georgia, Louisiana, and Texas successively took the same action. Shortly afterwards on February 4 a congress of delegates from these states met at Montgomery, Alabama, and set up a de facto government, called the Confederate States of America. A desperate attempt at conciliation was made under the leadership of Virginia; on that same February 4 a Peace Convention, which delegates from twenty-one states attended, assembled at Washington with ex-President Tyler of Virginia presiding. It was in vain; everything seemed futile in those mad days of February, 1861. Lincoln slipped into Washington incognito, and was inaugurated on March 4, a disagreeable and stormy day, an omen of dark and stormy days soon to follow.

Though Farragut's name in the *Navy Register* was always followed by Tennessee as his native state, for many years he had made his home in Norfolk and looked upon Virginia as his adopted state. Mrs. Farragut was also a Virginian. So during these weeks of dread and dismay, the Farraguts, like other Virginians among whom they lived, hoped and prayed that civil war might be avoided. Virginia's history had been closely joined with that of the union; Virginians had given indispensable aid in winning independence and in framing the Constitution, and five Virginians had been President of the United States. Though there was great disappointment in Norfolk over the election of Lincoln, the majority of the citizens were opposed to secession then; and later, when the election was held on that eventful February 4 to choose delegates for the convention which was to decide whether Virginia was to secede, the Unionist delegate from Norfolk was elected by a majority of two to one. The Farraguts passed through all these hectic days of political discussion and political speeches, and when the Convention met in Richmond they anxiously followed its proceedings.

Through all the mad turmoil of debate and discussion, Farragut steadfastly opposed secession. Though he had close relatives living in Louisiana and Mississippi and most of his wife's relatives, either by blood or marriage, were sympathetic to the South, Farragut could not feel the attachment to Virginia that he might have felt if he had been born in that state. His native state, Tennessee, had not at that time seceded, and besides he had been born in the eastern portion of the state, where the sympathy for the Union was very strong. It should be remembered that he had left both Tennessee and New Orleans when he was a child and had spent so much of his life on shipboard that he could not feel that strong allegiance to any particular state, which was so common in the South; the only allegiance which he felt strongly was for the United States under whose flag and in whose ships he had served since childhood.[5]

It should be remembered also that Farragut was on duty at Charleston when General Scott through a wise combination of diplomacy and force had carried out President Jackson's mandate to preserve the Union when it was threatened by the Nullifiers. He had observed the results of civil war in the Argentine, Uruguay, Brazil, and Mexico, and had watched with disapproval the anarchism attendant on the operations of the Vigilantes in California. So when he met with a group of naval officers and citizens, which gathered at a store in Norfolk to discuss the daily events, particularly the news from the convention in Richmond, he tried to point out to them the horrors of civil war towards which the country seemed to be drifting. For this he was called a "croaker" and ridiculed.

There were many naval officers then in Norfolk and its vicinity. A large number were on duty at the Navy Yard just across the Elizabeth River; there were others who resided in Norfolk and were then at home waiting orders. There was hardly an old family in the town who did not have a son in the naval service or a daughter married to a naval officer. Most of the officers then stationed at the Navy Yard were Southern in their sympathies. Commanders Robert G. Robb, Thomas R. Rootes, and Richard L. Page, Lieutenants Charles F. M. Spotswood, William Sharp, George T. Sinclair, and Carter B. Poindexter, and Surgeon R. F. Mason were all Virginians. Commander Frederick Chatard and Lieutenants Alexander A. Semmes and Edward Donaldson were from Maryland. Though born in the District of Columbia, Commander John R. Tucker was really a Virginian. Among those who were in Norfolk at that time were Surgeon James Cornick and Commander Arthur Sinclair.[6] Farragut knew all these men, and was particularly intimate with Commanders Sinclair and Page. Some of these officers, no doubt, were among those who gathered at the store to discuss the political situation and called Farragut a croaker for pointing out the probability of a civil war.

Farragut's hope that Virginia would not secede was gradually made dimmer. President Lincoln's inaugural speech, in which he made plain that he would use force, if necessary, to maintain the Union, played into the hands of the secessionist leaders. Resolutions from cities and towns all over Virginia, demanding immediate withdrawal from the Union, began to pour into the convention in Richmond. An immense crowd gathered in Mechanics Hall in Norfolk, where fiery addresses were delivered and a resolution was adopted, instructing their delegate to vote for secession, though he had been elected as a Union Conservative.[7] Farragut no doubt attended this meeting, as he had been doing, for he was greatly interested in the outcome and could not follow the debates very well in the newspapers, as he could then scarcely read at all because of his weak eyes.[8] He left the hall late at night a tired and a sadder man.

Then came Lincoln's attempt to reenforce Fort Sumter, the firing on the fort, and its capture by Southern troops. On the Sunday following this memorable event, there was an under current of excitement even at church, for it was reported that the prayer for the President of the United States was to be omitted in the service. Farragut had determined to walk out of the church, if such omission was made in the ritual. But the service was read as usual. The psalter for the day began with the sentence, "Samaria is desolate," and Farragut remarked to his wife, "There's prophecy for you! God help the country."

Two days later, on April 15, came Lincoln's call for 75,000 volunteers. This caused a more rapid increase in secession sentiment, and on April 17 the convention, amid scenes which approximated hysteria, passed an ordinance of secession by a vote of eighty-five to fifty-five. Since the firing on Fort Sumter, business had practically come to a stop in Norfolk; people assembled in the streets to discuss the last news or to listen to popular harangues. On the day of the vote, the militia, in anticipation of the result, paraded the streets with music and Southern flags. "When the telegraph flashed the announcement that the secession ordinance had been passed, it was greeted with great cheering, the firing of guns, and every demonstration of excited enthusiasm."[9]

Farragut heard the news with forebodings for the immediate future. Though he should not have been, he was astonished at the result and felt that "Virginia had been dragooned out of the Union."[10] He had become the victim of wishful thinking, and had not been in a position to accurately estimate the situation and foresee the rapid change in public opinion. Though he must have already discussed with Mrs. Farragut possible eventualities and had already made up his mind that he would not resign from the navy, he did not decide on an immediate step until the morning after the convention passed the ordinance of secession. When he went that morning to the store to talk over the latest developments with the naval officers who had been gathering there for political discussions, he at once sensed a change in their attitude towards him. He soon learned that most of the Southern naval officers had already sent in their resignations, though some had done so with great regret. When Farragut endeavored to defend Lincoln's call for volunteers to defend government property, he was very bluntly told by a former brother officer that Virginia had seceded and that he must either resign or leave Norfolk. Farragut replied, "I can not live here, and will seek some other place where I can live, and on two hours' notice."[11]

At last fully realizing that the situation was serious and that he had come to the parting of the ways, he returned to his home on Duke Street. As he walked along, he was not conscious of the perfume of the spring flowers which were just bursting into blossom in the lovely Virginia gardens. His mind was on things warlike, not on scenes of peace and beauty. Extremely downcast because of what he had to tell his wife, he resolutely entered the house and as quickly as possible announced to her that he had made up his mind to stick to the flag. After relating to her what had happened at the store, he said, "This act of mine may cause years of separation from your family; so you must decide quickly whether you will go North or remain here."[12] He reminded her of the situation at the Navy Yard, how Captain McCauley, too old to cope with the situation, had procrastinated until it was dangerous to try to remove the *Merrimac* and the *Germantown*, as the Navy Department had ordered. Farragut feared that there would be fighting, and he did not want to be called upon to fight against the people of Norfolk. He might be ordered soon to report for duty at the Navy Yard. He must leave and quickly too, that very day.

It was a difficult decision which Farragut had made; but it was a much more difficult one which he was calling upon his wife to make. She was being asked suddenly to leave friends she had known all her life and her nearest and dearest relatives.[13] Her devotion to her husband and her courage were equal to the demands of the crisis, and she promptly told Farragut that she would go with him. Hurried preparations were made and a few most prized valuables were hastily collected. There were sad farewells at Grandfather Loyall's home and at Uncle George Loyall's house on Granby Street. Then Mrs. Farragut, her sister Mrs. Ashe[14] with her two small children, and the old family Negro servant woman Sinah got into a carriage and rode down to the wharf. Farragut and his son walked somewhat uneasily to the same destination. Though it had been rumored that Captain Farragut might be arrested, they received only dark looks and mumbled threats. All were soon safely on board the steamer for Baltimore.

As the steamer, in the late afternoon, chugged down the river and out into Hampton Roads, Farragut and his party of tearful women and children gazed sadly at the receding familiar shore line. They did not know when they would be able to return. They would have felt even sadder, had they known how many years of civil strife were to intervene before they all saw Norfolk again. A few days before, every man in Norfolk was Farragut's friend; now most of them were his enemies.

Farragut was then nearly sixty years old, and he was beginning to show his age. He still had his athletic figure, and weighed only about one hundred and fifty pounds, not too much for his height of five feet and six and a half inches. His dark brown hair had turned almost black in middle life and then began to turn gray; baldness also appeared, which Farragut somewhat concealed by the way he combed his hair. His face had become deeply lined and his naturally swarthy skin appeared like leather, so tanned and weather-beaten had it become from exposure. His features were prominent; ears, nose, and mouth were large. His eyes, because of their weakness, gave a quizzical, half-smiling appearance to his face.[15] There was nothing striking about his appearance, and his unpretending mildness of manners and speech gave no hint of the rugged courage and fearless determination of the man.

The Farraguts arrived in Baltimore in the early afternoon of the 19th of April a short time after the Massachusetts troops had been attacked in the streets as they passed through on their way to Washington. Blood had been shed and the city was in a turmoil of excitement. Railway connections between that city and Philadelphia had been severed by the destruction of the bridge across the Susquehanna River. After many inquiries, Farragut managed to secure passage for his party on a canal boat, which they found to be crowded with over three hundred passengers, many of whom were also refugees. After reaching Philadelphia, they had no further inconveniences in traveling on to New York. After placing Mrs. Farragut's sister and her children on the steamer for California and spending a few days in the city amid the noisy preparations for war, Farragut went with his family to the village of Hastings on Hudson where he rented a small cottage. There we leave him for a while as he waited for the orders from Washington, which he was to carry out so brilliantly that his name was to be placed among the greatest naval leaders of history.

He had already lived a long life, filled with interesting experiences and adventures. It had extended from the age of sail into the new age of steam. He had served under, or in the same squadron with, David Porter, William Bainbridge, Oliver Hazard Perry, Charles Morris, Charles Stewart, Jacob Jones, Jesse D. Elliott, Isaac Chauncey, John Downes, and others who had distinguished themselves in the wars against the Barbary Corsairs and in the War of 1812, and had thus been nourished on the glorious traditions of that early period of the American navy. The cruise of the *Essex*, in which he actively participated, from the sailing of the vessel to her loss in the harbor of Valparaiso, was an odyssey of adventures in itself. But that was by no means the end of his voyaging. In several cruises he had become quite familiar with most of the Mediterranean ports, fought pirates in the Caribbean, spent several years on the

Brazil Station when there was trouble in eastern South America caused by civil strife, and perhaps become more familiar with the Mexican people and the eastern coast of Mexico than any other officer in the United States Navy. He had been off Vera Cruz when the French took the Castle of San Juan de Ulloa, and later had taken part in the war between Mexico and the United States. He had been on the *Brandywine* when that vessel was given the honor of transporting General Lafayette back to France after his visit to the United States. He was on the *Natchez* off Charleston during the Nullification crisis, where he had witnessed the wise use of force and diplomacy.

During his long life Farragut had met many distinguished people outside the circle of the navy. These included the Grand Duke of Tuscany, for whom a grand ball was given in Pisa, which Farragut attended; the Emperor of Austria, for whom Farragut interpreted when he visited the *Franklin* at Naples in company with Prince Metternich and the King of Naples; and Dom Pedro I of Brazil and the Royal Family. He had met General Santa Anna of Mexico and had been on very intimate terms with General Rosas and his family at Buenos Aires. He had known General Lafayette and Admiral Baudin of France; and had been intimately associated with American Ministers to Mexico Poinsett and McLane, General Winfield Scott, and many others who were not so famous.

Farragut's life was not one long string of continuous romantic adventure. No man's life is such except in the biographies written by romancers. He had long months of dull routine and monotony when the future seemed to have little to offer in the way of promotion and professional distinction. He had afflictions and sorrows too. He had sunstroke in Tunis which weakened his eyesight and thus handicapped him greatly all the rest of his life; he had to flee that country because of the plague; he was attacked by the yellow fever three or four times; and barely recovered from the cholera. He lost his first wife after she had been an invalid for many years and Farragut had exhausted all the resources of medical science in trying to save her.

He was not without faults, for after all he was a human being and not a demigod. A youthful indiscretion gained for him the ill will of the powerful Perry family, delayed his promotion, and probably kept him from any opportunity to distinguish himself in the Mexican War. Ill-considered criticism of Admiral Baudin by Farragut, which appeared in an American newspaper, brought down upon him the wrath of the Secretary of the Navy. A too hasty departure from New York after the unfortunate death of seaman Ritter on the *Brooklyn* and his prolonged unpleasant quarrel with Lieutenant Jeffers certainly left black marks on his record. But these things were of little consequence compared to what is found on the other side of the ledger. He was a remarkable seaman; he had commanded every kind of ship of war, from schooner to ship of the line under sail and the steam sloop *Brooklyn,* then one of the most powerful ships in the United States Navy; and though he had been confronted with dangerous situations on treacherous coasts, he had never had an accident. As opportunities were afforded, he had observed all new developments in foreign navies, particularly in guns; and eventually became recognized by the Navy Department as an ordnance expert. He had become thoroughly acquainted with every activity of the Norfolk Navy Yard, an experience which led to his appointment as commandant of the Mare Island Navy Yard, which he founded and organized. With trifling exceptions he had demonstrated his ability, both on shore duty and at sea, as a leader of men, who was both loved and respected.

That he was a man of courage was shown over and over again during his long life, as exemplified in his diplomatic handling of the delicate situation which arose in San Francisco during the trouble with the Vigilantes and later when his hour of decision struck at Norfolk. He had strong religious convictions, by which his life was guided. Family ties were very real to him, though his own home was broken up by his mother's death when he was a little lad; he often visited his sisters, as opportunity was afforded, and wrote a strong letter to the Secretary of the Navy in defense of his brother, who he thought had been unjustly treated by the Retiring Board. He was a devoted husband to both of his wives. Though he enjoyed the society of women, his relations with them were always above reproach. He was popular in society at home or on foreign stations because of his good humor, his ready smile, his gentlemanly manners, and his ability as a linguist.

Such was Captain David Glasgow Farragut, as he approached his sixtieth birthday and completed the first period of his remarkable life, the longest part but by no means the most interesting and the most important. Few men, at that age, could have looked back upon a fuller and richer life and but few indeed ever stood on the verge of more thrilling achievements than did Farragut as he waited at Hastings on Hudson for orders from Secretary Welles.

SOURCES AND BIBLIOGRAPHY

I. MANUSCRIPTS

United States Navy Department, Naval Records and Library
 Letters to Officers, Ships of War
 Officers' Letters, *passim*
 Masters Commandant Letters, *passim*
 Captains' Letters, *passim*
 Appointments, Orders, and Resignations
 Muster Rolls of *Essex* and *Spark*
 Logbook, Mare Island Navy Yard, September 16, 1854 to March 22, 1856
 Memorial of George Farragut to Secretary of the Navy William Jones, May 20, 1814
United States Navy Department, Bureau of Navigation
 Orders, *passim*
Library of Congress, Manuscript Division
 David Dixon Porter Papers
The National Archives
 Logbooks: *Erie, John Adams, Peacock, Brandywine, Vandalia, Boxer, Constellation, Delaware, Decatur,* and *Saratoga*. (Logs of the *Natchez* and a few other ships in which Farragut served before the Civil War have been lost.)
United States Naval Academy Museum
 Farragut Letters and Other Papers
Mr. and Mrs. George G. Hall
 Letters and Other Papers (Bequeathed by Loyall Farragut)
Dr. Ellsworth Eliot, Jr.
 Some Reminiscences of Early Life by D. G. Farragut, Captain, The U. S. Navy (Loyall Farragut, in his biography of his father, quoted from this as the *Journal*, with frequent changes from the original language.)
 Farragut Letters and Miscellaneous Papers
Court Records of Blount and Knox Counties, Tennessee, March and April, 1797
Records of Clerk of Courts, Norfolk, Virginia
Register of Trinity Church, Portsmouth, Virginia

II. PERIODICALS AND MAGAZINES

American Historical Magazine and Tennessee Historical Society Quarterly, Vols. II and III. Nashville, Tennessee.

American Historical Review, Vol. IX. New York, 1904.
Baltimore *Sun*, June 22, 1846.
East Tennessee Historical Society Publications, Vol. I. Knoxville, Tennessee, 1929.
Gulf States Historical Magazine, September, 1903: "Major George Farragut" by Marshall De Lancey Haywood.
Harper's New Monthly Magazine, August, 1859: "Cruise of the *Essex*."
Journal of the Royal Service Institution, November, 1921: "Naval Costume Past and Present" by R. N. Suter.
Knoxville (Tennessee) *Sentinel*, April 9, 1910: "Farragut's Beginnings" by George P. Mellon.
Maryland Historical Magazine, March, 1924: "Reuben James or Daniel Frazier?" by Charles Lee Lewis.
Maryland Historical Magazine, March, 1940: "Privateering from Baltimore during the Spanish American Wars of Independence" by Charles C. Griffin.
Mariner, The, January, 1934.
Nashville (Tennessee) *Dispatch*, November 11, 1866.
Nashville (Tennessee) *Republican Banner*, December 3, 1868 and November 17, 1879.
National Intelligencer, January 28, 1839.
Navy League Journal, October, 1904.
New Orleans *La Gazette*, June 24, 1808.
New Orleans *Times*, November, 1866.
New York *Evening Post*, November, 1859, and February-March, 1860.
New York *Times*, March, 1860.
New York *Tribune*, November, 1859.
Niles' Register. The Weekly Register, Baltimore, 1814.
Norfolk *Virginian-Pilot*, June 26, 1940: "David Glasgow Farragut" by Dr. W. H. T. Squires.
St. Nicholas, July, 1924: "Little David" by Don G. Seitz.
Taylor-Trotwood Magazine, July, 1907: "David Glasgow Farragut" by Robert L. Taylor.
United States Naval Institute Proceedings, December, 1923: "Farragut" by Rear Admiral C. F. Goodrich.
United States Naval Institute Proceedings, February, 1931: "The Crossroads" by Albert Mordell.
United States Naval Institute Proceedings, February, 1940: "First Contacts—The Glorious Cruise of the Frigate *Essex*" by Captain A. S. Merrill, U. S. Navy. (Translated from *La Actuación de los Oficiales Navales Norte-Americanos en Nuestras Costas, 1813-1840* by Eugenio P. Salas. 1935.

III. BOOKS

Adams, William Henry Davenport. *Farragut and Other Great Commanders*. London and New York (n. d.).

SOURCES AND BIBLIOGRAPHY

Alden, Carroll Storrs. *Lawrence Kearny: Sailor Diplomat.* Princeton, 1936.
Alden, Carroll Storrs and Ralph Earle. *Makers of Naval Tradition.* Boston, 1925.
Allen, Gardner W. *Our Navy and the Barbary Corsairs.* Boston, 1905.
American State Papers. *Documents, Legislative and Executive of the Congress of the United States, 1789-1825. Naval Affairs.* Four volumes. Washington, 1834-1861.
Annales Maritimes et Coloniales. Paris, 1839.
Annual Reports of the Secretary of the Navy, passim.
(Asbury) *Journal of the Reverend Francis Asbury, Bishop* . . . , Vol. III. New York, 1821.
Bancroft, H. H. *Works.* Vol. XIII. New York, 1883-1887.
Barnes, James. *Farragut.* Boston, 1899.
Barnes, James. *Midshipman Farragut.* New York, 1899.
Barnes, James. *Naval Actions of the War of 1812.* New York, 1896.
Barrows, E. M. *The Great Commodore: The Exploits of Commodore Matthew Calbraith Perry.* Indianapolis and New York, 1935.
Bassett, John S., ed. *Correspondence of Andrew Jackson.* Vol. I. Washington, 1926-1935.
Benjamin, S. G. W. "Captain Porter and the *Essex*" in *Stories of Our Navy Retold from St. Nicholas.* New York, 1929.
Beebee, M. B. *Four American Naval Heroes: Paul Jones, Oliver H. Perry, Admiral Farragut, and Admiral Dewey.* New York, 1899.
Bennet, Frank M. *Steam Navy of the United States.* Pittsburgh, 1896.
Blanchard, P. et A. Dauzats. *San Juan De Ulùa ou Relation de L'expedition Francaise au Mexique* . . . . Paris, 1839.
Bolton, Sarah K. *Lives of Poor Boys Who Became Famous.* New York, 1937.
Bowen, Abel, ed. *The Naval Monument.* Boston, 1816.
Brockett, L. P. *Our Great Captains: Grant, Sherman, Thomas, Sheridan, and Farragut.* New York, 1866.
Bulloch, James D. *The Secret Service of the Confederate States in Europe.* Vol. I. New York, 1884.
Cady, John F. *Foreign Intervention in the Rio de la Plata, 1838-1850.* Philadelphia, 1929.
Callcott, Wilfrid H. *Santa Anna: the Story of an Enigma Who Once Was Mexico.* University of Oklahoma Press, 1936.
Calogeras, J. P. *A History of Brazil.* University of North Carolina Press, 1939.
Campbell, Peter Colin. *Account of the Clan-Iver.* Aberdeen, 1873.
Chesney, Charles C. *Essays in Military Biography.* New York, 1874.
Claiborne, J. F. H. *Mississippi as a Province, Territory, and State.* Jackson, Mississippi, 1880.
Clark, Thomas. *Naval History of the United States.* Second edition. Philadelphia, 1814.
Cooper, James Fenimore. *A History of the Navy of the United States.* Two volumes. Philadelphia, 1839.

Davis, Charles L. . . . *North Carolina Troops . . . in the War of the Revolution*. Philadelphia, 1896.
Dearborn, H. A. S. *The Life of William Bainbridge, Esq. of the United States Navy*. 1816. Reprint edited by James Barnes, 1931.
Dictionary of American Biography, passim. New York, 1928-1937.
Dunbar, Rowland, ed. *Official Letter Books of W. C. C. Claiborne, 1801-1816*. Jackson, Mississippi, 1917.
Emmons, Lieutenant George F. *The Navy of the United States from the Commencement, 1775 to 1853*. Washington, 1853.
Eggleston, George C. *The American Immortals*. New York, c. 1901.
Ellis, Edward S. *Dewey and Other Naval Commanders*. New York, 1899.
Encyclopedia Britannica, passim.
Farragut Family *Bible*.
(Farragut, David Glasgow.) *Experiments to Ascertain the Strength and Endurance of Navy Guns*. Washington, 1854.
Farragut, Loyall. *The Life of David Glasgow Farragut, First Admiral of the United States Navy* . . . . New York, 1879.
Forrest, William S. *Historical and Descriptive Sketches of Norfolk and Vicinity* . . . . Philadelphia, 1853.
Frost, Holloway H. *We Build a Navy*. Annapolis, 1929.
Frost, John. *American Naval Biography* . . . . Philadelphia, 1844.
Frost, John. *The Pictorial History of the American Navy: Comprising Lives of Its Distinguished Commanders*. New York, 1845.
Frothingham, Jessie P. *Sea Fighters from Drake to Farragut*. New York, 1902.
Glazier, Willard. *Heroes of Three Wars*. Philadelphia, 1884.
Grove, K. W. *American Naval Heroes: Jones, Perry, Farragut, Dewey*. Chicago, c. 1913.
Goldsborough, Charles W. *The United States Naval Chronicle*. Washington, 1824.
Hale, Will T. and Dixon L. Merritt. *A History of Tennessee and Tennesseans*. Chicago and New York, 1913.
Hamersly, Lewis Randolph. *List of Officers of the Navy of the United States and of the Marine Corps, from 1775 to 1900*. Edited by Edward W. Callahan. New York, 1901.
Hanighen, Franck C. *Santa Anna: The Napoleon of the West*. New York, c. 1934.
Harris, Thomas. *Life and Services of Commodore William Bainbridge*. Philadelphia, 1837.
Headley, P. C. *Life and Naval Career of Vice-Admiral David Glascoe* (sic) *Farragut*. New York, 1865.
Headley, J. T. *Farragut and Our Naval Commanders*. New York, 1867.
Hill, Frederic S. *The Romance of the American Navy as Embodied in the Stories of Certain of Our Public and Private Armed Ships from 1775 to 1909*. New York and London, 1910.
Hill, Jim Dan. *Sea Dogs of the Sixties* . . . . University of Minnesota Press, 1935.

SOURCES AND BIBLIOGRAPHY 301

Homans, J. E. *Our Three Admirals* .... New York, 1899.
Heads of Families: At the First Census of the United States Taken in the Year 1790: North Carolina. Washington, 1908.
Hosmer, James K. *A Short History of the Mississippi Valley.* Boston and New York, 1901.
James, William. *A Full and Correct Account of the Chief Naval Occurrences of the Late War between Great Britain and the United States of America* .... London, 1817.
James, William. *The Naval History of Great Britain.* Vol. V. London, 1837.
(Jones, George) A "Civilian." *Sketches of Naval Life* .... New Haven, 1829.
Journal of the United States House of Representatives. 1797.
Jurien de la Graviére, Edmond. *L'Amiral Baudin.* Paris, 1888.
Kimball, H. *The Naval Temple* .... Boston, 1816.
King, Grace. *New Orleans, the Place and the People.* New York, 1895.
Knox, Dudley W. *A History of the United States Navy.* New York, 1936.
Lane-Poole, Stanley. *The Story of the Barbary Corsairs.* New York, 1896.
Lewis, Charles Lee. *Admiral Franklin Buchanan: Fearless Man of Action.* Baltimore, 1929.
Lewis, Charles Lee. *Famous American Naval Officers.* Boston, 1924.
Lewis, Charles Lee. *Matthew Fontaine Maury: Pathfinder of the Seas.* Annapolis, 1927.
Lewis, Charles Lee. *The Romantic Decatur.* University of Pennsylvania Press, 1937.
Lossing, Benson J. *The Pictorial Field Book of the War of 1812.* New York, 1868.
Lossing, Benson J. *The Story of the United States Navy* .... New York, 1881.
Macdonough, Rodney. *Life of Commodore Thomas Macdonough.* Boston, c. 1909.
Maclay, Edgar S. *History of the United States Navy from 1775 to 1894.* Two volumes. New York, 1894.
Mahan, Alfred Thayer. *Admiral Farragut.* New York, 1892.
Mahan, Alfred Thayer. *Sea Power in Its Relation to the War of 1812.* Boston, 1905.
Marshall, John. *Royal Naval Biography.* Vol. II. London, 1824.
Mechlin, A. H. and Charles H. Winder, compilers. *A General Register of the Navy and Marine Corps of the United States* .... Washington, 1848.
McLane, Robert M. *Reminiscences.* Privately Printed. 1903.
Morris, Charles. *The Autobiography of Charles Morris.* Boston, 1880.
Morris, Charles. *Heroes of the Navy in America.* Philadelphia, 1907.
Navy Register. Washington, 1812-1861.
Nordhoff, Charles. *Man-of-War Life.* Cincinnati, 1856.
North Carolina State Records. Vols. XVIII, XIX, XXII.

Official Records of the Union and Confederate Navies in the War of the Rebellion. Series II, Vol. I, Parts 1 to 4.
Paine, Ralph D. *Ships and Sailors of Old Salem.* New York, 1909.
Paullin, Charles Oscar. *Commodore John Rodgers. A Biography.* Cleveland, Ohio, 1910.
Paullin, Charles Oscar. *Atlas of the Historical Geography of the United States.* New York, 1932.
Paullin, Charles Oscar. "George Farragut" and "David Glasgow Farragut" in *Dictionary of American Biography.*
Paullin, Charles Oscar. "Father of Admiral Farragut" in *Louisiana Historical Quarterly,* January, 1930.
Peterson, Charles J. *American Navy* . . . . Philadelphia, 1857.
Phelan, James. *History of Tennessee.* Boston and New York, 1888.
Porter, David. *Journal of a Cruise Made to the Pacific Ocean by Captain David Porter in the United States Frigate Essex in the Years 1812, 1813, and 1814.* New York.
Porter, David Dixon. *Memoir of Commodore David Porter.* Albany, New York, 1875.
Pratt, Julius W. *Expansionists of 1812.* New York, 1925.
Preble, George Henry. "The First Cruise of the U. S. Frigate *Essex* . . . with a Short Account of Her Origin and Subsequent Career . . ." in *Essex Institute Historical Collections,* Vol. X. Salem, 1870.
Preble, George Henry. "Naval Uniforms" in *United Service: A Monthly Review of Military and Naval Affairs,* Vol. II. June, 1880.
Ramsey, J. G. M. *The Annals of Tennessee.* Philadelphia, 1853.
Regulations for the Uniform and Dress of the Navy of the United States. Washington, 1841.
Regulations for the Uniform and Dress of the Navy and Marine Corps of the United States. Washington, 1852.
Reynolds, J. N. *Voyage of the United States Frigate Potomac . . . 1831-1834.* New York, 1835.
Ridgely, David. *Annals of Annapolis.* Baltimore, 1841.
Riley, Elihu S. *The Ancient City: History of Annapolis* . . . . Annapolis, 1887.
Roosevelt, Theodore. *The Naval War of 1812* . . . . New York, 1882.
(Ruschenberger, W. S. W.) An Officer of the United States Navy. *Three Years in the Pacific* . . . . Philadelphia, 1834.
Sands, Benjamin F. *From Reefer to Rear Admiral* . . . . New York, 1899.
Shine, John W. *History of the Shine Family in Europe and America.* Sault Ste. Marie, Michigan, 1917.
Skinner, Constance Lindsay. *Pioneers of the Old Southwest: A Chronicle of the Dark and Bloody Ground.* Yale University Press, 1919.
Smith, J. J. *American Naval Battles.* Boston, 1831.
(Smithsonian) *Board of Regents of the Smithsonian Institution for the Year 1851.* Washington, 1852.
Snider, C. H. *Glorious "Shannon's" Old Blue Duster.* Toronto, 1923.
Soley, James Russell. *The Boys of 1812 and Other Naval Heroes.* Boston, 1886.

SOURCES AND BIBLIOGRAPHY

Spears, John Randolph. *David G. Farragut*. Philadelphia, 1905.
Spears, John Randolph. *The History of Our Navy from Its Origin to the Present Day, 1775-1898*. Five volumes. New York, 1897-1899.
Squires, W. H. T. and M. E. Bennett. *Through the Years in Norfolk* .... Norfolk, 1937.
Stevenson, Burton E., ed. *Poems of American History*. Boston, 1908.
Stewart, C. S. *A Visit to the South Seas in the United States Ship Vincennes during the Years 1829 and 1830* .... Two volumes. London, 1832.
Stowe, Harriet Beecher. *Men of Our Times*. New York, 1868.
Streeter, Gilbert L. "Historical Sketch of the Building of the Frigate *Essex*" in *Essex Institute Proceedings*, Vol. II. Salem, Mass., 1856.
Tucker, George H. *Abstracts from Norfolk City Marriage Bonds, 1797-1850*. (Norfolk), 1934.
Turnbull, A. D. *Commodore David Porter, 1780-1843*. New York, 1929.
Uniform Dress of the Captains and Certain Other Officers of the Navy of the United States. Washington, 1802.
Uniform Dress of the Officers of the Navy of the United States. Washington, 1814.
Uniform Dress for Officers of the United States Navy: Regulations. Washington, 1830.
Werner, Reinhold, *Berühmte Seeleute*. Vol. II. Berlin, 1884.
Wertenbaker, Thomas J. *Norfolk: Historic Southern Port*. Duke University Press, 1931.
West, Richard S., Jr. *The Second Admiral: A Life of David Dixon Porter*. New York, 1937.
Whitlock, Brand. *La Fayette*. Vol. II. New York, 1929.
Williams, Samuel C. *Early Travels in the Tennessee Country, 1540-1800*. Johnson City, Tennessee, 1928.
Wilson, Thomas. *The Biography of the Principal American Military and Naval Heroes*. Two volumes. New York, 1817.
Wines, E. C. *Two Years and a Half in the American Navy*. London, 1833.
Wise, John S. *The End of an Era*. Boston, 1901.
Wyatt, Thomas. *Memoirs of the Generals, Commodores, and Other Commanders . . . during the Revolution and 1812*. Philadelphia, 1843.

NOTES

I. OF FIGHTING BLOOD

1. As recorded in the Farragut Family Bible, belonging to Mrs. George G. Hall, Admiral Farragut's grandniece; as entered on the books of the ecclesiastical court of Ciudadella, Island of Minorca, Balearic Islands. Both are cited in the *Life of David Glasgow Farragut* by Loyall Farragut, p. 1.
   The following excerpt from the New Orleans *Times* was quoted in the Nashville *Dispatch* of November 11, 1866 (Sunday): "The Farragut family was originally Spanish, natives of Barcelona. Before the Revolution the grandfather of the Admiral emigrated to the neighborhood of Norfolk, Virginia. He was probably induced to do so by Colonel William Leigh, cadet of a well known family in England, who in early life had served in the Spanish infantry, and afterward settled in Sussex County, Virginia as a planter. His son, Fernando Leigh, married a Miss Farragut, who died without issue. He was the ancestor of the late eminent Virginia statesman and jurist, Benjamin Watkins Leigh, and in the maternal line, of the Claibornes of Louisiana and Mississippi. George Farragut (father of the Admiral) and this Fernando Leigh were close friends, and he received his commission in the U. S. Navy on the recommendation of the Honorable Thomas Claiborne, then and for near thirty years a Member of Congress from Virginia. It was after the brother of this gentleman, Colonel Augustine Claiborne that young Farragut was named. Shortly afterwards the Farragut family removed to Tennessee, where they found Wm. C. C. Claiborne just elected to represent the state in Congress. He was soon afterwards appointed Governor of Mississippi Territory, and thence transferred to Louisiana. Subsequently the Farragut family removed to this city, where the father of the Admiral and one of his brothers, a naval officer of high standing, died; here he passed his early youth; and here, some fifty years since, he received his appointment in the navy of the U.S. on the application of Governor Claiborne, his steady and devoted friend. . . ." This appears quite confused and unreliable, when checked by the facts as set forth in the text and notes of this biography.
2. *George Farragut's Memorial to Secretary of the Navy William Jones*, May 20, 1814. In this, he states that he was born in the year 1756.
3. As recorded in the ecclesiastical court of Ciudadella.
4. The name was originally spelled "Ferragut." As to Farragut's ancestry,

there is good reason to disregard the following: "It is said on authority that the brave Admiral Farragut was a descendant of a Portuguese of that name," quoted from an article by Mrs. Eliza N. Heiskell of Memphis, Tennessee, in the Arkansas *Gazette* of January 14, 1912, in *A History of Tennessee and Tennesseeans* by Will T. Hale and Dixon L. Merritt (Chicago and New York, 1913), I, 185. Equally without good foundation is the implication drawn by Hale and Merritt that George Farragut was a Melungeon, which was the name given by tradition to a strange people in North Carolina and East Tennessee, thought to have descended from Portuguese mutineers who beached their ship on the coast of North Carolina and fled into the interior.

5. From the translation by Henry Howard Brownell, as quoted in Loyall Farragut's *Life of David Glasgow Farragut*, p. 2.
6. *George Farragut's Memorial*, in Navy Department Archives and Library.
7. *Ibid.*
8. *Ibid.*
9. The only detail of this service which is mentioned by John Randolph Spears's *David G. Farragut*, p. 26, is connected with Farragut's part in the Battle of Cowpens. According to Spears, in this battle Farragut saved the life of Colonel William Washington. But this is not mentioned in Farragut's *Memorial to the Secretary of the Navy*, already referred to; and it seems incredible that he would have failed to make the most possible out of such an exploit if he had really performed such a heroic deed. It is mentioned, however, in *George Farragut* by Samuel C. Williams in *The East Tennessee Historical Society Publications*, I, 77 (Knoxville, 1929). As authorities, Williams cites Marshall's *Life of General Washington*, IV, 347, and "Light Horse Harry" Lee's *Memoirs of the War in the Southern Department*, I, 258, Note. But George Farragut is not mentioned by name, only "one of his sergeants."
10. *North Carolina State Records*, XIX, 309. This service to the state was recognized by the General Assembly of North Carolina on November 27, 1786, when it ordered the payment of a sum due George Farragut as a volunteer captain, with "the conviction of his faithful, voluntary, and public-spirited services." *Ibid.*, XVIII, 24 and 257.

Admiral Farragut knew but little of his father's early life, and apparently never saw the *Memorial to the Secretary of the Navy*. In the Admiral's letter of September 20, 1853, to Lyman C. Draper (quoted in *American Historical Review*, IX, 538) he admits his lack of knowledge of his father's early career. In *Some Reminiscences of Early Life by D. G. Farragut, A Captain, The U. S. Navy*, still extant in manuscript form, he wrote, "I only know that my father was an officer in the Revolutionary struggle for our independence; but whether on land or sea, I do not know." This statement, slightly changed, will be found in Loyall Farragut's life of his father, p. 6, where he calls the manuscript the *Journal*. The original manuscript, chiefly in the handwriting of amanuenses, is now owned by Dr. Ellsworth Eliot, Jr. Only six of the two hundred twenty eight pages were written by Admiral Farragut's own hand. Long quotations from this source were made by Loyall Farragut in his biography of the Admiral, though hardly a sentence has escaped the changes which he saw fit to make in his editing and revising. Most of the quotations in this book will be cited from the original *Some Reminiscences of Early Life*. Those that are paraphrases by Loyall Farragut will be cited from his biography.

Mahan's Admiral Farragut gives no details regarding George Farragut's revolutionary service. Apparently he had not seen the *Memorial to the Secretary of the Navy*.

11. *Memorial to the Secretary of the Navy.* In this connection he states that he was at sea until 1792; this, as proved below, was surely a slip of his memory.

12. Geo. Farragut, on November 3, 1790, was appointed by Gov. Blount second major of the cavalry regiment of Washington District of the Southwest Territory, according to *American Historical Magazine* (Nashville), II, 77; while on March 1, 1792, he was promoted by the Governor to be muster-master of all the militia forces of that district (now all of East Tennessee), according to *George Farragut* by Samuel C. Williams in *The East Tennessee Historical Society Publications*, I, 77, et seq.

In 1797 George Farragut petitioned Congress for back pay from March 1, 1792, to October 26, 1793. This petition was supported by Senator Andrew Jackson and Representative W. C. Claiborne, according to Bassett's *Correspondence of Jackson*, I, 23 note and *Journal of the U. S. House of Representatives* for 1797. See also Loyall Farragut, p. 5.

Hale and Merritt's *History of Tennessee*, I, 192, is clearly in error in stating that the date of George Farragut's first appointment was November, 1791.

13. *George Farragut* by Samuel C. Williams, already mentioned. Admiral Farragut, in his letter of September 20, 1853, to Lyman C. Draper (*American Historical Review*, IX, 540), in recounting a meeting which he had in Norfolk in 1827 with Colonel McKee, then a member of Congress from Alabama, states that "he informed me that a Mr. Ogden, himself, and my Father were the three first settlers of Tennessee, that they lived in a log cabin for some time (I don't remember how long) until my Father took it into his head that he would get married and that broke up their brotherhood."

This story seems exaggerated alongside the fact that in 1790 the population of Tennessee, according to the Federal Census of that year, was 25,691, as cited in James Phelan's *History of Tennessee* (Boston and New York, 1888). The first permanent settlements on the Holston River in what later became known as Tennessee were made in the year 1768, according to *Pioneers of the Old Southwest: A Chronicle of the Dark and Bloody Ground* by Constance Lindsay Skinner (Yale University Press, 1919), p. 159.

14. *George Farragut's Memorial.*
15. In 1791, this county which was named after Arthur Dobbs, Royal Governor of North Carolina in 1754, was divided into Lenoir and Glasgow, the latter being changed to Greene in 1799.
16. Williams's *George Farragut* gives this on the authority of *Bishop Asbury's Journal*, III, 83, in an entry for the year 1802.
17. Executive Journal of Governor Blount and Correspondence of General James Robertson, *American Historical Magazine*, Vols. II and III, *passim*. I have the following receipt, signed by George Farragut at Knoxville, October 24, 1794: "For riding Express from Knoxville to Richmond with public dispatches from Governor Blount to the Secretary of War, distance there and back 900 miles at 2 dollars and 50 cents for every 40 miles—$56.25."
18. There are no facts to substantiate the statement in Spears's *David G. Farragut*, p. 26, that while George Farragut "was yet living in North Carolina he had become enamored of a maiden named Elizabeth, the daughter of Captain John Shine of Dobbs County, and at a forgotten date he returned to the Old North State, married her, and carried her to Tennessee." The date, 1795, certainly has not been forgotten.
19. In describing George Farragut, George W. Sevier, a son of Governor John Sevier, stated that he was "a short, chunky man; very brave and a funny genius. He was on the Hightower Campaign under General Sevier, probably as quarter-master. He concluded to marry an old maid, and announced the event in a characteristic letter to his friend Willie Blount: 'Dear Willie: I is married and my wife's name is Shine; and by heavens, he (referring to himself) shine wherever he go'." *Draper Manuscripts*, Madison, Wisconsin, XXX, 328.
20. *North Carolina State Records*, XXII, 315-317.
21. *Our Living and Our Dead*, in State Library, Raleigh, North Carolina, as cited by John W. Shine's *History of the Shine Family in Europe and America*.
22. The name is written McIven in the Farragut Family Bible, apparently; and is so given in Loyall Farragut's life of his father, p. 1. But as there were no McIvens and many McIvers in the section of North Carolina where the Shines settled, it probably is McIver.
23. The Holston River south of its confluence with the French Broad River above Knoxville is sometimes referred to as the Tennessee River.
24. The records of the Knox County Court for the April session of 1797 show a license to have been granted Major Farragut to "keep a public ferry at his own landing on Holston River called Stony Point." The place eventually was sold to Elisha Jarnagin and by him to Abraham Lowe from whom it came to be known as Lowe's Ferry.

Blount County Court Records for March 13, 1797, show similar permission for the other side of the river.
25. Founded in 1787 and named after David Campbell, its founder. See *Early Travels in the Tennessee Country* by Samuel C. Williams.

II. THE LOG CABIN BY THE RIVER

1. *Pioneers of the Old Southwest* by Constance Lindsay Skinner, p. 35.
2. *Major George Farragut* by Marshall De Lancey Haywood in *The Gulf States Historical Magazine*, September, 1903.

   An old log house, claimed to be the original Farragut home, was moved from the vicinity of Stony Point, several years ago, to Chilhowee Park, Knoxville. There unfortunately it was totally destroyed by fire a few years ago. There is good authority for the belief that the log house in Chilhowee Park was merely a replica and not the original.

   A marker was placed on the spot of Farragut's birthplace by the Bonny Kate Chapter of the Daughters of the American Revolution, and dedicated by Admiral Dewey on May 15, 1900. A new dam, soon to be constructed on the Holston River below Knoxville, will flood a part of the Farragut Farm, and change the site of the Admiral's birthplace to an island.

   An extremely large elm tree, probably standing there when Farragut was born, still spreads its huge branches over the place of his birth.
3. James Glasgow was indicted for, and convicted of, fraud in his official capacity. But this, as will be seen, had no connection with the change of young Farragut's name from James to David. It was made entirely through the association of the youth with David Porter. For many years there was great confusion in recording the lad's name on ships' rolls and at the Navy Department. The Muster Roll of the *Essex*, 1809-1811, p. 193, has *James G. Fagerly* (or *Fagerty*) as having joined her at Norfolk, August 9, 1811; the roll, August 18, 1811 to February 9, 1812, p. 219, has *David G. Farragatt* as having joined at Norfolk August 14, 1811; the roll, August 16 to September 24, 1812, p. 238, has the name of *James G. Farragut* with no other data; the roll, September 25, 1812, to July 27, 1814, p. 256, shows *David G. Farragut* was detached from the *Essex* at New York on July 11, 1814; the Muster Roll of the *Spark*, July 12, 1814, to April 15, 1815, carries the name as *David G. Farragut*. But the Bureau of Navigation records, covering the period up to 1817, carry his name as *James Glasgow* and *James G. Farragut*; but in the second book, 1813 to 1817, the name *James* is scratched out and *David* substituted without explanation. In *American State Papers, Naval Affairs*, I, 260, the *Navy Register* for February, 1812, has both *J. G.* and *Glasgow Farragut*; the *Register* of February, 1814, p. 303, has *James G. Farragut*; *Registers* for January, 1818, 1819, 1820, and 1821 respectively, pp. 462, 596, 634, and 705, have David C. Farragut; and the *Regis-*

ter of January, 1822, has for the first time the correct *David G. Farragut,* on p. 752. George Farragut, unaware of a change of his son's name, in his *Memorial to the Secretary of the Navy,* May 20, 1814, states that his second son is James G. Farragut and that he was at that time with Captain Porter on the *Essex.* The name is, strange to say, curiously spelled David Glascoe in David Dixon Porter's *Memoir of Commodore David Porter,* p. 83.

4. This cradle was purchased by Mr. Edward S. Sheppard, father of Mrs. Bruce Keener, Senior, of Knoxville, Tennessee, at the auction of some of Admiral Farragut's effects after his death. Mrs. Keener presented it to the William Blount Mansion Association in 1931. Mr. Bruce Keener, Junior, wrote from Knoxville on September 16, 1937, that his mother was then dead, that he was unable to give any papers proving the authenticity of the cradle, but that "I can remember my grandfather telling me as a child that Admiral Farragut was rocked in the cradle. . . . At least that was the conviction of my grandfather." Admiral Farragut's niece, Mrs. George G. Hall of Ashfield, Massachusetts, has no knowledge of the cradle, but doubts its authenticity.

5. William A. C. Farragut was born August 23, 1797, and died December 19, 1859; Nancy Farragut was born January 20, 1804, married 1826 Louis Gourlie, resided at Pascagoula, Mississippi, and died June 6, 1883; George Antoine Farragut was born November 29, 1805, and was drowned in the vicinity of New Orleans on July 25, 1815.

6. Letter from David Glasgow Farragut to Lyman C. Draper, September 20, 1853. A much shorter but less vivid account of this incident is quoted from Farragut's *Journal* in *Life of Admiral D. G. Farragut* by Loyall Farragut, p. 8.

7. Though Haywood's *George Farragut in Gulf States Historical Magazine,* September, 1903, states that "after coming to America, he showed himself quite proficient in the language of his adopted country," the contrary seems evident from the letters written by George Farragut which are extant. See *American Historical Review,* IX, 797, note.

8. Claiborne was appointed Governor of Mississippi Territory, 1801-1805; and then Governor General of the Province of Louisiana, 1803-1805, moving his headquarters from Natchez to New Orleans in 1803. In 1805 Louisiana became the Territory of Orleans, and then the state of Louisiana in 1812. Until 1816 Claiborne remained Governor, having filled this office without break until that time.

9. "The petition of George Farragut, praying that he may be allowed the balance of pay due to him for services rendered the United States as Muster Master of the Militia of the District of Washington (East Tennessee), employed in actual service for the protection of the frontiers of the United States south of the Ohio, from the 1st of March, 1792, to the 26th of October, 1793." *Journal of the House of Representatives of the United States* for 1797.

10. The following letter of acknowledgment is of great interest: "Knoxville, April 1, 1807. Sir, Your letter of March 2 inclosing me a warrant of appointment, as Sailing Master, together with other inclosures therein contained, was handed me by General Daniel Smith, a few days since. I have accepted the appointment, and In conformity with your directions, I have this day taken the oath prescribed, which you you will receve inclosed, I have on the stocks small craft intended for the removal of myself and family, to New Orlians; some short time will be requisite for her complition so soon as I can git it Lanch I shall prosed to New Orlians without delay, and rest assured, Sir, that it shall be my endevor to fullfil the duty assingned to me in conformity with the rules and regulations of the Navy of the United States,—I am, Sir, with respect Your Obedient Servant, Geo. Farragut. The Honorable Robert Smith, Secretary of the Navy of the United States." From Navy Department Archives.
11. Apparently there was no suspicion of George Farragut because of his Spanish race, and no connection of him with the Spanish intrigues which for many years centered in New Orleans, with General James Wilkinson as the villain of the plan for delivering southwestern territory to the Spanish government. These intrigues had come practically to a close with the Treaty of 1795 opening the Mississippi River to the free navigation of both nations. The whole problem was settled for once and all with the Louisiana Purchase in 1803.

III. THE VOYAGE ON THE FLATBOAT

1. Letter of April 1, 1807, from George Farragut to Secretary of the Navy Robert Smith.
2. David Glasgow Farragut to Dr. Lyman C. Draper, September 20, 1853, in *American Historical Review*, IX, 538. Muster Rolls, New Orleans Station indicate he reported there July 1, 1807.
3. From Callot's *Atlas*, reproduced in James K. Hosmer's *A Short History of the Mississippi Valley*, opposite p. 96.
4. Farragut's letter to Draper, September 20, 1853.
5. *History of Tennessee* by James Phelan, p. 179.
6. *Pioneers of the Old Southwest* by Constance Lindsay Skinner, p. 186, et seq.
7. *History of Tennessee* by Phelan, p. 179. Only four years after the Farragut voyage, the first steamboat was built on the Ohio in 1811, and that same year steamed from Pittsburgh to New Orleans.
8. From the *Arrowsmith Map, 1814* in *Atlas of the Historical Geography of the United States* by Charles O. Paullin.
9. In this connection, one readily recalls that another Kentucky youth when nineteen years old made a voyage to New Orleans as a hired hand on a flatboat. He was Abe Lincoln, and the voyage was made in the year 1828.
10. *A Short History of the Mississippi Valley* by James K. Hosmer, p. 125.

NOTES 311

IV. THE BREAKING UP OF THE HOME

1. According to the *Encyclopedia Britannica,* the population of New Orleans was about ten thousand in 1803 when the United States took over Louisiana. Grace King's *New Orleans, the Place and the People,* p. 179, states that the inhabitants numbered about twenty-four thousand in 1812.
2. The Lafittes lived on the north corner of St. Philip and Bourbon Streets, and had a blacksmith shop on St. Philip Street. During the embargo of 1808 Jean Lafitte opened a shop on Royal Street. *New Orleans* by Grace King, pp. 190, 193.
3. Hosmer, *op. cit.,* p. 126.
4. David Porter's warrant as sailing master was dated August 4, 1807. It was sworn to in Baltimore on September 9, 1807. On September 3, 1807, he was ordered to proceed to New Orleans with his son Master Commandant Porter, but on September 16, 1807, he was ordered to Washington to command a gunboat fitting out there. He may have proceeded from here in this gunboat to New Orleans, though no later orders to him are in the archives of Naval Records and Library, Washington.

    The statement in D. D. Porter's *Memoir of Commodore David Porter,* p. 83, that David Porter, Senior, was appointed sailing master on September 3, 1807, is an error; it was then he was ordered first to New Orleans.
5. Farragut's *Journal,* as quoted in Loyall Farragut's *Life of David Glasgow Farragut,* p. 10, states, "This, as well as I can remember, occurred in 1809." Obviously, this is an error. See *Memoir of Commodore David Porter* by David Dixon Porter, p. 83, and *Commodore David Porter* by A. D. Turnbull, p. 81.

    There is an error in J. R. Spear's *David G. Farragut,* p. 31, which states, "In this condition (sunstroke) he was found by Sailing Master Farragut, who took him home to the plantation on the Pascagoula." At that time, the plantation had not yet been purchased.
6. Letter of September 20, 1853, from Farragut to Lyman C. Draper, in *American Historical Review,* IX, 539.
7. A letter from Mr. George G. Hall of September 13, 1937, cites the following from the New Orleans *La Gazette* of June 24, 1808: "Died Wed. June 22 after a lingering illness Capt. David Porter of Baltimore. On the same day Mrs. Farragut. Their remains were interred yesterday morning in the Protestant Cemetery." Letter of Master Commandant David Porter of June 25, 1808, to the Secretary of the Navy states that his father had died on June 22, 1808. Loyall Farragut's biography of his father, p. 9, declares, "Her funeral, according to a letter of the late Commodore Daniel T. Patterson, U.S.N., who was a pallbearer, occurred at the same time with that of Sailing Master David Porter." John R. Spears is wrong in recording in his *David G. Farragut,* p. 31, that Mrs. Farragut was buried on June 22, 1808.

8. Farragut's letter to Draper, September 20, 1853.
9. *American Historical Review*, IX, 539, Farragut to Draper. *Some Reminiscences* says Elizabeth was placed in care of Mrs. Dupont.
10. The Muster Rolls of the New Orleans Station bear the name of W. A. C. Farragut as acting midshipman from March 14, 1808, to June 15, 1810, during which period he drew $164.80. He was not appointed a regular midshipman until January 16, 1809. His warrant was sent him February 10, 1809. (Archives, Naval Records and Library.) Of interest is this letter from Secretary of the Navy R. S. Smith to Governor Claiborne, of June 13, 1808: "I have received your letter of the 4 inst. soliciting warrant of midshipman in the U. States Navy for Michael Perrault and Wm. A. C. Farragut." He goes on to explain that there are no vacancies at that time, but that probably in the ensuing autumn there will be, and then his letter will be "respectfully considered." *General Letter Book*, No. 9, p. 228, Naval Records and Library.
11. In *Letters to Secretary of the Navy: Masters Commandant*, Naval Records and Library, Porter writes that he left Chester, Pennsylvania, March 16, 1808, and Pittsburgh on April 15, and that he arrived at New Orleans on June 17, 1808, when he writes, "The shock your letter (complaining of Porter's purchases for the expedition down the river) has given me, added to my distresses for the expiring situation of my Father, has allmost (sic) overcome me." Farragut was incorrect in writing in his letter to Draper, September 20, 1853, "Shortly after (death of Mrs. Farragut and David Porter, Senior) Comdre. Porter arrived to take command of the station, and learning the particulars of his Father's death, etc., etc." Also incorrect is the statement in D. D. Porter's *Memoir of Commodore David Porter*, p. 83, "While in command at New Orleans his father, David Porter, senior, was ordered to report to him for duty." Equally incorrect is this from A. D. Turnbull's *Commodore David Porter*, p. 80: "(Commodore Porter) was comfortably established in it (his house in New Orleans) with her (his wife) and with his own father when he lost the latter. The old gentleman, recommissioned as sailing master in the Navy, had been contentedly serving under his son in the gunboats." This error is found also in Farragut's *Journal* as quoted in Loyall Farragut's life of his father, p. 10, "Not long after his father's death, Commander David Porter took command of the Naval Station at New Orleans, and having heard that his father died at our house, etc., etc." It is essentially the same in the original *Some Reminiscences*.
12. D. D. Porter's *Memoir of Commodore David Porter*, p. 78.
13. *American Historical Review*, IX, 539, Farragut's letter to Draper, September 20, 1853.
14. David Porter wrote the Secretary of the Navy on September 13, 1808, "I have placed Sailing Master Geo. Farragut in the Navy Yard

under orders of Lieutenant Commanding Carroll and given Lieut. Dan G. Patterson command of gun vessel No. 11. I consider Mr. Farragut too old and infirm a man to perform the active duties required of the commander of a gun vessel and I believe he possesses talents well suited to perform the duties required of him in the Navy Yard." However, George Farragut was then not quite fifty-three years old; and on November 14, 1808, Porter wrote an order to Sailing Master John Owings to deliver over gunboat No. 21 to Geo. Farragut, and in a letter of the following day to the Secretary of the Navy he mentions Geo. Farragut as the commanding officer of this gunboat. On July 9, 1809, Porter gives a list of gunboats to the Secretary of the Navy among which he cites "gunboat 13, Mr. Farragut, condemned, a sheer hulk." *Letters to Secretary of the Navy: Masters Commandant*, Naval Records and Library.

15. This place is in Jackson County, Mississippi. Here descendants of Farragut lived for many years, according to J. F. H. Claiborne's *Mississippi* . . . , p. 251.
16. Farragut's letter to Draper. September 20, 1853.
17. Farragut's *Journal* in Loyall Farragut's *Life of David Glasgow Farragut*. p. 11. The original *Some Reminiscences* says he "was rather more tickled with his uniform than any of the rest."
18. Farragut's letter to Draper; *Dictionary of American Biography*, article on Samuel Davies Heap.

    Heap was ordered away from New Orleans and to the Mediterranean in 1817. According to a letter of September 13, 1937, from Mr. George G. Hall, early in May, 1817, Nancy Farragut was adopted by William Boswell; in 1826 she married Louis Gourlie, resided at Pascagoula, Mississippi, and died on June 6, 1883.
19. Glasgow has been used as young Farragut's name to avoid confusion in the mind of the reader, unaccustomed to the name James Farragut. As a matter of fact, however, it was this single name that his friends used. A letter from Commodore David Porter, written on June 20, 1835, from Constantinople, begins with "My Dear Glasgow." See Loyall Farragut's biography of his father, p. 121. Also his signature on his oath of allegiance, dated December 19, 1810, is "G. Farragut." He is called Glasgow also in a letter from Porter to the Secretary of the Navy, August 12, 1811.
20. There is not the slightest foundation in fact for the insinuation, sometimes heard, that Glasgow Farragut was Commodore David Porter's natural son. During the year previous to young Farragut's birth David Porter was at sea. There is no evidence that Porter was ever in East Tennessee, nor that he ever saw Mrs. Farragut except perhaps a few days before her death and that of his own father in New Orleans. David Porter was born in 1780; Mrs. Farragut in 1765; and Glasgow Farragut on July 5, 1801.
21. Farragut in a letter to Commodore Porter, December 12, 1818, from Leghorn, Italy, concludes with "Your most affectionate young friend."

Other letters, in the same way, show that he was not an adopted son.
22. Farragut's *Journal*, as quoted by Loyall Farragut in his life of his father, p. 11. The original *Some Reminiscences* has it, "He has been to me all that he promised, a 'friend, a protector.'"
23. *Ibid.*, p. 9.
24. In *American Historical Review*, IX, 540, Farragut's letter to Draper, September 20, 1853, is as follows: "He (Colonel McKee with whom he had an interview in Norfolk) spoke of him (George Farragut) as a man of great wrecklessness (sic) of character and just suited for the life of a Pioneer. I replied that he paid the forfeit of his wrecklessness, that he had died of a cough contracted in that way when only sixty years of age at Pascagoula in Mississippi; he had purchased a tract of land and located his family there. It was his habit to cross lake Pontchartrain in a small Boat and sleep on the Beach when night overtook him. I well remember his wrapping we (sic) children up in the boat sails on one of these trips only a short time before I left him."

V. A MIDSHIPMAN AT THE AGE OF NINE

1. Mahan's *Admiral Farragut*, p. 5, has the following incorrect statement: "A few months later (after taking charge of Glasgow) Commander Porter appears to have made a visit to Washington on business connected with the New Orleans station, and to have taken Farragut with him to be placed at school, for which there were few advantages at that time in Louisiana." Also incorrect is a statement in Mahan, p. 8, as follows: "In the latter part of 1810 he (Porter) finally left New Orleans and went north again, this time by the Mississippi River and in a gun-boat. The voyage to Pittsburgh against the swift current took three months." Similar errors appear in Spears' *David G. Farragut*, p. 35, and in Turnbull's *Porter*, p. 89, all of them being based on the original incorrect source, D. D. Porter's *Memoir of Commodore David Porter*, p. 85. The facts, as found in *Letters to Secretary of the Navy, Masters Commandant*, 1810-1811 (Naval Records and Library), are that Porter did not return to Washington after assuming command of the New Orleans Station until his final departure about June 21, 1810, when he wrote that he was on the point of sailing on the *Vesuvius;* that he arrived in Washington about July 23, 1810; that he did not afterwards return to New Orleans but was in Chester as late as January 27, 1811, and on February 1, 1811, was granted a furlough to make a voyage on a merchant vessel; and that he was in Havana on June 19, 1811, and back in Chester on July 21, 1811.
2. George F. Emmon's *Statistical History of the Navy of the United States*, p. 10. The vessel was purchased in 1806 at a cost of $29,659. Her tonnage was not given. In her passage to New Orleans in 1806 she went aground and her guns had to be thrown overboard. She

went to New York in 1807 where she lay until 1829, when as a decaying hulk alongside the steamship *Fulton* she was blown up.
3. Farragut's *Journal* in Loyall Farragut's biography of his father, p. 11. The following letter written soon after the incident by Stephen Decatur to Secretary of the Navy Hamilton is of interest: "I have this day learned from a schooner nine days from Havana that the *Vixen*, Lieutenant Trippe, whilst off that place, was fired into by a British brig of war, and had his main boom shot away. The commander of the British vessel, it is stated, sent his boat on board to apologize for what had occurred, stating that he was ignorant of her national character and that he regretted much what had happened. Lieutenant Trippe sent the officer back to his commander to inform him that he would receive none but a written apology, which was acceded to. I cannot answer for the truth of this statement, but am of the opinion that something of the kind has taken place. And if it be true, Trippe has lost a glorious opportunity to cancel the blot under which our flag suffers, and to distinguish himself. From my knowledge of Lieutenant Trippe, I am perfectly satisfied that, although he may have shown *great* moderation in this affair, he has not lost sight of what is due the honor of the flag." As quoted in *The Romantic Decatur* by Charles Lee Lewis, 105.
4. Paul Hamilton Hayne, the poet, was the son of Paul Hamilton Hayne, an officer of the U. S. Navy who was named after Paul Hamilton.
5. This warrant was worded as follows: "JAMES MADISON, PRESIDENT OF THE UNITED STATES OF AMERICA. To all who shall see these presents, GREETINGS: KNOW YE, That reposing special Trust and Confidence in the Patriotism, Valour, Fidelity and Abilities of GLASGOW FARRAGUT I do appoint him a Midshipman in the NAVY OF THE UNITED STATES:

He is therefore carefully and diligently to discharge the duties of a Midshipman by doing and performing all manner of things thereunto belonging. And I do strictly charge and require all Officers, Seamen and others, under his command, to be obedient to his orders as a Midshipman. And he is to observe and follow such orders and directions, from time to time, as he shall receive from me, or the future President of the United States of America, or his superior officer set over him, according to the Rules and Discipline of the Navy. This Warrant to continue in force during the pleasure of the President of the United States for the time being. GIVEN under my Hand, at the City of Washington, this seventeenth day of December in the year of our Lord one Thousand eight hundred and ten and in the thirty-fourth year of the Independence of the United States.

JAMES MADISON

By the President.
Paul Hamilton."

In acknowledgment of this warrant, Farragut had the following oath executed: "I, Glasgow Farragut, appointed Midshipman in the

Navy of the United States, do solemnly swear to bear true allegiance to the United States of America, and to serve them honestly and faithfully against all their enemies or opposers whomsoever; and to observe and obey the orders of the President of the United States of America, and the orders of the officers appointed over me, and in all things to conform myself to the rules and regulations which now are or hereafter may be directed, and to the articles of war which may be enacted by Congress, for the better government of the navy of the United States, and that I will support the constitution of the United States.

G. Farragut

SWORN BEFORE ME
Chester, Dec. 19th, 1810
Isaac Eyre Justes (sic) of the
Peace in the County of Delaware
State of Pennsylvania."

6. Naval Records and Library, Navy Department, Washington, D.C.

According to the records of the Navy Department, Farragut was always accredited to Tennessee, the state of his birth.

Two other officers who were appointed midshipmen when very young were Samuel Barron and Louis M. Goldsborough. Barron, born November 28, 1809, was appointed a midshipman on January 1, 1812, when he was still only two years old; but he was eleven when he went on his first cruise. Goldsborough, born February 18, 1805, was appointed a midshipman June 18, 1812, at the age of seven, though he saw no active service until he was eleven.

VI. FARRAGUT JOINS THE *ESSEX*

1. As quoted in *The First Cruise of the U. S. Frigate Essex ... with a short account of her origin and subsequent career ...* by Captain George Henry Preble, U.S.N. in *Essex Institute Historical Collections* (Salem, 1870), X, 20. Also quoted in *David G. Farragut* by J. R. Spears, p. 45, who states that the letter is preserved at the Boston Navy Yard.

David Tittimary's name does not appear as an officer of the U. S. Navy on any navy list, but in a list of the officers and crew of the *Essex* in Captain David Porter's *Journal of a Cruise Made in the Pacific Ocean* it does appear as a midshipman, though it is spelled "Tittermary." He might have been taken on the *Essex* as a ship's boy and then employed as an acting midshipman.

Loyall Farragut's life of his father, p. 12, states that the trip from Chester to Norfolk was made by stage and packet, and that it was described in Farragut's *Journal* as "a long and tedious one, with only the upsetting of a stage to vary its monotony." The upsetting of this stagecoach had no such serious consequences as did a similar incident somewhat later which completely changed Matthew Fontaine Maury's naval career.

2. His father was short in stature also.
3. *The Uniform Dress of Captains and Certain Other Officers of the Navy of the United States*, 1802. These regulations were in force until others were approved in November, 1813, and published in 1814. These later regulations substituted pantaloons and half boots for breeches and shoes, and required midshipmen to wear a plain cocked hat with full dress instead of the gold laced cocked hat. The midshipman's undress was changed to "A short coat, rolling cape, with a button on each side," and permitted blue pantaloons, round hats with cockade, and dirks.

The buttons were "of yellow metal with foul anchor and American eagle surrounded by fifteen stars," both in 1802 and 1814.

In the *Life of Commodore Thomas Macdonough* by Rodney Macdonough, pp. 42, 43, there is a description of the uniform which he wore as a midshipman, taken from a memorandum left by Macdonough. It agrees exactly with the specifications of 1802 except that he wore "a single breasted *blue* vest with flaps" and "*blue* or white breeches."

For contemporary British uniforms, see "Naval Costume Past and Present" by Commander R. N. Suter, Royal Navy in the *Journal of the Royal Service Institution*, Vol. 66, pp. 559, *et seq.* (November, 1921).
4. "Historical Sketch of the Building of the Frigate *Essex*" by Gilbert L. Streeter in *Essex Institute Proceedings*, II, 76 (Salem, Mass., 1856).
5. *The First Cruise of the United States Frigate Essex, under the Command of Capt. Edward Preble* . . . by Capt. George Henry Preble, in *Essex Institute Historical Collections*, Vol. 10, p. 12, states that the original battery "consisted of 26 twelve-pounders on her gun decks, and 10 six-pounders on the quarter-deck, making 36 guns in all."

A. D. Turnbull's *Commodore David Porter*, p. 90, states that Captain John Smith in 1810 changed the *Essex's* battery to 24 thirty-two pounders and 2 long twelves on her main deck and 4 long twelves and 16 thirty-twos on the spar deck, and that Porter expressed in vain to the Secretary of the Navy his objections to the large ratio of carronades over long guns.
6. *Essex Institute Proceedings*, II, 74 (Salem, 1856).
7. *The Statistical History of the Navy of the United States* by George F. Emmons, p. 8, states that the total cost was $139,362. According to Mahan's *Admiral Farragut*, p. 15, her "cost, independent of guns and stores," was "somewhat over $75,000." According to *Essex Institute Proceedings*, II, 74, the total subscription amounted to $74,700, and the total cost, including guns and stores is given on p. 78 as $154,687.77. The government paid the remainder.
8. Turnbull's *Commodore David Porter*, p. 90, is in error in stating that Decatur was one of the distinguished commanding officers of

the *Essex*, though she was once a member of a squadron which he commanded.
9. As quoted in Loyall Farragut's *Life of David Glasgow Farragut*, p. 12.
10. From *Admiral Franklin Buchanan: Fearless Man of Action* by Charles Lee Lewis, pp. 21, 22. Based on *Sketches of Naval Life . . .* by A "Civilian" (George Jones), New Haven, 1829, and *Two Years and a Half in the American Navy* by E. C. Wines, London, 1833. The experiences set forth in these books were had on board the frigates *Constellation*, *Constitution*, and *Brandywine*, all contemporary with the *Essex*.
11. "The Yarn of the *Nancy Bell*" by Sir William S. Gilbert.
12. Mahan's *Admiral Farragut*, p. 11.
13. *Ibid.*
14. *Midshipman Farragut* by James Barnes, p. 13.

VII. PEACE TIME CRUISING IN THE *ESSEX*

1. *Masters Commandant Letters*, Naval Records and Library, Navy Department.
2. *Sketches of Naval Life* by George Jones and *Two Years and a Half in the American Navy* by E. C. Wines.
3. *Masters Commandant Letters*, Naval Records and Library.
4. *Sketches of Naval Life* by George Jones.
5. *Masters Commandant Letters* and *Letters to Officers: Ships of War*, Vol. IX, Naval Records and Library, Navy Department.
6. *The Second Admiral: A Life of David Dixon Porter* by Richard West, Jr., p. 3.
7. In Loyall Farragut's *Life of David Glasgow Farragut*, p. 13.
8. *Commodore John Rodgers . . .* by Charles Oscar Paullin, p. 172, gives this description: "He was a muscular, vigorous man, buoyantly alive, brave and modest, capable of deep feelings and strenuous energy; a little above the average in height, abundant coal-black hair, dark eyes and dark shaggy eyebrows; a handsome face bronzed by sea-winds and sunshine, an open countenance as befitted a sailor, and a look of firmness and resolution with a touch of imperiousness."
9. Loyall Farragut, p. 12.
10. *Ibid.*, p. 13.
11. *Commodore John Rodgers*, Paullin, p. 246.

VIII. FARRAGUT'S FIRST SEA FIGHT

1. *Commodore John Rodgers* by Charles Oscar Paullin, p. 250. D. D. Porter in his *Memoirs of David Porter*, p. 92, is in error in stating that Rodgers' squadron sailed on July 21 and the *Essex* on August 3.
2. *Journal* in Loyall Farragut's *Life of David Glasgow Farragut*, p. 15.
3. A letter by the purser of the *Essex*, Melancton W. Bostwick, dated

"17 April, 1812, on board the U. S. frigate *Essex*, at the Narrows below New York," states, "We are now, sir, going to sea, in every respect prepared for action." This is cited in John R. Spears's *David G. Farragut*, p. 47. Apparently the weakness in the mast was discovered after this date.

4. As quoted in Loyall Farragut, *op. cit.*, pp. 14, 15, which states, "The man, however, who really was an American and only wanted a frolic on shore, which he might have had by asking, as great liberty was allowed to the men, afterwards served all through the war on the Lakes, where he died about its termination."

The Naval History of Great Britain by William James, V, 363, quotes at length from a New York newspaper of June 25, 1812, "the formal deposition of the victim of Captain Porter's unmanly treatment" in which the sailor gave his name as John Erving of Newcastle-upon-Tyne in England, and claimed that, though he had resided in the United States since 1800, he had never become naturalized.

5. *Two Years and a Half in the American Navy* . . . by E. C. Wines, I, 344; *Sketches of Naval Life* . . . by George Jones, II, 17. A. D. Turnbull's *Commodore David Porter*, p. 97, is in error in stating that Porter's commission reached him on July 4 while the *Essex* was still in New York harbor.

6. *The Navy of the United States (Statistical History)* by Lieutenant George F. Emmons, U.S.N., p. 64; William James, *op. cit.*, V, 364, 365. Emmons is in error in stating that the escort was the *Nimrod*. James Fenimore Cooper's *Naval History of the United States* (one volume edition, 1847), p. 255, is in error in stating that the engagement took place "a few weeks from port" and that "150" soldiers were taken.

See Farragut's *Journal* in Loyall Farragut, *op. cit.*, p. 15.
7. *Ibid.*
8. William James, *op. cit.*, V, 365.
9. Emmons, *op. cit.*, p. 64, and *Captains' Letters*, Naval Records and Library, Navy Department.
10. Loyall Farragut, *op. cit.*, p. 15.
11. *Captains' Letters*, 1812. D. D. Porter's *Memoirs of David Porter*, p. 93, is in error in stating that the *Alert* was taken "a few days" after the *Minerva* affair; it was more than a month afterwards.
12. Cooper, *op. cit.*, p. 255.
13. *Ibid.*, p. 256.
14. William James, *op. cit.*, p. 366. Turnbull's *Commodore David Porter*, p. 100, has the British captain's name incorrectly spelled as "Langhorne."
15. Porter to the Secretary of the Navy, as quoted in the appendix to William James, *op. cit.*, V, xii. On p. 366 in this work the author states that the *Alert* was "in search of the *Hornet*"; but in the same author's *Naval Occurrences*, p. 81, it is stated that Porter had made

the false assertion that "the *Alert* was out for the purpose of taking the *Hornet*."
16. James, *op. cit.*, appendix, xii.
17. Loyall Farragut, *op. cit.*, pp. 15, 16.
18. *Ibid.*, pp. 16, 17.
19. D. D. Porter's *Memoirs of David Porter*, p. 94, states that the prisoners numbered 300 men; and on p. 95 declares that the cartel was placed in charge of Lieutenant Wilmer and Midshipman (sic) Stephen Decatur McKnight.

    William James, *op. cit.*, p. 366, states that, when the *Alert* was handed over to the United States, she was found unfit for a cruiser and was sent "to New York to grace the harbour as a block-ship, and to be pointed out to the citizens as one of the national trophies of the war."

    A letter by Purser Melancton W. Bostwick in Spears's *David G. Farragut*, pp. 50, 51, as quoted by Admiral George Dewey in the *Navy League Journal*, October, 1904, gives his personal account of the capture of the *Alert*. He states that the *Alert* had 13 men killed and thrown overboard before she was boarded.
20. Farragut's *Journal* in Loyall Farragut, *op. cit.*, p. 17, says the three ships were the *Shannon*, the *Acosta* (a misspelling of *Acasta*), and *Ringdove*. William James, *op. cit.*, p. 367, claims that the log of the *Ringdove* proves she was then in a harbor of the island of St. Thomas and that the log of the *Acasta* shows that this vessel could not have been there on August 30. He was confused by an error in Thomas Clark's *Naval History of the United States*, p. 180, as to the date and other details. By James's own data, however, the *Acasta* could have been on the scene on September 4, the correct date of the incident.
21. A. D. Turnbull, *op. cit.*, p. 103; and D. D. Porter's *Memoir of Commodore David Porter*, p. 97.
22. J. R. Spears, *op. cit.*, p. 46.

IX. DELAWARE BAY TO VALPARAISO

1. *Journal of a Cruise Made to the Pacific Ocean by Captain David Porter in the United States Frigate Essex* . . . I, 1.
2. *Commodore John Rodgers* by C. O. Paullin, p. 260.
3. To Samuel Hambleton, October 19, 1812.
4. Porter's *Journal*, I, 1.
5. *Life and Services of Commodore William Bainbridge* by Thomas Harris, p. 138.
6. The story in A. D. Turnbull's *Commodore David Porter*, p. 107, concerning the disciplining of Reuben James on the *Essex* is a good yarn, but unfortunately without foundation. First, the claim that he saved Decatur's life has been long exploded. See "Reuben James or Daniel Frazier?" by Charles Lee Lewis in *Maryland Historical Magazine*, March, 1924. In the second place, Reuben James was

not a member of the crew of the *Essex* under command of Porter. See Porter's *Journal*, I, 4-11, for a list of the crew.
7. *David G. Farragut* by J. R. Spears, p. 46.
8. Porter's *Journal*, I, 12.
9. *Ibid.*, p. 15.
10. *Ibid.*, p. 18.
11. *Sketches of Naval Life* . . . by George Jones, p. 36.
12. The story of the two shotes which had been taught to drink grog, found in A. D. Turnbull's *Commodore David Porter*, p. 112, is without foundation in Porter's *Journal* and Farragut's *Journal*. It is not in the original *Some Reminiscences* either.
13. Porter's *Journal*, I, 32. Mahan's *Admiral Farragut*, p. 20, is in error in stating that the *Nocton* had a crew of 40 men.

    "The command of this prize was given to Lieutenant Finch (afterward Captain Bolton), with orders to proceed home. She was captured on her way, between Bermuda and the Capes of Virginia, by a British frigate." Farragut's *Journal* in Loyall Farragut's *Life of David Glasgow Farragut*, p. 20.

    J. R. Spears's *David G. Farragut*, p. 55, is in error in stating that the *Nocton* was taken on December 11.
14. Spears's *David G. Farragut*, p. 55, is incorrect in stating that the *Essex* reached Cape Frio on December 29.

    Montagu is the spelling of the British ship of the line in Mahan's *Admiral Farragut*, p. 20.
15. Porter's *Journal*, I, 47, says nothing of the necessity of going in to refit, as stated in Mahan's *Admiral Farragut*, p. 20, and repeated in Spears's *David G. Farragut*, p. 55.

    The spelling of St. Catherines is from Porter's *Journal;* it may be spelled Santa Catharina or St. Catharines.
16. There is no foundation in Porter's *Journal*, I, 55, for the statement in D. D. Porter's *Memoir of Commodore David Porter*, p. 114, that Porter heard at St. Catherines "that an American frigate had sunk an English frigate" nor for the statement in Mahan's *Admiral Farragut*, p. 21, that at this place Porter heard "a rumor of the action between the *Constitution* and the *Java*." But see Porter's letter of July 3, 1814, to Secretary of Navy.

    The *Hornet* captured the *Peacock* off the mouth of the Demarara River in British Guiana on February 24, 1813. See *Life and Services of Commodore William Bainbridge* by Thomas Harris, p. 159.
17. Porter's *Journal*, I, 75.
18. *Ibid.*, p. 78. A. D. Turnbull's *Commodore David Porter*, p. 135, is incorrect in stating that Porter had replaced the guns before the last storm and that the rolling of the ship was thereby increased. Porter's *Journal*, I, 77, states that he had intended to do this but that the storm came before "we had effected this."
19. Farragut's *Journal* in Loyall Farragut's *Life of David Glasgow Farragut*, p. 20. "We lay off the Cape 21 days" is incorrect.

20. *Ibid.*, p. 21. Cf. Porter's *Journal*, I, 86. Porter's account varies in certain details from that of Farragut. The latter, which seems the more plausible, is followed here. But Farragut's statement that Spafford died two weeks after the accident is incorrect.
21. Porter probably out of consideration for the feelings of Commodore Stephen Decatur, who was Lieutenant McKnight's uncle, does not mention McKnight by name as the one who killed Spafford. But the name does appear in Farragut's *Journal*.
22. Farragut's *Journal* in Loyall Farragut's *Life of David Glasgow Farragut*, p. 21. Farragut is incorrect in stating that the *Essex* anchored on the 14th of March, when the crew had liberty. See Porter's *Journal*, I, 92, 93. D. D. Porter's *Memoir of Commodore David Porter*, 118, erroneously states that Porter reconnoitered Valparaiso on March 11. Mahan's *Admiral Farragut*, p. 22, repeats this error, as does also J. R. Spears's *David G. Farragut*, p. 58. A. D. Turnbull's *Commodore David Porter*, p. 142, adds details not having any foundation in Porter's *Journal* or in Farragut's *Journal*.

X. VALPARAISO AND GALAPAGOS ISLANDS

1. Not on March 22, as stated in Mahan's *Admiral Farragut*, p. 23.
2. The *Barclay* was commanded by Captain Gideon Randall of New Bedford; the *Walker* by Captain West of Nantucket.
3. Porter's *Journal*, I, 108-110. This was on March 25, and not on March 26, as stated in J. R. Spears's *David G. Farragut*, p. 58.
4. Porter's *Journal*, I, 117, 118. A. D. Turnbull's *Commodore David Porter*, p. 153, is incorrect in stating that it happened at the "end of April." Mahan's *Admiral Farragut*, p. 24, and J. R. Spears's *David G. Farragut*, p. 59, are both wrong in stating that the date was March 27.
5. The *Walker*, which had been taken from the Spanish (Peruvian) prize crew by the *Nimrod*, a British letter of marque, had been sent to England.
6. Porter's *Journal*, I, 148.
7. Farragut's *Journal* as quoted in Loyall Farragut's *Life of David Glasgow Farragut*, pp. 22, 23.
8. Porter's *Journal*, I, 150.
9. *Ibid.*, p. 149.
10. Loyall Farragut's *Life of David Glasgow Farragut*, pp. 23, 24.
11. *Some Reminiscences* by Farragut. Loyall Farragut, p. 24, paraphrases the account.
12. *Ibid.* Porter's *Journal*, I, 164, describes the grave of a sailor on this island under two lofty thorn-bushes, under which the sailors from the *Essex* used to gather. The pile of stones over the grave were used as both a seat and a table by them, "where they indulged themselves amply in their favorite food and quaffed many a can of grog to his poor soul's rest."

13. Porter's *Journal*, I, 167.
14. *Ibid.*, p. 174. Porter spells the name of the captain of the *Atlantic* "Wier"; Farragut's *Journal* has it "Weir."
    Spears's *David G. Farragut*, omits entirely the capture of the *Atlantic* and the *Greenwich*.
15. Spears's *David G. Farragut*, p. 59, is in error in stating that Porter captured six British whalers prior to June 1.
    Mahan's *Admiral Farragut*, p. 25, is wrong in stating that need of water compelled Porter to go to Tumbez; there is no foundation for this in Porter's *Journal*.
16. Farragut's *Journal* in Loyall Farragut's *Life of David Glasgow Farragut*, p. 25. Porter's *Journal*, I, 177, states that Porter thought the eruption was on Albemarle Island, and that this was confirmed the next day.
17. Porter's *Journal*, I, 191.
18. Farragut's *Journal* in Loyall Farragut's *Life of David Glasgow Farragut*, p. 25. Porter's *Journal*, I, 192, states that the animal was fifteen feet long; but at least one additional foot should be allowed in the retelling of such a story.
19. Farragut's *Journal* in Loyall Farragut's *Life of David Glasgow Farragut*, p. 25, is in error in stating that the *Georgiana* arrived on June 25 with the *Rose, Catharine*, and *Hector*. Porter's *Journal*, I, 198, gives the tonnage of these three vessels respectively as 220, 270, and 270. On p. 149, the tonnage of the *Georgiana* is given as 280 and the *Policy* as 275. The others were *Montezuma*, 270; *Greenwich*, 338; *Atlantic*, 355; *Seringapatam*, 357; *Charlton*, 274; *New Zealander*, 259; and *Sir A. Hammond*, 301.
20. Mahan's *Admiral Farragut*, p. 25.
21. Porter's *Journal*, I, 201.
22. *Ibid.* Mahan's *Admiral Farragut*, p. 27, J. R. Spears's *David G. Farragut*, p. 61, and D. D. Porter's *Memoir of Commodore David Porter*, p. 154, are all in error in stating that the two squadrons separated on July 4.
23. Farragut's *Journal* in Loyall Farragut, pp. 25, 26.
24. Porter's *Journal*, I, 241.

XI. AT NUKUHIVA IN THE MARQUESAS

1. As spelled in the *Encyclopedia Britannica* and on a map published by the National Geographic Society. Porter's *Journal*, II, 2, has it "Nooaheevah"; others spell it "Nukahiva" and "Nukahivah." It belonged to the Washington Group of the Islands, which were first discovered by Captain Joseph Ingraham of Boston in 1791.
2. Porter's *Journal*, II, 5.
3. This island is called Roohooga or Adams Island (written Huapu in the *Britannica*) in Porter's *Journal*, II, 7. In Farragut's *Journal* in

Loyall Farragut's *Life of David Glasgow Farragut*, p. 27, it is called Hood's Island and then confused with the Island of Nukuhiva.

J. R. Spears's *David G. Farragut*, p. 64, is in error in stating that the port was called Nukahiva.

4. Porter renamed them Massachusetts Bay and Madisonville respectively. Cf. His *Journal*, II, 14, 15.
5. Brother to the "Pathfinder of the Seas," Matthew Fontaine Maury, who also visited Nukuhiva many years afterwards on the *Vincennes* as a midshipman. See C. S. Stewart's *A Visit to the South Seas in the U. S. Ship Vincennes during the Years 1829 and 1830* and Charles Lee Lewis's *Matthew Fontaine Maury: Pathfinder of the Seas*, pp. 14-16.

    A. D. Turnbull's *Commodore David Porter*, p. 188, is wrong in stating there were only two white men.
6. Spelled "Hapas" and "Teiis" in Stewart's *A Visit to the South Seas*, I, 198, where "Typees" is written "Taipiis." Farragut's *Journal* in Loyall Farragut, 28, misspells "Happahs" as "Happars."

    The inhabitants of the island numbered about 20,000, according to Porter's *Journal*, II, 32.
7. Stewart's *A Visit to the South Seas*, I, 201, 262.
8. Porter's *Journal*, II, 22.
9. *Ibid.*, p. 63.
10. *Some Reminiscences*. Materially changed in Loyall Farragut, p. 27. Other midshipmen were Henry W. Ogden and William W. Feltus. See the *Journal* of Midshipman Feltus in the Historical Society of Pennsylvania.
11. *Ibid.*, p. 29; Porter's *Journal*, II, 74.
12. This was never ratified by the American government, and the island is now a French possession, France having taken possession of it about thirty years after Porter's visit.
13. Porter's *Journal*, II, Chap. xv, pp. 86-107.
14. For the troubles and disaster that befell Lieutenant Gamble and his men, see Porter's *Journal*, II, 178-231.

    On the 28th of December, the *New Zealander* sailed for the United States, and when within a day's sail of New York she was captured by a British man-of-war. Porter's *Journal*, II, 184.
15. His *Journal* in Loyall Farragut, p. 29.
16. Porter's *Journal*, II, 139, states simply: "I now called out White: he advanced, trembling. I informed them this was the man who had circulated a report so injurious to the character of the crew, and indignation was marked on every countenance. An Indian canoe was paddling by the ship; I directed the fellow to get into her, and never let me see his face again."
17. *Some Reminiscences*. Paraphrased in Loyall Farragut, p. 30.
18. *Ibid.* Porter's *Journal*, II, 161, states that the ships sailed on December 12, 1813; but this day was Sunday, and Farragut says they sailed on Monday, which would have to be December 13.

Mahan's *Admiral Farragut,* p. 30, is incorrect in stating that they sailed on December 9; D. D. Porter's *Memoir of Commodore David Porter,* p. 219, makes the same mistake; Spears's *David G. Farragut,* p. 65, makes a similar error in saying the date of departure was December 4. Mahan's *Admiral Farragut,* p. 30, is also wrong in stating that the *Essex* and the *Essex Junior* sailed for Valparaiso with one of the prizes.
19. Loyall Farragut, pp. 30, 31.
20. *Some Reminiscences.* Loyall Farragut, p. 31, has changed it to "I found them to be the best swordsmen on board."
21. Porter's *Journal,* II, 143. Spears's *David G. Farragut,* p. 68, incorrectly states that they arrived on February 4.

XII. THE LOSS OF THE *ESSEX*

1. Porter's *Journal,* II, 161, 162.
2. *Ibid.,* p. 144, states that "one half of my crew were on shore." D. D Porter's *Memoir of Commodore David Porter,* p. 220, makes the same statement. But Farragut's *Journal* in Loyall Farragut's *Life of David Glasgow Farragut,* p. 32, and Mahan's *Admiral Farragut,* p. 33, and Spears's *David G. Farragut,* p. 69, state that one third of the crew were ashore.
3. Porter's *Journal,* II, 164, and Loyall Farragut, p. 33.
4. Porter, II, 145; Porter's Letter to the Secretary of the Navy, July 13, 1814, in *Niles' Weekly Register,* VI, 352 (July 23, 1814). Farragut's *Journal* in Loyall Farragut, p. 33, phrases Porter's speeches differently. C. H. Snider's *Glorious "Shannon's" Old Blue Duster,* pp. 162, 163, giving the British point of view, tries to defend Hillyar's conduct.
5. Loyall Farragut, p. 33, as paraphrased from *Some Reminiscences.*
6. *Some Reminiscences.* Loyall Farragut, p. 33, has paraphrased it.
7. Porter's *Journal,* II, 145.
8. *Ibid.,* p. 162. William James's *Naval Occurrences,* p. 312, from British point of view, states that the *Phoebe* carried twenty-six long 18-pounders, fourteen carronades (32-pounders), one 18-pound and one 12-pound carronade, four long 9-pounders, and three 3-pounders and one 2-pounder in the tops, and carried only 300 men. He states that the *Cherub* had eighteen 32-pounder carronades, six 18-pounder carronades, one 12-pound carronade, two long 6-pounders, and a complement of only 121. He claimed, p. 314, the *Essex* had 265 men; but another English writer, Snider, pp. 174, 175, though greatly biased, admits that the *Essex* had 255 men and that the *Cherub* had 180. Theodore Roosevelt's *Naval War of 1812,* pp. 307, 308, gives a detailed comparative discussion of the strength of the two opposing sides.
9. *Some Reminiscences.* Porter's *Journal* does not mention this attempt. See J. Fenimore Cooper's *Naval History* . . . , p. 293.
10. *Some Reminiscences.* Porter's *Journal,* II, 165, states that the *Essex*

anchored "about three quarters of a mile to leeward of a battery on the east side of the harbor . . . within pistol shot of the shore." Cooper's *Naval History,* p. 294, states that the ship anchored "about three miles from the town, a mile and a half from the Castello Viego, which, however, was concealed by a bluff, half a mile from a detached battery of one 24-pound gun, and within pistol shot of the shore."

11. *Niles' Weekly Register,* VI, 351, 352, cites in detail from authorities on international law to prove that Hillyar violated the neutrality of Chile. This is substantiated in Mahan's *Admiral Farragut,* pp. 39, 40, and in Roosevelt's *Naval War of 1812,* pp. 300, 305, stating that Porter "could not anticipate Hilyar's (sic) deliberate and treacherous breach of faith." James does not attempt to defend Hillyar's attack on the *Essex* in Chilean waters, but on p. 308 he makes the false impression that the *Essex* brought on the attack by firing the first shot. Snider, p. 168, says, "Capt. Hillyar of H.M.S. *Phoebe* had no hallucinations about the obligations of respecting neutrality," and then makes the false statement that Porter had burned British vessels before Hillyar's eyes in neutral waters. Porter's *Journal,* II, 154, shows that the *Hector* was taken to sea beyond the three mile limit before she was burned. Porter's *Journal,* II, 172, discusses the reasons why the Governor of Valparaiso did not protect the *Essex* with his land batteries and order Hillyar to cease firing, as requested during the action by the American Consul General, Mr. Poinsett.

12. *Some Reminiscences.* Loyall Farragut, p. 35, is a paraphrase.

13. Porter's *Journal,* II, 164. Farragut's *Journal* in Loyall Farragut, p. 35, is probably incorrect in stating that springs had been gotten ready before the action began; also Mahan, *Admiral Farragut,* p. 41, makes the same error.

14. Porter's *Journal,* II, 165.

15. Loyall Farragut, p. 36, and Porter's *Journal,* II. 165, state that the enemy soon repaired damages and returned to the attack. Hillyar's report in William James's *Naval Occurrences,* Appendix, cvii, states that "on closing the *Essex,* at 35 minutes past 5, the firing re-commenced." This would have given the British a whole hour for repairing damages, and besides the careful distance which they kept to be out of range of the *Essex's* carronades could hardly be called "closing the *Essex.*" Snider, p. 169, states that the *Phoebe* returned, anchored, and began firing broadsides at five o'clock, but cites no authority for the statement.

16. Porter's *Journal,* II, 165. Farragut's *Journal* in Loyall Farragut, p. 36, says the position was on the larboard side, and Roosevelt, p. 295, follows this authority. But Mahan, p. 42, follows Porter's *Journal.*

17. Loyall Farragut, pp. 40, 41, paraphrases the account.

18. *Some Reminiscences.* The name is spelled Adam Roach in the list of the crew of the *Essex* in Porter's *Journal,* I, 5, but Adam Roche in the list of the missing in Porter's *Journal,* II, 235. Farragut's *Journal*

follows the former spelling. Farragut, p. 40, further states, "The most remarkable part of the affair was that Roach had always been a leading man in the ship, and, on the occasion previously mentioned, when the *Phoebe* seemed about to run into us in the harbor of Valparaiso, and the boarders were called away, I distinctly remember this man standing in an exposed position on the cathead, with sleeves rolled up and cutlass in hand, ready to board, his countenance expressing eagerness for the fight: which goes to prove that personal courage is a very peculiar virtue. Roach was brave with a prospect of success, but a coward in adversity."

Farragut, p. 45, states further that William Call, who lost a leg in the action, "while he was weltering in his blood, and it yet hung by the skin . . . discovered Adam Roach skulking on the berth deck, and dragged his shattered stump all around the baghouse, pistol in hand, trying to get a shot at him." No seaman by this name appears on the lists in Porter's *Journal*, though there was a William Cole and he might have been the man.

19. Loyall Farragut, p. 43, slightly paraphrased from *Some Reminiscences*.
20. *Ibid.*, p. 42. Ralph D. Paine's *Ships and Sailors of Old Salem*, pp. 308, 309, on the authority of one of the seamen of the *Essex* who returned to Salem after the capture of the ship, cites other examples of bravery, as follows: John Ripley, after losing his leg, said: "Farewell, boys, I can be of no use to you," and flung himself overboard out of the bow port. John Alvinson received an eighteen-pound ball through the body; in the agony of death he exclaimed: "Never mind, shipmates. I die in defence of Free Trade and Sailors' Rights," and expired with the words *Rights* quivering on his lips. James Anderson had his left leg shot off and died encouraging his comrades to fight bravely in defence of liberty. After the engagement, Benjamin Hazen, having dressed himself in a clean shirt and jerkin, told what messmates of his that were left that he could never submit to be taken as a prisoner by the English and leaped into the sea where he was drowned."

As the names of these four men appeared on the list of killed in Porter's *Journal*, II, 234, and the name of Bissley, mentioned by Farragut, does not appear on any of the lists, Farragut probably confused the name with that of John Ripley, the circumstances being similar. Alvinson, however, was Alvison on the list. See also *Niles' Weekly Register*, VI, 420.
21. Porter's *Journal*, II, 167.
22. Loyall Farragut, pp. 43, 44.
23. Porter's *Journal*, II, 167, 168. Loyall Faragut, p. 37, says that Porter went below "to ascertain the quantity of powder in the magazine. On his return to the deck, he met Lieutenant McKnight, the only commissioned officer left on duty, all the others having been killed or wounded." Porter does not mention his having gone below.

24. *Ibid.*, p. 168. Loyall Farragut, p. 37, says the flag came down at 6:30. See James's *Naval Occurrences*, p. 309, for the British answer to Porter's accusation that the *Phoebe* fired ten minutes after the *Essex* surrendered.

    According to a letter by Lieutenant Edward Barnewalle, of March 28, 1814, "Capt. P. now seeing no hopes left, gave orders to fire the Ship, but humanely considering that many of his brave companions were lying wounded below, he countermanded this order, and gave the painful one to lower our ensign, which was executed precisely at half past six. The enemy did not cease firing until some minutes afterwards; during this interval some of our men were wounded and four shot dead." As advertised for sale by Retz & Storm, Inc., 598 Madison Avenue, New York.

    He is carried in the *Navy Register* as Edward Barnewell, who became a master January 29, 1814, and a lieutenant on July 22, 1814. He was probably acting as lieutenant during the battle. In 1815 he was lost with the *Epervier*.
25. Loyall Farragut, pp. 41, 42. Loyall Farragut, p. 42, has "O Davy," but *Some Reminiscences* has "O Gatty," evidently another nickname.
26. *Ibid.*, p. 42. Neither he nor Porter say anything about drunkenness on the *Essex* during the battle. But James, p. 311, says that "buckets of spirits were found in all parts of the main-deck; and most of the prisoners were in a state of intoxication." On p. 314, he says that "the majority of the unwounded men that remained in the *Essex* were such as either could not swim, or were incapacitated by liquor." Snider, p. 172, probably getting his information from James, says, "Brandy by the bucketful stood between the guns, and added to the chaos below decks. Men who were not crazed by burns and wounds were fighting drunk."
27. Porter's *Journal*, II, 169, and *Some Reminiscences*, according to which Cowell lived twenty-one days.
28. Porter's *Journal*, II, 17, 235; James, pp. 314, 315.
29. Captain James Hillyar's report of March 30, 1814, from Valparaiso, in James, Appendix, cvii, and in *Royal Naval Biography* by John Marshall (Lieutenant in the Royal Navy), London, 1824, II, 862, states that the action with the *Essex* began a little after 4:00 P.M., and ended at 6:20, but minimizes all but the last 45 minutes of the engagement. In part, he wrote, "The defence of the *Essex*, taking into consideration our superiority of force, the very discouraging circumstance of her having lost her main-topmast, and being twice on fire, did honor to her brave defenders, and most fully evinced the courage of Captain Porter, and those under his command. Her colours were not struck until the loss in killed and wounded was so awfully great, and her shattered condition so seriously bad, as to render further resistance unavailing." His report shows that he felt under obligation to respect the port of Valparaiso only.

30. Loyall Farragut, p. 39, paraphrased from *Some Reminiscences*.
31. Porter's *Journal*, II, 169. This is the only mention made by him in the *Journal* except in the list of the officers and crew of the *Essex* and in the list of those paroled by Captain Hillyar.
32. Loyall Farragut, p. 32, paraphrased from *Some Reminiscences*.
33. *Ibid.*, p. 38.
34. Porter's *Journal*, II, 174.
35. Loyall Farragut, p. 44, paraphrased from *Some Reminiscences*.
36. Porter's *Journal*, II, 241, says there were 132; but Loyall Farragut, p. 45, explains how two were left behind.
37. Snider, p. 176, states that the *Essex*, as a British prize, arrived in Plymouth Sound, November 13, 1814. According to Mahan's *Admiral Farragut*, p. 50, the vessel was there bought into the British Navy, in which she served as a frigate until 1837, when she was sold and all trace of her history thereafter was lost.

Paine's *Ships and Sailors of Old Salem*, pp. 307, 308, quotes the following from a broadside published in Salem after the news of the loss of the *Essex* reached that town:

> "The *Essex* sorely rak'd and gall'd;
> While able to defend her
> The *Essex Crew* are not appall'd
> They DIE but *don't* SURRENDER!
> They fearless FIGHT, and FEARLESS DIE!
> And now the scene is over;
> For *Britain*, Nought but *Powers* on high
> Their DAMNING SINS can Cover.
> They MURDER and refuse to *save!*
> With Malice Most infernal!!
> Rest, *England's Glory* in the Grave,
> 'Tis INFAMY—ETERNAL!!!
> Brave HULL and LAWRENCE fought your Tars
> With honorable dealings;
> For great as Jove and brave as Mars
> Are hearts of Humane Feelings.
> Our tears are render'd to the brave,
> Our hearts' applause is given;
> Their Names in Mem'ry we engrave,
> Their spirits rest in Heaven;
> Paroled see Porter and his crew
> In the ESSEX JUNIOR coasting;
> They home return—hearts brave and true,
> And scorn the *Britons* boasting—
> Arrived—by all around belov'd,
> With welcome shouts and chanting,
> Brave Tars—all valiant and approv'd,
> Be such Tars never Wanting.

Should Britain's *Sacrilegious* band
The 'Millions' be for sparing;
Yet tell her in her native land
Her *Deeds* are like her *Daring*,
That should she *not* with WISDOM haste
Her *miscreant* CRIMES undoing,
Her *Crown, Wealth, Empire*, all must waste
And sink in common RUIN."

Another poem, not so fiery but written by a better poet, though an anonymous one, was entitled "The Battle of Valparaiso." It is quoted in full below from *Poems of American History* by Burton E. Stevenson, pp. 307, 308:

"From the laurel's fairest bough,
  Let the muse her garland twine,
To adorn our Porter's brow,
  Who, beyond the burning line,
Led his caravan of tars o'er the tide.
  To the pilgrims fill the bowl,
  Who, around the southern pole,
  Saw new constellations roll,
    For their guide.

Heave the topmast from the board,
  And our ship for action clear,
By the cannon and the sword,
  We will die or conquer here.
The foe, of twice our force, nears us fast:
  To your posts, my faithful tars!
  Mind your rigging, guns, and spars,
  And defend your stripes and stars
    To the last.

At the captain's bold command,
  Flew each sailor to his gun,
And resolved he there would stand,
  Though the odds were two to one,
To defend his flag and ship with his life:
  High on every mast display'd,
  'God, Our Country, and Free Trade',
  E'en the bravest braver made
    For the strife.

Fierce the storm of battle pours:
  But unmoved as ocean's rock,
When the tempest round it roars,
  Every seaman breasts the shock,
Boldly stepping where his brave messmates fall.
  O'er his head, full oft and loud,

Like the vulture in a cloud,
As it cuts the twanging shroud,
   Screams the ball.

Before the siroc blast
From its iron caverns driven,
Drops the sear'd and shiver'd mast,
By the bolt of battle riven,
And higher heaps the ruin of the deck—
   As the sailor, bleeding, dies,
   To his comrades lifts his eyes,
   'Let our flag still wave,' he cries,
      O'er the wreck.

In echo to the sponge,
   Hark! along the silent lee,
Oft is heard the solemn plunge,
   In the bosom of the sea.
'Tis not the sullen plunge of the dead,
   But the self-devoted tar,
   Who, to grace the victor's car,
   Scorns from home and friends afar
      To be led.

Long live the gallant crew
   Who survived that day of blood:
And may fortune soon renew
   Equal battle on the flood.
Long live the glorious names of the brave.
   O'er these martyrs of the deep,
   Oft the roving tar shall weep,
   Crying, 'Sweetly may they sleep
      Neath the wave.' "

XIII. AN INTERLUDE

1. While the *Essex Junior* was en route to New York with Midshipman Farragut on board, his father George Farragut, who had been officially dismissed from the naval service on March 25, 1814, wrote his *Memorial to the Secretary of the Navy*, dated May 20, 1814. It has already been quoted from at length, but the concluding portion covering the career of the old man after Glasgow left New Orleans is as follows: "I have five children; my Eldest son William A. C. Farragut is a midshipman in the Navy and serving I believe on board the new Sloop of War *Frolic;* my second son James G. Farragut (His father apparently did not know that he had changed his name to David Glasgow Farragut) is a midshipman on command, under that Gallant officer, Captain Porter of the *Essex*, and the happiest moment of my Life was when I noticed in the public Papers the honorable

mention Captain Porter made of my Boy. I trust in God my two Sons may deserve well of their Country; I have always given them a good example and patriotic precepts; my dismission *is the most terrible to my feelings*, lest it may hereafter be cast up to my Boys as a reproach. I ask of the President and of you, Sir, the Justice to reinstate me in my Command and with Instructions to the Naval Commander of this Station that, when age and Infirmities incapacitate me for active duty, to allow me half pay; I have served my Country long and faithful; now that I am getting old and am poor, my Country should serve me—*one good turn deserves another*. Be at the trouble, Sir, to ask the Tennessee Representatives in Congress and they will assure you that I have in my time been an active and zealous friend of the United States. General John Sevier, the Honorable Mr. Campbell, Secretary of the Treasury, Governor Claiborne of Louisiana, Governor Blount of Tennessee, the Honorable Mr. Anderson of the Senate and the Honorable John Rhea of the House of Representatives have long known your Memorialist and he is proud to believe that they all believe him an honest Man and deserving well of the Country.

Your Memorialist tenders to you his best wishes for the honor of your administration and for the continuance of the Successes and the Glory of the American Navy."

The following incident apparently happened after Farragut left his father, as he makes no mention of it in his *Journal*. It is recounted in the following letter from George W. Sevier (Draper Manuscripts, XXX, 328): "A vessel in which (George) Farragut was sailing from New Orleans to Pascagoula Bay was attacked by pirates. The crew was for giving up. Farragut flew around; loaded and fired his gun rapidly, calling to the others: 'By heavens, fight, fight like de devil.' This inspired confidence in the crew, and on becoming active the pirates were repulsed."

At this time the country between Lake Pontchartrain and Pensacola was in a state of anarchy, because it was claimed by the United States as a part of Louisiana Territory and by Spain as a portion of West Florida. As George Farragut's plantation was located in this disputed territory and he was conversant with conditions, he was entrusted by Governor Claiborne with responsibilities there. He accompanied Dr. William Flood as an interpreter in January, 1811, to establish the parishes of Viloxy and Pascagoula (*Claiborne Official Letter Books*, V, 83). A little later Dr. Flood appointed him Justice of the Peace in the latter parish (*Ibid.*, p. 133). On April 4, Claiborne wrote George Farragout (*sic*) approving the establishment of a military post on the Dog River (*Ibid.*, p. 206); and on July 9 he wrote Colonel Maximilien Maxent referring to Captain Farragout as the bearer of dispatches from him to the officer commanding the U. S. naval force near Mobile (*Ibid.*, pp. 297, 298). This is substantiated by a letter of January 5, 1811, from Commodore John Shaw, in command of the Naval Station in New Orleans, to George Farragut: "Public service requires your presence on the Pascagola (*sic*). I have therefore to direct that you will proceed immediately on board the U. S. *Fallacca Allegator* (*sic*) bound for that port, and obey such Lawful instructions as you may receive from time to time through me, from his Excellency Governor Wm. C. C. Claiborne. It is considered from your knowledge of that country that your services and presence are of considerable import there, and having every confidence in your ability as an Officer, you are selected on that service. The *Allegator* has been ordered to remain at Pascagola six days provided important circumstances forbid her return: you are required to write me on all opertunities (*sic*)." As late as October 10, 1812, Shaw wrote Farragut from Bay St. Louis: "I find it out of my power to undertake the building of a Blockship, consequently you are at liberty to return to Pascagola; on your arrival there I must request you to send us on, as soon as possible to this place, two pairs of good sawyers, the ash oars must be of a good quality, otherwise they will be rejected. A moderate compensation will be allowed you for your passage to this place."

George Farragut refers to this service in his *Memorial* as follows: "Your Memorialist enjoying bad health was ordered in 1811 by Commodore Shaw to the Bay of Pascagoula, where for the most part your Memorialist has since resided. Whenever his health permitted, your Memorialist was ready and willing to enter on active Service. But it is too true that the Constitution of your Memorialist is much impaired and *that with increase of years and hard Service,* his Lamp would some time since have burnt out, but for the little relaxation he lately experienced at Bay of Pascagoula." This admission of ill health is the reason why nothing apparently was done by the Secretary of the Navy to restore him to active service. It was a good reason, however, for giving him half pay; but this too apparently did not materialize.

2. Porter's *Journal*, II, 176.
3. Loyall Farragut, p. 46, as slightly paraphrased from *Some Reminiscences*.
4. Porter's *Journal*, II, 176.
5. Loyall Farragut, p. 47, as slightly paraphrased from *Some Reminiscences*.
6. *Some Reminiscences*.
7. *Niles' Weekly Register*, VI, 349. *Some Reminiscences* mentions the ox cart and makes the doubtful statement that Porter took a hack in Brooklyn in which he went across to New York. A. D. Turnbull's *Commodore David Porter*, p. 236, states, "Men dragged his boat out of the water, set it on wheels and drove it into Brooklyn, where he launched it and pulled across to New York."
8. The *Essex Junior* was sold into the Navy of the United States for the sum of $25,000 (Porter's *Journal*, II, 243).

In Valparaiso, after the battle, Lieutenant Stephen Decatur Mc-

Knight, Chaplain David P. Adams, Midshipman James Lyman, and eleven seamen were exchanged for a part of the crew of the captured British whaler *Sir Andrew Hammond*. They were not permitted to return home on the cartel ship *Essex Junior* but were obliged to get passage on merchant vessels. McKnight and Lyman transferred from the Swedish brig *Adonis* (in which they had embarked) to the sloop of war *Wasp* of the U. S. Navy, in lat. 18°35′ north and long. 30°10′ west. The *Wasp* was never heard of again, and is supposed to have been shipwrecked and lost at sea. See Porter's *Journal*, II, 172 and 245-256.

9. Farragut's *Journal* in Loyall Farragut, p. 50, is incorrect in stating, "On the last of November, 1814, I was exchanged." In Porter's *Journal*, II, 244, 245, letters from the Commissary General of Prisoners and the Secretary of the Navy prove that on August 10 and 11, 1814, the officers and crew of the *Essex* were "discharged from their paroles, and are as free to serve, in any capacity, as if they had never been made prisoners," on account of the conduct of Captain Nash, commander of the *Saturn*. The same error is in Mahan, p. 52, and Spears, p. 88.

10. *Some Reminiscences*.

11. Porter's *Journal*, II, 245. Richard West's *The Second Admiral: A Life of David Dixon Porter*, p. 4, is in error in stating that "the hero of the *Essex* reached Green Bank (Porter's home at Chester) in September, 1814."

   Niles' Weekly Register, VI, 356, gives the following reception given Porter as he passed through Philadelphia: "He entered the city in a carriage with the mayor, preceded and followed by an immense cavalcade of officers, civil and military, and citizens of all ranks. The streets were hung with the stripes and stars. When the crowd arrived opposite Christ Church in Second-street, it was met by a large body of respectable seamen, who hitched another rope to the carriage in which the people were hauling the gallant fellow (for long before they had unyoked the horses) and the whole went through the city with continual shouts. When they arrived at the Mansion House Hotel, the sailors took him on their shoulders and carried him in with huzzas. He stopped but a few minutes, and taking a private carriage proceeded to his family at Chester." Though Farragut makes no reference to this incident in his *Journal*, he probably shared in it. No date is given, though it occurred previous to July 23, 1814.

12. Loyall Farragut, 49. *Some Reminiscences* has only the words, "All of which I have since found useful."

13. Mahan's *Admiral Farragut*, p. 51.

14. The Muster Roll of the *Spark* carries Farragut's name from July 12, 1814, to April 15, 1815.

15. From *Some Reminiscences*. Loyall Farragut, p. 50, omits most of the details.

XIV. CRUISING IN THE MEDITERRANEAN

1. Gardner W. Allen's *Our Navy and the Barbary Corsairs*, 276, et seq.
2. Not razeed until 1836. A. D. Turnbull's *Commodore David Porter* refers to the *Independence* as a razee at the time Farragut served on her.
3. George F. Emmons's *Statistical History of the Navy of the United States*, p. 24; and *The Mariner*, January, 1934.
4. The description is based on Charles Nordhoff's *Man-of-War Life*, 1855, an account of a voyage round the world in the *Columbus*, a sister ship to the *Independence*.
5. *The Autobiography of Commodore Charles Morris*, p. 73. Morris, on p. 74, states that the *Congress* met the *Independence* at Carthagena on August 1; but Allen's *Our Navy and the Barbary Corsairs*, pp. 292, 293, states that Bainbridge's squadron arrived August 5, and the *Congress* on August 9; Thomas Harris's *Life ... of Bainbridge*, p. 199, also states that Bainbridge arrived on August 5.
6. *The Romantic Decatur* by Charles Lee Lewis, pp. 156-174.
7. *The Life of William Bainbridge, Esq. of the U. S. Navy* by H. A. S. Dearborn, 1816 (reprint edited by James Barnes, 1931), p. 202.
8. Farragut's *Journal* in Loyall Farragut, p. 50.
9. Harris's *Life of Bainbridge*, pp. 200, 201.
10. Loyall Farragut, p. 50. Not in *Some Reminiscences*.
11. *Some Reminiscences*. Among the ships which he mentions as being present is the *Epervier*. This is an error, for that vessel passed Gibraltar on the way home with the treaty on July 12 (Allen's *Our Navy and the Barbary Corsairs*, p. 289). She was, however, lost at sea and never reached the United States. In her perished Captain William Lewis and his brother-in-law, Lieutenant B. J. Neale, returning home as passengers, together with the captives recently released from bondage in Algiers.
12. Loyall Farragut, p. 51.
13. Charles Lee Lewis's *Romantic Decatur*, p. 216.
14. Loyall Farragut, p. 51.
15. *The Autobiography of Commodore Charles Morris*, p. 75. He states that there were fifteen, but forgets that both the *Epervier* and *Guerrière* were not present.
16. See the illustration in Allen's *Our Navy and the Barbary Corsairs*, p. 292, showing Bainbridge's fleet in sailing formation.
17. *The Autobiography of ... Morris*, p. 75.
18. Loyall Farragut, p. 51. Farragut is wrong in the impression that Captains Ridgely and Crane exchanged commands after the squadron arrived at Newport, for the *Erie* had been left at Gibraltar as a part of Commodore Shaw's squadron (Allen's *Our Navy and the Barbary Corsairs*, p. 294). *Some Reminiscences* states that Taylor afterwards died a martyr to the vice of drunkenness.
19. Charles Lee Lewis's *Admiral Franklin Buchanan*, p. 29. William Pinkney was a distinguished citizen of Annapolis.

20. *The Ancient City: History of Annapolis* . . . by Elihu S. Riley, p. 253.
21. *Some Reminiscences*. Farragut would not have referred to Porter as his "friend," if he had been his adopted son, as some claim him to have been.
22. Loyall Farragut, pp. 52, 54.
23. Mahan's *Admiral Farragut*, footnote on p. 54, relates a tradition that on this ship a midshipman in full dress with cocked hat together with a full crew was constantly stationed in each boat at the booms so that no time would be lost in dropping alongside when called away.
24. Allen's *Our Navy and the Barbary Corsairs*, p. 297, footnote 2. Loyall Farragut, p. 54, is in error in stating that this happened at Port Mahon several months later.
25. Loyall Farragut, p. 53, as paraphrased from *Some Reminiscences*. The treaty with Algiers was signed under pressure on December 23, 1816.
26. *Ibid.*, pp. 54, 55.
27. Farragut's father died at Pascagoula on June 4, 1817, though the son did not learn about his passing until many months afterwards. According to Farragut's letter to Lyman C. Draper of September 20, 1853, in *American Historical Review*, IX, 540, his father died of a cough contracted through careless exposure.

After the writing of his *Memorial to the Secretary of the Navy* on May 20, 1814, his financial condition seems to have declined, according to the following letters which he wrote to General Andrew Jackson. From Mobile, he wrote March 24, 1815 (The Battle of New Orleans was fought on January 8, 1815): "I regret not been with you at New Orleans, but owever, I did my duty on this quarter, for two months I have been imploed by General Winchester as Spy from Pascagoula to pas cristian, and den I come to this place, and becos I had a public Horse, did no alowed me but twenty Dollars per month. I anderwent a great dil of fatig, in that place, from the 15 day of December to the 15 day of February and I both (bought) a public Horse, he dyd, so it his that my pay dont pay for the Horse, and ten Dollars that I had from Capt Fils, the quarter master, so it his that I am indeted to the quarter master sixteen Dollars bisis my pay, so I go home with out money, nor provision, and without horse to plow my corn, or to geder my Catlet (cattle?), I mos go to New Orleans in a few days to git my friends to asist me in giteen provision until I can sell som of my stok or work hard for it, if I could git eny thing to do in the line of my profetion on this cost, I would be glad, if dont I chell be oblige to lebour hard to support me and my smol childrens. My respects to your Lady and friends I am Respectfully your obt Servant Geo Farragut." This is substantiated by a receipt signed by George Farragut at Mobile, February 15, 1815, for payment for services rendered the U.S. as a spy; it is countersigned by General James Winchester. Cited in the *American Clipper* for March, 1940 (American Autograph Shop, Merion Station, Pennsylvania).

This letter apparently met with a favorable response from the General, according to a second letter which George Farragut wrote Jackson from Pascagoula, March 30, 1816, a year later, in which he wrote: "I hope this will met you well, I write you this to let you no that I am in the land of the living and working ard to mak some thing to supist on. I have totat rels (toted rails) on my shoulder, until my sholders could ber no more, owever my fences are all don, but now I must tak the owe (hoe) to plant my corn, for I have no Horse, and my Catlet I must hont on foot—God bles you and Seft Return to your famely. I am Respectfuly your obt Servant Geo Farragut."

Both these letters are quoted in *American Historical Review*, IX, 767. Glasgow Farragut apparently knew nothing of these letters, for in his long letter to Draper he declared: "He (father) was in the battle of New Orleans but what part he bore I know not. I only know that if he had not borne an honorable part Genl. Jackson would never have acknowledged him as a friend, or have been disposed to befriend his son as he ever did me."

28. Loyall Farragut, pp. 56, 57.
29. *Ibid.*, p. 57. In *Some Reminiscences* he mentions seeing the opera, *Bluebeard*, at the San Carlos Opera House.
30. *Ibid.*, pp. 58, 59. Farragut's *Journal* is in error in stating that the *Washington* went then to Port Mahon for the winter. According to her log, she did not even touch at Minorca on her return to Syracuse where she wintered. Other errors in the itinerary of the cruise appear on p. 59. Mahan's *Admiral Farragut*, p. 57, makes the same mistake regarding the *Washington*.
31. Folsom, in a few years, returned to the United States and gained distinction as a teacher and librarian at Harvard College.
32. Dated October 14, 1817, and quoted in full in Loyall Farragut, pp. 61, 62. The letter shows clearly that David Porter was merely the "patron" of Farragut and not his legal foster parent.
33. Log of the *Erie*. Loyall Farragut, p. 62, is in error in stating that Farragut went on board the *Erie* in November, and later stopped at Marseilles only ten days.
34. Loyall Farragut, p. 56, is in error in stating this happened on board the *Washington*, in the spring of 1817. According to her log, she did not visit Malaga then or later while Farragut was aboard her.
35. Loyall Farragut, pp. 62, 63.
36. Log of the *Erie* states the arrival was on December 28, 1817. Mahan's *Admiral Farragut*, p. 58, is in error in stating that Farragut and Folsom arrived early in 1818.
37. *Some Reminiscences*.
38. Farragut to David Porter from Leghorn, December 12, 1818. In Navy Department Archives and Library.
39. Loyall Farragut, p. 75.
40. Folsom to Farragut from Cambridge, Massachusetts, October 9, 1865, quoted in full in Loyall Farragut, p. 73.

41. Loyall Farragut, p. 71.
42. *Ibid.*, p. 76, as paraphrased from *Some Reminiscences*.
43. Farragut to Folsom, November 2, 1818, from the Lazaretto, Leghorn; quoted in full in Loyall Farragut, p. 76. On p. 58, Farragut relates that on his first visit to Leghorn when the *Washington* called there in the summer of 1817 many of the officers went to Rome but he had to be contented with a view of the dome of St. Peter's as the ship sailed along the coast.
44. Folsom to Farragut from Tunis, November 4, 1818, quoted in full in Loyall Farragut, pp. 78, 79.
45. Loyall Farragut, p. 80, as paraphrased from *Some Reminiscences*.
46. Farragut to David Porter from Leghorn, December 12, 1818. This letter, as does his correspondence in later life, shows that Farragut never mastered English spelling and grammar. Loyall Farragut, p. 80, is in error in stating that he left Leghorn for Messina on December 1. It may have been as late as January, 1819, for Spears's *David G. Farragut*, p. 99, quotes the following letter which Farragut wrote to Danish Consul Gierlew, January 27, 1819: "I am happy to inform you that I had a pleasant ride out last evening with a young Jewess, who was very easy and agreeable in her conversation, so that I did not repent in the least my late ride, as we contrived to make the time pass." Spears, however, neglects to state the place from which the letter was written, though he implies that it was from Pisa.
47. Crane to Porter, written on board the *United States* at Tunis, September 28, 1818. In Navy Department Archives and Library.
48. Letter from Commodore Charles Stewart, in Captains' Letters, Navy Department Archives and Library. Spears's *David G. Farragut*, p. 99, is in error in stating that he reported "late in January."
49. Log of the *Franklin*. Loyall Farragut, p. 57, is incorrect in the statement that this incident took place on the *Washington* during her visit to Naples in the year 1817. Spears's *David G. Farragut*, p. 93, repeats the same error, and without authority states that one of the sailors remarked, "One of them kings has fallen down a hatch, sir." Farragut's *Journal* does not mention this detail.
50. *Some Reminiscences*.
51. *Ibid.*, p. 81, is incorrect in stating that this was the *Shark*, which according to Emmons's *Statistical History of the Navy of the United States*, p. 14, was not built in Washington until the year 1821. On p. 12, the *Spark* is said to have been purchased in Baltimore in 1814. She carried 14 guns and 90 men, and had a tonnage of 300. She had only two masts and square sails like a frigate; but all the guns were carried on the spar deck. Mahan's *Admiral Farragut*, pp. 60, 61, makes the same mistake.
52. Loyall Farragut, p. 81, must be incorrect in stating that it was the spring of 1820, for Bainbridge's arrival, referred to in the same connection, was on June 4, 1820.
53. Loyall Farragut, p. 82, paraphrased from *Some Reminiscences*.

NOTES 339

54. *Ibid.*, p. 83, is incorrect in stating that the *America* arrived in Washington on November 20, 1820. Mahan's *Admiral Farragut*, p. 62, and Spears's *David G. Farragut*, p. 100, make the same error.

The *America* arrived in New York and not Washington. See Farragut's letter to Secretary of the Navy, of February 26, 1821, in the Navy Department Archives and Library.

XV. CRUISING IN THE GULF OF MEXICO

1. Loyall Farragut, p. 83.
2. Farragut to Secretary of the Navy Smith Thompson, from Norfolk, November 24, 1820. Navy Department Archives and Library.

    Loyall Farragut, p. 83, covers up Farragut's failure as follows: "It appears that Farragut did not pass his examination so well as to satisfy his own ambition." Mahan's *Admiral Farragut*, p. 62, incorrectly states, "His examination soon followed, and was passed; but apparently not quite to his own satisfaction."
3. *Some Reminiscences* also states that Farragut had learned that Raymond Perry "was both a fool and a drunkard" while he served under him as captain of the *Spark*. His name appears as Raymond H. Perry, in the *Navy Registers*; he was the brother of Oliver Hazard and Matthew Calbraith Perry and the brother-in-law to Captain George Washington Rodgers. He died March 12, 1826. Oliver Hazard Perry also drank. See *The Great Commodore* by E. M. Barrows, p. 54.
4. *Some Reminiscences.*
5. Thomas J. Wertenbaker's *Norfolk: Historic Southern Port* (1931), p. 139.
6. *Ibid.*, p. 143.
7. *Ibid.*, 179. According to letters in the Navy Department Archives and Library, Farragut took his examinations in New York between September 28 and November 17, 1820, and went to Norfolk between November 17 and 23, 1820.
8. Navy Department Archives and Library. Captain Arthur Sinclair was in command of the Norfolk Station.
9. *Ibid.*
10. Navy Department Archives and Library has a letter of June 21, 1913, from Worthington C. Ford, Massachusetts Historical Society, to Charles W. Stewart, Superintendent of Naval Records and Library, stating, "I have a letter of Admiral Farragut, dated New York, October 28th, without year. In he states that he has passed his examination: 'I aimed at the head but was glad to catch at number 20 out of 53. A. Bainbridge passed next above me.' Will your records give me the year of this letter?" Stewart replied, "The date . . . is October 28, 1820. . . ." This answer was incorrect, for among Farragut manuscripts recently given to the Naval Academy Museum is a form letter from Secretary Smith Thompson to Farragut, dated November 6, 1821, as follows: "You are hereby notified that on your late examina-

tion you were found qualified for promotion." The correct date for the Worthington Ford letter must have been October 28, 1821.

In the *Navy Registers* of 1821 and 1822 Farragut's name appears among the lists of midshipmen; but in the *Register* of 1823 his name appears 15th in a list of 44 of "Midshipmen Passed for Promotion 1821." This was the first *Navy Register* to carry such a list. Resignations and deaths changed his number 20 out of 53 in 1821 to 15th out of 44 in 1823.

11. Officers' Letters, Navy Department Archives and Library.
12. Navy Department Archives and Library.
13. George F. Emmons's *Statistical History of the Navy of the United States*, p. 8, states that it "was cut down twice and raised once to a jackass frigate." She was also called a corvette.
14. Log of *John Adams*. Loyall Farragut, p. 84, is incorrect in stating that she called at Charleston in June. *Some Reminiscences* states that Poinsett had business in Puerto Rico.
15. Ibid. *Some Reminiscences* calls the passenger Mr. Todd and says he was transferred to the *Spark* in Mona Passage.
16. He was crowned emperor on July 21, 1822, was forced to abdicate on April 19, 1823, and returning to Mexico the following year from Italy, was taken prisoner and shot on July 1, 1824. The dates in Loyall Farragut, pp. 84, 85, are all wrong.
17. Loyall Farragut, p. 84, as paraphrased from *Some Reminiscences*.
18. The Poinsettia was named after him, though this fact is not stated in the *Encyclopedia Britannica*. This might be considered a penalty for not having been born an Englishman. Poinsett was a native of South Carolina. He was American Consul at Santiago, Chile, at the time of the Cruise of the *Essex*.
19. Log of the *John Adams*.
20. It is really a continuation of the Panuco River.
21. A Spanish coin originally worth sixteen silver dollars, but later much reduced in value.
22. Loyall Farragut, p. 85; not in *Some Reminiscences*.
23. *Ibid.*, p. 86. The distance to Tampico is said to have been three leagues, a measure differing in different times and countries from 2.4 to 4.6 miles. *Some Reminiscences* states that he reached "the river" and does not call it the Tampico River, as it is called in the edited version in Loyall Farragut, p. 86. A careful examination of a detailed map of the environs of Tampico shows that Farragut, depending on his memory, was in error as to the geography of the vicinity.
24. *Ibid.*, p. 87, as paraphrased from *Some Reminiscences*.
25. *Ibid.*, p. 89, as paraphrased from *Some Reminiscences*.
26. Log of *John Adams*. Loyall Farragut, p. 89, is incorrect in stating she arrived "about the first of December."

Mahan's *Admiral Farragut*, p. 63, devotes only six lines to this entire cruise; Spears's *David G. Farragut* omits it entirely.

XVI. HUNTING PIRATES IN THE CARIBBEAN

1. Letter of Porter, February 5, 1823, in Captains' Letters, Navy Department Archives and Library. Letter of February 4, 1823, in Naval Academy Museum, ordering Farragut to the West Indies Squadron as lieutenant or acting master.
2. Log of the *Peacock*. D. D. Porter's *Memoirs of Commodore David Porter*, p. 282, states that the *John Adams, Hornet, Spark, Shark*, and *Grampus* were then in the West Indies and were also placed under Porter's command. But, according to *American State Papers: Naval Affairs*, I, 1103, Commissioner John Rodgers, November 24, 1823, recommends that the *Independence, John Adams, Hornet, Spark, Grampus, Porpoise, Wild Cat*, and five or six barges be substituted for those *then* in use in the West Indies. According to letter of Secretary of the Navy to Porter, September 27, 1823, the *Shark* was *then* in New York. These vessels, however, according to Emmons, were in the West Indies at different times while Porter was in command there.
3. Log of the *Peacock*. Mahan, p. 64; Spears, p. 113; and D. D. Porter, p. 282, incorrectly give the date of sailing as February 14. Loyall Farragut, p. 91, has it February 12.
4. Loyall Farragut, p. 92, as paraphrased from *Some Reminiscences*, which states that John Porter had to be sent home on account of drunkenness.
5. The entire Island of Haiti was then under one government.
6. Loyall Farragut, p. 93.
7. *American State Papers: Naval Affairs*, I, 1103, et seq. A. D. Turnbull's *Commodore David Porter*, p. 259, does not mention the sending of the *Greyhound* into the harbor; and very strangely Farragut's *Journal* omits this also, though he was on this schooner.
8. Charles Lee Lewis's *Admiral Franklin Buchanan: Fearless Man of Action*, p. 48, et seq.
9. Loyall Farragut, p. 93.
10. *Ibid*. Farragut is incorrect in stating that Kearny "had distinguished himself in conquering the Greek pirates," as this service came later. See Carroll S. Alden's *Lawrence Kearny: Sailor Diplomat*, p. 64, et seq.
11. *Some Reminiscences*. As an acting lieutenant, he wore a single epaulet on the left shoulder.
12. *Some Reminiscences*.
13. Kearny's Report to Commodore Porter, August 10, 1823, Navy Department Archives and Library. In this he reports that a woman and some children belonged to the gang; the former he called a second "Helen McGregor."
    Loyall Farragut, p. 97, states that only one old man was captured.
14. D. D. Porter's *Memoirs of Commodore David Porter* (1875) gives many details of this cruise, but does not even mention Farragut's name

in connection with his account. *Some Reminiscences* says they had no bread or meat and only a few gallons of beans.
15. According to *Some Reminiscences*, Lieutenant Gardner's wife, who in a few months was to be Farragut's sister-in-law.
16. Loyall Farragut, p. 94. George F. Emmons's *Statistical History of the Navy of the United States*, p. 78, states that the pirate "Diaboleto" was killed in July, 1823, in Sigaumpa Bay, and Domingo was taken near Havana on April 8, 1823.
17. *Some Reminiscences.*
18. Both letters, in the Naval Academy Museum.
19. *Some Reminiscences.*
20. The date was about September 1, 1823. D. D. Porter's *Memoir of Commodore David Porter*, p. 292, says his father had yellow fever in June, 1824. Apparently he had two attacks. Farragut's attack of fever is related in *Some Reminiscences*.
21. Loyall Farragut, p. 99. Incorrect in stating the voyage took forty-three days. *Some Reminiscences* states that stops took up twenty days.
22. Officers' Letters, Navy Department Archives and Library.
23. Probably the Dry Tortugas near Key West rather than the island of Tortuga north of Haiti.
24. A letter of May 20, 1824, by Commodore Daniel T. Patterson, then in command at New Orleans, has this sentence: "We have been gratified by the visit of young Farragut, of whom we have formed a high opinion." Quoted in Spears's *David G. Farragut*, p. 123.
    In Farragut's letter to Lyman C. Draper, September 20, 1853, he writes that he visited his sister in New Orleans for eight or ten days in 1823. His memory was at fault.
25. She afterwards married Celestant Dupont, and "lived in New Orleans or Pascagoula," according to a letter from George G. Hall, September 13, 1937.
26. Loyall Farragut, p. 100. Additional details relating to his visit taken from *Some Reminiscences*.
27. *Some Reminiscences.*
28. *Ibid.*, p. 100; not in *Some Reminiscences*.
29. Loyall Farragut, p. 101, is incorrect in stating that the date was August 1, 1823. It was near the last of June, 1824.
30. According to the report of Captain W. C. Finch (W. C. Bolton), in *American State Papers: Naval Affairs*, II, 301, this incident happened on July 10, 1824. He gives the name of the deserter as James Fredenburg, and states that he was given over to Captain Du Maigue, commanding H.B.M. Ship *Kangaroo*, who had returned an American deserter to the *Wild Cat*.
    Spears's *David G. Farragut*, p. 124, relates an incident he claims was told him by Loyall Farragut, in which Farragut manhandled two pirates at the same time on a hotel veranda in Havana. It may have some basis of fact, but the details are so exaggerated as to raise a question. Farragut does not mention it in *Some Reminiscences*.

31. No explanation is given for Farragut's having been sent to Washington. Porter had already gone north, and was in Washington about June 24, 1824. The ship was apparently sent north on account of the fever.

Though there is no mention in Loyall Farragut, p. 98, of a previous attack of yellow fever, he states, in a letter to the Secretary of the Navy, February 9, 1825, and later to the Secretary on August 6, 1825, that he had had the fever two successive summers preceding. Mahan, p. 67, and Spears, p. 122, state that he had escaped the fever while in the West Indies.

Loyall Farragut, p. 101, is mistaken in saying that it was the middle of September before Farragut had recovered sufficiently to go to Norfolk to visit friends.

XVII. MARRIAGE, PROMOTION, AND THE *BRANDYWINE*

1. Register of Trinity Church, Portsmouth, Virginia. A curious error in Farragut's *Some Reminiscences* gives the marriage date as September 24, 1824; Loyall Farragut, p. 103, makes it even worse as September 24, 1823. Mahan's *Admiral Farragut*, p. 67, follows Loyall Farragut. Tucker's *Marriage Bonds* says John H. Wingfield married them.
2. Farragut's letter of September 16, 1824, is no longer extant; but Porter's reply of October 1, 1824, is in the Naval Academy Museum.
3. He was permitted to wear the uniform of a lieutenant also. See p. 188.
4. *Appointments, Orders, and Resignations,* Navy Department Archives and Library. Form letter from Secretary of Navy Southard to Farragut, dated February 16, 1825, inclosing commission, "dated January 13, 1825," in Naval Academy Museum.

   Loyall Farragut, p. 103, and Mahan, p. 71, state that he was promoted to lieutenant in August, 1825.

   In Naval Academy Museum is a letter of recommendation of August 15, 1824, from Captain James Renshaw to Southard, stating that Farragut's "uniform correct deportment of the Officer and Gentleman together with his knowledge and experience of his profession made manifest on all occasions induces me to ask your attention to a lieutenancy which he is desirous of receiving."
5. *Navy Uniform, General Order, May 10, 1820,* effective January 1, 1821. This was worn until 1830 when certain changes were ordered. It was then that the single epaulet was shifted to right shoulder.
6. Letter to Secretary of the Navy, Navy Department Archives and Library.
7. Navy Department Archives and Library.
8. *Ibid.*
9. *La Fayette* by Brand Whitlock, II, 280.
10. George F. Emmons's *Statistical History of the Navy of the United States,* p. 24.

11. Log of the *Brandywine*. Loyall Farragut, p. 103, is probably incorrect in stating that a Mr. Somerfield was also a member of the party.
12. *The Autobiography of Commodore Charles Morris, U. S. Navy*, p. 92.
13. Log of the *Brandywine*. Loyall Farragut, p. 103, and Spears, p. 132, state that the ship sailed on the "13th of September"; while Morris's *Autobiography*, p. 92, gives the date as September 4.
14. Log of the *Brandywine*.
15. Morris's *Autobiography*, p. 93.
16. *La Fayette* by Brand Whitlock, II, 288, giving the impression of Duke Victor de Broglie.
17. *Ibid.*, p. 287.
18. Log of *Brandywine*.
19. *Ibid.*
20. Farragut's *Journal* as quoted by Loyall Farragut, p. 104.
21. Commodore Chauncey to Farragut, May 7, 1826, in Naval Academy Museum.
22. Navy Department Archives and Library.
23. Log of the *Brandywine*. Farragut was detached on June 24, 1826, according to Navy Department Archives and Library.
24. Farragut's *Some Reminiscences*. Loyall Farragut does not give this.
25. See picture in *Through the Years in Norfolk* by W. H. T. Squires and M. E. Bennett, p. 38.
26. *Norfolk: Historic Southern Port* by Thomas J. Wertenbaker, p. 179.
27. Farragut's *Some Reminiscences*. Loyall Farragut, p. 105, quotes it thus: "He'd be damned if he would learn."
28. Farragut's *Journal* as paraphrased by Loyall Farragut, p. 106. *Some Reminiscences* says the school was on board the *North Carolina* at Norfolk.
29. Barron, who had killed Decatur in a duel, became Commandant of the Norfolk Navy Yard May 25, 1825, where he remained until 1831. He lived on until 1851, and is buried in Trinity Churchyard, Portsmouth, Virginia.
30. *The Great Commodore: The Exploits of Matthew Calbraith Perry* by Edward M. Burrows, p. 119.
31. February 21, 1827, Porter Papers, Manuscript Division, Library of Congress. The letter ends with "Your most sincere young friend"; this hardly suggests that he was Porter's legally adopted son.
32. December 30, 1826. The letter is owned by Dr. Ellsworth Eliot, Jr., of New York City.
33. Letter of May 25, 1828. Navy Department Archives and Library.

XVIII. ON THE BRAZIL STATION

1. Navy Department Archives and Library.
2. George F. Emmons's *Statistical History of the Navy of the United States*, pp. 26, 106.

3. Log of the *Vandalia*. Loyall Farragut, p. 107, states the date to have been December 28.
4. Benjamin F. Sands's *From Reefer to Rear Admiral*, p. 21. He was then a midshipman, appointed April 1, 1828. Lieutenant Joshua R. Sands, appointed April 1, 1818, was also on the ship.
5. Log of the *Vandalia*. All dates of the cruise are from the ship's log. Loyall Farragut, p. 107, states that the ship soon sailed, but it was really after about two months.
   The description of Rio is based on J. N. Reynolds's *Voyage of the U. S. Frigate Potomac, 1831-1834*, pp. 34 et seq.
6. John F. Cady's *Foreign Intervention in the Rio de la Plata, 1838-1850*, pp. 7-9.
   Encyclopedia Britannica.
7. Loyall Farragut, pp. 110, 111.
8. *Ibid.*, p. 110. Cady, *op. cit.*, p. 9, states that this was in June, 1828; but Farragut says he was present, and the log of the *Vandalia* states that the ship sailed May 24 and did not return until September 4.
9. *A History of Brazil* by J. P. Calogeras, p. 114.
10. Loyall Farragut, p. 111.
11. *Ibid.*, p. 112.
12. Log of *Vandalia*. Letter of Captain John Gallagher to Farragut, December 22, 1829: "As you are about to leave this ship to return to the United States in consequence of ill health, it affords me much pleasure to say that since you have been under my command your conduct as an officer and deportment as a gentleman has met my entire approbation, and I will always be happy to meet you either on duty or in private life. Wishing you a safe and speedy passage and a happy meeting with your family and friends." Naval Academy Museum.
13. Court-martial of Commodore Creighton for receipting for his pay three months in advance. He was reprimanded. See *Some Reminiscences*.
14. *Officers; Ships of War*, XVII, Navy Department Archives and Library.
15. Mahan's *Admiral Farragut*, p. 73.
16. Navy Department Archives and Library.
17. August 13, 1832, Navy Department Archives and Library.
18. August 18, 1832, Naval Academy Museum.
19. August 21, 1832, Navy Department Archives and Library.
20. August 29, 1832, Naval Academy Museum.
21. Letter of that date to Secretary of Navy was written by Farragut in Washington. Navy Department Archives and Library.
22. Navy Department Archives and Library.
23. Charles W. Elliott's *Winfield Scott: The Soldier and the Man*, pp. 274 et seq.
24. D. D. Porter's *Memoir of Commodore David Porter*, p. 391.
25. Loyall Farragut, p. 114.

26. Charles W. Elliott, *op. cit.*, p. 284.
27. *Some Reminiscences.*
28. Loyall Farragut, p. 115.
29. Joel R. Poinsett wrote Farragut from Charleston, April 15, 1833: "This letter will be put in your hands by my young relative, Robert Poinsett Lovell, who will make his first cruise under your auspices. He is very modest and retiring; but you will cure him of all excess in such matters and make a man of him. For the sake of long acquaintance and I hope I may say our old friendship, I beg you will take him under your especial charge and teach him his profession. He could not have a better master nor a better friend, and I trust he will merit your kindness, which I bespeak for him and for which I thank you in advance." Naval Academy Museum.
30. John F. Cady, *op. cit.*, p. 12.
31. Not mentioned in Loyall Farragut's paraphrase, which he called the *Journal*.
32. Charles Lee Lewis's *Romantic Decatur*, pp. 216 et seq.
33. *Some Reminiscences.*
34. Woolsey's letter to Farragut, February 11, 1834. Naval Academy Museum.
35. Reminiscence of one of Farragut's officers in Loyall Farragut, p. 115. Repeated by Spears's *David G. Farragut*, p. 133, though Spears omits the entire cruise of the *Natchez* to South America.
36. George F. Emmons, *op. cit.*, p. 14.
37. Log of the *Boxer*. Loyall Farragut, p. 119, states the date to have been March 6.
38. Captain Thomas Taylor, who began privateering out of Baltimore under the flag of Buenos Aires in 1816. *Maryland Historical Magazine*, March, 1940.
39. Loyall Farragut, p. 119.
40. Matthew Fontaine Maury, then a midshipman, was aboard the *Potomac*, having been transferred to her from the *Falmouth* at Callao. See Charles Lee Lewis's *Matthew Fontaine Maury: Pathfinder of the Seas*, pp. 24, 25.
41. Loyall Farragut, p. 120.
42. J. N. Reynolds, *op. cit.*, p. 518.
43. *Some Reminiscences.* Not in Loyall Farragut.
44. Reynolds, *op. cit.*, p. 519.
45. Letter of Salter to Farragut. Naval Academy Museum.
46. Log of *Boxer*.
47. *Some Reminiscences.* Not in Loyall Farragut.

Loyall Farragut, p. 120, describes a race of the *Boxer* and the *Pigeon*, reputed fastest English packet. There is no reference to such a race in the log of the *Boxer*. It would have been a remarkable coincidence if Farragut had raced the same English ship which he outran off Malta when he was executive officer on the *Spark* more than twenty years previous.

XIX. AN EBB TIDE IN HIS LIFE

1. Charles Lee Lewis's *Matthew Fontaine Maury: Pathfinder of the Seas*, p. 39.
2. Letter of June 20, 1835. Naval Academy Museum. Porter's spelling is reproduced. Loyall Farragut, pp. 121-123, edited it.
3. St. Stephano, or San Stefano, a village seven miles west of Constantinople, on the Sea of Marmora.
4. Loyall Farragut, p. 124, and letter of Farragut to the Secretary of the Navy, written at Georgetown, June 17, 1835, in Navy Department Archives and Library.
5. On December 15, 1832, Farragut signed the marriage bond for Jane Edna Marchant and William D. Porter, according to Clerk of Courts, Norfolk, Virginia.
6. A lieutenant commanding a ship received $1,800 a year; on other duty, he received $1,500; on waiting orders, he was paid $1,200. *Navy Register*, 1836.
7. William S. Forrest's *Historical and Descriptive Sketches of Norfolk and Vicinity*, p. 206.
8. Navy Department Archives and Library. A rendezvous was a recruiting office.
9. Loyall Farragut, p. 124. Lieutenant Edmund Byrne, third above Farragut on the list of lieutenants, who was Commodore Dallas's first lieutenant in 1836, and Lieutenant Frederick Engle, fourteenth below Farragut, who was the Commodore's first lieutenant in 1837, were both detached and placed on waiting orders. *Navy Register*, 1838, 1839.
10. Navy Department Archives and Library. On March 21, 1838, Farragut acknowledged receipt of his orders of March 14, 1838.

XX. ON THE WEST INDIA STATION

1. Based on Thomas J. Wertenbaker's *Norfolk: Historic Southern Port*, pp. 155-157.
2. Log of the *Constellation*.
3. *Some Reminiscences*. This states that, after her mother's death, Elizabeth Farragut was placed in the care of a Mrs. Dupont near Pascagoula. She may have become the girl's mother-in-law.
4. Log of *Constellation*.
5. *Some Reminiscences*. Mahan's *Admiral Farragut* makes no mention of the cruise of the *Constellation;* nor does Spears's *David G. Farragut*.
6. Log of the *Erie*.
7. George F. Emmons's *Statistical History of the Navy of the United States*, p. 10.
8. All dates are from the log of the *Erie*. The paraphrase of *Some Reminiscences* in Loyall Farragut, p. 127, combines the two visits

to Tampico, as though there were only one, with great resulting confusion.
9. Log of the *Erie*.
10. Farragut to Commodore Barron, March, 1839, from the U. S. Ship *Erie*, as published in Loyall Farragut, pp. 132 *et seq*. The date must be incorrect, for Farragut left the *Erie* in January, 1839. It was probably written in November, 1838.
11. *L'Amiral Baudin* par Le Vice-Amiral Jurien de la Graviére, p. 142, and other French authorities state that the bombardment took place on November 27. Mahan's *Admiral Farragut*, p. 79, gives November 28 as the date.
12. Jurien de la Graviére, *op. cit.*, pp. 138 *et seq*. and plan of engagement.
13. *San Juan De Ulùa ou Relation de L'expedition Française au Mexique* . . . par Mm. P. Blanchard et A. Dauzats, p. 311.
14. *Ibid.*, p. 313. Loyall Farragut, p. 128, states that this magazine blew up before the Prince de Joinville shifted his position, and disagrees with regard to several other details of the engagement.
15. Loyall Farragut, p. 128.
16. Blanchard and Dauzats, *op. cit.*, pp. 315, 318.
17. Jurien de la Graviére, *op. cit.*, p. 149. Loyall Farragut, p. 130, exaggerates in stating that "a shower of 200 shell and shot a minute" fell upon the castle. Simple arithmetic shows that the total of shot and shell would at that rate have lasted only 41 minutes; whereas the duration of the engagement was over five hours during which the firing was continuous. An excerpt from Baudin's report in *Annales Maritimes* . . . , 1839, p. 160, states that "302 bombes, 177 obus et 7,771 boulets ont été lancés contre la forteresse," and that of the approximately 8,000 projectiles about 500 were "creux" (hollow). There is, accordingly, an error in Farragut's letter to Barron to the effect that the "French threw almost entirely shell-shot," for only a little more than six per cent of the total were shell and bombs. Loyall Farragut, p. 130, is also mistaken in stating that the bomb vessels threw only 150 bombs, and that each French ship had two 8-pounders and a dozen carronades firing only shells. In Farragut's letter to Barron he states that each French ship had two or four 80-pounders. Blanchard and Dauzats, pp. 336, 337, state that each ship had two "canons obusiers Paixhans de 80," and Jurien de la Graviére, p. 151, states that the 177 shells were 80 pounds. Mahan's *Admiral Farragut*, p. 80, states that the French fired "7,771 round shot, and 177 shell, the mortar-vessels at the same time throwing in 302 bombs."
18. Blanchard and Dauzats, *op. cit.*, p. 333. Jurien de la Graviére, p. 150, says 17 officers and 207 men were killed and wounded. H. H. Bancroft's *Works*, Volume XIII, 195, footnote, says that the list of Gaona, commander of the Castle, totaled 65 killed and 147 wounded.
19. Loyall Farragut, p. 130. This was doubtless an exaggeration, and does not agree with the statement in Loyall Farragut, p. 129, that the Mexicans lost 200 men.

20. Letter to Barron. Farragut's poor opinion of bomb vessels was held by him even during the Civil War.
21. Loyall Farragut, p. 129, says that one midshipman was killed, and two lieutenants and three men were injured, on the flagship; but Jurien de la Graviére, p. 150, and Blanchard and Dauzats, p. 333, agree that one was killed and fourteen were wounded.
22. Letter to Barron.
23. Spelled "Rincion" in Loyall Farragut, p. 131. He was the governor of Vera Cruz.
24. Paraphrased from Loyall Farragut, p. 131. John Forsyth was then Secretary of State.
25. W. H. Callcott's *Santa Anna*, p. 158, says, "Santa Anna seems not to have been near the barracks where something like active resistance was offered the French." Loyall Farragut, p. 132, says that Santa Anna joined the troops there.
26. Jurien de la Graviére, *op. cit.*, p. 159. Mahan's *Admiral Farragut*, p. 83, says that the cockswain was also killed.
27. As an interesting tissue of errors the following is cited from Franck C. Hanighen's *Santa Anna: The Napoleon of the West*, p. 153: "But the French frigates had now come in to cover the rowboats and when they saw the horde of Mexicans approaching the pier they loaded their guns and took aim. . . . Just then a French gunner on a ship fired an historic shot. . . . Bursting at the head of the comically heroic little column, it killed our hero's white stallion, shattered his own left leg and disabled a soldier beside him."
28. Jurien de la Graviére, *op. cit.*, pp. 161, 162. Blanchard and Dauzats, *op. cit.*, p. 380, state that the French losses were eight killed and 60 wounded; the Spanish losses were from 25 to 150, the casualties on the mole alone being 74. W. H. Callcott's *Santa Anna*, p. 159, gives Santa Anna's own figures as 25 men killed and wounded on his side, and the French had lost over a hundred dead on the streets and "a multitude of wounded." Loyall Farragut, p. 132, estimates that the French had nearly a hundred killed and wounded, and the Mexicans twenty or thirty. He closes with this opinion: "When the disparity of force (the French landed in a dense fog with twelve hundred men, in three divisions) and the other circumstances are fairly considered, I think it will be found that Santa Anna's defense was highly creditable to himself and his countrymen."
29. Bancroft, *op. cit.*, pp. 203, 204.

XXI. HOME AND TROUBLE

1. Farragut's letter to Lyman C. Draper, September 20, 1853, states that he spent two weeks with his sister in New Orleans in 1838. The visit must have been in January or February, 1839.
2. *Some Reminiscences*. Not in Loyall Farragut.
3. *Ibid.*

4. Farragut inclosed Baudin's letter in one he wrote to the Secretary of the Navy, April 2, 1839. Baudin's letter is now missing from the Navy Department Archives and Library.
5. April 13, 1839. Navy Department Archives and Library.
6. April 22, 1839. Navy Department Archives and Library.
7. April 27, 1839. Navy Department Archives and Library.
8. June 25, 1839. Navy Department Archives and Library.
9. July 3, 1839. Navy Department Archives and Library.
10. August 1, 1839. Navy Department Archives and Library.
11. August 6, 1839. Navy Department Archives and Library.
12. One of the officers in charge of ships laid up in ordinary.
13. *Some Reminiscences* states that Mrs. Gardner died of dropsy and numerous complications on March 2, 1841, only three months after Mrs. Farragut's death.
14. *Some Reminiscences*. Paraphrased in Loyall Farragut, p. 136.
15. Loyall Farragut, p. 136.
16. Bureau of Navigation, Navy Department. Mahan's *Admiral Farragut*, p. 89, and Loyall Farragut, p. 137, state that the date was February 22, 1841.

XXII. ON THE BRAZIL STATION AGAIN

1. George F. Emmons's *Statistical History of the Navy of the United States*, p. 24. Loyall Farragut, p. 137, says that 450 men were transferred to her, which probably was her peacetime complement.
2. Log of the *Delaware*.
3. Adapted from *Three Years in the Pacific* . . . by An Officer of the United States Navy (Dr. W. S. W. Ruschenberger), pp. 10-12.
4. David Ridgely's *Annals of Annapolis*, p. 230, states that the population was then about 3,000.
5. Loyall Farragut, p. 140.
6. The pay of a commander at navy yards and on other duty was $2,100; pay while on leave was $1,800, according to *Navy Register*, 1841. The rank of commander took the place of master commandant first in the *Navy Register* of 1838.

   Farragut was commissioned a commander on September 21, 1841, to date from September 8, 1841, according to Bureau of Navigation records. Spears's *David G. Farragut*, p. 137, is incorrect in stating that Farragut was promoted to commander on September 8, 1841. Spears devotes only one sentence to Farragut's service in South American waters in 1841-1842.
7. Uniform Regulations for Officers of the U. S. Navy, in effect after February 19, 1841.
8. Log of the *Delaware*.
9. Loyall Farragut, p. 140.
10. Log of the *Delaware*. Mahan's *Admiral Farragut*, p. 90, says she arrived on January 12, 1842.

11. For a description of the harbor and its surroundings, see Ruschenberger's *Three Years in the Pacific*, pp. 18 et seq.
12. Log of the *Delaware*.
13. George F. Emmons, *op. cit.*, pp. 26, 110.
14. Log of the *Decatur*.
15. Loyall Farragut, pp. 143-145.
16. Log of the *Decatur*.
17. This was Giuseppe Garibaldi, the Italian patriot, who fled from Italy to escape execution by the Austrians. After aiding in establishing the freedom of Uruguay, he returned to Italy and played a leading role in the liberation of his country.
18. Loyall Farragut, pp. 150, 151. Cf. James D. Bulloch's *The Secret Service of the Confederate States in Europe* I, 93. He was a midshipman in the *Decatur* under Farragut's command. Commodore Morris entrusted to Farragut forty doubloons and a small box for Mrs. Morris. "If opportunity should offer," wrote the Commodore from Montevideo, December 5, 1842, "it would give me pleasure to hear from you in the Mediterranean, as it will at all times, to hear of your prosperity and happiness." Letter in Naval Academy Museum.
19. Log of the *Decatur*.
20. *Ibid.* Loyall Farragut, p. 152, is incorrect in stating that she sailed on the 21st of January.

XXIII. SHORE DUTY AND SECOND MARRIAGE

1. Loyall Farragut, p. 153.
2. See pp. 140-142.
3. *Some Reminiscences*.
4. Records of the Norfolk Corporation Court, and Tucker's *Marriage Bonds*. There is no record of the marriage on the register of Christ Church.
5. Records of Bureau of Navigation, Navy Department.
6. George F. Emmons's *Statistical History of the United States Navy*, p. 6.
7. Loyall Farragut, p. 155, is mistaken in stating that Commodore William C. Bolton was in command of the station; he was "Port Captain." Commodore Jesse Wilkinson was in command of the Navy Yard.
8. President Tyler married, on June 26, 1844, Julia Gardiner, daughter of David Gardiner of New York, who was killed on board the steam man-of-war *Princeton* when a large gun exploded during trials, in February, 1844. President Tyler narrowly escaped death on that occasion, though Secretary of State Upshur and Secretary of War Gilmer were both killed.
9. *Some Reminiscences*.
10. *Ibid.*
11. The additional six pages covered Farragut's career down to September 14, 1850. The original manuscript was owned in 1941 by Dr. Ellsworth Eliot, Jr., of New York City.

XXIV. IN THE MEXICAN WAR

1. Letter of August 19, 1845. Navy Department Archives and Library. There is no record of an earlier letter written in July, which is referred to in a letter to Farragut from the Secretary, on November 10, 1846.
2. See pp. 217-220.
3. See pp. 214-215.
4. Mentioned in Farragut's letter to the Secretary of the Navy of November 3, 1846, though the original letter is not in the Navy Department Archives and Library. Farragut may have made this application in person, as the Secretary on May 7, 1846, ordered Farragut to Washington to assist, not later than May 25, in preparing a set of rules and regulations for the government of the navy. The latter original letter is in the Naval Academy Museum.
5. Letter quoted in full in Loyall Farragut, p. 156; but not found in the Navy Department Archives and Library. It is referred to, however, in the Secretary's letter of November 10 to Farragut, which is in the Archives.
6. In September, 1846, Bancroft was succeeded as Secretary of the Navy by John Y. Mason.
7. Letter of November 10, 1846.
8. In Navy Department Archives and Library.
9. Records of Bureau of Navigation, Navy Department. Loyall Farragut, p. 158, is incorrect in stating that Farragut received the command in February, 1847.
10. E. M. Barrows' *The Great Commodore*, p. 189.
11. See pp. 140-141.
12. Commanding Norfolk Navy Yard and the Receiving Ship, respectively.
13. George F. Emmons's *Statistical History of the United States Navy*, p. 6.
14. *Ibid.*, p. 100. See also Charles Lee Lewis's *Admiral Franklin Buchanan*, p. 114.
15. Log of *Saratoga*.
16. Vera Cruz was occupied by Scott's army on the 29th of March. *Winfield Scott: the Soldier and the Man* by Charles W. Elliott, p. 459.
17. *Some Reminiscences*. Loyall Farragut, p. 157, records that Farragut said, "I urged that I could take the Castle of San Juan with the *Pennsylvania* and two sloops of war like the *Saratoga*"; but such declarations do not appear in his letters to the Secretary of the Navy.
18. Farragut to Secretary of the Navy Mason, January 25, 1848. Quoted in Loyall Farragut, p. 162.
19. Log of *Saratoga*.
20. Loyall Farragut, p. 163: Letter of Farragut to Secretary Mason, January 25, 1848.

21. Farragut to Secretary of the Navy, January 25, 1848, is incorrect in stating the date of Perry's letter as August 15, 1847.
22. According to Loyall Farragut, p. 158, Farragut declared, "I took the yellow fever while there (in Mexican waters), and was near losing my life." The same appears in his *Some Reminiscences*. But in his letter of January 25, 1848, to Secretary Mason, Farragut wrote, "My own case . . . was pronounced a high state of bilious fever . . . ." Mahan's *Admiral Farragut*, p. 96, states that Farragut had yellow fever.
23. Log of *Saratoga*, and letter of Perry to Secretary of Navy of December 28, 1847, in Navy Department Archives.
24. Letter of December 12, 1847, in Navy Department Archives. Quoted in Loyall Farragut, p. 159.
25. Letter of December 17, 1847, in Navy Department Archives. Quoted in Loyall Farragut, p. 160.
26. Perry to Secretary of the Navy, December 28, 1847, stating that he had sent the *Saratoga* to Pensacola on the preceding day. The log of the *Saratoga*, however, records that she sailed on the 29th of December.
27. Farragut to the Secretary of the Navy, on January 31 and February 20, 1848, both in Navy Department Archives.
28. On the 25th of January, 1848, in Navy Department Archives. Quoted in Loyall Farragut, pp. 161-164.
29. Loyall Farragut, p. 158.

XXV. AN ORDNANCE EXPERT

1. Loyall Farragut, p. 159.
2. Letter from Farragut to Secretary of the Navy, February 21, 1848. Navy Department Archives.
3. Letter from Farragut to Secretary of the Navy, from Gosport Navy Yard, July 22, 1848. Navy Department Archives. On the 10th of April, 1848, Farragut was ordered to report to serve on a court-martial at Annapolis.
4. Letter of November 23, 1849. Navy Department Archives.
5. Records of Bureau of Navigation, Navy Department.
6. Letter of May 24, 1850, to the Secretary of the Navy. Navy Department Archives.
7. Farragut's letter from Norfolk to the Secretary of the Navy, October 6, 1850. Navy Department Archives.
8. March 15, 1851, according to the records of the Bureau of Navigation, Navy Department. Loyall Farragut, p. 164, is incorrect in stating that Farragut was ordered to Washington in October, 1850, and has confused Lieutenant Barron with Lieutenant Stephen C. Rowan.
9. *Some Reminiscences*. According to the Sixth and Seventh Annual Reports of the Board of Regents of the Smithsonian Institution for the Years 1851 and 1852, the following lectures were delivered: six on History as a Science and one on Poetry by Dr. Samuel H. Cox of

Brooklyn, New York; two on Induction and Association by Dr. John Ludlow, Provost of the University of Pennsylvania; five on Entomology and one on the Alps by Dr. John G. Morris of Baltimore; two on History of the Forms of the English Language by Professor W. C. Fowler of Amherst College; one on Architecture of the Middle Ages by Dr. A. H. Vinton of Boston; two on the Mechanism of Speech and Its Bearing on the Natural History of the Human Race by Professor S. S. Haldeman of Columbia, Pennsylvania; twelve on the Structure and Function of Insects by Dr. Henry Goadby; three by Dr. E. K. Kane, U.S.N., on Arctic Exploration; three by President Mark Hopkins of Williams College on Method Applied to Investigation; four by Professor W. B. Rogers of the University of Virginia on Phases of the Atmosphere; twelve by Dr. Benjamin Silliman of Yale and later six by Dr. Silliman on the Four Ancient Elements—Earth, Air, Fire, and Water; two by Professor C. C. Felton of Harvard on Greek Literature; one by Job R. Tyson, Esq. of Philadelphia on Queen Elizabeth and Oliver Cromwell, Their Characters and Times, Contrasted and Compared; six by Dr. B. A. Gould of Cambridge on the Recent Progress of Astronomy; and six by Professor Louis Agassiz of Cambridge on the Foundation of Symmetry in the Animal Kingdom. These lectures, given in the evening, covered the entire years 1851 and 1852. Farragut attended those which came between March 15, 1851 and April 30, 1852. The exact dates of the lectures were not reported.
10. Letter to Secretary of the Navy of September 11, 1851. Navy Department Archives. The Rendezvous was the recruiting office.
11. Letter of November 19, 1851, to the Secretary of the Navy. Navy Department Archives. The Ordinary refers to the ships out of commission stationed at a Navy Yard.
12. Letters to Farragut from the Secretary of the Navy, of April 19 and July 13, 1852. Navy Department Archives. The *Pennsylvania* was then the receiving ship at Norfolk.
13. Letter from Morris to Farragut, September 3, 1852. Navy Department Archives. Loyall Farragut, p. 165, is incorrect in stating that Farragut was ordered to this duty in the summer of 1852.
14. Loyall Farragut, p. 166.
15. Letter to Secretary of the Navy, of April 12, 1854. Navy Department Archives. Quoted in Loyall Farragut, pp. 166-167.
16. The Secretary of the Navy wrote to Farragut April 15, 1854, that his suggestion would receive "careful consideration."
17. Mahan's *Admiral Farragut*, p. 99.

XXVI. ESTABLISHES MARE ISLAND NAVY YARD

1. Mahan's *Admiral Farragut*, p. 99.
2. Records of the Bureau of Navigation, Navy Department.
3. Farragut to Secretary of Navy, July 29, 1854. Navy Department Archives. "I left Washington on a litter, just recovering from cholera,

in a state of salivation; and in that state crossed the Isthmus with my family," wrote Farragut to the Secretary, May 19, 1858. Navy Department Archives.
4. *Some Reminiscences.*
5. Thomas J. Wertenbaker's *Norfolk: Historic Southern Port,* pp. 210 et seq.
6. *Some Reminiscences.*
7. *Log Book, Mare Island Navy Yard,* September 16, 1854, to March 22, 1856, written in Farragut's hand. Navy Department Archives.
8. Farragut to Secretary of the Navy, August 11, 1854. Navy Department Archives.
9. *Log Book, Mare Island Navy Yard.*
10. The copper plate on the corner stone had the following inscription: "This Navy Yard was founded September 18, 1854. Franklin Pierce, President of the United States, J. C. Dobbin, Secretary of the Navy, Jos. Smith, U.S.N., Chief of Bureau of Docks and Yards, D. G. Farragut, Commandant of Yard, D. Turner, Civil Engineer, A. Powell, Master Carpenter, R. S. King, Master Blacksmith, Mr. Warner, Master Mason. The corner stone of this building was laid Jany. 23d, 1855."
11. Letter to Loyall Farragut from one "who had close official relations" with Farragut in California. As quoted in Loyall Farragut, p. 171.
12. According to *Log Book, Mare Island Navy Yard,* Farragut received his commission as Post Captain on November 15, 1855. On November 19, 1855, he acknowledged his commission as "Post Captain in the Navy of the U. S.," to the Secretary. According to the records of the Bureau of Navigation, he was recommissioned captain on August 1, 1856. At this date he, no doubt, became a regular captain in the Navy.
13. October 18, 1855. This letter has not hitherto been published.
14. *Navy Register,* 1858.
15. Boutwell to Secretary of the Navy, July 3, 1856. Navy Department Archives. Loyall Farragut, p. 170, is incorrect in stating that a letter demanding the release of Dr. Ashe "was forwarded to Commander Boutwell, then in command of the *John Adams,* which had been sent to take a position off the city in case of emergency, with instructions to enforce it."
16. As quoted in Loyall Farragut, pp. 176, 177.
17. *Ibid.,* pp. 179, 180.
18. *Ibid.,* pp. 178, 179.
19. Letter of July 2, 1856, in Loyall Farragut, pp. 180, 181.
20. In Loyall Farragut, pp. 181-183.
21. Farragut to Secretary of the Navy Dobbin, July 17 and August (?), 1856, in Loyall Farragut, pp. 184-187.
22. Secretary of the Navy to Farragut, August 2, 1856, in Loyall Farragut, pp. 189-190.
23. Secretary of the Navy to Boutwell, August 2, 1856, in Loyall Farragut, p. 189.

24. Of August 18 and 30, 1856. Navy Department Archives.
25. Farragut to Secretary of the Navy, October 4, 1856.
26. Farragut to the Secretary of the Navy, February 19, 1857. Navy Department Archives.
27. *Ibid.*, December 2, 1857.
28. *Ibid.*, May 19, 1858. Statements in Loyall Farragut, p. 171, are not found in the correspondence between Farragut and the Secretary of the Navy, in the Navy Department Archives.
29. Farragut to Secretary of the Navy, July 16, 1858. Navy Department Archives.

XXVII. COMMANDS THE STEAM SLOOP-OF-WAR *BROOKLYN*

1. Farragut to the Secretary of the Navy, September 4, 1858. Navy Department Archives.
2. *Ibid.*, December 11, 1858. Navy Department Archives.
3. Thomas J. Wertenbaker's *Norfolk: Historic Southern Port*, p. 214.
4. *Regulations for the Uniform and Dress of the Navy and Marine Corps of the United States*, 1852.
5. Navy Department, Bureau of Navigation records. Farragut to Secretary of the Navy, December 11, 1858. Navy Department Archives.
6. Frank M. Bennett's *Steam Navy of the United States*, p. 154. Mahan's *Admiral Farragut*, p. 101, is in error in stating that there were six of these steam sloops-of-war.
7. *Official Records of the Union and Confederate Navies in the War of the Rebellion*, Series II, Vol. I, Parts 1 to 4, p. 48. Bennett's *Steam Navy of the United States*, 157.
8. *Navy Register*, 1859.
9. Secretary of the Navy to Farragut, January 3 and 10, 1859. Navy Department Archives.
10. Farragut to Secretary of Navy, January 26, 1859. Navy Department Archives.
11. *Ibid.*, February 5, 1859.
12. *Ibid.*, February 11, 1859.
13. *Ibid.*, February 17, 1859.
14. *Ibid.*, February 26, 1859. Saluke is also sometimes spelled Soulouque, as in Loyall Farragut, p. 195.
15. Farragut to Flag Officer McCluney, March 11, 1859, as quoted in Loyall Farragut, pp. 195, 196. Mahan's *Admiral Farragut* and Spears's *David G. Farragut* omit entirely the cruise of the *Brooklyn* to Haiti and Panama. Aspinwall is now called Colon.
16. Farragut to Secretary of the Navy, April 4, 1859. Navy Department Archives.
17. *Ibid.*, April 22, 1859.
18. Governor Robert M. McLane's *Reminiscences*, privately printed, 1903, *passim*.
19. To Farragut from E. Behn, F. W. Shueke, Fuentes Canarol, and C. Markoe, June 28, 1859, as quoted in Loyall Farragut, pp. 198, 199.

NOTES

20. Farragut's reply, July 31, 1859, as quoted in Loyall Farragut, p. 199.
21. Farragut to Secretary of the Navy, June (?), 1859. Navy Department Archives.
22. This is the first record of the use of the telegraph in official communications by Farragut. The telegram was marked as having been received in Washington on July 18; so it was not a very rapid communication.
23. Farragut to Secretary of the Navy, July 28, 1859. Navy Department Archives.
24. *Ibid.*, September 7, 1859.
25. Telegram from Farragut to Secretary of the Navy, September 14, 1859. Navy Department Archives.
26. *Ibid.*, September 26, 1859.
27. Lieutenant Jeffers to the Secretary of the Navy, November 2, 1859. Navy Department Archives, where are to be found all letters relating to this episode.
28. Commander Thomas Turner, in command of the *Saratoga*.
29. Farragut to the Secretary of the Navy, November 21, 1859.
30. New York *Evening Post*, November 7, 1859. Many details relating to the incident are taken from this paper.

    Farragut to Flag Officer Samuel L. Breese, November 8, 1859: "I regret to inform you that on our way down from the yard we blew out the joints of the heaters (work newly made at the yard) and we were compelled to stop at this place to repack them."
31. Farragut to Breese, November 8, 1859.
32. *Ibid.*
33. Farragut to the Secretary of the Navy, November 21, 1859, and Farragut to Breese, November 8, 1859.
34. New York *Evening Post*, November 9, 1859.
35. New York *Tribune*, November 10, 1859, as quoted from the *Staten Island Gazette*, November 10, 1859.
36. Date of death, as found in Farragut's Bible, is December 19, 1859. Loyall Farragut, p. 200, Mahan's *Admiral Farragut*, p. 104, and Spears's *David G. Farragut*, p. 146, confuse the time of William Farragut's death with Captain Farragut's later visit to New Orleans.

    Date of arrival of *Brooklyn* in New Orleans, according to Farragut's telegram to Secretary of Navy, December 21, 1859. Navy Department Archives.
37. Farragut to Secretary of the Navy, January (?), 1859. Navy Department Archives.

    Loyall Farragut, p. 196, is incorrect in stating that this force was landed on January 2, 1860. The entire account of the movements of the *Brooklyn*, under Farragut's command, is greatly confused in Loyall Farragut's biography of his father.
38. Telegram and letter of Farragut to the Secretary of the Navy, January 30, 1860. Navy Department Archives.
39. Cooper to the Secretary of the Navy, December 7, 1859, from the *North Carolina*, the station ship.

40. Secretary Toucey to Winant, January 28, 1860. Navy Department Archives.
41. New York *Evening Post*, February 27, 1860.
42. Farragut to Winant, February 27, 1860, from Brooklyn. Navy Department Archives.
43. New York *Evening Post*, March 7, 1860.
44. Loyall Farragut, p. 194.
45. New York *Times*, March 9, 1860.
46. Captain A. N. Brevoort to Headquarters of Marine Corps, Washington, April 17, 1860. Navy Department Archives.
47. Loyall Farragut, p. 194.
48. *Ibid.*, p. 195.
49. Farragut to Breese, March 12, 1860. Navy Department Archives.
50. Farragut to Secretary of the Navy (no date). Navy Department Archives.
51. Secretary of the Navy to Farragut, March 17, 1860. Navy Department Archives.
52. Farragut to Secretary of the Navy, April 1, 1860. Navy Department Archives.
53. *Ibid.*, April 25, 1860.
54. Loyall Farragut, p. 195.
55. *Ibid.*, p. 197.
56. The Secretary of the Navy to Farragut, August 3, 1860. Navy Department Archives.
57. Seventeen of the eighteen letters by Farragut, according to the index, have been torn from the book of *Captains' Letters*, July-September, 1860, in Navy Department Archives.
58. Loyall Farragut, p. 200. His letter of protest is now not in the Navy Department Archives, and is probably one of the missing letters.
59. Loyall Farragut, p. 201.
60. Letter of Engle to the Secretary of the Navy, October 19, 1860. Navy Department Archives.

XXVIII. WAITING ORDERS

1. Letter of Farragut to Secretary of the Navy, from the Metropolitan Hotel, November 2, 1860.
2. Secretary of the Navy to Farragut, November 12, 1860. The order stated that naval officers were to keep the Navy Department informed of their change of address.
3. Farragut to Secretary of the Navy, November 17, 1860. Spears's *David G. Farragut*, p. 148, and Albert Mordell's "Farragut at the Crossroads" in *United States Naval Institute Proceedings*, February, 1931, Vol. 57, p. 152, are incorrect in stating that Farragut returned to Norfolk in October, 1860.
4. In Norfolk, Bell received a clear majority over the three other candidates, according to Thomas J. Wertenbaker's *Norfolk: Historic South-*

ern Port, p. 221. Mordell, *op. cit.*, p. 153, states that Farragut was for Douglas, but cites no proof.
5. See "David Glasgow Farragut" by Robert L. Taylor in *Taylor-Trotwood Magazine* (Nashville, Tennessee), July, 1907, V, 347-351.
6. Samuel Barron was on duty in Washington as a member of the Lighthouse Board and not merely visiting there; Surgeon Wm. B. Sinclair, Arthur's brother, was not on duty then in Norfolk but was on the receiving ship at Philadelphia; Lieutenant Robert B. Pegram did not serve on the *Saratoga* under Farragut, as stated in Mordell, *op. cit.*, p. 153.
7. Thomas J. Wertenbaker's *Norfolk: Historic Southern Port*, p. 226.
8. Mordell, *op. cit.*, p. 156, is incorrect in stating that Farragut "was a great reader of newspapers."
9. John S. Wise's *End of an Era*, p. 160. Mordell, *op. cit.*, p. 160, is mistaken in stating that "the next morning, the 18th, the news came" to Norfolk, and incorrect on p. 159, in stating that the "news had leaked out" the night of the 17th that the vote was in favor of secession. He is also mistaken in stating that the vote was 88 to 55.
10. Farragut's speech at a reception given him by the Union people of Norfolk after the fall of Richmond, as quoted in Loyall Farragut, pp. 481-482.
11. *Ibid.* Other reported statements by Farragut, as in Spears, p. 152, and in Mordell, *op. cit.*, pp. 160 and 161, are not well founded.
12. Loyall Farragut, p. 204. "The house which he (Farragut) called his home for more than twenty years was a plain, frame dwelling on the eastern side of Duke Street midway between College Place and Freemason Street, torn down about twenty years since and now a parking station." *David Glasgow Farragut* by Dr. W. H. T. Squires in Norfolk *Virginian-Pilot*, June 26, 1940.
13. Her cousin Margaret Loyall was the wife of Commander A. M. Pennock, who fought on the Union side; her cousin Eliza was the wife of Commander John K. Mitchell, who joined the Confederate navy; they were the daughters of Mrs. Farragut's uncle, George Loyall, Navy Agent at Norfolk, whose son, Lieutenant Benjamin P. Loyall, resigned and fought with the South. Letter from W. H. T. Loyall of Norfolk to the author, January 6, 1940. Virginia Loyall Farragut "was the oldest of five daughters and two brothers—none of them Union except Virginia." Letter from George G. Hall of June 23, 1940.
14. Farragut to Welles, May 1, 1861: "I have the honor to inform the Department of my change of residence to this place (Hastings on Hudson). On the afternoon of the 19th ult. I left Norfolk for the purpose of taking my Sister to New York and there placing her on the California Steamer to return to her husband. I hurried my departure, perceiving that things were fast culminating to a crisis, by which she might be indefinitely detained and my position as a United States officer be rendered uncomfortable: I therefore determined to change my residence for the present." According to a letter of June

27, 1940, from George G. Hall, in Farragut's reference to a sister's accompanying them to New York to catch a boat, "he probably meant Mrs. R. P. Ashe of San Francisco (married Dr. Ashe of that city)," who was a sister to Mrs. Farragut.

15. Farragut's mouth was not unusually small, as stated in Mordell, *op. cit.*, p. 153. See photo of Farragut, made by Anthony of New York in 1862. Some of his portraits present his lips as compressed, and this makes his mouth appear small.

INDEX

Adams, Chaplain David P., 85, 334
Adams, President John Quincy, 173
Agassiz, Professor Louis, 253
Agincourt, British ship of the line, 229
Albany, U.S. sloop, 247
Albatross, U.S. East Indiaman, 86, 87
Alcibiades, French ship of war, 208
Alert, British sloop, 44, 45, 319, 320
Alert, U.S. sloop, 178-80, 189
Algiers, 114, 117, 122-24, 126, 170, 190, 196, 335
Allen, Lieutenant William H., 153
America, U.S. merchantman, 137, 138, 144
Annapolis, Maryland, 120, 121, 224, 335
Antelope, British ship of war, 43
Argus, U.S. brig, 40, 49
Armide, French frigate, 227
Armstrong, Captain James, 227
Ashe, Doctor R. P., 261, 360
Aspinwall (Colon), 285
Atlantic, British whaler, 73, 74, 76, 323

Badger, Secretary of the Navy G. E., 224, 225
Bahia, Brazil, 60, 188, 195, 201
Bainbridge, Captain William, 23, 49, 50, 51, 55, 58, 60, 114, 115, 118, 119, 137, 196, 293, 338, 339
Balearic Islands, 1, 304
Baltimore, Maryland, 43, 138, 205, 293, 311, 338
Bancroft, Secretary of the Navy George, 242, 243
Barcelona, Spain, 2, 304
Barclay, U.S. whaler, 67, 68, 71, 73, 77, 78

Barnegat, U.S. merchant brig, 188
Barnewall, Edward, 101, 328
Barney, Commodore J. N., 47
Barron, Commodore James, 180, 189, 197, 242, 252, 349
Barron, Commander Samuel, 251, 316
Baton Rouge, 15
Baudin, French Admiral, 211, 213, 215, 216, 218, 220, 221, 242, 294
Bazoche, French Commodore, 209
Beall, The Reverend Upton, 239
Beaufort, South Carolina, 270, 271
Bell, Lieutenant C. H., 167
Bell, Lieutenant Henry H., 254
Bell, John, 287
Berryman, Lieutenant O. H., 225
Bey of Tunis, 128, 130-32
Biddle, Commodore James, 152
Bison, French brig, 227
Blacknall, Surgeon George, 251
Bland, Quartermaster Francis, 99
Blount, Governor William, 4, 5, 8, 306, 309
Bolton, Captain William C., 28, 31, 58, 165, 321
Bonaparte, Louis Napoleon, 206
Bonaparte, Napoleon, 65, 111, 120, 134
Bonne Citoyenne, British ship of war, 58, 60
Boston, Massachusetts, 51, 114, 115, 117, 119, 188
Boston, U.S. sloop, 184, 186, 208
Boutwell, Commander E. B., 261-64
Boxer, U.S. schooner, 117, 197-202, 229, 346
Brady, Merrill, 12, 13
Brandywine, U.S. frigate, 172-77, 294, 318

Page 361

362   DAVID GLASGOW FARRAGUT

Breese, Captain S. L., 247, 269, 274, 279, 281, 357
Brooklyn, U.S. steam sloop, 269-86, 295
Brothers, British merchantman, 43
Brown, Admiral (Brazilian Navy), 234
Brown, John, 287
Brownell, Henry Howard, 305
Buchanan, Commander Franklin, 156, 265
Buenos Aires, 184, 186, 196, 197, 230, 234, 294
Burr, Aaron, 11
Butakoff, Captain (Russian Navy), 265
Byng, John, English admiral, 3

Calhoun, John C., 190, 194
Callao, Peru, 68
Campbell, Judge David, 4, 308
Campbell, Thomas, 163
Campbell's Station, 6
Campeche, Mexico, 284
Cape Cruz, 157
Cape Frio, 58, 59, 182
Cape Horn, 60, 61, 62, 65, 70, 100, 107
Cape San Antonio, Cuba, 157
Cape Verde Islands, 49, 51, 55
Cassin, Commodore Stephen, 134, 135, 153, 188
Catharine, British whaler, 76, 77, 323
Charles, U.S. whaler, 67, 68
Charles X, King of France, 175
Charleston, South Carolina, 2, 3, 145, 146, 180, 192-95, 217, 256, 288, 294, 340
Charlton, British whaler, 79, 323
Chatard, Commander Frederick, 289
Chattanooga, Tennessee, 14
Chauncey, Commodore Isaac, 120, 122-26, 135, 145, 220, 293
Cherokee Indians, 5, 13
Cherub, British sloop, 79, 94, 96, 97, 102, 104, 151, 325

Chesapeake, U.S. frigate, 49
Chesapeake Bay, 112, 121, 143, 173, 205, 207, 236
Chesme, 2
Chester, Pennsylvania, 18, 23, 24, 36, 38, 46-49, 111, 112, 182, 190, 312, 314, 316
Chiriqui Expedition, 284-86
Ciudadella, Minorca, 1, 304
Clack, Captain John H., 227
Claiborne, Governor William C. C., 10, 11, 304, 306, 309, 312, 313, 332, 333
Clark, Daniel, 11
Claxton, Captain Alexander, 188
Clay, Henry, 257
Cochrane, Admiral Sir Thomas, 156
Cocke, Lieutenant William H., 113, 156
Columbia, U.S. frigate, 115, 202
Concepcion, Chile, 63, 90
Congress, U.S. frigate, 40, 49, 117, 119, 152, 189, 335
Conner, Commodore David, 243, 244, 246
Conover, Midshipman Thomas H., 58
Constellation, U.S. frigate, 23, 27, 117, 119, 122, 206-8, 318
Constitution, U.S. frigate, 49, 51, 172, 208, 318
Cooper, Charles, 276, 277, 279, 280
Coquimbo, Chile, 67
Cornick, Surgeon James, 289
Cornwallis, General, 4, 111
Corsica, 133, 134
Cortez, U.S. steamer, 258
Cowan, Midshipman John, 68
Cowell, Lieutenant John G., 101, 102
Cowes, Isle of Wight, 176
Cowpens, Battle of, 4, 305
Crane, Captain William M., 114, 119, 135, 335
Creek Indians, 5, 13

INDEX 363

Creighton, Captain John O., 120, 121 124, 184, 186, 188
Créole, French frigate, 212
Cropper, Captain, 258
Cumberland River, 13, 14
Cunningham, Captain R. B., 266
Dahlgren, Lieutenant John A., 254
Dallas, Commodore Alexander J., 206, 207, 243, 347
Decatur, Commodore Stephen, 27, 28, 40, 49, 114, 117, 145, 172, 189, 194, 196, 315, 317, 322
Decatur, U.S. sloop, 229, 230, 232, 234-37, 244, 248, 263
Delaware, U.S. ship of the line, 144, 221, 224, 227-29, 232
Dewey, Commodore George, 308, 320
Diablito, pirate, 161
Dickens, Charles, 176
Dobbin, Secretary of the Navy J. C., 256
Dolphin, U.S. brig, 202
Dom Pedro I, Emperor of Brazil, 187, 199, 200, 294
Dom Pedro II, 195, 197-200, 228
Domingo, pirate, 161
Donaldson, Lieutenant Edward, 289
Donelson, Captain John, 13
Donelson, Stockley, 6
Dornin, Commander T. A., 252
Downes, Commodore John, 25, 28, 32, 38, 55, 58, 59, 65, 68-70, 72, 75-79, 83, 84, 87, 90, 91, 95, 100, 108-10, 119, 199, 293
Downing, Lieutenant Samuel W., 184, 195
Drake, Sir Francis, 75, 271
Drayton, Lieutenant Percival, 254
Dublin, Ireland, 6
Duckworth, Admiral Sir J. Y., 45
Duncan, Lieutenant Silas, 165
Dupont, Celestant, 208, 342
Dupont, Mrs. Celestant (Elizabeth Farragut), 208

Dwina, Russian ship, 265

Eliot, Ellsworth, Jr., x, 306, 351
Elliott, Commodore Jesse D., 192, 194, 293
Engle, Captain Frederick, 284, 347
Enterprise, U.S. schooner, 23, 117, 197, 198, 202
Emperor of Austria, 136, 294
Erie, U.S. sloop, 119, 122, 127, 208-10, 213, 216, 229, 242, 243
Essex, U.S. frigate, 24-29, 31, 33, 34, 36, 38-44, 46, 47, 49-57, 58-63, 65-71, 73, 74, 76, 79-82, 84, 85, 88-92, 94-98, 101-3, 105, 112, 114, 115, 119, 143, 161, 170, 199, 205, 207, 293, 308, 316, 318, 322, 325, 326, 328-31
Essex, Junior (formerly the Atlantic), 77-79, 81, 83, 84, 86-88, 91, 93, 94, 98, 100, 105, 107, 108, 110, 331
Evans, Captain Samuel, 141
Exmouth, Lord, 122
Experiment, U.S. schooner, 23, 192

Fairfax, Lieutenant A.B., 252
Fajardo, Puerto Rico, 168, 169, 172, 180, 192
Farragut, Anthony, 1
Farragut, David Glasgow (James Glasgow), 5, 22, 23, 28, 29, 109-12, 308, 313, 331
  Birth, 7
  Life at Stony Point, Tennessee, 7-11
  Voyage to New Orleans on the Tennessee, Ohio, and Mississippi Rivers, 12, 15
  Life in New Orleans, 16, 21
  Death of His Mother, 17
  Adoption by David Porter, 19
  Becomes a Midshipman, 24
  Joins the Essex, 25
  His Appearance, 25, 26, 292

Cruises in the *Essex* in Peace Time, 33-39
His First Sea Fight, 40-48
He Saves the *Essex* from Mutineers, 45
Famous Cruise of the *Essex*, 49-90
Loss of the *Essex*, 91-106
Cruise in the Mediterranean in the *Independence*, 114-20
Mediterranean Cruise in the *Washington*, 120-26
Cruising in the *Franklin*, 135, 136
He Commands the *Spark*, 136, 137
Several Months Spent in Tunis, 126-33
Failure to Pass the Examination for Promotion, 140-42
On the *John Adams* in Mexican Waters, 145-51
Passing His Examination for Promotion to Passed Midshipman, 144
Hunting Pirates in the Caribbean with Porter, 152-68
His Marriage to Susan Caroline Marchant, 169
His Promotion to Lieutenant, 170
Cruise in the *Brandywine*, 172-77
Establishment of a School for Seamen in the *Alert* at Norfolk, 178-81
Service in the *Vandalia* on the Brazilian Station, 182-88
At the Norfolk Navy Yard in the *Alert*, and Later in the *Java*, 188-91
Cruise in the *Natchez*: at Charleston during the Nullification Affair and then Again on the Brazil Station, 191-98

Commands the *Boxer*, 198-201
At the Rendezvous, Norfolk Navy Yard, 202-6
Service in the West India Squadron,—*Constellation* and *Erie*, 206-16
Observes the French Bombardment of the Castle of San Juan de Ulloa, 211-14
Controversy with Admiral Baudin, 217-20
Death of Mrs. Farragut, 221
Cruise in the *Delaware* as First Lieutenant, 222-27
Promotion to Commander, 225
Cruise to Brazil in the *Delaware*, 227-29
Commands the *Decatur*, 229-36
Marriage to Virginia Loyall, 239
Executive Officer in the Receiving Ship Pennsylvania, Norfolk Navy Yard, 239-41
Birth of Son, Loyall Farragut, 240
The Writing of *Some Reminiscences*, 241
Commands the *Saratoga* in the Mexican War, 244-50
Controversy with Commodore Matthew Calbraith Perry, 246-49
On Ordnance Duty at Norfolk, Washington, and Old Point Comfort, 251-55
Establishment of Mare Island Navy Yard, of Which He Becomes First Commandant, 256-66
Promotion to Captain, 260
Trouble with the Vigilantes, 261-64
Commands the Steam Sloop *Brooklyn* and Cruise in the Gulf of Mexico, 269-85
Controversy with Lieutenant Jeffers, 273-76

INDEX 365

The George Ritter Affair, 276-78, 279-82
Leaves Norfolk at the Secession of Virginia, 286-92
Waiting for Orders at Hastings on Hudson, 293
Farragut, Mrs. David Glasgow (Susan Caroline Marchant), 169, 170, 177, 178, 181, 182, 188, 190, 191, 221, 238
Farragut, Mrs. David Glasgow (Virginia Loyall), 239, 240, 256, 265, 266, 279, 288, 291, 292, 359
Farragut, Elizabeth (wife of George Anthony Magin Farragut), 6, 7, 8, 10, 12, 13, 16, 17, 18, 307, 311
Farragut, Elizabeth (daughter of George Anthony Magin Farragut), 13, 165, 208, 312, 347
Farragut, George Antoine, 9, 13, 165, 309
Farragut, George Anthony Magin, 1-8, 10, 11, 16-18, 20, 124, 190, 304-7, 309, 314, 331-33, 336, 337
Farragut, Loyall, vii, 240, 265, 267, 279, 286
Farragut, Nancy, 9, 13, 164, 217, 309
Farragut, William A. C. (Augustus Claiborne?), 6, 8, 13, 17, 19, 162, 164, 260, 261, 278, 304, 309, 310, 312, 313, 331, 357
Febrer, Mossen Jaime, 1
Feltus, Midshipman William H., 85, 87, 324
Fernando de Noronha, 55, 56, 58
Ferragut, Don Pedro, 1
Ferret, U.S. schooner, 165, 166, 167, 198, 229
Field, Cyrus W., 266
Finch, Captain William C. (Bolton), 28, 31, 58, 165, 321
Fittimary, David, 25

Flying Cloud, U.S. clipper, 265
Flying Fish, U.S. clipper, 265
Follansbee, Chief Engineer Joshua, 270
Folsom, Charles, 126-29, 132-34, 139, 337
Fort Jefferson, 15
Fort Pickering, 15
Fort Patrick Henry 13
Franck, Barbara, 6
Franklin, U.S. ship of the line, 115, 135-37, 222, 294
Fulton the First, first U.S. steam man-of-war, 111

Galapagos Islands, 66, 68, 70, 77, 79, 82
Gallagher, Captain John, 135, 182, 184
Gamble, Lieutenant John M., U.S. Marines, 87
Gamble, Master Commandant Thomas, 112, 127
Gardner, Lieutenant William H., 182, 185, 221
Gardner, Lieutenant William Ross, 217
Garibaldi, Guiseppe, 234, 351
Gattanewa, Chief of the Taeehs, 83
Geffrard, President of Haiti, 271
Geisinger, Captain D., 198
General Armstrong, U.S. privateer, 46
George Law, U.S. steamer, 266
Georgiana, British whaler, 70, 71, 76, 77, 79, 323
Gibraltar, 53, 117-19, 121, 122, 124-26, 136, 137, 176, 177, 238, 335
Gierlew, Danish Consul at Tunis, 128, 132, 133, 338
Glasgow, James, 7, 308
Glisson, Lieutenant Oliver S., 252
Gloire, French frigate, 212
Golden Age, U.S. mail steamer, 266

Gordon, Captain Charles, 122
Gourlie (also spelled Gurlie), Louis, 313
Gourlie (also spelled Gurlie), Mrs, Louis (Nancy Farragut), 279, 313
Grand Duke of Tuscany, 134, 135, 294
Great Smoky Mountains, 8
Greeley, Horace, 281
"Green Bank," 38, 46, 111, 182, 190
Greene, Elizabeth, 6
Greene, General Nathaniel, 4
Greenwich, British whaler, 74, 76, 77, 87, 323
Gregory, Lieutenant F. H., 175, 176
Greyhound, U.S. schooner, 153-55, 157, 162
Guerriére, U.S. frigate, 34, 117, 118, 137, 184
Gulf of Guyaquil, 75
Gunboat No. 13, 12
Gurlie (also spelled Gourlie), Louis, 313
Gurlie (also spelled Gourlie), Mrs. Louis (Nancy Farragut), 279, 313

"Hail Columbia," 37
Halifax, 43
Hall, Mr. George G., x, 304, 311, 313, 342, 359, 360
Hall, Mrs. George G., x, 304, 309
Hamilton, Secretary of the Navy Paul, 23, 24, 44, 315
Hamlet, U.S. merchant ship, 164
Harrison, Midshipman C. P. C., 158
Harwood, Commander Andrew A., 252
Hastings on Hudson, 293, 296, 359
Havana, 1, 20, 22, 24, 47, 55, 151, 166, 167, 314, 315
Havre, France, 174, 175
Hawkins, Captain Richard, 42
Hayne, Robert Y., 190

Heap, Doctor Samuel Davies, 19, 134, 313
Heath, Lieutenant John, U.S. Marines, 122
Hector, British whaler, 76, 77, 94, 323
Henry, Joseph, 253
Herman, French frigate, 209
Hero, British merchant ship, 43
Hillyar, Captain James (British Navy), 92-94, 96, 102-5, 107, 326, 328, 329
Holston River, 4, 6, 13, 14, 306-8
Hopkins, Mark, 253
Hornet, U.S. sloop, 40, 44, 49, 51, 60, 319
Horta, Azores, 46
"Huck Finn," 14
Hudson, Captain W. L., 266
Hudson, U.S. frigate, 181, 184-88
Hyperion, U.S. brig, 196

Independence, U.S ship of the line, 114, 116-20, 222, 335
Ingram, Lieutenant William (British Navy), 102, 103
Insurgente, French frigate, 23
Iphigenie, French frigate, 209, 212, 214
Island of Maranham, 235
Ives, Doctor Eli, 177

Jackson, President Andrew, 190-92, 194, 288, 306, 336, 337
James I, King of Aragon, 1
Java, U.S. frigate, 60, 124, 189, 191
Jeffers, Lieutenant W. N., 273-76, 278, 283, 284, 295
Jefferson, Thomas, 10, 173, 191
Jeremie, Santo Domingo, 23
John Adams, U.S. frigate, 112, 120, 144-46, 149-52, 156, 163, 202, 261, 262, 264
John Hancock, U.S. steamship of war, 263
Joinville, Prince de, 215, 227, 348
Jones, Captain Jacob, 53, 293
Juarez, Benito, 272

INDEX 367

Kane, Doctor Elisha K., 253
Kearny, Lieutenant Lawrence, 157-60, 162
Kelly, Commander J., 255
Kennedy, Captain Edmund P., 178
Key West, 157, 162, 163, 165, 166, 181, 278
King, Thomas, 5
King George, British merchant ship, 43
King of Naples, 294
Kingsbury, Boatswain's Mate William, 61, 100
Kinston, North Carolina, 5
Knoxville, Tennessee, 4, 6, 8, 14, 307-9

Lafayette, Marquis de, 172-75, 294
Lafayette, George Washington, 173
Lafitte, brothers, 16, 311
Lake Nicaragua, 257
Lake Pontchartrain, 17-20, 34, 332
Lamprey, British merchant brig, 42
Laugharne, Captain Thomas L. P. (British Navy), 44
Laurel, French brig, 208
Lavalle, General, 184-86, 230
Lawrence, Captain James, 40, 51
Le Perouse, French frigate, 208
Leander, British merchant ship, 43
Lee, Robert Edward, 287
Leghorn, Italy, 125, 132, 134, 135, 136, 313, 337, 338
Leigh, Benjamin W., 193, 194
Levant, U.S. sloop, 206, 207
Levasseur, Auguste, 173
Lewis, Lieutenant Arthur, 210
Lewis, Captain William, 335
Lexington, U.S. store ship, 195
Lincoln, Abraham, 287-91, 310
Little Belt, British sloop, 34
Lookout Mountain, Tennessee, 14
Lowe's Ferry, 307
Loyall, George, 292, 359
Loyall, Virginia Dorcus, 239, 240,

256, 265, 266, 279, 288, 291, 292, 359
Loyall, William, 239, 240, 292
Lugeol, Rear Admiral (French Navy), 265

Macedonian, U.S. frigate, 117, 119, 120, 145, 152
Mackelwean, Sarah, 6
Madison, James, 114, 120, 122, 173, 315
Mahan, Captain Alfred T., vii, viii, 189, 255
Marjorca, 1, 2, 124, 136
Malaga, Spain, 117, 127, 337
Marchant, Jane Edna, 205, 347, 350
Marchant, Susan Caroline, 169, 170, 177, 178, 181, 182, 188, 190, 191, 221, 238
Mare Island, California, 258, 265, 295
Marion, General Francis, 3, 4
Marquesas Islands, 79, 80, 202
Marseilles, France, 125, 127, 337
Marshall, Midshipman E. Y., 162
Martin, Chief Engineer Daniel B., 270
Mary, British merchant ship, 43
Masefield, John, 61
Mason, Secretary of the Navy John Y., 244, 250, 251, 255
Mason, Surgeon R. F., 289
Maury, Midshipman John Minor, 82
Maury, Commander Matthew Fontaine, 173, 203, 237, 238, 253, 270, 316, 324
McAllister, Judge, 264
McCauley, Captain Charles S., 222, 225, 228, 291
McClung, Charles, 4
McCook, Midshipman J. J., 229
McIntosh, Lieutenant J. M., 207
McIver, Ellenor, 6
McKee, John, 4, 306, 314
McKnight, Lieutenant Stephen

Decatur, 28, 45, 63, 73, 93, 101, 320, 322, 327, 333
McLane, Robert M., 272, 273, 276-79, 283, 284, 294
Mediterranean Sea, 1, 2, 114, 117, 121, 125, 139, 144, 145, 189, 196, 222, 273, 313
Merida, Mexico, 284
Meridian Hill, 142, 169
Mervine, Commodore William, 263
Mesquida, Juan, 1
Messina, 117, 122, 125, 135, 338
Metternich, Prince, 136, 294
Miller, Surgeon Robert, 75
Minerva, British frigate, 42
Minorca, 1, 3, 122, 304, 337
Miramon, General, 272, 278, 283
Mississippi, U.S. side-wheeler, 238, 244, 248
Mississippi River, 15, 33, 208, 278, 314
Mississippi Sound, 18
Mitchell, Lieutenant William, 280, 281
Montague, British ship of the line, 59, 60
Montevideo, 184, 187, 197, 199, 200, 228, 235
Montezuma, British whaler, 70, 71, 73, 75, 323
Morgan, General Daniel, 4
Morris, Captain Charles, 117, 119, 172, 174, 175, 227, 230, 253, 293, 351
Morse, S. F. B., 240
Mt. Vernon, U.S. steamer, 175

Nancy, British merchant ship, 43
"Nancy Bell," 30
Naples, 117, 120, 122, 125, 135, 136, 294
Nash, Captain (British Navy), 107-9, 334
Nash, Governor of North Carolina, 4
Nashville, Tennessee, 13, 304
Nassau, New Providence Island, 166, 167

Natchez, Mississippi, 11, 12, 15
Natchez, U.S. sloop, 188, 191-95, 197, 199, 201, 208, 217
Nautilus, U.S. schooner, 39
Neale, Lieutenant B. J., 335
Neif, Mr., 111
Néréide, French frigate, 212
Nereyda, Peruvian privateer, 67, 68
Neuse River, 5
New Bern, North Carolina, 6
New Haven, 177, 178
New Madrid, 15
New Orleans, 1, 2, 10-12, 14-22, 24, 33, 55, 144, 162, 164, 208, 218, 242, 246, 254, 278, 280, 310-14, 331-33, 336, 337
New York, 39, 53, 110-12, 114, 119, 140, 144, 156, 163, 177, 180, 239, 250, 256, 266, 267, 270, 273, 279, 282, 295, 315, 319, 320, 333
New Zealander, British whaler, 79, 87, 323
Newport, Rhode Island, 38, 39, 119, 335
Newton, Lieutenant J. T., 157
Niagara, U.S. steamer, 266
Nimrod, British privateer, 67, 68
Nocton, British packet, 58, 61
Norfolk, Virginia, 25, 36, 38, 143-46, 152, 154, 163, 169, 174, 177, 178, 180, 188-91, 201, 203, 205, 207, 216, 217, 221, 236, 238, 239, 244, 245, 250-52, 254, 269, 282, 284, 286, 288-92, 295, 308, 316, 339
North Carolina, U.S. ship of the line, 177, 279
Northern Light, U.S. steamer, 286
Nukuhiva, 81, 82, 89, 323, 324

O'Conor, Charles, 281
Ogden, Midshipman Henry W., 85, 229, 324
Ogden, Titus, 4, 306

INDEX 369

Odenheimer, Midshipman William H., 101
Ohio River, 14, 15, 33
Old Point Comfort, 254
Ontario, U.S. sloop, 117, 119, 122, 124, 201, 208

Page, Commander Richard L., 289
Palermo, 136
Palma, Majorca, 2
Pandora, British ship of war, 166
Para, 235
Parades, General, 247
Pascagoula River, 18-20, 165, 208, 279, 311, 313, 332, 333, 336, 347
Patterson, Captain Daniel T., 177, 311, 313, 342
Paulding, Commander Hiram, 207
Paulding, Secretary of the Navy J. K., 218, 219
Payta, Peru, 68
Peacock, U.S. sloop, 122, 153, 198, 199, 202
Pennsylvania, U.S. ship of the line, 239-41, 251, 253
Pensacola, 206, 208, 216, 248, 249, 273, 279, 280
Pernambuco, Brazil, 195, 201
Perry, Christopher Raymond, 140, 245, 339
Perry, Commodore Matthew Calbraith, 180, 237, 238, 243, 244, 246-51, 255, 265, 339
Perry, Captain Oliver H., 122, 145, 152, 194, 293, 339
Persevante, French frigate, 265
Philadelphia, 3, 112, 188, 190, 196, 240, 293, 334
Philadelphia, U.S. frigate, 23, 172
Phoebe, British frigate, 79, 94, 96-98, 102-4, 161, 325, 327
Pigeon, British packet, 137
Pinkham, Lieutenant Alexander B., 194
Pinkney, William, 28, 120-22, 335
Pisa, 135, 294, 338
Pittsburgh, 14, 18, 314

Plymouth, U.S. sloop, 255
Poindexter, Lieutenant Carter B., 289
Poinsett, Joel R., 65, 145, 147, 149, 150, 194, 294, 340, 346
Policy, British whaler, 70, 71, 77, 79
Polk, James K., 240
Port Mahon, 122, 123, 137, 175, 177, 337
Port-au-Prince, 2, 271
Porter, David, Senior, 17, 312
Porter, Commodore David, Jr., 22-24, 32, 107, 108, 110, 111, 114, 120, 135, 169, 182, 189, 194, 199, 293, 308, 309, 311-14, 319, 321, 326-28, 332, 334, 337
  Command of the New Orleans Station, 18-21
  Adopts Glasgow Farragut, 19
  Takes Command of the *Essex*, 24, 26
  Cruising in the Atlantic, 33-43
  Capture of the *Alert*, 43-46
  Famous Cruise of the *Essex*, 49-90
  Loss of the *Essex*, 91-106
  Becomes a Navy Commissioner, 142-45
  Hunting Pirates in the Caribbean, 152-68
  The Fajardo Affair, 168, 169, 172, 180, 192
  In the Mexican Navy, 170, 180, 181
  In the Consular and Diplomatic Service, 170, 190, 203-5
  Death, 240
Porter, Mrs. David, Jr., 19, 22, 23, 38, 50, 169, 180, 182, 190
Porter, David Dixon, 111, 181
Porter, Elizabeth, 50
Porter, John, 153-55
Porter, Margaret, 19
Porter, William D., 50, 181, 205, 347

Porto Bello, 271
Portsmouth, England, 176
Portsmouth, New Hampshire, 120
Portsmouth, Virginia, 169, 176, 178, 207
Potomac, U.S. frigate, 199, 200, 202, 229
Poughkeepsie, 267, 286
Powhatan, U.S. steam frigate, 252
Preble, Captain Edward, 27
President, U.S. frigate, 34, 39, 40, 49
Princess Royal, Brazilian Navy, 198
Princeton, U.S. steam propeller, 242

Read, Captain George C., 175, 177
Renshaw, Captain, 145-47, 150, 343
Richmond, Virginia, 220, 237, 239, 290, 307
Ridgely, Captain Charles C., 119, 335
Rincon, General, 215
Rio de Janeiro, 58, 59, 66, 79, 183, 186, 187, 195, 197-99, 201, 228, 229, 235, 280
Ritter, George, 276, 277, 280, 282, 295
Robb, Commander Robert G., 289
Robertson, General James, 13, 307
Robles, General, 277
Roche, Adam, 98, 327
Rodgers, Captain George Washington, 140, 141, 339
Rodgers, Commodore John, 34, 38-40, 49, 120, 145, 162, 177, 318
Rootes, Commander Thomas R., 289
Rosas, Emanuelita, 231, 234
Rosas, Juan Manuel de, 184-86, 196, 230, 232, 233, 294
Rose, British whaler, 76, 323
Rossie, U.S. privateer, 47

Rousseau, Captain Lawrence, 162, 261
Rowan, Lieutenant Stephen C., 252

Salem, Massachusetts, 27, 327
Salter, Lieutenant William D., 201
Saluke, Emperor, 271
Samuel and Sarah, British transport, 42
San Francisco, 258, 259, 261-65, 295
San Juan, Puerto Rico, 146
San Juan River, 257
San Juan de Ulloa, 146, 209, 211-13, 242-46
San Juan del Nord, 257
San Juan del Sur, 258
Sands, Lieutenant Joshua R., 182, 345
Santa Anna, General, 146, 215, 216, 218, 294
Santiago, Chile, 65, 66, 340
Santiago, Cuba, 164
Saratoga, U.S. sloop, 244, 245, 247-50, 283
Sardinia, 133
Satellite, British ship of war, 209, 210
Saturn, British ship of war, 107, 108
Saunders, Commander John L., 238
Savannah, 3
Scott, General Winfield, 191, 194, 245, 288, 294
Sea Gull, U.S. steamer, 153, 162, 163
Semmes, Lieutenant Alexander A., 289
Seringapatam, British whaler, 79, 87, 323
Sevier, General John, 5, 13, 307, 332
Shaler, William, 122, 123
Shannon, British frigate, 46, 320
Shark, U.S. schooner, 163
Sharp, Lieutenant William, 289

INDEX

Shaw, Captain John, 119, 122, 335
Shields, Lieutenant William F., 198
Shine, Daniel, 6
Shine, Elizabeth (Mrs. George Anthony Magin Farragut), 5, 6
Shine, John, 6
Silliman, Benjamin, 178, 253
Sinclair, Lieutenant Arthur, 40, 289
Sinclair, Lieutenant George T., 289
Sir Andrew Hammond, British whaler, 79, 86, 87, 323
Skinner, Commodore Charles W., 245
Sloat, Commodore John D., 252
Smith, Captain John, 40
Smith, Commodore Joseph, 256, 266
Smithsonian Institution, 253, 353, 354
Smoot, Commodore Joseph, 216, 239, 241
Sommerville, Lieutenant G. W., 158-60
Southampton, British frigate, 47, 48
Southard, Secretary of the Navy Samuel L., 172, 180, 343
Spafford, James, 63
Spark, U.S. brig, 112, 117, 122, 137, 308, 338
Spitfire, U.S. brig, 34, 117
Spotswood, Lieutenant Charles F. M., 289
St. Catharines, 59, 187, 321
St. Helena, 49, 60, 76
St. Louis, U.S. sloop, 184
St. Salvador, 58, 60, 188
St. Sebastians, 59
Stanly, Lieutenant Fabius, 225
Star of the West, U.S. steamer, 256, 257
Stewart, Commodore Charles, 135-37, 293
Stockton, Captain R. F., 242, 243
Stony Point, 6, 10, 307, 308

Stowe, Harriet Beecher, 256
Stribling, Lieutenant C. K., 161, 227, 245
Swartwout, Commander Samuel, 263
Sumter, General Thomas, 4
Susquehanna, U.S. steam frigate, 265
Syracuse, Sicily, 125, 337

Tabasco, Mexico, 243
Tampico, 147-49, 208-10, 216, 250, 278, 283, 340
Taney, Roger Brooke, 225
Taylor, Commodore, 198
Taylor, Midshipman William, 119
Taylor, Lieutenant William Rogers, 254
Taylor, Zachary, 243, 267
Tennessee River, 13, 14, 33, 307
Terry, D. S., 261, 262, 264
Teviot, British steamer, 247
Tippoo Sahib, 79
"Tom Sawyer," 14
Toucey, Secretary of the Navy, Isaac, 279-81
Treaty of Ghent, 113
Tripoli, 23, 117, 122, 125, 126, 133, 172
Trippe, Lieutenant John, 22, 315
Truxtun, U.S. brig, 240
Truxtun, Commodore Thomas, 23, 145
Tucker, Commander John R., 289
Tunis, 117, 122, 125-28, 131, 132, 294
Turkey, 2, 170, 190, 255
Turner, Commander Thomas, 275
Tuspan, Mexico, 246-48
Tyler, John, 206, 225, 227, 239, 351
United States, U.S. frigate, 40, 49, 117, 119, 121, 122, 124
Upshur, Secretary of the Navy Abel P., 237, 238, 351
Valagie, French brig, 209
Valencia, 1
Vallejo, California, 259

Valparaiso, 63, 64, 68, 76-78, 90, 91, 94, 95, 105, 161, 263, 293, 325-28, 330, 333
Van Buren, Martin, 202, 215
Vandalia, U.S. sloop, 182-85, 188, 191
Vera Cruz, 1, 146, 209, 211, 215, 216, 218, 242, 244-48, 271-75, 278, 283, 284, 294
Vesuvius, U.S. bomb brig, 22, 34, 314
Vixen, U.S. brig, 22

Walker, U.S. whaler, 67
Walker, Captain W.S., 285
Warren, U.S. sloop, 258, 263-65
Warrington, Commodore Lewis, 137, 252
Washington, D.C., 22-24, 33, 55, 112, 114, 139, 142-44, 163, 167, 169, 175, 177, 191, 195, 205, 238, 246, 252, 253, 261, 262, 278, 281, 293, 314
Washington, George, 6, 173, 174, 343
Washington, U.S. ship of the line, 115, 120, 123, 126, 127, 135, 186, 187, 222, 337, 338, 352
Wasp, U.S. sloop, 28, 49, 53, 334
Watson, Lieutenant William A., 161
Webster, Daniel, 190
Welles, Secretary of the Navy Gideon, 296, 359
White, James, 5
Wilkinson, Commodore Jesse, 241
Willard Hotel, 256
Wilmer, Lieutenant James P., 101, 320
Wilmington, North Carolina, 217
Winant, District Attorney, 279, 280
Winchester, General James, 336
Woodbury, Secretary of the Navy, 191
Woolsey, Commodore M. T., 190, 197, 199, 201

Yale College, 177, 178, 253
Yeo, Sir James, 47, 48
Yorktown, Battle of, 174

Zantzinger, Captain J. P., 191, 192, 195, 197

www.ingramcontent.com/pod-product-compliance
Lightning Source LLC
Chambersburg PA
CBHW022210090526
44584CB00012BA/373